History of Crime and Criminal Justice Series

CRIME, JUSTICE, HISTORY

ERIC H. MONKKONEN

THE OHIO STATE UNIVERSITY PRESS

Columbus

Library of Congress Cataloging-in-Publication

Monkkonen, Eric H., 1942–
   Crime, justice, history / Eric H. Monkkonen.
     p. cm.—(History of crime and criminal justice series)
  Includes bibliographical references and index.
   ISBN 0-8142-0902-5 (cloth)
   1. Crime—United States. 2. Crime—Great Britain. 3.
  Violence—United States. 4. Violence—Europe. 5. Police—United
  States. 6. Sociology, Urban—United States. I. Title. II. Series.
HV6789 .M63 2002
364.973—dc21   2002008374

   Jacket design by Bookcomp, Inc.
   Type set in Adobe Garamond by Bookcomp, Inc.
   Printed by Thomson-Shore, Inc.

   The paper used in this publication meets the minimum requirements of the
   American National Standard for Information Sciences—Permanence of Paper for
   Printed Library Materials. ANSI Z39.48-1992.

9 8 7 6 5 4 3 2 1

Contents

Acknowledgments

I gratefully acknowledge the original publishers for permission to reprint the following material:

"Crime and Punishment," in Jack P. Greene, ed., *Encyclopedia of American Political History* (New York: Scribner, 1984), 443–54.

"The Violence Conundrum," *Los Angeles Times,* November 30, 1997; "Crossing the (Blue) Line," *Los Angeles Times,* September 26, 1999; "The Power of 'Excuse Me,'" *Los Angeles Times,* March 8, 1998. All reprinted with the permission of the *Los Angeles Times.*

"Homicide over the Centuries," in Lawrence Friedman and George Fisher, eds., *The Crime Conundrum* (New York: Westview Press, 1997), 163–70. Reprinted by permission of the publisher.

"The American State from the Bottom Up: Of Homicides and Courts," *Law and Society Review* 24 (1990). Reprinted by permission of the Law and Society Association.

"Racial Factors in New York City Homicide, 1800–1874," in Darnell Hawkins, ed., *Ethnicity, Race, and Crime: Perspectives across Time and Space* (Albany, NY: SUNY Press, 1995), 99–120. Reprinted by permission of the publisher.

"New York City Homicide Offender Ages: How Variable? A Research Note," *Homicide Studies* 3 (August 1999): 256–71. Reprinted by permission of Sage Publications, Inc.

"The Dynamics of Police Behavior: A Data Reanalysis" (with Catrien Bijleveld), *Historical Methods* 24 (Winter 1991): 16–24. Reprinted by permission of Historical Methods and Hedref Publications.

"Policing in the United States since 1945," in *The State, Police and Society* (Brussels: Editions Complex, 1997). Reprinted with permission of Editions Complex.

"History of Urban Police," in M. Tonry and N. Morris, eds., *Modern Policing,* vol. 15 of *Crime and Justice: An Annual Review of Research* (Chicago: University of Chicago Press, 1992), 547–80. Reprinted by permission of the University of Chicago Press.

"Nineteenth-Century Institutions Dealing with the Urban Underclass." First published in Michael Katz, ed., *The "Underclass Debate"* (Princeton: Princeton University Press, 1992). Reprinted by permission of Princeton University Press.

"A Disorderly People? Urban Order in Nineteenth- and Twentieth-Century America," *Journal of American History* 68 (1981): 539–59. Reprinted by permission of the publisher.

"American Cities and the Creation of Order," in Herbert Reinke, ed., *"Nur für die Sicherheit da?" Zur Geschichte der Polizei im 19. und 20. Jahrhundert* (Düsseldorf, 1993), 206–21. Reprinted by permission of the publisher.

Foreword

One of the major virtues of this collection of essays is that it reflects some of the breadth of Eric Monkkonen's work. Historians of criminal justice are as specialized as other scholars, many of them confining themselves to cops, crooks, or courts; to one side of the Atlantic or the other; to the twentieth century or perhaps the nineteenth. But Monkkonen has made important contributions in all these areas, and is equally versatile in terms of approach. Sometimes he has re-imagined what had seemed familiar subjects simply by approaching them from unfamiliar angles, or by drawing unexpected comparisons. Equally often he has done the grunt work of collecting the data at ground level, producing surprising new information through analyzing statistical series. These eighteen pieces, some published here for the first time in English, illustrate all these strengths and more, under four suggestive heads. It is impossible to introduce them all, but a few examples will illustrate the points about both diversity and insight.

The first essay of Section I, published for the first time here, deals with postwar American crime as entertainment. As it happens much of that entertainment, an increasingly large share of American exports to the world, and not incidentally increasingly important to our image abroad, is produced in the movie and television studios of Culver City, California, Monkkonen's home. Historians as private citizens are often fans of one subgenre of crime-as-entertainment in particular: the detective story speaks to us in our own language. Much like detectives we, too, are in the business of sifting whatever clues have been left behind by some past event or events, whether eyewitness testimony, official records, or physical remains, and then reconstructing the story in some convincing fashion. What Monkkonen argues here is that as professionals it pays us to revisit this whole branch of our popular culture, as through several media and genres it provides its own clues to the times in which it was produced, reflecting preoccupations and fears sometimes universal, sometimes ephemeral, always suggestive.

The next section, into another gear entirely, is even more characteristic of Monkkonen's work. A long-term leader in cross-Atlantic conversations, he is more conversant with European studies in crime than is any other American.

"Searching for the Origins of American and European Violence Differences" goes back many centuries to evaluate the insights of the theorist Norbert Elias. Currently in vogue on the continent, where he has traced the progressive civilization of Western manners and mores from the Middle Ages into the twentieth century, Elias was long forgotten in the United States. Monkkonen is principally responsible for his recent revival in this country.

In this section, several additional pieces are drawn from Monkkonen's recently published study of all the homicides officially counted in the city of New York between the late eighteenth century and the late twentieth. This monumental work, the most ambitious longitudinal study of its type ever published, is full of suggestive material. One intriguing statistical tidbit is that while violent crime in the contemporary city is heavily associated with very young males, even teenagers, nineteenth-century killers, while equally male, were on average markedly more mature. The puzzle is addressed in the last essay in this section, "New York City Homicide Offender Ages: How Variable over Time?"

The four pieces in Section Three, "Police," are, together, remarkably comprehensive. "Crossing the (Blue) Line" analyzes the several rather different varieties of police corruption; timely as well as insightful, it is all too natural a subject for a resident of Los Angeles County, home of the currently beleaguered LAPD. Two of the other pieces cover what scholars, including Monkkonen himself, have had to say about American police in two different eras. Among historians, paradoxically, the varied nineteenth-century origins of police work are better known than the more recent developments, after World War II, which these historians and the rest of the public have actually lived through.

The final section, "Cities and Crime," revisits several earlier themes and puts them, properly, into one of the most appropriate contexts of all: the growth of cities, and the impact of that growth on disorderly or criminal behavior and the means of dealing with it. Monkkonen is one of several scholars who, over the past long generation, has put to rest the once conventional wisdom that crime was and is above all an urban problem. When he began his scholarly career, in the 1970s, politicians, pundits, and much of the public tended to echo the founding fathers of sociology in explaining much criminal behavior as the result of the anomie, the anxiety, and the opportunities for anonymity created by the move out of stable rural communities into the dog-eat-dog world of the city. But even apart from the fact that the stability of the traditional order is in large part a myth, Monkkonen has helped to show, in part using Norbert Elias as a guide, that most kinds of cities (although not all) have served literally to civilize their inhabitants, in small ways as in large. And in this country, above all, the great urban-industrial revolution which took hold in the nineteenth century had a powerful effect in creating an orderly population, acting predictably and generally peacefully, out of the continual waves of often desperate immigrants from Europe and the countryside which continually battered it.

Under his dual title, Professor of History and Public Policy at UCLA, Monkkonen has done much work with obvious policy implications. But while his sympathies are clear, his politics are not; he approaches history with too many tools and from too many angles, and has too much respect for its ironies and complexities, to try to force it into any predictable ideological box. What can, however, be said with confidence is that everyone who studies the history of cops, crooks, and courts in this country is indebted to Eric Monkkonen, as editor, commentator, organizer, and guide. This volume of essays should consolidate his reputation among longtime admirers and introduce him to new ones.

Roger Lane
Benjamin R. Collins Research Professor of Social Sciences
Haverford College

■ PART I:

BIG ISSUES

Crime entertains us; crime terrifies us; crime sets the United States apart from the rest of the wealthy world. How can we watch mayhem in the movies, yet lock up those who actually do it? How can we fear it, yet be so timid in our policy making about it? How can one of the world's richest, freest, and legalistic nations suffer so much violence?

Elite American universities and social theorists seldom devote resources to research and teaching on crime and violence. Outspoken thinkers on crime are all too often connected with political ideologies and partisanship. Academic scholarship is so highly fragmented that experts on one campus may not even be aware of their colleagues in other departments.

It may be that the very nature of crime, diverse and sometimes completely contextual, fragments our approaches to and understanding of it. Perhaps the lack of coherent policies, research, and public opinion simply reminds us that our understanding of people still struggles to surmount the enormous complexity, variety, and creativity inherent in humans.

Certainly the essays in this section—and this book—do not pretend to bring forward fundamental changes in how we conceptualize crime. Rather, my hope is to pick things apart, to bring history to bear on our thinking, and to help build a basis for a greater understanding and for better policies. As I see it, the American challenge is to reduce crime, yet to preserve our freedoms; to look for justice and keep people from being victimized; to prevent rather than punish, and to punish sensibly when prevention fails.

We have to begin with humility and a recognition that the American problem of crime is very old, very deep, and of necessity, more complex than we want it to be.

1

Postwar American Crime as Entertainment

One might think that those who study crime have a special attitude toward crime entertainment, laughing cynically at TV shows or rejecting out of hand mystery stories. Instead, my informal survey shows that criminal justice experts are as likely to be fans of a TV series as any other person; their special knowledge clearly stays compartmentalized.

Yet, when looking back only a few years, the popular genre of crime entertainment gives considerable leverage on understanding the recent past. A huge proportion of crime fiction, when only slightly distanced from today, is unremittingly stupid. My personal favorites are the Dick Tracy "Crime Stoppers," little graphics that appeared in the color comic strips. With two holes indicated so that the avid reader could assemble the tips into a notebook, one can only hope that their readers laughed hysterically (as I did), or that they were never more than nine years old. Will the same thing happen to our current entertainment? This should give us pause: no doubt every generation thinks, at least secretly, that it is the coolest ever to exist. Will our popular entertainment look as extravagantly foolish and lowbrow in forty years? No, of course not.

Crime fiction, whether in movies or comic books or novels, has been popular in the United States since before World War II. Some fictional characters and conventions which became popular in the immediate postwar era have had influence on subsequent forms of entertainment until very recently. Dick Tracy, for instance, metamorphosized from over a half-century-old comic strip into a 1990

First presented as a conference paper at the Institut des Hautes Etudes de la Sécurité Intérieure, Paris, 1999.

feature film which many considered stylish and au courant (or, perhaps, "post-modern"?). Some of the persisting powers of these conventions and characters have to do with generational power and influence. For instance, until the most recent presidential election, a substantial degree of power in the United States remained in the hands of men whose formative experiences had been in World War II and the years immediately following. President George H. W. Bush, for instance, had been a wartime pilot and had attended college *after* the war, graduating from Yale in 1948.

This essay explores the themes and conventions of popular crime fictions which were set before and during the war years and have since become imprinted in popular entertainment. In the 1990s these themes can be seen influencing popular fiction and visual media, and even the appearance of the relatively new, such as docudramas (*Rescue 911*) or *cinéma vérité* (*Cops*), often uses these older images and conventions. The first part of this essay discusses some of the big-name crime fighters of fiction, the second examines juvenile delinquency, and the third describes those few new trends which have emerged in more recent times.

It is important to keep in mind that crime as a problem and that the various entertainment formulas about crime do not intersect precisely, if at all. That is, people enjoying a crime story or a detective movie are not gaining enjoyment because that entertainment helps explain or solve problems in their real life. Presumably, criminals can watch a cop movie just as cops might watch a movie that romanticizes crime (e.g., *Butch Cassidy and the Sundance Kid*, 1969, or the 1972 bank robbery film, *$*).

The relationship between fictions on crime and criminal justice issues needs to be considered with some care if we are trying to use entertainment fiction as a way to actually understand crime. It is, in fact, a very poor way to understand crime. We need to remember that the earliest and most popular crime fiction came out of Victorian England, which by the second half of the nineteenth century had experienced a dramatic decrease in crime. By the mid-twentieth century, when Agatha Christie wrote her classic murder mysteries, England had a very low homicide rate. Why should such a tame and safe country gobble up such improbable tales? One explanation lies in the nature of the narrative itself. The classic murder mystery shows evil (or at least wrong) intruding into an ordered scene; its resolution is the finding of that evil and its expulsion from the scene. Order is thus restored. Equally important, the irrational is shown to be rational after all, and, once the detective has had her (or his) way, there turns out to have been no mystery at all. The only mystery is why we persist in calling them that.

Perhaps the deeper appeal of mystery stories is that they, like religion, show the design behind disorder, and having shown that design, they then show a powerful figure manipulating it to save the innocent and punish the bad. Like religion, the element of choice for the believer is in the nature of the powerful figure—here everything goes, whether style, gender or race. The early-nineteenth-century detectives were masters of perception, ratiocinative power, and deception. In the twentieth century, the detective flavors have expanded enormously, so that gender, race, sexual preference, and even the incompetent bumbling detective have a place.

The underlying premise of all these fictions is still the same: apparent disorder shown to be order and evil punished. Perhaps knowledge has expanded so far it is now difficult not to be aware of both our own expanding boundaries of ignorance and the great difficulty in understanding what is known. Presumably even astrophysicists exploring the fundamental nature of the universe experience this, for they, too, must be aware of their own ignorance of other aspects of life and vast regions of human knowledge. So the mystery story flourishes, even as those entertained by it know in their daily lives that few mysteries are mysterious, and those that are, are not solved.

Other points also separate crime fiction from the real thing. The fictional criminal, in order to bring out the "best" in the detective, must be smart, sinister, planning, persistent, and independent. Typically their flaws reflect larger social flaws: greed, predatory calculation, and a hypocritical flaunting of traditional values from family to the consideration of others. The detectives, on the other hand, only *seem* to knock these values; their cynicism comes from sensitivity. They have been wounded by exposures to life's cruel underbelly. Thus the detective acknowledges central cultural ideals while the criminal flaunts them.

I. FICTION'S CRIME FIGHTERS

The wide variety in kinds of fictional crime fighters greatly exceeds that of their real world analogs. Some of these fictional characters belong to literary conventions stretching back to the nineteenth-century origins of the detective story: Charles Dickens, Edgar Allan Poe, Wilkie Collins, and Arthur Conan Doyle. These kinds range from the purely cerebral crime fighters like Rex Stout's Nero Wolfe, to the ever observant Miss Marple of Agatha Christie, to the careful and psychologically subtle detectives like Dashiell Hammett's Sam Spade, to those like Sara Paretsky's V. I. Warshawski, who intervenes in a web of continuing action in order to see what actions result. Here, we examine five of the best known and most popular detectives or the television series associated with them. We see how they fit into or contrast with their cultural and historical contexts.

The J. Edgar Hoover Vision

American GIs returning home in 1945 could have seen movies about cops and G-men, read hard-boiled detective novels, listened to radio shows like Johnny Dollar, or looked at comics like Dick Tracy. Millions of these readers would have been familiar with the name of J. Edgar Hoover, for as head of the FBI, he had been a master of self-publicity as a great detective. Shamelessly promoting himself and his agency, he used "true life" cases as the basis for popular literature. However, these ex-GIs would have been disappointed if looking for some exciting reading under J. Edgar Hoover's name, for he had turned from his prewar ghostwritten "Take that, you dirty rat!" school to more serious (if still ghostwritten) analyses of communism.

J. Edgar Hoover's name had been big in the sleazy crime fiction market in the late 1930s and early 40s. Teenagers had read *Junior G-Men* while their parents participated in the volunteer fingerprinting rage.[1] Always at the center of the crime-fighting image was J. Edgar Hoover himself, his carefully managed image a strange combination of genius, moral superiority, and nasty streetwise toughness. Courtney Ryley Cooper, his privileged ghostwriter and publicist, said of Hoover, "His brain is one of the most rapidly functioning mechanisms I ever have encountered."[2] In addition to this massive brain, Hoover also possessed a bit of the magical, "a sixth sense which allows him instantly to find the flaw in seeming perfection," the clue leading to another evildoer's arrest.

Hoover had created his incredible tough-guy image during the Depression. He manipulated the public fear of crime, so that it seemed as though violence and criminal anarchy were about to sweep away the nation and its customary crime-control mechanisms. Again, Hoover's ghostwriter shows how this image was created:

> Kidnaping was growing worse. Bank robbers ran about the country, drinking champagne between machine-gun holdups. Great gangs of hoodlums, through their ability to commit major crimes hundreds of miles from their hideouts, went at their depredations with almost a spirit of playfulness. The public temper grew more and more strained. Finally patience broke with the news of a happening in Kansas City, Mo. A group of gangsters, in attempting to deliver from arresting officers, one of their pals, a bank robber named Frank Nash, had engaged in a machine-gun massacre of local police, state officers, and a member of the Federal Bureau of Investigation. Public opinion crystallized. The Federal Government should do something about crime— especially that beyond the power of local law enforcement.[3]

To clean up the country, Hoover saw that he had to also combat the image of the gangster as Robin Hood, to keep "boys from playing at being machine-gun bandits."[4] According to Cooper, Hoover proclaimed boldly, "I'm going to tell the truth about these rats. I'm going to tell the truth about their dirty, filthy, diseased women. I'm going to tell the truth about the miserable politicians who protect them and the slimy, sob-sister convict lovers who let them out on sentimental or ill-advised paroles. If people don't like it, they can get me fired. But I'm going to say it."[5]

In Hoover's language, in the reams of popular crime stories published to promote the image of the FBI, and in the seeming success of his attack on the crime wave, Hoover had cemented a whole sequence of events and an analysis of crime that still inhabits much popular thinking about crime and the way to fight it. This comic book and pulp fiction magazine version of crime and crime control created in the Depression by Hoover and others provided the framework for postwar crime thought. The basic elements of the story are not difficult to master: dirty rats did the crime; unscrupulous politicians gulled the weak-willed and naive public about these dirty rats; and only the Federal Bureau of Investigation had the physical bravery, the mental force, and an uncanny street knowledge that made them capable of saving the nation. This force depended on genius, science, a sixth sense, and incredible toughness, and it did its job. The story is compelling in its clarity and optimistic fantasy about a much messier reality.

So in this fictional world, the fight against crime was not only feasible, it got done. And returning GIs needed not to worry about gangsters in the United States. From Hoover's point of view, the new threat was external and internal— communism. Thus, the fictional discourse about crime began a subtle shift. The FBI stayed in the crime-fighting picture; in fact through television, it continued for a long time. But in the postwar era, the popular vision of crime and crime fighting became much more diffused, though not much more complicated.

Dragnet

Dragnet, which began on radio in 1949, moved to television in 1952, and became a feature film by 1954, elevated the Los Angeles police into the scientific, crime-fighting position from which Hoover and the FBI had retreated. This new image for the Los Angeles Police Department came with the new broadcast media, and quickly replaced the image of Los Angeles and its police as corrupt and latently violent (an image that remains associated with the prewar era, as depicted, for instance, in the 1974 movie *Chinatown*).

Dragnet began as a radio show on NBC in 1949. A typical early *Dragnet* radio drama began with an announcer introducing the Los Angeles Police Department as just one of a city's services, along with parks, schools, libraries, and fire departments. This was a shocking statement, designed to bring the auditor up short by introducing crime and violence so matter-of-factly. The programs emphasized verisimilitude: real street names and places appeared constantly.

The plots were drawn from real felony crimes: in one of the earliest episodes, a stickup man kills a clerk while robbing a grocery store and escapes in a taxi. The police check some records, use their impressive memories of previous crimes and MOs (modus operandi, or as explained by Sergeant Joe Friday, method of operation), figure out who drove and who did the stickup, and arrest both. The badness of the bad guys is emphasized by the goodness and incredible bravery of the police, while well-intentioned bystanders are considerably weaker—morally and physically—than the police.

By the end of 1949, *Dragnet* had a regular sponsor, Fatima cigarettes. Therefore, shaky witnesses would be calmed by Sergeant Friday's "Here . . . have a cigarette." The shows continued to emphasize the bravery, incorruptibility, and special knowledge of the police. For instance, in "Spring St. Gangs—Juveniles," gang members come from families that neglect to instill proper values, while the police outsmart the fences who run the gangs by using a map with pins and their knowledge of the criminal underworld.

The best-remembered image *Dragnet* promoted was that of the tough, fair, and dispassionate cop. The program's music and phrases became popular passwords of the time: "Just the facts, Ma'am," were the words with which key police officer Joe Friday would calm a distraught victim. With its deadpan delivery, the phrase elevated the police and put the victims down as members of the helpless class. Jack Webb, the principal actor in the series, developed a close relationship with the Los Angeles Police Department, in particular with its reformer, Chief William Parker. The Los Angeles Police Department, historically corrupt and inept, had become under Parker's leadership a showpiece department—its brutality masked by its squeaky clean image of no political or financial corruption. Webb solicited stories for his program from police officers; in turn he paid them and sent 6 percent of the show's profits back to capital costs for the department.[3] *Dragnet* did for policing what Hoover's approved print and film entertainment had done for the FBI. Chief Parker became a nationally respected figure in police science, and his *Parker on Police* became the "Bible" in many police science courses.

Chief Parker made clear that the *Dragnet* image was his ideal; a case perhaps of life mimicking art. In a 1962 interview, he brushed aside a gingerly put question about police and race brutality, claiming that this was a press-created problem which exaggerated a "very small number of cases." When the interviewer then asked how the public should get an accurate picture of the police if not through the press, Parker replied: "*Dragnet*. . . . This program showed the true portrait of the policeman as a hardworking, selfless man."[7]

This image—tough, scientific, and fair—was precisely that by which Los Angeles Police Department Chief Parker wanted the police to be viewed. (He wanted it to be the reality, too.) Parker and Webb wanted to show how a no-nonsense policing could lead the way to the future.[8] The popular image the series *did not* continue was that of the friendly, happy, and not too bright Irish cop. Community policing was to be ended by truly professional crime fighters, and the Los Angeles Police Department became the national symbol of that kind of crime fighting.

The "FBI Story"

In this shift of media images, from the federal level to the Los Angeles Police Department, the FBI had lost out. A fan writing after early radio episodes of *Dragnet* made as his first point: "Unlike the FBI lad [the announcer on "This Is Your FBI"], your announcer doesn't intone unctuous bunk."[9]

Richard Gid Powers shows how the television series *The FBI* (1965) tried to turn toward family values and away from the passé tough guy, "take that you dirty rat" genre.

> A skeleton of the old action-detective formula remained in [the movie] *The F.B.I. Story* [1959] and 'The F.B.I.,' but a new set of conventions had been superimposed on it. This was the domestic formula, a concoction with two main ingredients—a warm, secure family group and an intrusion from the outside that disrupted it. . . . This domestic formula is perfectly suited to an audience whose interests are overwhelmingly private in orientation, an audience that has turned away from public affairs to immerse itself in the drama of private life. . . . By turning the G-men into a symbol of morality Hoover made them vulnerable to precisely the kind of allegations that began to surface in the 1960s. . . . With the first stain on his cloak of moral perfection he [the G-man] forfeited that claim.[10]

Although the FBI and national political attention shifted to a focus on the cold war and communism, popular media continued to portray images of crime and crime fighting, for crime as a problem had not disappeared. And the formula stories for thinking about crime continued to enjoy mass popularity.

Perry Mason

In Erle Stanley Gardner's Perry Mason we meet one of the well-known postwar detectives who successfully crossed from one form of media to another. Mason, introduced in a wildly popular series of serialized stories and novels in the mid-1940s, had a bit of everything. Sophisticated and urbane, he could dish out tough talk and had a way of sizing up women, whether they were "dames" or real ladies. His sidekick and secretary, Della Street, could handle everything he dished out, and, not only that, she was "sympathetic, loyal and understanding."[11] Mason worked hard, was not terribly brainy, was brave and action-oriented and, Gardner let his readers know, could handle himself in the most sophisticated company even though his dialogue never included polysyllabic words.[12]

Mason did not appeal to the fireside virtues: he sniffed at rural bumpkins and rural ways. Sophisticated big-city people in these stories go to bed late and sleep late; only simple rural folk go to bed with the sun. He snaps about a rural store owner who protests about doing him a favor late at night: "If he wants to live out in the country and go to bed with the cows and chickens he'll have to realize that *we* can't gear *ourselves* to *his* schedule."¹³

Though a lawyer, Mason does not exemplify the rule of law. Rather, the law and the courtroom form the stage on which he can practice his individual heroism. Part of his urbanity comes from sly legal manipulation and deception. Because he has to lie and deceive to overcome other liars or incompetents, the reader accepts it as a part of his cleverness.

As a guide to the actual world of crime and justice, the Perry Mason stories typify a fictional world very different from the real one. Most cops are simple and vain, if not thuggish and brutal; the higher levels of the system are so influenced by "politics," *always* an ominous word in a mystery, that there is only the occasional flash of honest intelligence. Bad guys are best punished prior to prison, a fatal accident while escaping is especially just. And the offenders themselves are always grasping, cowardly, and plotting. None are poor, ill-educated, alcohol-damaged, unpredictable or purely predatory. Few are the age of the typical offender and most tend to be more near the age of Mason himself.

Mickey Spillane and the Hard-Boiled

If Perry Mason worked through deception and cleverness, another wildly popular postwar detective took a very different route. Mike Hammer just killed, smashed, pulverized, or tortured the bad guys he encountered. The ultimate "hard-boiled" detective, Hammer detested evil, saw women as meat, and hated homosexuals. Hammer also hated killers (except himself), "I couldn't think of anything I'd rather do than shoot a killer and watch his blood trace a slimy path across the floor" (1951).¹⁴ His kind, of course, has continued into today's violent movie superheroes, who talk even less effusively than Mike Hammer.

And, to complete his worldview, Hammer also wanted to kill all Communists. As Spillane had him subtly comment on Communists: "Kill 'em left and right, show 'em that we aren't so soft after all. Kill, kill, kill, kill!"¹² Unlike most mystery writers in the postwar period, Spillane came from a comic book background, which accounts for his simple, graphic violence and emphasis on action. His ultraconservative worldview earned him the approval of libertarian Ayn Rand, and Spillane's philosophy about writing sounds as though it had been lifted from Rand herself:

> Spillane has never made extravagant claims for his fiction. He self-
> deprecatingly describes himself as the "chewing gum of American literature."
> To those who say his work is garbage, he replies, "but it is good garbage." The
> fact that he has been scorned by the critics doesn't particularly bother him,
> given his success with readers. "The only award I've ever gotten is the ringing
> of the cash register from the public." Characterizing himself as a writer rather

than an author, he acknowledges that his primary urge is money: "Creative urge, hell—I get a money urge."[16]

II. POSTWAR YOUTH CULTURE

Two of the most powerful and long-lasting treatments of youth and crime came in the years *before* the baby boomers had reached any meaningful age so as to change the larger society. If anything, these fictional treatments are more about the parents of the baby boomers, yet they became the reigning narratives about postwar youth.

The Baby Boom

It is important to pause here a moment and remember just how much the world of the fiction detectives was a fantasy world. Postwar detectives gained their enormous readership just as the baby boom occurred: in reality their readers were embarked on an extraordinary burst of family formation unmatched by any other period in the twentieth century. Most adult males married and had families; most people, including unmarrieds, lived in a family context. Although a vast proportion of the fictional detective heroes are single males, when authors do create women or gay detectives, they usually place them as living alone and always on the edge of a romantic relationship. As fictional devices, the single adult gives the author the ability to have a romantic tension and play throughout a series—will Parker ever find true love? Most readers probably would acknowledge this, but by bracketing what they read as fiction, they enjoy this long-standing convention.

But in the context of the larger families and increased affluence—more single-family homes and widespread automobile ownership—vague Communist plots did not intersect with life experiences of most people. But the increased number of young people did make themselves felt. And well before the actual numbers of teenagers increased, public concern about them and about youth life did. Thus was born the crime fear phenomenon of the 1950s: *juvenile delinquency*.

Juvenile Delinquency

Historian James Gilbert has shown how the postwar concern about juvenile delinquency was a veritable media explosion.[17] This explosion and the films, literature, and research which had created it, dissected the reality, causes, and feelings about youth crime. In fact, there was little good evidence that an actual outbreak of juvenile crime was indeed occurring. Ironically, the reality of such crime became much more severe and socially threatening two or even three decades later—well after the panic.

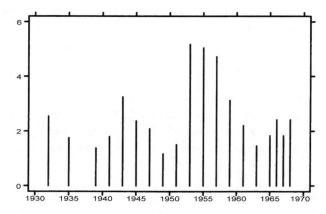

Figure 1.1 Articles per month on Juvenile Delinquency. Source: calculated from data in J. Gilbert, *A Cycle of Outrage,* 65.

Gilbert asserts that this outpouring of concern came from agitation of researchers, writers, and government officials (including J. Edgar Hoover) during World War II. Hoover evoked particular concern in a series of articles during and after the war. He claimed that crime by girls had skyrocketed, that marijuana smoking gangs were depredating Los Angeles, and that the postwar period would experience these youthful gangs awakening to vent their rage. "Like the sulphurous lava which boils beneath the slumbering volcano—such is the status of crime in America today."[18]

The Los Angeles Zoot Suit Riot of 1943, which was a series of attacks by sailors on Latino teenagers dressed in zoot suits, was (mis)interpreted often as a juvenile delinquency problem. The "problem," young people wearing flashy suits with baggy pants, is hard for us to see except that the clothing reflected a countercultural expression. Nevertheless, the Los Angeles city council made the wearing of the zoot suit a misdemeanor after the riots. When California governor Earl Warren appointed a "Youth in Wartime Committee" in 1943, he stated: "Normal life and living conditions have been dislocated, and as a result youth problems are greater and more complex than ever before."[19]

Rebel without a Cause

Robert Lindner's novel, *Rebel without a Cause*, published in 1944, explicitly yoked the more moralistic government crusade against lawless youth with the wartime fear of fascism. The youth in his book represented an "embryonic Storm-Trooper."[20] Though fascism itself did not develop as a postwar threat, communism did. And as historian James Gilbert has shown, the delinquency scare could as easily be linked to communism as fascism. In 1954 Senator Hendrickson told a conference on delinquency that "Not even the Communist conspiracy could devise a more effective way to demoralize, disrupt, confuse, and destroy our future citizens than apathy on the part of adult Americans to the scourge known as Juvenile Delinquency." In the same year Lois Higgins told Congress that delinquency was actually a part of the Communist conspiracy. To combat it, the United States had to tell its children "about the secret weapons of our enemy. Let us tell them, too, that the obscene material that is flooding the Nation today is another cunning device of our enemies, deliberately calculated to destroy the decency and morality which are the bulwarks of society."[21]

When translated to film over a decade later, *Rebel without a Cause* (1955) shifted in its focus from a warning about fascism to a critique of the American family, a warning about rootlessness and wealth. The film's main character, Jim, played by James Dean, captured (or created) the personal rebellion of an only child whose family life is a series of torments. In one family argument, the TV set, a symbol of consumer wealth, blinks in the background. But the TV is only a small part of the problem, for there is a deeper cause: a weak father and excessive power of women, both Jim's mother and *her* mother. He turns to his father for guidance but the father is unable to do more than make a wimpy list of alternatives. Jim's father wears an apron in the home and brings the mother breakfast in bed. His best advice to his son is to avoid standing out: "You can't be idealistic all your life." Juvenile delinquency as such is only a minor part of the film; its root causes are the focus, and the root causes are a corrupt and woman-dominated society.

Jim, his girlfriend, Judy, and their disturbed young friend, Plato, all have a short moment of happiness when they make up a symbolic nuclear family inhabiting an abandoned mansion in the Hollywood hills—the image is that of a proper nuclear family with a strong father, forced to live a furtive existence in the decaying mansion of a decadent society. In contrast to the slightly later *West Side Story,* police come off well in this film, which may reflect its origin in a wartime novel. At worst, the police are bumbling: when the delinquents taunt the police, they call them Nazis. The only authority figure of hope is a sympathetic (male) detective, who genuinely understands and sympathizes with the kids.

The actual images of delinquency come when the bad guys try to get Jim to fight with switchblades, challenge him to playing "chicken" with cars (again, the sign of a corrupt affluent society), chase him and his friends with chains. The weapons the juveniles don't have are important: guns appear in the hands of the police and Plato (Sal Mineo), who is a victim of the gang. Perhaps most interesting today is the issue of race: there is one African American in the film, the maid who takes care of Plato. Bad guys and good guys are all white.

West Side Story

By the late 1950s, the poetic and romantic vision of youth crime and gangs reached its remarkable peak and turning point in *West Side Story.* With a brilliant score by Leonard Bernstein and a libretto by Stephen Sondheim, based on an idea of Jerome Robbins, the musical was a Broadway sensation in 1957. (As a film, it won an Oscar in 1961.) The story, loosely modeled on Shakespeare's *Romeo and Juliet,* offered an entree into the world of rival gangs. Capturing the tensions of the cold war, the film subtly tells us that gang warfare over turf is as old as conflict in the fifteenth century, and as foolish as the carefully orchestrated turf violence in cold war Europe. The musical's parallel between the fifteenth century and the 1950s has some historical accuracy: access to weapons and rival group violence did belong to the upper classes in the early modern urban world. High society *was* violent then, and only the wealthy could afford weapons of quality. Access to weapons has drifted downward, as have the codes which govern the behavior of an armed class. Called the "civilizing process" by sociologist Norbert Elias, rules governing interpersonal violence began in late medieval courtly codes (hence the word "courtesy").

The explicit conflict in the musical is over turf and ethnicity—Puerto Ricans versus "whites" who, we are reminded carefully, are themselves second-generation immigrants. The police in it, represented by Officer Krupke, are careerist and racially prejudiced; Officer Krupke is a part of the problem in driving apart racial groups. There is no hope from intellectuals either: a sociological analysis of juvenile delinquency as a "social disease" is mocked. The only saving virtue is in young love, which obliterates racial barriers.

Two exchanges of the gang members with Doc, owner of the candy store hangout, make these themes clear. He chides them for the escalating violence, "You kids'll make this world lousy," which is rebuffed by their "We didn't make it, Doc." And later, he asks them, "Why do you kids live like there's a war on?" Here the underlying causes are shifted to the adult world and paralleled with the geopolitical fears of the cold war era.

The popularity of this particular vision of youth crime clearly marks a new attitude for the 1960s—rebellious youth as pure people in a corrupt society. Just as Hoover had the FBI image (and practice, to a certain extent) turn away from crime control in the immediate postwar era, by the end of the 1950s, juvenile delinquency had begun to be redefined. No longer a threat, it presented a potential force for the good.

Analysis and Reflection

Through all of the postwar outpouring on juvenile delinquency, three anomalies confound an analysis of juvenile delinquency that would only use fiction as a source of information.

The first is something that cannot help but strike some readers in the twenty-first century as odd: the race of the juvenile delinquents—they are almost all white. *West Side Story* did have Puerto Ricans, but the overall whiteness of the topic is best suggested by Gilbert's study: his index has no entry for race. The Zoot Suit Riot victims were Mexican-American. But were there no African American, Chicano, or Asian gang members in the 1950s? Or were there as many as now, and did the outpouring of concern reflect something else?

The second is the question of demography, the baby boom which began in 1946. The delinquency scare cannot have reflected the baby boom, because the first seventeen-year-old baby boomers would have been visible about 1963, *after* the peak in the juvenile delinquency scare.

The third anomaly has to do with patterns in urban growth. The 1950s witnessed an enormous expansion of small cities built near older, larger ones. In vast tract housing developments and in the many smaller developments, parents of the baby boomers, financed by subsidies to ex-GIs, moved out of old housing and into new. Suburbanization, the turn to smaller cities, characterized huge segments of the American residential shift. What did this have to do with the images of rebellious teenagers?

Today, fictional images of juvenile delinquents have been replaced by the occasional vision of armed gang members, usually Latino or African-American. But these images are not as popular for film media as the explosively dangerous super cop. This super cop has his predecessor in Mike Hammer, so the idea of an unbelievably aggressive killer on the side of good is not new. Mike Hammer simply did not have the imaginary technology of the new bloodthirsty savior—no artificial body parts or super weapons.

III. CRIME PAYS—AT THE BOX OFFICE

Since the late 1960s, the consumer of crime entertainment has had a vast choice which no one could have anticipated in the late 1950s. Only two crime-related films had won Oscars before 1971 (*On the Waterfront* in 1954 and *West Side Story* in 1961). But by the early seventies, crime was big in the movies in a fashion never before seen. For four years in a row crime movies won Oscars: *The French Connection* (1971), *The Godfather* (1972), *The Sting* (1973), and *The Godfather, Part II* (1974). These films paid homage to graphic violence in ways at which *West Side Story* had only faintly hinted.

Since then, these hints and tendencies have been magnified into dozens upon dozens of thematic variations. From robot police (in the film *Robocop*, 1987) to gay detectives (Joseph Hansen's Brandstetter) to African Americans (Walter Mosley's Easy Rawlins) to Navahos (Tony Hillerman's Joe Leaphorn) to hard-boiled women (Sarah Paretsky's V.I. Warshawski) to organized crime and on and on. Whole books are available which analyze subgenres. Richard Meyers's very useful *TV Detectives*, for example, covers with scholarly care the pre-1980s television era. Dozens of dissertations on mystery stories have been and are being written. And soon, given the continuing crises in the former Yugoslavia, one can predict new analyses of Rex Stout's detective hero Nero Wolfe and his constant oblique references to Montenegro and the evils of Balkan politics.

Expansion of the Popular Media

Not only has crime fiction expanded in the post-sixties era, so have movies and television shows. Some of the greatest talents in the entertainment industry have turned to making varied forms of crime-based entertainment. From acting to cinematography to script writing, television viewers today have a feast of options. This section examines what does seem to be the one truly new genre of popular crime entertainment, the docudrama and other "live"-footage formats.

Docudramas like *Rescue 911* or live-footage shows such as *Cops* all work on the notion that what is being seen is reality. Lest it not be clear, it should be pointed out that such shows are closer to reality only in the sense that what is shown is less likely to be fabricated than in fiction. The reenactments in docudramas mix professional actors with original participants, but even then, the normal stuttering, dead time in conversations, and the general ineptness of human life are not displayed. More to the point, docudramas are most typically used for those stories whose narrative structure has some relationship to conventions of rising action, climax, and resolution. There are exceptions, however, which do contribute something new. The exceptions, such as *America's Most Wanted* or *Unsolved Mysteries,* come from a violation of narrative convention—no closure or resolution. These can only come when the bad person is found, turned in, and reported on subsequent shows. Here, then, is an interesting turn, for the shows that have dramatized reality actually do intervene in everyday life so that the evildoers are caught and life gives previous shows a kind of closure.

In crime and crime fighting as entertainment, the idea of showing the real dates back to at least the eighteenth century, when printed versions of sermons given at executions were popular. In these sermons readers could be sure to get graphic descriptions and lurid etchings of hideous crimes, criminals, and their just punishments. Then, in the early nineteenth century, the stories of infamous murders (such as that of Mary Rogers in New York in 1841) were turned into inexpensive books. Mary Rogers also becomes a fictional victim in one of America's early mystery stories, Poe's "The Murder of Marie Roget."

By the middle of the nineteenth century, popular newspapers had begun to print extensive details about particularly lurid crimes. The innovative *Police Gazette* (begun in 1845) amplified on such stories with pictures of the most hideous or sexy crimes.[22] By drawing on the whole United States, it was able to keep its readers abreast of sensational events across the country, rather than an occasional burst from a single community. Its pictures were a considerable improvement over the images from execution sermons, gave a sense of action hard to convey until moving images of the twentieth century, and could only be supplanted by photographs of the actual crime in progress.

All these genres included details so as to give the greatest semblance of reality: quotations, testimony, eyewitness accounts, and artists' renderings of the action.

Photography made less of an impact on such true-life stories than might be imagined because the actual event could not be pictured and because the mass reproduction of photographs in inexpensive media had to wait until the twentieth century. Well known today, the exposé photographs such as those taken by Jacob Riis at the end of the nineteenth century were carefully reproduced for middle-class viewers of his day. Further, photographs had to be incorporated into a

Figure 1.2 *Police Gazette,* ca. 1860, "New York's Deadly Dives," shows a fight in progress, something unavailable in real-time images until very recently.

narrative, which, in his case, was for a middle-class, reform-oriented audience. In any case, a lightweight camera was not available for good-quality photography until the 1930s, with the German Leica, which used 35mm motion picture film as its stock. Furthermore, its price restricted it to well-off journalists. This restriction left action drawings, including comic books, to carry the weight of visual representation of most crimes.

The Advent of Real-Time Images

A slow change began with the advent of amateur 8mm movie cameras. Again, their cost, low only when compared to professional-quality 16mm cameras, the costliness of film and its typical time limit of three minutes, their technical complexity and relatively narrow range of light all severely limited the likelihood of amateurs capturing action as well as an artist's representation. But certain major social/political crises of the 1960s turned on the careful examination of both amateur and professional photographic images.

During the Cuban missile crisis, the public was treated to the photo magic of aerial reconnaissance spying on shipboard Soviet missiles being unloaded in Castro's Cuba. In order to bolster the case for the U.S. blockade, widely circulated enhanced aerial photographs became a part of the public domain. Shortly thereafter, Arnold Zapruder captured on film the assassination of President Kennedy, and the subsequent investigation made prominent frame-by-frame analyses of this amateur film. Following on this tragic event was the television news live filming of Jack Ruby murdering Kennedy's assassin. In the interests of political persuasion, a new usage of visual representation began in the early sixties which within a decade would become a means of criticizing the government. The era of the image as unmanipulated truth had begun.

Live footage from the Vietnam War came into the country's living rooms every night on the television news. These images ran counter to the official version of events; slowly the country took the new attitude toward pictures as evidence to heart and the government's story on Vietnam began to ring hollow. Many commentators argue that the Vietnam War would not have been so widely resisted had not the television brought some aspects of it back to the United States.

At the same time, a literary reinvention occurred which helped provide narrative conventions for such real-time images. Well-known writers began to explore real events, including heinous crimes, in a form sometimes called "faction." Truman Capote told in novelistic form the grisly story of two serial killers in *In Cold Blood* (1965): based on his extensive prison interviews and personal acquaintance with the killers, the work made special truth claims because of its reporting of reality.

Toward the end of the sixties, the notion that film could be used to unmask reality took even stronger hold of the public imagination. Antonioni's 1966 film *Blow Up* expressed this notion most clearly: the film's plot revolves around a fashion photographer's careful darkroom enlargement of an accidental series of images. With his technical expertise, they reveal a murder in progress behind what seemed to be a romantic encounter. A new visual vocabulary had emerged: objective reports on real events could bring observers into real social crises.

Given this new power of film footage, the advent of the camcorder filled a niche waiting to be exploited. Unlike the movie camera, the camcorder can operate in a wide range of lighting, it requires no costly film processing, it shoots two hours as opposed to three minutes, its technology allows sound recording, and the automation of focusing and light sensing has made the amateur able to capture moving images nearly impossible twenty years ago. The capturing of real-time, moving images has given a whole new means of expression to a vast public. And commercial entertainment has begun to capture this, following the convention established in the usage of the Zapruder footage of Kennedy.

Already there are at least three conventions for the use of real-time images: (1) The incorporation in fiction of well-known amateur footage of a serious, real event, such as the killing of Kennedy (as in *JFK*) or the beating of Rodney King in Los Angeles (*Malcolm X*); this convention is of interest for what it affirms: what we see is real. This convention carries with it the notion that events can be understood, can be uncovered and interpreted. That this is a convention is made most clear when such images are taken apart, often with the purpose of unmasking some deeper reality. (2) The dramatic re-creation of a real event with a mix of live footage, professional actors, and original participants—docudramas, such as *Rescue 911*. (3) A complete story told with live-action footage, such as on *Cops*. While claims to authenticity had been the hallmarks of many earlier television shows, this new convention makes much more authentic claims on the viewer's sense of reality.

Even if these new claims are greatly exaggerated, they may have the consequence of changing some aspects of the reality they purport to represent. East German police, unfamiliar with civil rights or bank robbery or the idea of helping in emergencies, were shown programs like *Rescue 911* in order to learn what it is that police and emergency workers are supposed to do.[23] In 1998, in Los Angeles, some *Cops* sequences got reused in police training, this time as a bad example. This suggests that even as the new conventions of television are truly convincing, they also may have the consequence of making certain features of reality conform to television. The difference between a reality show like *Cops* and *Dragnet* is that reality shows are not nearly so crisp and conclusive.

This new genre raises an interesting possibility: that the public is willing to be entertained by nontraditional narrative, by open-ended, ambiguous, unflattering portraits of both offenders and the police. Or, will the urge to narrative closure narrow this kind of story to a more traditional plot: the mystery which leaves viewers and readers satisfied that there is no mystery after all?

NOTES

1. Richard G. Powers, *G-Men, Hoover's FBI in American Popular Culture* (Carbondale: Southern Illinois University Press, 1983).

2. J. Edgar Hoover, *Persons in Hiding* (Boston: Little, Brown, 1938), Hoover was never troubled by excess modesty! *Persons in Hiding*, ix.

3. Ibid., xv.

4. Ibid., xvii.

5. Ibid., xvii–xviii.

6. David Shaw, "The Media and the LAPD: From Coziness to Conflict," *Los Angeles Times*, May 24, 25, 1992.

7. The LAPD actually had women officers, and they had been given small roles in the earliest radio versions of *Dragnet. The Police: An Interview by Donald McDonald with William H. Parker* (Santa Barbara: Center for the Study of Democratic Institutions. Fund for the Republic, 1962), 13–14.

8. One can question the artlessness and strict attention to facts in the Webb series. For instance, Webb dedicated his book *The Badge* (Englewood Cliffs: Prentice-Hall, 1958) to Lew, presumably Ross McDonald's detective Lew Archer.

9. Letter, October 1949, from B.J.R. Stolper bound in Volume 1 of *Dragnet* scripts in AAUPL Special Collections at UCLA, URL. Curiously, Stolper, about fifty-five at the time, was a scholar, perhaps a high school teacher, and the author of two books, one on Stephen Crane and the other on high school teaching of history, art, and social studies.

10. Powers, 248–254.

11. Gardner, *The Cautious Coquette* (New York: Morrow, 1949), 95.

12. Today's readers would be shocked only by one thing: he smoked. But then, in the postwar era, almost all authority figures smoked, and in public—even President Eisenhower.

13. Gardner, *The Cautious Coquette*, p. 87.

14. Mickey Spillane, *Vengeance Is Mine* (New York: New American Library, 1950).

15. *One Lonely Night* (New York: New American Library, 1951).

16. Gehern, 128–29.

17. James Gilbert, *A Cycle of Outrage* (Oxford: Oxford University Press, 1986).

18. All from Gilbert, *A Cycle of Outrage*, 28.

19. Ibid., 31, for sources and citations.

20. Ibid., 40.

21. Ibid., 75.

22. Here, taken from Edward Van Every's *Sins of New York* (New York: Stokes, 1930), 212.

23. Tamara Jones, "East German Police Face Arresting Obstacles," *Los Angeles Times* (January 5, 1993), H 6, for *Rescue 911* reference; Dan Cray, "Inside Story; The LAPD's Reality Check; Somehow, Altercations Don't Play Out like They Do in Movies and TV. That's Why the Department Has Revolutionized Its Officer Training," *Los Angeles Times Magazine* (December 13, 1998), 22:

Jack Webb has been dead for 16 years, but you couldn't convince Greg Dossey of that. A 27-year veteran police officer, Dossey can't get away from the man who created *Dragnet* and transformed the LAPD into a brand name. Every time Dossey mingles with the public, he is confronted with the specter of the Webb ubercop. . . .

Cheeks are puffing, eyes are red, and the clock on the wall is the focus of attention as the thought of a break begins to enter weary minds. It's 6:30 a.m., and police officers are already 30 minutes into their daylong training sessions at the LAPD's 13,000-square-foot "dojo center" downtown. The "center" is actually rented space in the offices of the Holy Hill Korean-American Church, and other than a sign for LAPD parking, there is no indication the training center exists. Inside, the room is awash in confrontation and sweat. Bodies slam hard on mats as instructors shout guidance to officers. In an adjoining classroom, Dossey watches *Cops*. . . . Most of the officers love *Cops,* but Dossey especially enjoys it since it makes for great training material. In this particular clip, one officer is pulling a suspect's arm, attempting to throw him down. Problem is, another officer is attempting the same maneuver . . . from the opposite side. The result: They're pulling him in opposite directions, accomplishing nothing. The wrestling match veers into comedy as several officers reach for the suspect's flailing arms. In the first attempt, a handcuff is accidentally slapped on an officer's wrist—there are so many arms in the same place, no one is sure which belong to the suspect.

2

Crime and Punishment

When I wrote the following essay, nearly twenty years ago, an overview of the criminal justice system and crime itself seemed to be something that could be squeezed into twenty pages. Now we have Lawrence Friedman's much more comprehensive *Crime and Punishment in American History* (Basic, 1993) which comes in at just under six hundred pages. Yet this piece stands the test of time well, with one unfortunate exception: the problem of crime.

I was able to comment on the long-term decline in Western violence without a caveat about the current climate. We were actually at the front end of what would be two very bad decades of criminal violence in the United States. My comments in this piece were meant to be in the context of the high violence rates in the Middle Ages, but I should have made this clearer.

On the other hand, the story of imprisonment, of crime-control agencies, and the yet-to-be-solved puzzles of whether or not we can actually control crime remain. The tone attributed to scholars and conveyed in this piece probably is still prevalent amongst crime historians: optimistic criminal justice reformers lived and still live in cloud-cuckoo-land. It is difficult, studying the past, to find anything that seemed to work, to find any reform of the systemic problems that did not ultimately fail. It should always be remembered that this difficulty is an intellectual challenge. Just because our means of analysis are not quite up to the task, we have no justification to conclude that all crime-control policies are doomed to failure: we have to work even harder to discover this.

First published in Jack P. Greene, *Encyclopedia of American Political History* (New York: Scribner, 1984), 443–54.

One small comment in this paper was as prescient as the missing of a huge crime wave was not: criminal justice, even done badly, is very expensive. As the twenty-first century opens and states stagger under the burdens of costly prison systems, one wonders what the future holds in store: a disinvestment in the criminal justice system, a shrugging off of the commitment to keeping the nation crime-free, or a lack of any concern with a problem so difficult as to defy clear answers?

A traditional, relatively static system of criminal justice characterized English colonies in North America. The laws, the apparatus for enforcement and punishment, and the organizations all resembled the traditional models provided by the English Middle Ages. The nineteenth and early twentieth centuries saw a dramatic transformation, and virtually all of the modern tools of crime control had been created by 1930. On the other hand, the actual offense rate, the number of criminal acts per capita, did not change so abruptly or dramatically. Rates of serious crime apparently have been gradually declining since the Middle Ages, throughout the Western world. To be sure, there have been periods of dramatically increased crime rates—the 1850s, 1960s, and 1970s, for instance—but the best evidence is somewhat encouraging, suggesting that for unknown reasons our world has witnessed continuously less criminal violence.

Historians in general act with caution when making claims about the utility of lessons from the past; few of them have the temerity to expect their work to speak to—much less change—the present (Rothman 1981). Yet historians of crime cannot help but feel that their work does have lessons for the present. Of course, the history of crime is never studied primarily for purely utilitarian reasons. Like other forms of historical analysis, its main goals are to explain and understand the past in order to gain deeper social knowledge. But, as opposed to many other historical topics, crime and criminal justice carry an invisible policy imperative.

It is important, therefore, to make explicit the reasons for studying the history of crime and criminal justice. This ensures that the goal of our analysis will not obstruct our understanding of the subject. Thus there are two conceptual frameworks with which to structure criminal justice history. The first is purely historical, to understand the past for its own sake and to understand society. The second is more pragmatic, to achieve analytic insights into the control of crime and to use the crime rate and our handling of crime as a social barometer.

The notion that crime rates provide a social barometer with which to compare societies was challenged and rejected by Émile Durkheim at the turn of the twentieth century. Arguing that a society needs crime to define the boundaries of acceptable behavior, Durkheim maintained that the amount of crime should be constant, although the kind of crime would change as the society changed. Durkheim's notion has inspired both historical and criminological research, covering the whole span of American history. Most notable have been Kai Erikson's provocative work (1966) on crime in colonial Massachusetts and the research of Alfred Blumstein, his associates, and his critics (1979), who have analyzed long-range trends in imprisonment rates.

As used by historians and sociologists, Durkheim's argument speaks less to offense rates than to punishment rates. Thus one can assert the constancy of punishment while examining variations in the per-capita rate of offenses. We can use crime to see not only how we are doing but also how we are changing. This dualistic aspect of criminal justice history, therefore, is less contradictory than it may appear.

The purposive change of the criminal justice system has always been rife with argument and conflict. Indeed, the issues posed by "law-and-order" advocates in the late 1960s mirror only very faintly those of an earlier age. As elaborated in England in the eighteenth century, the most significant issue was centered on the apparently irreconcilable conflict between liberty and order. Those measures perceived as necessary to control public crimes of violence—the creation of a regularized police, more systematic surveillance, and a generally more intrusive criminal justice system—seemed to subtract from private liberty as they added to public order. Given this apparent trade-off, the English elite long resisted any criminal justice reforms that appeared to intrude on their liberties. The French police were always pointed to as a bad example of the consequences of greater organization in the name of crime control: they spied, they constantly trespassed on political liberties, they oppressively maintained the status quo. Thus when Sir Robert Peel created the London police in the late 1820s, he carefully avoided the word *police,* cautiously invoking notions of "public safety" instead.

That the criminal justice system underwent such great transformation in the nineteenth century suggests that the process was an aspect of modernization, of the ascent to power of the bourgeoisie, and of the evolution of Western society from agrarian to industrial. Each of these changes did indeed affect the criminal justice system, which by its very nature is political. Crime is most reasonably, if circularly, defined as behavior that violates the criminal law. And organized systems of control and a body of laws created by political systems cannot help but reflect the major socioeconomic changes of an age. Yet the political aspect of crime does not account for the criminal behavior of individuals, and here a conundrum appears. For, although the crime control system was transformed, there is little evidence of such transformation in criminal behavior. That is, there is no good reason to find any cause-and-effect in either direction between the actions of criminal offenders and change in the system designed to control them. This makes the historian's job both interesting and difficult: changes in the system cannot be analyzed simply as passively responsive, nor can the directional variations of crime rates be analyzed as responding to the system.

Recent work on the policy of criminal justice has highlighted this conundrum and its disturbing implications for modern policy makers. One might conclude from Silberman's study (1978) of crime and crime control, for instance, that "nothing works," that policy directed toward crime is bound to fail. But a more accurate appraisal is that the relationships between crime control and crime cannot be established with any confidence. In a sense, the strength of history, working through tradition, makes us fear to deal with crime in new ways; at the same time we are not convinced that the means given to us by the past are adequate.

Yet a centuries-long, gradual decline in Western per-capita felony rates contrasts with the comparatively abrupt transformation of the criminal justice system in the nineteenth century. The contrast suggests that, at least on the grand scale, the simplest message to be drawn from the past is as unclear as that of recent criminal justice research. There is no immediately visible relationship between actual crime and the system intended to control it. How, then, can the crime control system be effectively manipulated? Are crime rates driven by causal mechanisms independent of those implemented by the control system? Is crime control merely whistling in the dark? Only a careful and tentative look at the history of criminal justice can begin to help us to understand the past for its own sake and to think with some clarity about current options.

THE CRIMINAL LAW

Most of what we call crime today would have been recognized as such by our colonial forebears, just as we would consider criminal most of the offenses that they prosecuted. Unlike the civil law, which some historians argue underwent a capitalist "transformation" in the late eighteenth and early nineteenth centuries, criminal law changed slowly and imperceptibly (Horwitz 1977; Fletcher 1976)—so subtly as to escape most legal and historical analysts. Even if its history has not been filled with sudden or surprising developments, it is important to start with the law itself.

In a formal and important sense, crime begins with the criminal law. When criminologists define crime as behavior proscribed by the criminal law, they are expressing more than a circular argument. Before behavior can be criminal, there must be a state. The wrongful action of an individual becomes an offense against the state when it threatens the state's power. When the state has little power, or its power is limited in geographical scope, the range of criminal offenses is likewise limited. In English law the notion of the king's peace in the Middle Ages at first applied only to the area near the king, then later to the king's highways, and finally to the country as a whole. As the scope of criminal law expanded, so did the power of the state. In a state with limited power, even homicide is a private wrong; not until the state itself gains the right to take an individual life does it become criminalized.

Therefore, only because it is proscribed by law is criminal behavior raised from the level of private wrong to a wrong against the state. Specifically created as a behavioral category by law, crime is essentially political. Here *political* does not mean that offenders of the law act with political intentions but that the political system has given their actions conceptual significance. And this sense of *political* is far from trivial, for the incorporation of private wrongs into the criminal law created a new sense of rights in the Western world, the right to freedom from criminal violence.

By the mid-nineteenth century, American criminal justice officials had grouped all offenses into three categories for the purpose of tabulation: crimes against property, crimes against persons, and crimes against morality or statutes. As far as the first two categories are concerned, the law and perception of criminal behavior have not changed very much. In the late twentieth century most forms of theft and personal violence still look about the same, even if the technology associated with them has become more sophisticated. Most seventeenth-century crimes against morality still exist, even if they go unprosecuted. And statutory crimes have expanded, but they make up a tiny proportion of all criminal behavior.

This rather surprising stability in legal and perceived definitions of serious criminal behavior may be epitomized in the Federal Bureau of Investigation's *Uniform Crime Reports*. In spite of criticism and the FBI's own disavowal of the statistical utility of the first thirty-five years of the series, the reports have become the bench mark for definitions of crime in the United States. Since 1930 they have given monthly updates and annual indices of seven different offenses, or "index crimes," known to the police: homicide, rape, robbery, burglary, larceny, assault, and auto theft. Only the last would be incomprehensible to colonial Americans, although they might perhaps have included some moral offenses— adultery, for instance—that the FBI has dropped from the statistical forefront.

Theft, which has changed only slightly on the surface, has undergone an interesting and subtle shift in the common law since the sixteenth century. Its definition has had to encompass forms of property and economic life radically different from those that the law originally protected. Yet its essence has remained trespass and the concept of thief-like behavior. That is, the thief has had to act like a thief, to be defined under the law as a thief. In the sixteenth century these basic principles covered most forms of theft. If the owner of a piece of portable property gave it to someone who converted it for personal gain, this action would not constitute theft under the common law, for the receiver had "possessorial immunity." Carrier's case in the late fifteenth century dealt with this problem, establishing that if the receiver broke the bulk of the other's property—that is, broke into a package removing some or all of its contents—then a felonious trespass had occurred.

The law of theft tried to accommodate increasingly complex forms of property relationships until the late eighteenth and early nineteenth centuries, when what Fletcher has called a "metamorphosis" occurred. This metamorphosis refocused the law away from the specific moment of the criminal act—for example, a delivery person's breaking into a package—and away from possessorial immunity. The new object of scrutiny became the actor instead of the act. Although acting "like a thief" may seem to attend to the actor, it did so only at the instant of the offense—when the offender violently broke into a house, for instance. The new focus turned away from the instant of the action to accommodate planning, execution, and consequences.

A subtle conceptual metamorphosis with only modest consequences for the vast bulk of thefts, this shift does have a direct analogue to modes of punishment. As delineated by Foucault, the changing modes of punishment can be related to a whole new notion, the rise of the individual, and a conception that the individual's "career," rather than particular acts, is the object of importance. In Foucault's formulation, this change came about as a consequence of growing state power and its simultaneous disappearance behind the mask of bureaucracy. In the case of larceny, this conceptual shift had little visible effect on the definition or day-to-day aspects of criminal behavior. On the other hand, the parallel change in punishment was indeed dramatic: torture declined, public executions disappeared, and penitentiaries began to dot the landscape.

A more practical problem for the criminal law arose as theft became commercialized in a mass urban setting, particularly in London in the early eighteenth century. Jonathan Wild, the self-proclaimed "thief-taker general" for London, epitomized and made famous the role of the fence, flamboyantly capitalizing on the demands of both the thief and his victim: the thief wanted to convert stolen goods to money, the victim wanted to recover the goods. In an age before personal property insurance, the fence provided a useful function, returning the missing items to the owner—for a fee. Thus the victim recovered the goods, and the thief and fence made a small profit. Since Wild's time fences have caused legal difficulties. They do not act like thieves; they act like merchants. (For their actions to be criminal they must know that the goods they receive have been stolen.) Yet, the fence provides a critical nexus in supporting the economic enterprise of larceny. The criminal receiver legislation enacted in the mid-eighteenth century confronted but could not solve this persistent problem. Convicting a fence continues to be very difficult, often requiring perjury on the part of law enforcement officials (Hall 1952; Klockars 1980).

Although the history of the law of larceny is conceptually exciting, like most of our criminal law it is hardly filled with stunning reversals. Witchcraft might be considered a major and sensational exception to this generalization. Few people today believe in witches, and as a result, their trials and executions in the seventeenth century appear fanatical and wrong. One must not presume the innocence of seventeenth-century witches, however (Butler 1979). In an age that took its religion seriously, witches could use their powers in ways as malevolent as other felons. The problem with the Salem witchcraft trials of 1692–1693 was not witchcraft itself but the admission of the "spectral evidence" of accusers. This troubled Cotton Mather; for, although the witches may have been real, there was no way to corroborate their accusers' visions.

Two other aspects of criminal law from the colonial period, which seem equally foreign today, remind us that ours is a secular world. Many criminal offenses in the colonies retained "benefit of clergy" until the end of the eighteenth century. A common-law device, the benefit of clergy had been designed to preserve the division between ecclesiastical and secular law. Many common-law offenses were stipulated as clergiable, indicating that clergymen could not be prosecuted for them. In practice, the determination of a defendant's clergiable status amounted to a literacy test, the reading aloud of a section of the Bible. Such a test, particularly given jailed defendants' powers of memorization, ensured the acquittal of many. An equally peculiar practice persisted into the seventeenth century. This was deodand, a nonhuman object, such as an animal or tool, that had been instrumental in a criminal act (resulting in death). It was not formally abolished in England until 1846, when the application of the concept to train accidents could have proven very costly. The deodand, if an animal, might be executed or, if a tool or instrument, confiscated by the state. Although interesting, these practices were only a small part of the criminal law or criminal behavior. But crimes of magic and conjuring, the benefit of clergy, and deodand serve to remind us of our tacit acceptance of a material world unsuffused with spiritual meanings.

Fornication by unmarried people is still an offense in many states. Virtually unprosecuted today, more court cases of fornication were prosecuted during the mid-eighteenth century than cases of theft or interpersonal violence (Nelson 1975; Hindus 1980; Greenberg 1976). But these prosecutions had motives rooted in local economies: local courts could establish paternity to remove the women and children involved from local welfare rolls. These prosecutions served as a way to evade the local obligation to support poor residents (Jones 1983). Thus, rather than interpreting fornication statutes as signs of intrusive colonial concern with private morality, they might instead be seen as a means of transferring nominal public obligations to private individuals.

In the nineteenth century, legal reformers struggled to rationalize state legal systems that seemed to defy Enlightenment principles of criminal law. To deter crime, the thinking went, the list of proscriptions and punishments must be public, rational, and easily understood. The existing criminal laws, built by accretion on a common-law inheritance, were exactly the opposite of such a system. In this context, it is easier to understand the passion that surrounded the codification movement, which its supporters envisioned as a rationalizing, liberal reform. Massachusetts led the way in codification. Although reformers never enacted a code, they did get a collection of revised statutes in 1835 that served as a reasonable substitute. South Carolina, ever conservative, resisted codification or even a rational compilation until forced to do so during Reconstruction (Hindus 1980; Friedman 1973).

By the end of the nineteenth century, the rationale behind much criminal law had become buried, as Friedman points out, in legal "inflation." In many states the number of specific offenses enumerated in the criminal code had become large and hopelessly detailed; for example, section 2121 of the 1881 Indiana code prohibiting the selling of grain seed that harbored the seeds of Canada thistle (Friedman 1973). But the apparent irrationality of these codes actually preceded the creation of the law of regulation. To give bite to regulatory law, legislators by the end of the nineteenth century often criminalized the behavior under question, as in the grain seed example above. Thus the apparent plethora of criminal conducts represented the more detailed regulation of the economy. The control of monopolies illustrates this best. The Sherman Antitrust Act of 1890, for instance, seemed ineffectual until given a criminal bite by the Clayton Antitrust Act twenty-four years later. Fines enforced the Sherman Act; the Clayton Act added imprisonment—presumably a greater deterrent for corporate representatives.

Finally, public and legislative concern about the morality and efficacy of capital punishment increased. By the mid-nineteenth century, Wisconsin had entered the Union without any capital offenses; Maine and Michigan abolished capital punishment in the 1880s. In contrast, South Carolina reduced its capital offenses from 165 in 1813 to a mere 22 by 1850 (Friedman 1973). In related developments, northern states reduced or ended corporal punishment, whereas southern states tended to retain it. These legal differences should not automatically be attributed to conservative southern attitudes toward crime. Most southern states had weak governments and very low levels of public services. Criminal justice reforms, such as the codification of laws or the creation of more just criminal justice systems, are costly. Southern states spent little money or legislative time on any aspect of their governmental apparatus. Under such circumstances one must not be surprised to find corporal punishment; it is not only inexpensive but also emphasizes the power of the state.

The United States now has fifty-one criminal codes, one for each state and one for the federal government; regulatory law, too, often prescribes criminal punishment for its offenders. These codes alone define crime—but they do not tell us what occurs in the outside world, to which the laws apply. For this, we must examine policing systems and the behavior of criminal offenders.

POLICE

Police are uniformed officers whose task it is to enforce local ordinances and the criminal laws of the government. As the Greek root (*polis*) suggests, the police are urban in locus, although in the early twentieth century contradictorily labeled "rural police" appeared. American cities began to create police departments in the mid-nineteenth century. The first uniformed police, in Boston and New York, were explicitly modeled on the Metropolitan Police of London, established in 1829 (Lane 1967; Miller 1977; Monkkonen 1981). These organizations replaced an ancient and traditional system, the constable and night watch. The constable-and-watch system had long been criticized for its bumbling ineffectiveness and, since Shakespeare's time, had furnished material for comedies. This system and the police that followed it exemplify the dramatic transition from an organic to a rational system. Conceptually, organizationally, and behaviorally, the contrast between the two forms of crime control highlights the differences between the modern and premodern world.

In theory, the constable and the night watch represented the community. The constable served the court, his remuneration coming from fees attached to the individual services he performed. The watch, on the other hand, represented community members, who each took his turn at night patrolling the town. Their guidance came from the constable, their legal authority from the notion of posse comitatus, which required that all adult males in the community be responsible for pursuing felons. Whereas the night watch was "proactive," patrolling to prevent disturbances as well as to report anything untoward, the constable was "reactive," not actively seeking offenses or offenders but responding to complaints made either to him or to the courts.

The night watch had ceased to be composed of volunteer townsmen long before the English brought the institution to North America. By then it consisted of hired "substitutes," usually unemployable or—quite literally—moonlighting men. Virtually every reference to the night watch pokes fun at them, citing their cowardice, drunkenness, laziness, and overall ineptness. No historian has yet tried to ascertain the accuracy of these charges, but one thing is clear: the differing patrol and scheduling traditions of the constable and the watch led to great organizational inefficiency. The night watch patrolled from sunset to sunrise; the constables usually served from 8 A.M. until 5 P.M. In the summer, as a consequence, no one served for the long daylight periods in the morning and evening.

Moreover, the reactive nature of the constables, the requirement of paying them fees, and the apparent inefficiency of the watch resulted in a passive policing system that not only had little or no investigative capacity and no responsibility to seek out offenses, but also placed the burden of law enforcement on the victims. For the poor in particular, seeking the constable's assistance would be far more costly than suffering the damages. Until the introduction of non-fee-based policing, the state's power in crime control was only nominal. A passive agent, the criminal law came into action only when the seriousness of the offense outweighed the costs of calling on the state for assistance.

The creation of the uniformed urban police made the criminal law active. This did not necessarily mean that the creators had wanted an active law, for the reasons that had led to the uniforming of the police did not often portend their functions once they began to patrol. Americans traveling in England had often admired London's orderliness and apparent lack of crime, which observers often attributed to Robert Peel's Metropolitan Police. Both in Boston and New York, a small number of wealthy, educated reformers began working to replace the antiquated constable-and-watch sytem with a police modeled on the bobbies or peelers. The reformers wanted polite policemen who would bring order to the streets.

The new police, they hoped, would replace the loosely organized watch with efficient, well-organized, and uniformed officers. They would follow orders, deter crime through their uniformed presence, and detect unreported crimes. The uniforms symbolized the importance of the goals and provided the means to implement them. Before the new form of policing was adopted, the constables and watch wore what they pleased and, when given stars or other badges, placed them on easily covered parts of their jackets. The plain clothes gave them freedom to be their own boss, once out of the sight of their superiors. Anonymity preserved their independence and made them virtually masterless in the streets. Like the urban artisans whose own autonomy was being eroded at the same time, the police vigorously resisted any constraint on their independence. Bringing them under tight control and making them regularly visible and available constituted the central vision of their creators. The intimidating sight of the uniformed officer, it was confidently predicted, would deter the potential criminal. The almost military command structure would swiftly direct and coordinate police actions; regular, aggressive patrolling would find and prosecute criminals who had operated undiscovered under the looser systems.

The transition from one system to another came about slowly in the first cities making the change, but by the 1860s and 1870s the rate of change began to accelerate. In Boston and New York, a separate night police, headed by a constable or captain, mirrored the day police, but each operated independently. The two forces served as a transitional form and probably provided increased resistance to the final unification of New York's police in 1853, Boston's in 1859. Although the reformation of the police was opposed in all quarters, the most vigorous protest came from the police officers themselves. They saw the change as degrading their autonomy and status, for in the antebellum United States, only servants wore nonmilitary uniforms. City governments themselves resisted the new police, for the earlier police were far less costly, because they paid themselves with the fees they collected.

England's example provided the prototype for the urban police, but Americans introduced significant modifications, perhaps unknowingly. No one considered organizing the police from the top down, at the federal or even state level. In each city the reform began locally and stayed local, and from the beginning the police acted as agents of local government. This difference accompanied another structural shift. The constable had been an agent of the courts, doing both civil and criminal work, like the sheriff at the county level. In contrast, the new police had their allegiance to the executive branch of city government, partly because the city courts had complete jurisdiction only over minor criminal offenses and partly because the new police worked around the clock. Unlike courts, which adjudicate only what comes to them, the new police did not wait to respond but were, rather, active agents in the administration of urban order.

These seemingly subtle differences signaled a profound change in the nature of criminal justice. The police made the justice system an active shaper of the social system, and their purview included a broadly defined world of public and private behavior. The criminal law contributed a significant component of their guidelines for action, of course, but local ordinances increased the scope of their charge so that arresting criminal offenders represented only a small portion of their activity.

Police looked after the welfare of indigents, inspected boilers, shot stray dogs, reported open sewers, returned lost children to their parents, and sometimes even ran soup lines, and, while doing these jobs, unintentionally expanded the role of city government in providing services. Never before had the city offered an easily identified representative on the street, and in the era of pre-electronic communication this constituted a service revolution. Whereas earlier, the parents of lost children had located them with great difficulty, with the police organization they could go to precinct or central headquarters and recover them. This centralization affected all areas of police activity; officers could more easily be on the alert for known offenders, public health threats, or other potential problems. In a sense, the creation of the police had opened a Pandora's box.

As a formal organization of social control the police often took partisan political action, and they had an electoral role as well, as an important part of urban political machines. Their jobs provided patronage. By the end of the nineteenth century they were the final arm of urban political machines, literally standing at the ballot boxes to ensure proper voting outcomes. But when machines lost, so did the police officers. For other reasons as well, the typical police officer did not stay long on the job, and his loyalty was not, as it is today, to the organization or the job culture. The police often took sides in class conflicts, usually protecting the rights of property against the demands of labor. But sometimes they refused to side with property owners in strikes, and the reasons illustrate one of the consequences of their localism. Individually, police officers were recruited from and related to the working class. Few officers stayed on the job long, partly because they were political appointees and partly because most did not see themselves as careerists. As a result, especially in smaller cities, strikes involved their relatives and centered on issues of wages that the police themselves might soon face. Thus they could not always be relied upon to protect scabs or break strikes; sometimes they did—but sometimes they did not (Harring 1981; Walkowitz 1978).

Even though their organizational structure seemed to favor military-like action and control, police behavior in strikes and riots showed the hopelessness of depending on them in any kind of group action. Major riots usually ended with the arrival of the national guard or army as, most spectacularly, in the New York City Draft Riots of 1863. The individualistic, day-to-day reality of police work, although centrally organized, featured an independent or small-group working pattern that impeded the formation of an army.

The very features of policing that made it precipitate a broad range of urban functions finally led, in the early twentieth century, to a narrowing of police duties. The primary intention had been for the police to deter crime—a problematic charge, to say the least, for how does one determine if an imminent criminal offense did not occur? Nevertheless, as police lost their broader role, they fell back on their crime-control responsibility. The various national organizations of police chiefs emphasized crime fighting, and officers began to conceive of themselves as crime fighters. And the very public that had made so many kinds of demands on the police also wanted them to be the primary force against crime.

As the police's crime-fighting image grew, so did their image of corruption, violence, and politicization. In 1894 the Lexow Commission in New York created a sensation by exposing police corruption, both political and vice-related. Investigations in other cities and on the federal level, culminating in the Wickersham Commission's investigation (1929), echoed these findings (Fogelson 1977). The nature of the corruption and its exposure varied little. But there was a clear trend toward the removal of police both from political action and from the patronage system. In large part this dissociation came about as a part of the decline of political machines, rather than as a result of change in the police departments themselves. In addition, the use of torture in forcing confessions, euphemistically referred to as the "third degree," fell into disrepute. The role of the forensic expert in investigation came to the fore as the public acceptance of a brutal police declined.

Seen in this context, the *Miranda* decision (1966), limiting the duplicitous gathering of evidence, constituted one more step in the forced decline of inquisitorial tactics. Somehow, we still expect our police to be wiser than Maigret and braver than Dick Tracy. Since 1894 at least, we have been asking the police to act as subtly as their fictional counterparts. Each outraged exposé, each failure to deter crime, has been counted as an indictment of the police. The consequence has been to cement the singular image of the police as crime-control agents. Most police historians today, and certainly the police themselves, recognize that crime-related work occupies only a small fraction of their time. But the rich and complex history of the police has been one of constant yet unrealistic narrowing of function, so that the institution has acquired both a public image and a self-image at odds with reality.

A classic social contradiction fosters another kind of police corruption, unrelated to electoral politics. For most vice offenses, for instance, those in a position to provide prosecutorial evidence have also been willing participants in the criminal behavior. Known as "victimless crimes," all of these offenses, with the exception of receiving stolen goods, require the police to place themselves in compromising positions to gather evidence (Skolnick 1966). They must participate in drug buys, visits to prostitutes, selling stolen goods, and gambling, and must present evidence of this. Perjury almost becomes a prerequisite for conviction, and evidence on pimping and other higher levels of vice is even more difficult to get.

In these cases, the contradiction is that the criminal law creates nominal "victims" but the expectation is that a certain number of proscribed offenses is tolerable. Police are asked to limit, not eliminate, vice. The limitation creates the opportunity for bribery, because limiting suggests that only some offenders should be arrested, that the offense is only partially criminal. Thus the police in vice control internalize the social and legislative contradiction, sometimes at personal profit if at a moral loss.

PRISONS

Since the 1833 publication of the Beaumont and Tocqueville volume on American prisons, the United States has had an international reputation for its model penitentiaries. In the twentieth century this reputation has suffered, and few international commissions come today to learn from our system. Yet early in the nineteenth century the penitentiaries were often a part of an American tour; Tocqueville came on a specific government mission to learn from the prison system. From the European perspective, the United States had invented a place to reform rather than to punish. That American penitentiaries should have institutionalized the Enlightenment vision of human perfectibility seemed to fulfill the highest European hopes, and visitors arrived prepared to find innovation, optimism, and the successful reformation of human character. Not that these penitentiaries coddled the inmates. Tocqueville observed: "They are unhappy, they deserve to be so; having become better, they will be happy in that society whose laws they have been taught to respect" (Beaumont and Tocqueville 1964).

The notion of locking up offenders as punishment was ancient; the seemingly unique American contribution to penology was to construe the prison as a place for more than punishment. David Rothman (1980) considers this innovation an outcome of the optimistic social expectations of the Jacksonian era. Jacksonian culture, says Rothman, assumed that human nature could be changed. And the democratic Jacksonian United States, which had raised the common man, could also change the habitual criminal offender, the mentally ill, or the pauper. In the proper institutional setting these defects could be remedied, and after treatment, the miscreant could be released, ready to participate fully in normal society. Human nature itself could be changed.

In the early nineteenth century two models of penitentiaries developed, the Auburn system and the Walnut Street Jail, or Philadelphia, system. Both demanded silence, daily productive work, and heavy doses of Bible reading. The Auburn system, implemented in the 1820s at Auburn (N.Y.) prison, allowed prisoners to work in groups, whereas the Philadelphia system required complete physical isolation. Hence they were often referred to as the silent system and the separate system. Both assumed that an inherent and universal moral sense, if given the opportunity, would convince the offender of the wrongness of the criminal offense. Solitude provided the reflective opportunity; "alone, in view of his crime, he learns to hate it," and the subsequent remorse ensured that when released, the offender would never again turn to evil (Beaumont and Tocqueville 1964).

The view of human nature informing such expectations was indeed optimistic, if not naïve. Moreover, the assumption that a criminal offense is an easily isolated social act of inherent, universal wrongfulness virtually denied the existence of conflicting social values or the power of the state against which the offense was made. Foucault's observation (1977) that the modern punishment system masks state power is appropriate here. Both the silent and the separate penal systems tried to remove the offenders from all contact with society, insisting that the wrong was solely within the individual, that crime was not even a conflict between right social norms and wrong individual actions or power and powerlessness, but that the state's side of the conflict did not exist at all. In a sense, the ideology of the new form of prison dissolved the increased organizational power of the state in a cloud of words.

The innovational and rhetorical aspects of the American penitentiary system little affected the day-to-day reality facing most incarcerated offenders in the nineteenth and early twentieth centuries. They spent their hours in the county jail, the city jail, or the work farm; were hired out as contract labor; or worked on the chain gang. In the nineteenth century jails often held witnesses, the mentally ill, and those for whom there was no other place of confinement. In the 1840s, Dorothea Dix visited hundreds of jails, valiantly trying to have the insane and debtors placed elsewhere. Conditions in these places often made them a greater punishment than anything coming later. A national scandal down until the present time, they were usually overcrowded, understaffed, and dangerous. The county paid the costs of jail maintenance and construction and for the food and guards. Because jails were theoretically only temporary places of confinement, they had (and usually still have) no places for exercise and no facilities other than cells. In a sense, the county paid the costs of enforcing state law, and the taxpayers had no interest in spending money on jail facilities.

The idea that able-bodied men were locked up at the taxpayers' expense suggested that there was potential labor to be exploited. In fact, in most nineteenth-century institutions, the inmates were always expected to pay their own way, if not turn a profit. In the North, such exploitation usually failed. Inmates in prisons and poorhouses did indeed work, but only until they threatened the interests of labor in commercial business. Thus by the last third of the nineteenth century most inmate labor was to produce items used in the institution, such as food and shoes. Contemporary prison manufacturing of license plates continues this tradition of not threatening regular commercial enterprise. The irony here is that the Jacksonian principle of teaching the inmates to value honest and useful labor was frustrated by the limited range of skills that they could be taught.

In the South, things were different. Legislators resisted building prisons by substituting capital or corporal punishment. When this began to appear too inhumane, and when slavery was abolished, states began to rent out their convicts and counties created the infamous chain gangs (Carleton 1971; Conley 1981). Chain gangs did road work and other activities to maintain both urban and rural infrastructures. County sheriffs often received work orders indicating the number of men needed for work projects, which usually lasted from spring through fall, and they made enough arrests to procure these work gangs. The system, when abused, amounted to little more than forced labor. Convict leasing offered employers a chance to rent men and to extract their maximum labor value. This turned a profit for the state or county, while it simply used up prisoners. Unlike slaves, prisoners had no resale value to encourage the employer to keep them alive. In Louisiana, the death rate was 20 percent annually in 1896, and the system of convict leasing persisted until 1901. Until the 1960s the sugar mill at the state penitentiary continued to be a profit-making business, where prisoners worked under brutal and degrading conditions (Carleton 1971). No latter-day Tocqueville came to broadcast the praises of such a system.

The use of convict labor poses a continuing problem. We define useful and socially integrating work as a means of integrating people into society and deterring them from crime. For incarcerated offenders, the opportunity to learn and do useful work seems an appropriate mode of treatment. In a society where full employment is still a dream, why should prisoners be given an opportunity unavailable to law-abiding citizens? The puzzle is almost two centuries old.

In addition to providing a substitute for corporal punishment or banishment, the penitentiary also created a new problem, the socialization of released prisoners, mainly men who had often spent a formative decade in prison. Compared to their predecessors, these ex-offenders had a much more severe social-entry problem. Forms of ameliorating this new problem soon appeared, especially probation and parole. Both were aimed at reintegrating the ex-offender, a task presumably attendant on anyone who had been deliberately severed from society. Ironically, the penitentiary "solution" created a social problem that required the attention of the most humane social activists. The Boston shoemaker John Augustus, who between 1841 and 1858 aided ex-offenders in finding jobs, and to whom courts often delivered prisoners in an early form of parole, well deserves the attention he has been paid for his thankless and compassionate efforts (Hindus 1980).

The growing mid-nineteenth-century apparatus of police and prisons represented a socially costly means of dealing with offenders. Because police officers were public servants, it was difficult to stint on their pay; after all, they could quit. But the physical conditions of prisons and jails stayed at a minimally tolerable level. Similarly, the costs associated with full court trials were kept down with a means that is still familiar, the guilty plea or plea bargain. Although much research remains to be done, the practice of pleading guilty appears to have pervaded mid- and late-nineteenth-century criminal courts (Friedman 1981). The extent to which these pleas were exchanged for lesser sentences has not yet been systematically estimated, but preliminary work implies that the plea-bargaining "evil" so sensationalized today is well over a century old.

CRIME

Historians would like to know two very basic things about crime: how its rate has changed over time and how it has changed in kind. Both answers remain frustratingly elusive. What we can know with greatest certainty tells us least about these. The best data, available in limited range only since the federally sponsored National Crime Survey began in 1973, tell how many criminal offenses there have been. This survey regularly interviews a random sample of the general population and derives a rate of victimization. (Even in these best circumstances, we do not know how many offenders were responsible.) But if we had such estimated rates of victimization over the past centuries, we could analyze with some accuracy trends both in kind and amount of crime.

Next to victimization information is a measure called by the FBI "offenses known to the police," which includes all offenses known to and recorded as such by the police. The FBI has collected such data from local police departments with increasing coverage since 1930, publishing the statistics in the *Uniform Crime Reports*. The quality of these data has been controversial, as they depend on voluntary local collection and can be difficult to ascertain on a per-capita basis. This source comprises more than fifty years of crime information; but because most of the significant changes in crime control have occurred over a longer period, analysts still lack a sufficiently long perspective. The most useful data after offenses known are the arrest rates. These figures obviously measure police behavior and provide a murky reflection of actual crime. But these data stretch back to the earliest police departments and even to some constabulary systems, thus spanning over 150 years of change (Monkkonen 1981; Ferdinand 1980). Prison data begin in the 1830s of course, and court cases can be counted back into the early seventeenth century. But these latter two kinds of data tell us only about final outcomes, which bear an even more ambiguous relationship to actual crime than do arrest rates.

Just as the best data are furthest from that which we wish to understand, those crimes most completely recorded are the least common and most sensational. We can accurately count presidential assassinations and ransom kidnappings (Alix 1978), but for theft, for instance, uncertainty prevails. Homicide is most often taken by historians as an index crime, for most homicides are "cleared" by arrest and go to trial. As a result, the newspapers, arrest data, and court cases may be combed to establish something approximating a true homicide rate (Lane 1979). The results of various studies suggest that homicides per capita have long been declining, perhaps even since the fourteenth century.

One must be cautious in assessing such generalizations, of course, for several factors make comparison difficult. Medical care has presumably improved; accordingly, fewer assaults result in death. On the other hand, weapons have also improved, making it easier to kill with a gun than with a crossbow, for instance. To counter this, the anonymity of urban life creates opportunities for murderers to disappear and avoid arrest. Yet, in intimate communities, witnesses may be easily intimidated. Do these various factors negate each other? They appear to, and we may tentatively conclude that Anglo-American history is one with decreasing murder rates.

Similar but less reliable evidence suggests that the trend toward fewer murders parallels other crimes of violence (Gurr 1981). Theft is more difficult to analyze. It may have increased in the eighteenth century, perhaps even until the mid-nineteenth century. With a little more assurance we may say that since the mid-nineteenth century, both in England and the United States, theft appears to have been declining. Perhaps public disorders, breaches of the peace, and drunkenness have also been declining (Monkkonen 1981). Everybody can be thankful for such apparent declines, but historians would like to understand why they have occurred.

Several arguments have been advanced to account for them. They range from that of Lane (1974), who claims that one of the consequences of urbanization has been a "civilizing effect," to that of Gatrell (1980), who argues for the actual deterrent effect of the nineteenth-century transformation of the criminal justice system. Certainly, increased real wealth has had its effects. In the Middle Ages there simply was less personal property to steal, for instance, but on the other hand, depressions and famines probably forced the poor to steal grain. Through the late eighteenth, or perhaps early nineteenth century, subsistence crises probably did force the poor to steal but in gradually diminishing numbers. But by the Great Depression, destitution forced few people to steal for survival. Thus, amid growing opportunity for theft, the circumstances that required that the poor steal simply to survive diminished.

This analysis does not account for decreasing crimes of violence. The history of the police suggests that the service they provide, free criminal arrests, has promoted a new social right to live free from crime. Crimes of violence, whatever else they are, often represent ways of resolving disputes. In thinking of small-scale societies, we sometimes imagine that they have informal dispute-settlement mechanisms that somehow function better than the formal ones of urban society. Assaults and murders would have to be considered two such techniques. In a large-scale society, such direct, "informal," and drastic methods are no longer necessary or practical.

The long-run decline in crimes of violence may well be due to the relatively new organizational means of dealing with personal problems. In a very weak state, even murder may be a personal wrong rather than a criminal offense. In a strong state, even personal quarrels may find a resolution on an institutionalized basis. The criminal law that provides the basis for this absorption of individual action into bureaucratic solutions has not had to change, for its major outlines were established by the time the English settled North America.

It is the actual means of implementing the existing law that have changed and that have moved us from a world of personal action to one of state action. And the system of criminal justice created in the United States has proved unexpectedly costly. The police arrest too many people; court trials are too long and expensive; imprisonment requires huge capital investments; released prisoners need help; reformatories don't seem to reform people. These problems run parallel to the notion that the system, if only it were properly implemented, would work to deter crime and reform criminals. On this, the evidence is not yet in.

The data, poor as they are, suggest that over the centuries crime has declined and ordinary people are less victimized. Whether or not the criminal justice apparatus has had anything to do with this remains an open question.

REFERENCES

Alix, Ernest K., *Ransom Kidnapping in America, 1874–1974: The Creation of a Capital Crime* (Carbondale, Ill., 1978); Beaumont, Gustave de, and Alexis de Tocqueville, *On the Penitentiary System in the United States and Its Application in France* (Carbondale, Ill., 1964); Blumstein, Alfred, and Soumyo Moitra, "An Analysis of the Time Series of the Imprisonment Rate in the States of the United States: A Further Test of the Stability of Punishment Hypothesis," *Journal of Criminal Law and Criminology* 70 (1979); Butler, Jon, "Magic, Astrology, and the Early American Religious Heritage, 1600–1760," *American Historical Review* 84 (April 1979); Carleton, Mark T., *Politics and Punishment: The History of the Louisiana State Penal System* (Baton Rouge, La., 1971).

Conley, John A., "Revising Conceptions About the Origins of Prisons: The Importance of Economic Considerations," *Social Science Quarterly* 62 (1981); Durkheim, Émile, *Division of Labor in Society* (New York, 1947), and *Rules of Sociological Method,* 8th ed. (New York, 1950); Erikson, Kai, *Wayward Puritans: A Study in the Sociology of Deviance* (New York, 1966); Ferdinand, Theodore N., "Criminality, the Courts, and the Constabulary in Boston: 1702–1967," *Journal of Research in Crime and Delinquency* 17 (1980); Fletcher, George P., "The Metamorphosis of Larceny," *Harvard Law Review* 89 (1976); Fogelson, Robert M., *Big City Police* (Cambridge, Mass., 1977); Foucault, Michel, *Discipline and Punish: The Birth of the Prison,* trans. Alan Sheridan (New York, 1977); Friedman, Lawrence M., *A History of American Law* (New York, 1973), and "History, Social Policy, and Criminal Justice," in David J. Rothman and Stanton Wheeler, eds., *Social History and Social Policy* (New York, 1981).

Gatrell, V. A. C., "The Decline of Theft and Violence in Victorian and Edwardian England," in Gatrell, Bruce P. Lenman, and Geoffrey Parker, *Crime and the Law: The Social History of Crime in Western Europe Since 1500* (London, 1980); Greenberg, Douglas, *Crime and Law Enforcement in the Colony of New York, 1691–1776* (Ithaca, N.Y., 1976); Gurr, Ted R., "Historical Trends in Violent Crime: A Critical Review of the Evidence," in Michael Tonry and Norval Morris, eds., *Crime and Justice: An Annual Review of Research,* III (Chicago, 1981); Hall, Jerome, *Theft, Law, and Society,* 2d ed. (Indianapolis, 1952); Harring, Sidney L., "Policing a Class Society: The Expansion of the Urban Police in the Late Nineteenth and Early Twentieth Centuries," in David F. Greenberg, ed., *Crime and Capitalism: Essays in Marxist Criminology* (Palo Alto, Calif., 1981); Hindus, Michael S., *Prison and Plantation: Crime, Justice and Authority in Massachusetts and South Carolina, 1767–1878* (Chapel Hill, N.C., 1980).

Horwitz, Morton J., *The Transformation of American Law, 1780–1860* (Cambridge, Mass., 1977); Jones, Douglas L., "The Transformation of the Law of Poverty in Twentieth-Century Massachusetts," in Daniel S. Coquillette, et al., eds., *Law in Colonial Massachusetts* (Charlottesville, Mass., 1983); Klockars, Carl B., *The Professional Fence* (New York, 1974), and "Jonathan Wild and the Modern Sting," in James A. Inciardi and Charles E. Faupel, eds., *History and Crime: Implications for Criminal Justice Policy* (Beverly Hills, 1980); Lane, Roger, *Policing the City: Boston, 1822–1885* (Cambridge, Mass., 1967), "Crime and the Industrial Revolution: British and American Views," *Journal of Social*

History 7 (1974), and *Violent Death in the City: Suicide, Accident and Murder in Nineteenth-Century Philadelphia* (Cambridge, Mass., 1979).

Miller, Wilbur R., *Cops and Bobbies: Police Authority in New York and London, 1830–1870* (Chicago, 1977); Monkkonen, Eric H., *Police in Urban America, 1860–1929* (New York, 1981), and "The Organized Response to Crime in Nineteenth- and Twentieth-Century America," *Journal of Interdisciplinary History* 14 (1983); Nelson, William E., *The Americanization of the Common Law: The Impact of Legal Change on Massachusetts Society, 1760–1870* (Cambridge, Mass., 1975); Ransom, David, "Crime and Punishment Reconsidered: Some Comments on Blumstein's Stability of Punishment Hypothesis," *Journal of Criminal Law and Criminology* 72 (1981); Rothman, David, *Conscience and Convenience: The Asylum and Its Alternatives in Progressive America* (Boston, 1980); Rothman, David J., and Stanton Wheeler, eds., *Social History and Social Policy* (New York, 1981); Silberman, Charles E., *Criminal Violence, Criminal Justice* (New York, 1978); Skolnick, Jerome H., *Justice without Trial: Law Enforcement in Democratic Society* (New York, 1966); Walkowitz, Daniel J., *Worker City, Company Towns: Iron and Cotton-Worker Protest in Troy and Cohoes, New York, 1855–84* (Urbana, Ill., 1978); Wilson, James Q., "Crime and American Culture," *Public Interest* 70 (1983).

3

The Historiography of Criminal Justice
and Violence in Britain and the United States

This paper survived through several seminars in England, the Netherlands, and the United States. Unfortunately, I never tried to publish it, since it did not contain new research. Nonetheless, the material in the piece turns out to still be relevant; perhaps even more so than when I wrote it. The concern with Marxism dates the piece, but also serves as a reminder that theory—important as it is—is not a lodestar. One can think of only a few people who worked on explicitly comparative criminal justice themes: Franklin Zimring, Rosemary Gartner, and Wilbur Miller stand out. Yet the basic questions are still there: what, exactly, makes criminal behavior in different countries so different? The question drives in two directions, each important. It pushes one into defining what particular aspects of nationhood affect individual behavior—laws, institutions, traditions—and at the same time it turns up the apparent universals in humans—rage, violence, greed.

Elsewhere in this collection appears one recent piece (ch. 4) where I, in part, take up a detailed analysis, comparing the age distribution of homicide offenders in nineteenth-century Liverpool against those in New York City. And, in my book on long-term trends in New York City homicides (*Murder*

Earlier versions of this paper were read at the Seminar on Modern Social History, Institute of Historical Research, International Relations Room, Senate House, University of London, October 26, 1983; Institute of Criminology, Cambridge University, December 1984; The Second International Conference for the History of Crime and Criminal Justice, Maastricht, April 1984; Law and Society Conference, Boston, May 1984. I wish to thank Jon Butler, Michael Brogdon, Douglas Hay, and the members of the Modern Social History Seminar for their comments on the first draft of this paper.

in New York City), I explore some of the possible reasons for the differences in American and English homicide rates over time. However, none of these presents full-scale comparative efforts, which I still think make sense. A project under way by Gartner, comparing two Canadian and two U.S. cities, represents an excellent way to begin comparisons. My hope is that each comparative effort provides some guideways to future work, and that scholars will someday be able to identify the salient differences in crime rates. These, in turn, will lead to an understanding of where policy can make a difference, and where deep tradition and structure may impede social change.

To contrast crime and justice in the United States and Britain has become commonplace. One is violent, the other is not. This stark contrast then raises a series of explanatory puzzles. But the greatest puzzle is why, with only a few exceptions, historians have not seized on the issue as their own.

In the past two decades, historians have published a long list of books and articles on crime, criminal justice, and their social history in both Britain and the United States.[1] Although the number of books and articles is similar, the intensity and vitality of discussion on the British side is much greater. These differing levels of passion need explaining, for one might predict that historians in the two nations would pose similar questions, use similar methods, and compare their conclusions. This seems particularly true when one considers that the handful of studies consciously trying to establish comparative base rates of criminal violence emphasize strong parallels, especially in the decline in the rates of serious violent crimes starting in the mid-nineteenth century.[2] A comparison of the two histories suggests that the history of crime and criminal justice has itself certain fundamental assumptions which have not yet been examined by historians.

The first two centuries of American history seem intimately tied to British history, particularly in the case of law and legal procedures where innovation in North America was at best cautious and change from tradition glacial. Although there have been many studies of the relationship of American law to the common law, there have been only two explicitly comparative historical studies of the criminal justice apparatus, and only a few comparisons of criminal violence in the two countries.

This gap between the two written histories has a twofold origin, the first substantive and the second methodological. Primarily, two critical substantive differences, the low level of urbanization in the United States and its much less centralized political structure, gave rise to differences in criminal behavior and organized social control. These differences have been somewhat obscured by methodological differences in approaches to historical writing. In order to unravel these two pasts and two modes of writing about the past, it is necessary to argue backwards, from the historiography to the substantive history.

HISTORICAL WRITING

There is only one study on an American subject with a British flavor, and because it appears in a British journal explicitly identified with Marxist analysis, one might guess that at least one source of the difference is indeed theoretical, most American historians operating outside of a Marxist intellectual culture.[3] Yet the determination of the contour or impact of theoretical differences is difficult because to a certain extent they represent self-perceptions of the historians more than practice. Of those few American historians who do explicitly associate themselves with a Marxist tradition, none has yet produced work similar to that of Douglas Hay, for instance, either in depth or sophistication.[4] This I take to be a reflection of contemporary cultural and intellectual traditions, not of differential skills and abilities.

A second, related factor has also influenced U.S. historians of crime and justice. In the mid-1960s American cities saw sensational urban riots, outrageous police violence, and the growth of criminal violence. Historians looked to the past for an understanding of these crises. For models, methods, and theories these historians often looked to the other social sciences. By the time more sophisticated Marxist approaches offered alternative methods, the original impetus for criminal justice history had waned, with other facets of social history coming to the fore. As a result, only a handful of historians one can identify as Marxist work in criminal justice history. In the United States, it appears, in fact, as if the main work in explicitly Marxist criminal justice history may come from outside of the historical discipline, as Marxist sociologists and legal scholars reanalyze the past.[5]

The actual impact of theoretical differences has a murky outline, but not so the wide methodological gap separating almost all aspects of social history on both sides of the Atlantic. This obvious gap suggests that the difference may be methodological rather than theoretical or substantive. The written history of crime and justice in Britain contains thick, rich detail and narrative, while its American counterpart emphasizes local chronology, social science models, and a tendency to count. Even when British historians have gone to great effort to gather numbers, they regard them with suspicion and caution, arguing that because the numbers may not be correct, they should not be manipulated with statistics more powerful than percentages or rates.

In Britain, on the other hand, widespread interest in criminal justice history began about a decade later than in the United States. In response to a changing population, increasing crime problems, and the subsequent critical reanalysis of the police, the British studies from the beginning looked different. Early U.S. studies tended to show that the past had been a violent precursor to the violent present, that riots were not unusual, and that the police had always been brutal. These studies implied that things weren't falling apart, but were continuing to be bad. The American tradition itself was held responsible for current levels of violence, a point of view summed up nicely by H. Rap Brown, "Violence is as American as cherry pie." In Britain the new research tended to show that past criminal justice had been class-biased and established that the bias shown in the mid-1970s criminal justice system had been present for a long time. Both histories demystified, but in different ways. Americans, historians judged, had to be reminded of a historical continuity with their violent past, the British of an unjust past and a class-biased criminal justice system.

The British studies focused on the political context of legislation, on the organization and goals of the police, and on trials for political crimes. Trial transcripts proved to be a documentary entree into the function of law and criminal arrests concerning political conflict. The United States is not without such criminal trials, just without their criminal justice historians. The Haymarket Square massacre, for instance, generated a wealth of such material, including, finally, a brilliant book by Illinois governor and prison reformer John Peter Altgeld on the class nature of the penal system.[6]

Had American historians focused on their Haymarkets, the histories they wrote would still have been very different. For, in the end, most American historians treat the evidence left by the criminal justice system as though it were transparent, rather than an opaque mask. The terms "transparent" and "opaque" characterize the way in which the historian treats historical evidence. I make here a quasi-structuralist distinction (or is it deconstructionist?), that the evidence of the past, created through uneasy cooperation with the present, constitutes a text. An opaque text has an internal consistency which can be taken to imply a similarly consistent maker. Issues of the evidence's correspondence with reality do not arise, for one cannot, indeed need not, see behind or beyond the text. For all practical purposes, the text directly represents reality. Historical analysis, in this mode, can purport to be about past reality, but its test, in parallel with that of the evidence, is in its internal *coherence*. The written history becomes like literary criticism, a form of literature in itself which at the most relates to the body of evidence, but not to the ambiguous and past reality which produced the evidence.

A transparent text, through which one may see to past reality, is not necessarily internally coherent, nor does it assume a unitary maker. This text corresponds with reality, but in an ambiguous, incomplete, and perhaps varying way. This form of historical analysis has an uneasy epistemological stance because it cannot know its relationship to past reality. Yet as opposed to the other form of analysis, this is the essential question. The test of the historical analysis is in its *correspondence* with the past, for a transparent text, by definition, should permit direct access to the past. Thus, most American historians assume that people's actions and motives leave a transparent record through which the historian may look to the past.[7]

Michael S. Hindus's *Prison and Plantation* makes the problem of transparency versus opacity most apparent. Clearly Hindus had intended to read records surrounding the criminal justice systems of Massachusetts and South Carolina as opaque texts, showing how the liberal North ended up with a class control system as invidious as the slave control system of South Carolina. But somewhere along the way, the evidential texts of both states became transparent, at least as I read the book. The liberal industrial culture of Massachusetts reformers does indeed seem genuinely more concerned and more active in its concern than barbaric and inhuman South Carolina. Perhaps the contrast is simply too great, for the northern penitentiary which steals men's time comes off as at least fairer, if not more effective, than the southern system which mainly ignored crime or, when forced to pay attention, took men's lives. The "texts" produced by these two systems undoubtedly would have provided a Foucault with an opportunity to discover the workings of different forms of power.[8] But the texts themselves led Hindus into a less mediated analysis of the social intentions and actions that produced the criminal justice apparatus. He stops short of analyzing the differing nature of the state in these two socioeconomic systems, but he has provided the raw material out of which such an analysis can be constructed easily. And rather than finding in the South an instance of the pre-capitalist state emphasizing its own power over that of the individual offender, he has given us a state whose brutality comes out of its refusal to take power over criminal offenders.

Americans, when they adopt a critical attitude toward evidence, take one of two positions: one, that the relationship of the evidence with the reality which produced it is problematic, or two, that the evidence is a consistent, often intentionally so, misrepresentation of reality. The first position parallels modern measurement theory in hypothetico-deductive social science research.[9] The second amounts to sophisticated debunking and characterizes all too much work employing the social control thesis, for instance, that of David Rothman.[10] Neither approach comes close to the goal structuralists advocate and which Foucault most notably exemplifies, that of reading the past as an opaque text.

The attitude of U.S. historians toward the evidence forces them to engage in a dialogue with the past by researching yet one more empirical aspect of a subject. Few follow the lead provided by other social scientists and reanalyze the arguments or data of earlier studies. They opt instead to test arguments on *different* sets of data, almost always from different places.[11] Logically then, their revisions can establish only that the two places differ, not that either argument is wrong, especially if one does not assume a national unity. For instance, Steven Schlossman's *Love and the American Delinquent,* which provides a superbly documented and highly critical revision of Anthony Platt's work, exemplifies this problem.[12] In conjunction with Platt's work, it also demonstrates the difficulty of synthesizing American social/legal history, for Schlossman covers Milwaukee, Wisconsin, one hundred miles and one state away from Platt's Chicago. He convincingly demonstrates that the reformers there designed the juvenile justice system with the genuine needs of children in mind; that immigrant parents latched on to and used the system; and, at least to a limited and brief extent, that it actually achieved its goal, reforming children. But a conundrum arises. Does Schlossman's general argument revise Platt or simply show that Milwaukee was not Chicago?

Although one would not cast the British historians of criminal justice as structuralists, the best British work does, like Foucault, read the past as an opaque text.[13] That is, it takes the evidence from the past as a consistent and interrelated set of images, ideas, signs, symbols, concepts, and facts, and analyzes the evidence as a coherent whole. For instance, Brewer and Styles identify the methodological approaches exemplified by the influential Hay et al. collection and their own book as case studies. When, as in these books, case studies take a part to represent the whole without making any argument about the relationship of the two, we have the strongest possible instance of the assumption of a unitary culture, a unitary maker of texts. The text is inseparable from its maker.

Douglas Hay argues that the distinction made here on the basic approach to evidence reflects two different scholarly traditions. He contrasts the "rather sterile sociological tradition of positivist criminology" in the United States with the British tradition summed up in the apt phrase "knowing your period." I agree with Hay's distinction, but feel that his version of the difference is but another, and certainly clearer, way of labeling the distinction. For the very phrase "knowing your period" carries with it the significant epistemological assumption that it is in fact possible to know any period, that an immersion in scholarship and in primary sources will put the scholar in touch with the past in a way that other scholars will accept as equivalent, or at least similar, to their own knowledge of the past. I admire and envy the epistemological certainty carried by the phrase. But I also recognize that outside of artificially bounded subfields in United States history, one simply does not consider whether or not a scholar "knows" any one period.[14]

In fact, most U.S. historians would not very willingly defend the notion that there are clear periods to be known. Virtually any period stipulated by the textbooks has been recently criticized as a wrong understanding of some other larger or different time span. And because most periods in U.S. history are short, vague, and controversial, U.S. historians avoid the problem of epistemological uncertainty by avoiding the stress invoked by the phrase "knowing your period."

Because the British evidence so often speaks to class conflict, it is easy enough for Americans to misread history written from this basic position—especially as it analyzes the various sides, factions, and classes—as representing a society separated by unbridgeable chasms. This makes the British historian's implicit understanding of the past as an opaque text invisible to outsiders. Americans read the British histories of crime and justice as such outsiders, forgetting that the deep conflict can permeate a unitary culture at least as easily as it can a fragmented one.

Americans thus misapprehend the British approach as one determined by a different methodological approach to the past, rather than one determined by a different and continuous historical reality that determines the historical sense of how to understand the past. When Americans try to write a similar kind of history, they then fail for invisible reasons. It may be that here is the heart of the difference between the two criminal justice histories. If so, the two may conflate methodological and substantive differences inextricably, both historiographies thoroughly embedded in their own national histories. This gets us off the horns of the dilemma posed at the beginning of this essay, for the different historiographies arise from substantive differences which in turn give rise to methodological differences, and we are not forced to abandon the unique histories or the impact of method on outcome.

To read the past as an opaque text, one must assume that there has been a single text maker. To make this assumption with ease and confidence (or, as a guarantor of that ease and confidence, unconsciously), it is best to be a part of a culture that assumes its own consistency as a text maker. Thus the shared conception of reality determines what seems to an outsider to be a methodology.

Modern Americans, on the other hand, cannot make the assumption of a unitary culture producing a historical text, for even when they do, it becomes a conscious, even artificial, act. In the 1950s the American Studies movement tried consciously to confront this problem, asserting that there was such a thing as one unifying culture which could be analyzed. When cultural pluralism became the mode of understanding ethnic and racial differences in the 1960s, the American Studies movement was forced to quietly abandon this key assumption.

Note also that the principle of the single, opaque, evidential text does not assert a substantive difference between the two histories. Nor does it refer to the existence of national self-identity. Rather, the principle regards an aspect of that identity as it regards its own trail of evidence of self. In the arena of social history it is clear that for Americans, fragmentation is the order of the day. Traditional historical subjects worked well on the assumption of a unified history because they focused on subjects that in fact had unified texts of evidence—correspondence between elites, for instance. More recently, the attention paid to specific nonelite groups by the new social history has produced hundreds of analytic pieces on unrelated microcosms. Every focused social history turns up not just local variations, but variations so intense that to a society where geographical mobility has heightened the sense of fragmentation, historians seem fated to write more and more localistic history. Thus the history of criminal violence in the United States continues to struggle to rise above the particular and the local.[15]

THE HISTORICAL CONTEXTS

I. Legal Structures

To locate the differences between Britain and the United States in historical method seems unhistorical if very modern. It denies the role of the two pasts in shaping what now have become two very different nations. Even in the colonial era the criminal justice systems had begun to differ, if for no other reason, because of the presence of slavery and its embarrassing legal contradictions. By the beginning of the nineteenth century, the United States had many different criminal codes, one for each state, and at least three contrasting penal systems: the separate system in New York, the silent system in Pennsylvania, and no penitentiary at all in South Carolina. The contents of the state criminal codes varied only a little. There were very few federal criminal offenses—principally treason and piracy. Because the U.S. Constitution said little about crime other than forbidding "cruel and unusual" punishments, from the late eighteenth century on, the formal aspects of criminal justice practice differed in complexity and history from state to state.

If the multiple legal systems are difficult to understand, in principle they can be compared. It is on the level of social history where simple difficulty yields to an almost impossibly unnavigable complexity. In the United States there is no single Home Office, no police college, no Public Record Office to go to for archival material, but rather records are often widely dispersed even on the state level. The state of Massachusetts has the best preserved and most centralized records, both for the colonial and independence periods, hence the number of excellent pieces of research on it. Major justice archives lie uncatalogued in county and city offices, libraries, and historical societies across the United States. (One might note here that this lack of local research and an uncritical acceptance of the national paradigm is in fact a significant flaw in British work which is only recently being countered, as in Brewer and Styles.)

The major consequence of the highly fragmented justice systems in the United States has been that only a handful of historians have deliberately developed an approach comparing various states.[16] More typically one has a narrative history of the penal system of Louisiana, say, but nothing comparable for Texas or Mississippi.[17] There is one still useful overall history of the American penal system, Blake McKelvey's *American Prisons*. He takes an essentially progressive view of prison development, but the book is based on extensive empirical research which very nicely sketches in the main organizational and legal contours of state and federal prisons. Yet his study lacks the analysis of the local social, political, and economic context which a work like Mark Carleton's on Louisiana shows is necessary.[18] Thus, further substantive questions concerning the range of regional differences, ethnic and racial heterogeneity in the United States compared to Britain may be irrelevant, for the formal differences alone are daunting.

With the very large exception of the "peculiar institution" of slavery, the nature of the American and the British class systems suggests greater class homogeneity in the United States. While this is an old argument abandoned for its apparent barrenness, and for inherent problems of definition and operationalization, it bears heavily on the contrast between the two histories. The United States is both more unified and more diverse than Britain. Its white population may be less class riven but it is far more ethnically diverse. The presence of several racially distinct and legally discriminated-against groups—most notably, blacks, Native Americans, and Chinese—and constitutionally protected state-level legal differences make the picture complex. Although the United States may not have had clearly designed legislation criminalizing class behavior, both *de jure* and *de facto* its civil and criminal codes constrained minorities.[19]

Take the case of poaching legislation, for instance, which criminalized class behavior in Britain. Few Americans could have ever seen how such legislation could be class-based. Recent work indicates that in the post-bellum South landowners sought laws to exclude free roving stock, hunters, and fishers from their lands. This legislation demonstrates that hunting, fishing, and stock-grazing practices had been virtually unrestricted in the South until the late nineteenth century.[20] The expansion of the United States over the continent legalized the taking of what had been Native Americans' game. In recent times, Native American activists have challenged various laws regulating the taking of game and fish, sometimes successfully asserting their tribal rights. Such conflict highlights the major distinction in the regulation of hunting in the United States, where, from the white perspective there was a plenitude of game and fish, a plenitude which came under the control of the state acting in the interest of all white settlers, rather than a class. But the state was one in conflict with Native Americans, so that in the United States, crime-creating legislation may more often be characterized as racial or national, but not class-based.

II. Demography

One major demographic difference between the United States and Britain has had probably more influence on the actual directions of crime and crime control than all other historical factors combined. This is the proportion of the population living outside of cities. For reasons having to do with both socialization and repression, several studies suggest that in the long run people in cities commit fewer crimes than do those in the countryside. Because this is an effect over time, it is usually not apparent in cross section and may not even correctly describe the atemporal short run.

There exists, however, a common, powerful, and ahistorical misconception that urbanization causes an increase in criminal behavior. As the urban locus of uniformed policing, especially in the United States, is often overlooked, the criminal justice consequences of urban growth are usually misread or ignored. Increased urbanization, it is misconceived, should have caused increases in criminal behavior, and these falsely postulated increases, it may then be claimed, caused cities to create police. Presumably any nascent comparison of crime and justice in the two countries which accepted this common misunderstanding of crime and the city would also have to find Britain leading the United States in crime and violence, a notion probably contrary to the facts. This false analysis has created, in the United States, a functionalist misreading of police history, which claims that the natural increase in crime (from urban growth) stimulated the natural response of uniformed policing.[21]

Recent quantitative studies of crime rates in both the United States and Britain show a decline through the last two-thirds of the nineteenth century and the first half of the twentieth.[22] Both V. A. C. Gatrell in Britain and Roger Lane in the United States explicitly find declines in crimes of personal violence to be associated with an urban context, especially in the late nineteenth century.[23] My own work on the United States police shows how changing city government, not increasing crime rates or social conflict, influenced the organizational shape and strength of the police.[24] In any case, whether one claims that cities "civilized" their inhabitants, as does Lane, or more effectively repressed them, as does Gatrell, the outcome is the same—a decline in the rate of offenses.

As Britain led the United States in its proportions of urbanization by a factor of two, or about ninety years, an inescapable conclusion is that for all the similarities of the two countries, there has been a basic demographic difference impinging on both crime and the justice system. Not only has Britain led the United States in the proportion of the population living in cities, but the relative size of the cities, their political autonomy, and the proportion of the population living in their own houses differed greatly.

Figure 3.1 compares the proportions of persons living in urban places in the United States and England and Wales from the beginning of the nineteenth century until recently. The graphed values are very nearly parallel, with Britain's rising more quickly for the first four decades and apparently leveling off earlier. This figure also estimates the proportion of the population regularly scrutinized by uniformed police officers. Here the graphed values diverge in spite of their relatively similar origins. In about four decades Britain went from unpoliced to policed, whereas the process in the United States took almost a century longer. Probably it was not until the last decade of the nineteenth century that all United States cities had paid, uniformed police. The image of a raw, new society may well have reflected nothing more than the public aspects of an unpoliced society.

	Percent Urban		Percent Policed (estimated)	
	U.S.	Britain	U.S.	Britain
1800/01	6	34	1	10
1810	7	37	1	10
1820	7	40	1	10
1830	9	44	1	10
1840	11	48	1	30
1850	15	54	5	50
1860	20	59	10	75
1870	26	65	20	100
1880	28	70	20	
1890	35	74	30	
1900	40	78	40	
1910	46	79	50	
1920	51		55	
1930	56			
1940	56			
1950	60			
1960	70	81		
1970	74	79		
1980		77		

Figure 3.1
Source: C. M. Law, "The Growth of the Urban Population in England and Wales, 1801–1911," *Transactions of the British Institute of Geographers* 41 (1967): 125–43; *Preliminary Report for Towns: Urban and Rural Population, England and Wales* (London: HMSO, 1982), 7.

The impact of these urban differences, although perhaps not readily measurable, was substantial. In the United States, to live outside of a city was to live unpoliced. To live unpoliced meant that to file a criminal complaint one took on burdens of travel and the possibility of having to pay fees to the arresting officer, whereas in cities, filing a complaint was relatively easy, and certainly making court appearances did not require traveling great distances. Further, urban anonymity insured that a person making a complaint in the city had a greater chance of avoiding retaliation. Although the evidence is scant, Flaherty's work on privacy in the colonies shows how locals feared either prosecuting or serving as witnesses. Just as the United States lagged behind Britain by ninety years in its proportion of urban population, its formation of rural police lagged by a similar or greater extent. The first rural police departments in the United States developed in the 1920s, at about the same period that the population living in places of over 2,500 persons reached 50 percent.[25]

Britain, on the other hand, not only was more urban and therefore more policed, but had had formally organized rural police which spread slowly from eight counties in 1839 to 28 by 1851, a complete system being mandated in 1856. The actual rural orientation of these police forces is somewhat doubtful, as many were created by counties to police unincorporated but demographically urban areas. Moreover, there was not complete compliance with the law. Nevertheless, by mid-century a principle of complete police patrol had been established, a dramatic contrast with the United States.[26]

David Philips has studied the Black Country in the mid-nineteenth century, the prototypical industrial region which includes portions of Birmingham, which had both urban and rural non-farm constituencies. Focusing on the actual local functions of policing and crime, he highlights these points. He shows how the fear of having to pay costs of prosecutions that did not result in indictments appears to have deterred many victims from prosecuting.[27] The transition from a constable watch system to a paid police force took about twenty years in the coal mining and iron founding region of the Black Country, so that by the 1850s, the victim of a crime no longer had to pay the constables' fees to initiate an arrest and prosecution. By contrast, in the same decade in the United States, only three major cities—Boston, New York, and Philadelphia—had made the transition from fee-based constables to paid police.

The relative city sizes also differed between the two nations, as one might expect given the lag in American urbanization. Because, for a variety of reasons, large cities tend to have more police per capita, Britain had at any one time more dense policing of its urban population than did the United States. Again, the result was a more policed nation.

Another simple reason for the lag in American policing was fiscal. U.S. cities paid directly for their police out of taxes on real property. Throughout the nineteenth century these proved to be a sensitive political issue, and any innovations had to be powerful enough to convince local voters to support them. In Britain, on the other hand, the lower levels of home ownership, the much lower proportion of enfranchised working-class people, the complex and indirect property taxes, and national subsidization of local finance, especially for the police, meant that crime control was not as directly affected by ordinary local people.

Finally, American cities, particularly those not located along the East Coast, tended to have high levels of home ownership. Historians have yet to explore systematically the implications for social history of access to housing and forms of tenure, but one can guess that this variation affected the nature of policing in several ways, ranging from voter concern over police costs to less dense housing, which results in higher police patrol costs.[28] The consequence, again, is that the United States had less intense policing, even in those places that might at first appear to have been similar to Britain.

Although it is possible to enumerate many other differences between Britain and the United States which probably have affected their criminal justice histories, I think that these urban differences are primary. They set the demographic context for further change and growth. Within this context, historians have attended mainly to differences in sociopolitical circumstances, letting those alone account for the major differences in the two nations' histories and historiographies.[29]

CONCLUSION

Can one predict on the basis of these contrasts that if there were adequate historical data we would be able to trace a parallel, lagged decline in criminal violence in the United States? That the stark contrast between the contemporary United States and Britain in levels of violence derives from the much more recent and still incomplete transition to a policed society in the United States? Should contemporary New York be compared to a much earlier London? Such a view would be too mechanically developmental, yet it does suggest that the historical origins of contemporary American criminal violence may best be sought in a comparison with Britain. If there is a historical dynamic in the production and control of criminal violence, only a comparative view will allow its analysis.

In order to undertake a synthetic approach that does begin to grasp the historical dynamic of violent crime, we must begin with the historiography, for it represents both the means of understanding the past and also our contemporary blinders to one another. In a sense, the historians must understand how their colleagues conceptualize history in order to use the considerable amount of work done thus far and to move even further. The heroic summary by Ted Gurr of virtually all work done on trends in violent crime represents the plateau to which two decades of work have contributed.[30] Yet it is important to recognize the primitive level such work represents. How long of a time period do we need to apprehend in order to call upward and downward drifts a trend? The recent consensus that there is a U-shaped curve in homicides, with the mid-nineteenth century and the 1970s at the two high points, has a problematic interpretation within what may be a much longer downward drift in homicide rates since the thirteenth century. Gurr notes this problem, pointing out that the U-curve may be only a trivial fluctuation in a long decline in violence, and to confirm this he cites Norbert Elias on the "civilizing process."[31]

But it is critical to be doubly cautious when we undertake this all-important work of looking at long trends, for we must first agree in what ways it is meaningful to compare the fourteenth to the seventeenth and to the nineteenth centuries. Though it makes intuitive sense to draw a long downward curve in homicide rates in Britain from 1300 to 1980, few would agree that such a curve, were data available to draw it, would make sense for the North American continent. We assume that geocultural continuity underwrites the logic of such analyses for Britain and its colonies but not for the continent alone. Although this assumption should not cause many to squirm, it violates the most basic contextual sensitivities which we as historians should show. As pointed out above, the demographic and jurisprudential contexts of ninteenth- and early-twentieth-century Britain and America varied in significant ways. A similar variation existed between the fourteenth and nineteenth centuries in Britain, a variation to which the population's age structure must be added. In all probability the median age of medieval Britain was substantially lower than that of the nineteenth century. Our evidence is not yet nearly fine enough, but one must wonder if these three basic contextual variables—lower age, absence of cities, and irregular means of crime control—are not enough in themselves to account for much of the long decline in homicide rates. And if they are, then we must ask if this socially important phenomenon, the long-run decline in violent crime, has any meaning at the individual level. That there were fewer automobile accidents in the nineteenth century does not tell us very much about the nature of automobile drivers, or even about society. Although homicides are not so mechanically dependent on means as are automobile accidents, the analogy forces us to ask in what ways the long-run analysis of criminal violence is meaningful.

A historical comparison, then, leads us to a fundamental problem in the history of criminal violence in Western society: is violence, when closely examined, an ahistorical phenomenon that has taken on its historical character because historians have claimed it as a subject? Do not the actual fourteenth-century homicides studied by Barbara Hanawalt share more with those described for twentieth-century Houston by Henry Lundsgaarde than do the host cultures?[32] If so, then perhaps the history of criminal violence may be history only when it is about everything but the violence. And is this such a bad thing?

NOTES

1. Review essays on criminal justice history in the United States and Britain include Eric H. Monkkonen, "The Quantitative Historical Study of Crime and Criminal Justice," in James A. Inciardi and Charles E. Faupel, eds., *History and Crime: Implications for Criminal Justice Policy* (Beverly Hills: Sage, 1980), 53–73; also Monkkonen, "From Cop History to Social History: The Significance of the Police in American History," *Journal of Social History* (Summer 1982): 575–591; Victor Bailey, ed., *Policing and Punishment in Nineteenth-Century Britain* (New Brunswick, N.J.: Rutgers University Press, 1981); James A. Sharpe, "The History of Crime in Late Medieval and Early Modern England: A Review of the Field," *Social History* 7 (May 1982): 187–203.

2. Wilbur R. Miller, *Cops and Bobbies: Police Authority in New York and London, 1830–1870* (Chicago: University of Chicago Press, 1975); Clive Emsley, *Policing and Its Context, 1750–1870* (London: Macmillan, 1983); Ted R. Gurr, *The Politics of Crime and Conflict: A Comparative History of Four Cities* (Beverly Hills: Sage Press, 1977) and "Historical Trends in Violent Crimes: A Critical Review of the Evidence," in Norval Morris and Michael Tonry, eds., *Crime and Justice: An Annual Review of Research* 3 (1981): 295–353; Roger Lane, "Crime and the Industrial Revolution: British and American Views," *Journal of Social History* (1974): 287–303.

3. Sean Wilentz, "Crime, Poverty, and the Streets of New York City: The Diary of William H. Bell, 1850–51," *History Workshop Journal* (Spring 1979): 126–55; Rhodri Jeffreys-Jones, *Violence and Reform in American History* (New York: Franklin Watts, 1978).

4. Sidney Harring, *Policing a Class Society: The Experience of American Cities, 1865–1915* (New Brunswick: Rutgers University Press, 1984); Michael Katz, *The Social Consequences of Industrial Capitalism* (Cambridge: Harvard University Press, 1982).

5. The 1967 Presidential Commission on Civil Disorders, for instance, turned to historians for an understanding of urban race riots. David F. Greenburg, *Crime & Capitalism* (Palo Alto: Mayfield, 1981).

6. John Peter Altgeld, *Live Questions: Including Our Penal Mechanism and Its Victims* (Chicago: Donohue, 1890). Studies by Amy Gilman Srebnick and Patricia Cline Cohen show great progress since I made this assertion. See *The Mysterious Death of Mary Rogers: Sex and Culture in Nineteenth Century New York* (New York: Oxford University Press, 1995) and *The Murder of Helen Jewett: The Life and Death of a Prostitute in Nineteenth Century New York* (New York: Knopf, 1998).

7. Anthony Platt, *The Child Savers: The Invention of Delinquency* (Chicago: University of Chicago Press, 1969), might be considered an exception to this, for he shows how cynical reformers designed the late-nineteenth-century juvenile justice innovations in order to control the masses of new immigrant children. The fear of immigrants overwhelming white Protestant American culture fueled the rhetoric of concern for the welfare of children. The language of reform and the legislative battles make up the historical text which Platt strips away, as it were, from an underlying and different reality. Yet, his is an approach similar to one that reads the text of the past as though it were transparent, for it assumes a consistent misrepresentation, rather than representation. Thus, even when taking the text of the past as opaque, it is not complex, nothing more, really, than a directly reversed mirror of reality.

8. Michel Foucault, *Discipline and Punish: The Birth of the Prison* (New York: Vintage Press, 1979).

9. Hubert M. Blalock Jr., *Conceptualization and Measurement in the Social Sciences* (Beverly Hills: Sage, 1982).

10. Walter I. Trattner, ed., *Social Welfare or Social Control? Some Historical Reflections on Regulating the Poor* (Knoxville: University of Tennessee Press, 1983).

11. Colin Loftin and Robert H. Hill, "Regional Subculture and Homicide: An Examination of the Gastil-Hackney Thesis," *American Sociological Review* 39 (October 1974): 714–24.

12. Steven Schlossman, *Love and the American Delinquent: The Theory and Practice of "Progressive" Juvenile Justice* (Chicago: University of Chicago Press, 1977).

13. Douglas Hay on legitimacy in Hay et al., *Albion's Fatal Tree: Crime and Society in Eighteenth-Century England* (New York: Pantheon, 1975).

14. John Brewer and John Styles, eds., *An Ungovernable People: The English and Their Law in the Seventeenth and Eighteenth Centuries* (London: Hutchinson, 1980), 12–13. See Douglas Hay, "Comment," Law and Society annual meeting (1984), 7.

15. For an example of in-depth analysis of one sensational crime, see Boynton Merrill Jr., *Jefferson's Nephews: A Frontier Tragedy* (Princeton: Princeton University Press, 1976).

16. Michael S. Hindus, *Prison and Plantation: Crime, Justice, and Authority in Massachusetts and South Carolina, 1767–1878* (Chapel Hill: University of North Carolina Press, 1980).

17. Mark T. Carleton, *Politics and Punishment: The History of the Louisiana State Penal System* (Baton Rouge: Louisiana State University Press, 1971).

18. Blake McKelvey, *American Prisons: A Study in American Social History* (Montclair, N.J.: Paterson Smith, 1972).

19. Charles A. Tracy, "Race, Crime and Social Policy: The Chinese in Oregon, 1871–1885," *Crime and Social Justice* (Winter 1980–81): 11–25.

20. Note that Lawrence M. Friedman, *A History of American Law* (New York: Simon and Schuster, 1973), does not mention poaching. But see Steven Hahn, "Hunting, Fishing, and Foraging: Common Rights and Class Relations in the Postbellum South," *Radical History Review* 26 (October 1982): 37–67.

21. Lane, "Crime and the Industrial Revolution"; David R. Johnson, *Policing the Urban Underworld: The Impact of Crime on the Development of the American Police, 1800–87* (Philadelphia: Temple University Press, 1979).

22. Eric H. Monkkonen, "The Organized Response to Crime in the Nineteenth and Twentieth Centuries," *Journal of Interdisciplinary History* 14 (Summer 1983): 113–28.

23. V. A. C. Gatrell, Bruce Lenman, and Geoffrey Parker, eds., *Crime and the Law: The Social History of Crime in Western Europe since 1500* (London: Europa, 1980); Roger Lane, *Violent Death in the City: Suicide, Accident and Murder in Nineteenth-Century Philadelphia* (Cambridge: Harvard University Press, 1979).

24. Eric H. Monkkonen, *Police in Urban America, 1860–1920* (New York: Cambridge University Press, 1981).

25. Bruce Smith, *Rural Crime Control* (New York: Institute of Public Administration, Columbia University Press, 1933).

26. Emsley, *Policing and Its Context*, 68–75.

27. David Philips, *Crime and Authority in Victorian England: The Black Country, 1835–1860* (London: Croom Helm, 1977), 49–50, and chapter 3, which details the transition from traditional policing to a professional police force, both urban and rural.

28. Ibid., 83.

29. Note, for instance, that this urban context of the formal criminal justice apparatus is reflected in the high proportion of U.S. criminal justice historians who are urbanists, writing and teaching on many other urban historical topics, beginning with Blake McKelvey, who is better known as the official historian of Rochester, New York, than as the author of the first social history of U.S. prisons.

30. Gurr, "Historical Trends."

31. Ibid., 340–42.

32. Barbara A. Hanawalt, "Violent Death in Fourteenth- and Fifteenth-Century England," *Comparative Studies in Society and History* 18 (1976): 297–320; Henry P. Lundsgaarde, *Murder in Space City: A Cultural Analysis of Houston Homicide Patterns* (New York: Oxford University Press, 1977).

■ PART II:

VIOLENCE

The study of the criminal justice system—police, courts, laws—makes more sense than the study of crime itself, for the simple reason that the evidence left by the system about itself is much better than are the traces left by criminal behavior. And most of that behavior is lost to us, even as it was hidden from contemporaries. The special case of lethal criminal violence is different, however. Murder has generated formal notice and sanction for a long time. Murder victims are hard to hide. Murders are usually noisy, social, and visible. Generally, murders generate paper trails: we at least know the names of victims.

Murders, therefore, are top priority crimes to study both for themselves and for their contexts. We may never be able to study assaults or thefts across place and time, for too much in the context is different, but murders are all too much the same. The gain from studying murder goes toward broader intellectual goals of understanding people and society, understanding the impact of social and personal change, and thinking about questions like evolution and post-traumatic stress disorder. The gain from studying murder may also go in a different, future-oriented direction, toward the control of personal violence. It has not happened yet, exactly, but my hope is that a careful historical understanding of murder will assist future generations in shaping prevention policy.

For example, while gun control is an obvious beginning to dealing with the current dilemmas posed by American violence, it is my obligation as a historian to demonstrate that eliminating gun murders will not eliminate the high rates of American violence. The control of violence, the historical evidence makes abundantly clear, will not happen from any single policy; there may need to be a policy intervention for every different personal conflict. To understand this, to consider that starting with the obvious is only a start, may be one of the most important discoveries that violence historians can bring to future generations.

4

Searching for the Origins of American and European Violence Differences

The difference between American and other Western violence rates is so great and so persistent that it is a wonder there is not a whole field of study to account for it. Perhaps it is its magnitude and persistence that make it seem natural, not in need of explanation. There it stands, huge, even bizarre. Canadian cities are much safer than otherwise similar American ones. "World cities" like London, Paris, and Amsterdam are seas of safety compared to New York City or Chicago or Los Angeles. Yet one can hardly conclude that other Westerners are just nicer people, or less crime oriented. Franklin Zimring and Gordon Hawkins (1997) have shown that in recent years other forms of crime such as theft are as high in Europe as in the United States. And, if there is anything like an American character, it is our well-known penchant for friendliness. When it comes to wars, genocide, or collective violence, again, the American record would hardly point toward the personal violence that it has experienced for at least two centuries. It is specifically personal violence at which Americans excel.

One speculative paper hardly begins the work needed to understand this special American problem. This essay takes the theoretical work of Norbert Elias as the start of a comparison of violence differences. One problem it addresses in particular is that the empirical basis for the differences need not be carefully established: should the whole set of national excess come down to mass-manufactured and inexpensive weapons, for example, then the explanations turn in one direction. On the other hand, if weapons do not provide a full account, then

Originally presented at the Elias Centenary Conference, Amsterdam, December 18–20, 1997. I wish to thank the NSF, NIS, UCLA Academic Senate, and multiple research assistants for support on this project.

explanations turn another way.

The search for origins of the differences may prove long and difficult. But the payoff should be great. An American policy goal should be to reduce violence rates: American "world cities" will never achieve their economic and social potentials if they remain dangerous places. Violence helps maintain American economic inequality as well, its hidden costs in social stress, in dangerous schools, in children with post-traumatic stress disorder, and in streets rendered unfree by the dominance of violent gangs. If the United States had levels of personal safety comparable to other Western nations, its social and economic life would benefit from enormous, indeed unmeasurable, benefits in the long run (*New York Times* 2000).

With the exception of Russia, the United States has had the highest homicide rates in the Western world for at least the twentieth century, more probably for the past two centuries. There are many easy explanations for this, but none are complete or convincing. For example, the prevalence of guns since the mid-nineteenth century must be a large part of the difference, but even with gun murders removed from the data, the U.S. rate is still higher, though less dramatically so. Some think that racial and ethnic diversity causes higher homicide rates, but most homicides are within groups, not between them. A parallel argument undermines the notion that extremes of wealth and poverty cause higher homicide rates: that is, few murders are inter-class.

Because the higher violence rates in the United States are so well established, indeed several generations old, they make analysis difficult. A long-standing difference seems more "natural" than a quick change and therefore is less urgent in its explanatory demand. My research is designed to explore the differences in violence rates backward in time to establish, if possible, when these differences emerged. Once identified, this point in time is when the analytic effort should begin.

For international long-term comparisons, the United States and England make a reasonable comparative start due to their similar legal and law enforcement systems, as well as the more obvious colonial and demographic ties. Because of its youth, size, and agricultural wealth, the United States lagged behind England in many respects, urbanizing and industrializing some fifty to one hundred years later and getting uniformed police about fifty years later. It led England in other important respects, the white male franchise becoming open some half a century before England, the jury system opening up to nonelite men relatively quickly.

It is difficult to make a clear contrast between modes of punishment in the two countries: England seems to have been more likely to hang, and certainly it had the ability, unavailable to the United States, to transport felons. On the other hand, the United States did have a famous if ineffective penitentiary system from the early nineteenth century on.

Figure 4.1 displays the national homicide rates, U.S. and U.K., for the twentieth century. These two very different lines need some brief methodological discussion: while homicides are the best comparative indicators of personal violence, they may not relate to other forms of serious violence—since we have a good measure only of homicides, we are not really in a position to claim that they index assaults, say. A further difficulty may blur international differences: if one reporting locale systematically reduces murder to the accidental category, we may undercount. I have tried to correct for such possibilities throughout this essay, but even the best data are still vulnerable to definitional error.

Three things may be observed about the U.S./U.K. comparison:

1. First, the U.S. rates are something like ten times those of England. (The multiples have ranged from as little as 6 to as high as 19 through the twentieth century.) The high violence rates of Americans are not new, at least not new to the twentieth century.

2. There is a loose correlation between the two rates (R^2 = .28; .39 with WWI removed). In the 1940s and early 1950s, England's rate did not decrease nearly so much as did that of the United States, but clearly some global, or at least trans-Atlantic, forces were affecting both nations simultaneously.

3. Differences between the United States and the rest of the West apparently emerged prior to the twentieth century, perhaps even before it is possible to measure the differences. To continue the U.S./U.K. contrast becomes more difficult prior to the twentieth century, given the lack of national reporting for the United States, and probably incomplete reporting for England.

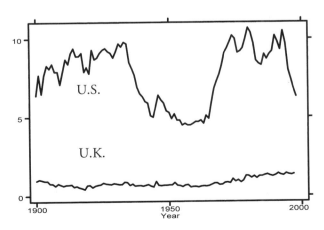

Figure 4.1 U.S. and U.K. homicide rates per 100,000 people, 20th century.[1]

Therefore, to refine my probe of the differences, I turn to more limited geopolitical units, New York City for the United States and London and Liverpool for England. New York City and London were the biggest cities in their nations, both were big even by twentieth-century standards, and both can be considered important for themselves even if they turn out to be unrepresentative of their nations (see Figure 4.2).

For the twentieth century, the city comparison looks almost exactly like the national one, with the dramatic exception of the 1970s through the 1990s when New York City's homicide rates soared. Their rates correlate more tightly than do the national ones (R^2 = .76 for the twentieth century, .69 for the nineteenth and twentieth). They differ by a similar factor for the twentieth century, a mean difference of 8, but by a higher factor when the nineteenth century is included: 15. Surprisingly, even for the nineteenth century, London's rates are very low, and it takes a step back to the seventeenth and eighteenth centuries before one can see high rates for London. Figure 4.2 therefore shows the very long-term comparison for the two cities. The picture is important for one reason: London did have high homicide rates in the seventeenth and early eighteenth centuries, suggesting that the international comparison is not preposterous, but indicating that London had become very different from its colonies by the mid-eighteenth century, prior to the time when the American data can be used.

London differed from the rest of England also. The homicide rate for all of England was considerably higher in the nineteenth century, about twice that of London for those years when it was nationally reported.

Liverpool turns out to be a better city to contrast to New York City, at least as far as homicides are concerned, with Liverpool's nineteenth-century rates

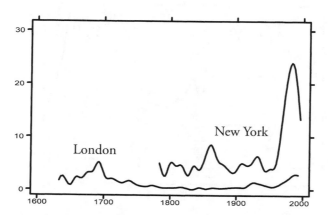

Figure 4.2 London and New York City homicide rates, 17th century to 2000. Source: see Note 1.

nearly equal to those of New York City (and as high as early modern London's). Figure 4.3 shows the two cities over time, and it shows how current high homicide rates in Liverpool mirror New York's, although at a lower level. More of interest, however, are the high rates in mid-nineteenth-century Liverpool. These rates nearly match those of New York.

Subjectively this is understandable: Liverpool was a new industrial port city, growing rapidly and filled with impoverished immigrants. Not far from the Manchester depicted by Dickens in *Hard Times* and Mrs. Gaskell in *Mary Barton*, the city's gritty reputation has persisted until today. Liverpudlians in the mid-century had the idea that Americans were particularly brutal and violent. The Liverpool *Mercury* often accused American sea captains of excessive violence.[2] At least one American sailor did experience such a cheating and brutal captain. The sailor, Herman Melville, wrote of his 1839 voyage to Liverpool ten years later in his novel *Redburn*. The nineteen-year-old Melville had seen things in Liverpool very differently from the *Mercury*. Horrified by the city's callous indifference to its poor, he reported the disturbing instance of trying to find help for a starving woman and her two children and failing. The woman and children subsequently died.

Melville creates a feeling for the city's violence by casually mentioning a murder of a prostitute ("a woman of the town") by a "drunken sailor from Cadiz" in the context of telling the more amazing (to him) story of a street balladeer. Impressed with the balladeer's skill, Melville mentions how he watched "the murderer carried off by the police before my eyes, and the *very next morning* [emphasis added]" the balladeer was singing the story and "handing round printed copies of the song, which, of course, were eagerly bought up by the

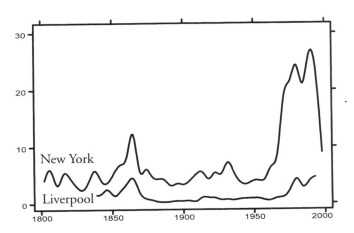

Figure 4.3 Liverpool and New York City homicide rates, 1800 to 2000.
Source: see Note 1.

seamen." Melville's description of part of Liverpool parallels the more famous description of the Five Points area of New York by Charles Dickens in his *American Notes*, published seven years earlier. Melville wrote: "the pestilential lanes and alleys . . . are putrid with crime and vice; to which, perhaps, the round globe does not furnish a parallel. The sooty and begrimed bricks of the very houses have a reeking, Sodomlike, and murderous look" (p. 184). All this he took in during a six-week visit.

Melville also distinctly set Liverpool and New York City apart from London. "As we rattled over the boisterous pavements . . . all the roar of London in my ears . . . I thought New York a hamlet, and Liverpool a coal-hole" (p. 218). He recognized that London's size, elegance, and level of civility made it a city of a wholly different character.

Figure 4.4 focuses on these high homicide years, showing New York City with the vertical bars, Liverpool with the horizontal line. There are significant, if crude, parallels between the two cities (R^2 =.26) and in two years almost identical rates. This has never happened since.

Could the relative similarity of New York City's and Liverpool's murder rates be due to the cities' demographic composition? In historical violence research we are usually unable to ask such questions. Typically we must rely upon the rate of homicides per 100,000 persons, even though we know we should look more precisely at the population's age and sex structure. A population with a heavy proportion of young men, for example, we would predict to be more homicidal than one of children or older women. Age- and gender-specific rates measure more precisely the relevant demographic features of violence, but for most early modern populations such figures are unavailable. For both cities here, however, such population data are available. Only a proportion of the offenders' ages are

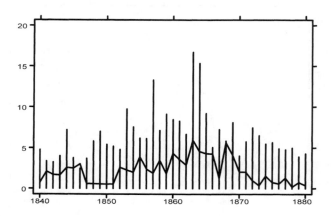

Figure 4.4 Liverpool (line) and New York City (bars), 1840–1880.
Source: see Note 1.

known, yet this seems to be due to the unimportance of the information rather than to reporting bias, so I have simply used the reported ages as a sample, which I have then inflated to adjust for missing information. In the case of Liverpool, the data are presented by age group, while a better population and offender sample for New York City allows for individual age rates. Figure 4.5 displays the resulting values, and includes for contrast the age rates of late-twentieth-century New York offenders as well.[3]

The two cities and two eras contrast sharply. The late twentieth century stands out for its extraordinary rate of violence by younger men. This is well known to contemporary criminologists, but this comparative context highlights the peakedness of age offending, which clusters tightly in a few years around age twenty.

Mid-nineteenth-century Liverpool, on the other hand, shows a peak of age offending at twenty-five and actually exceeds that of contemporary New York City for the forty-year-old group. Liverpool is much more peaked and also generally higher than nineteenth-century New York City, something Figure 4.4's overall picture would not have suggested.

The New York City rate per total population was higher than that of Liverpool even though Liverpool's young men were more violent. Therefore, it must be the case that New York City's low proportion of children gives it the high per capita rate for the mid-nineteenth century. That is, whether it be the result of lower birth rates or the swelling of the adult male population due to immigration, the city had more men in the group likely to commit murder.

The higher age-specific rates for males indicates that, all else being equal, Liverpool should have had a *higher* homicide rate than New York City. That it

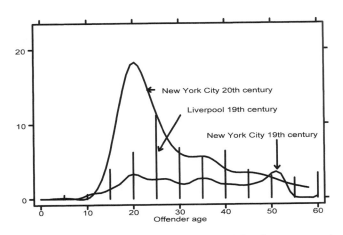

Figure 4.5 Liverpool (bars) and New York City (lines) age rates, 19th and 20th centuries. Source: see Note 1.

did not is due purely to demographic differences. New York City's 15–55-year-old males accounted for 30.5 percent of its population, but in Liverpool these men made up only 24.9 percent of the population. It was primarily the 20 percent additional males in the New York population that made it so dangerous, comparatively. (Today, for New York City, the proportion of such males is 27.4 percent.) The oft-used notion of American character and violence, prevalent since H. Rap Brown's 1960s utterance that "violence is as American as cherry [*sic*] pie," may have much more to do with demography than with anything more exotic.

Certainly the continuing and amplifying differences in interpersonal violence over the following century and a half cannot be laid to demography, but it is possible that American practices of personal violence were created in a demographically unusual era and then persisted through very different times. It is important to note that the post–U.S. Civil War, post-unification era did possibly have slightly lower homicide rates than the prewar era, but this long era of relative stability set a standard much higher than that of England.[4]

From the work of Norbert Elias we know that even a nicely fitted demographic explanation is not enough. We cannot pretend that the demographic differences between Liverpool and New York accounted for the whole story—they actually would not, for murder is not a natural occurrence, a weed appearing every so many thousand persons. Rather, it is the culminating event in a series of interactions, some over years, some over seconds. Murder is the result of individual actions, interpretations of those actions, and then reactions. These all occur in a cultural context tempered by broad political and state-based forms, practices, patterns. Spierenburg (1995) has reminded us that the American state formation process differed from that of European nations, thus affecting its criminal punishment structure. If we consider also that the whole criminal justice system was taking shape in the mid-nineteenth century, it is this that we must use to understand the emergence of very different national violence patterns.

Most Western nations went through an era of declining personal violence somewhere between the late seventeenth and early nineteenth centuries.[5] Liverpool was a bit unusual in its mid-century burst of violence. The United States, on the other hand, did not see a decline in violence until the post–Civil War era, and in this New York City may have been unusually early. Other evidence shows high violence rates in the rural South in the 1880s, in Western cities as late as 1900. Ignoring here the reasons for the decline, in these periods when normal institutional practices crystalized in other nations, the social expectations of personal violence were low. The United States, in contrast, went through its era of centralization and unification with high levels of personal violence the norm. It is irrelevant that the high rates of violence came not from some special national character, but rather from a demographic imbalance toward young males. If we conceptualize the period between American independence and the Civil War (1780s–1860s) as a period of state structure building, then the high violence era set the basic platform of social expectations.

Rather than conceptualizing violence as a product of abstract social forces, we can also see it as collective individual actions and responses, mediated by the state, which can grow under conditions of tolerance as well as for innumerable other reasons. In the case of the United States, tolerance occurred during state crystalization, as opposed to other nations that crystalized their state systems under conditions highly intolerant of many behaviors, including violence.[6] Americans had to be tolerant: they created a union half of which depended on slavery. Because immigrants formed an enormous part of this democratic society's social basis, the state system of the United States tolerated religious diversity, ethnic diversity, and incidentally, violence. Universal white male suffrage, which seemed safe in the deferential if not homogenous society preceding the wave of 1840 immigrants, opened the political world to Catholics, the Irish, Germans, other immigrants, and native-born working men. Jury pools too were opened up. While I do not wish to exaggerate, for elites still retained most of their power, the notion of state mediated "courtly behavior," especially in courtrooms, never obtained in nineteenth-century America.

A genre painting, *The First Mayor of Pittsburgh*, by David Blythe (ca. 1860), which shows a lower-level criminal court in Pittsburgh in the early to mid-nineteenth century, gives a rare glimpse of the criminal justice world. The scene is deliberately coarse. The judge, a stereotypical Protestant Yankee, pages through his legal manual. The police officer, an Irish caricature, club (and hat) in hand, seems simian in his cringing brutality. The offender, a pitiful creature in rags, is clearly more terrified by the police constable than by the judge or murky jury. The jury shows intense interest—this is their entertainment. On the other hand, two loungers seem to be sleeping on the bench in front of the jury box. A newsboy smoking a cigar seeks to find customers in the room, even as the officer testifies. In this scene, only the judge and his books embody the authority and dignity of the law. For the jurors and—through the newsboy—the media, the law is a source of entertainment. The offender appears as victim. And the law enforcer seems to be more beast than man.

This picture underlies the basis for American criminal justice practices of the nineteenth and twentieth centuries. The evidence I have gathered for New York City indicates that although over half of all murderers were arrested, less than half of these were tried, and less than half of these were convicted. Of this handful convicted, three-fourths were sentenced to less than five years in prison, and a large proportion of these were pardoned. Throughout the nineteenth century, as the practices that define the nation state were instituted and bureaucratized, an elaborate mechanism for tolerating personal violence became articulated. Juries sympathized with the offenders, not the judges or prosecutors or police.

In the middle of the nineteenth century, a whole armada of daily practices began to increase the violence rates that had originated in simple demographic differences. These all contributed to violence rates very different from the parent nations of most Americans. Newly mass-produced guns in the mid-nineteenth century became popular male consumer items. Politically open coroners' positions and coroners' juries tolerated violence. Trial juries continued this tolerance. A definition of normal became imbedded in the lower levels of state practices as well as in social practice, and this continued through the late twentieth century. And although the tolerance of violence is not the whole story, it is the essential place to start.

NOTES

1. Graphed data in Figure 4.1 come from three sources: the FBI, Douglas Eckberg (1995), and my own research. The FBI data are reported in the Uniform Crime Reports, which extend back to 1930. Homicides also comprise a part of vital statistics, which became national in the United States only in 1930. Douglas Eckberg has used partially reported vital statistics between 1900 and 1930 to estimate a national U.S. homicide series, and I use these to extend the U.S. series back to 1900. Data for England are reported in Home Office *Criminal Statistics* (various dates). The archived data and a full description are available from the Inter University Consortium for Political and Social Research

2. Paul Laxton and Joy Campbell, "Homicide and Manslaughter in Victorian Liverpool: A Research Report" (Liverpool University, Dept. of Geography, 1997).

3. I wish to thank Roger Schofield for the Liverpool population data and the IPUMS project for the New York population data.

4. The twentieth-century ratio of homicide rates between the two nations set the United States about five (4.8, R^2 of .37) times that of England (except for WWI). For the more specific and longer-term comparison of Liverpool and New York City, the ratio is a bit closer (3.2, R^2 of .43), and the time span nearly two centuries. (For London: a ratio of 7 and an R^2 of .65. Liverpool correlated *less* with London than with New York City.)

5. Johnson and Monkkonen, *The Civilization of Crime*, 9.

6. New York City has been called a place of more toleration than customary in the United States: "Because no single group was large enough to dominate city affairs, and because religious and ethnic strife was always possible, an ethic of toleration had evolved in New York City" (Hood, following Tiedemann, p. 539). Of course the least tolerant region of the United States, the South, was also the most violent, so this argument only goes so far.

REFERENCES

Eckberg, Douglas Lee. "Estimates of Early Twentieth-Century U.S. Homicide Rates: An Econometric Forecasting Approach." *Demography* 32 (February 1995): 1–16.

Home Department, Secretary of State for the. *Criminal Statistics, England and Wales.* London: H. M. Stationery Office, various dates.

Hood, Clifton. "New York City and the American Revolution." *Reviews in American History* 25 (December 1997): 537–44.

Johnson, Eric A., and Eric H. Monkkonen, eds. *The Civilization of Crime: Violence in Town and Country since the Middle Ages.* Urbana: University of Illinois Press, 1996.

Spierenburg, Pieter, ed. "Introduction" to *Men and Violence: Gender, Honor, and Rituals in Modern Europe and America.* Columbus: Ohio State University Press, 1998.

Tiedemann, Joseph S. *Reluctant Revolutionaries: New York City and the Road to Independence, 1763–1776.* Ithaca: Cornell University Press, 1997.

Zimring, Franklin, and Gordon Hawkins. *Crime Is Not the Problem: Lethal Violence in America.* (New York: Oxford University Press, 1997).

5

The Puzzle of Murder Statistics:
A Search for Cause and Effect

Los Angeles, 2001. Bad news for Los Angeles: after a nine-year decrease, murder rates have started to rise. In 2000, the decline had slowed, with only four fewer murders than in 1998. The current increase in Los Angeles is about 60 more victims than at this time last year. If 2001 ends with an increase of 100, that's far bigger than a blip. And Los Angeles is not alone: the news is also bad in Orange County, New Orleans, Boston, and even London.

However, not every place is suffering. The mixed picture from city to city, and the overall dramatically lower rates in Los Angeles and elsewhere, frustrate simple explanations and solutions. Back in June 2000, for example, it looked bad for New York. But now things are better there, and better also in Chicago and San Francisco. All three cities could well have lower homicide rates than last year.

Reasons for the scattered increases are not yet fully developed. Some experts suggest that young men, especially those in gangs, have forgotten lessons learned by the young a decade ago, when they saw their neighborhoods destroyed as rates went to all-time highs, so today's youth are again becoming more violent. Others suggest that police scandals—Ramparts in Los Angeles and several in New York—have caused cops to back off aggressive tactics, which, in turn, has emboldened criminals. But it could well be that long-term attitudes, part of the nation's traditional makeup, contribute to the increase.

Meanwhile, the Los Angeles Police Department and other police departments are vowing to fix things, but they are not disclosing their methods. The reasons they give for today's increase in murder rates differ starkly from those of a decade ago. No one is claiming big insights this time. In the late 1980s and early 90s, the most common reasons cited for the sharp rise were an abundance of high-powered guns, the coming of age of a generation of vicious young "super predators," intractable unemployment, not enough imprisonment, and drug use, especially crack.

We can hope current upturns in Los Angeles and New Orleans are only brief reversals in a longer decline. There is historical precedent for this. If we focus on the broader trends, previous declines were quite long, for example, in New York, from 1930 to 1952, and in Los Angeles, from 1932 to 1953. But there were slight increases during these periods, in New York, in 1939, and in Los Angeles, in 1937.

Both cities, and the nation as a whole, took a turn for the worse in the late 1950s. While the baby-boom generation has often been blamed for this increase, it actually accounts for only a small part. People, especially young men, just started murdering more. No one has ever offered a definitive reason why.

What can we say is feeding this current, scattered rise in the murder rate? For one thing, it could have nothing to do with the actual crime rate. An intricate web of factors contributes to homicide statistics, everything from funding for more high-quality trauma rooms to counseling programs for angry husbands to after-school athletic programs.

Other factors are related: Gun availability probably makes a huge difference, but shifts in availability and the likelihood of gun carrying surely swing over long periods of time, not over half-year spans. The current 23 percent increase in the number of homicides in Los Angeles can hardly be due to more guns.

What about invisible changes in unemployment? Here, the possibility is that unobservable microchanges can make a major difference. It's not the unemployment rate itself, but who is unemployed and what they do while unemployed. Maybe a small increase in unemployment among the kinds of people who kill has occurred in the past year. But how would we discover this?

Since increased harshness of prison terms was also given credit for the 1990s' overall decline in violence, what do we say now? Imprisonment hasn't eased. Is it a failure? Or would rates be really high were it not for the increased imprisonment?

If we could figure out all the relevant circumstances of the 326 murders in Los Angeles so far this year [2001], could we find the reasons why this is going on? In principle, yes; in practice, unlikely.

A key point is that America still lacks the clear, nonideological, and probably complicated set of policies to get rates down to those similar to the rest of the Western world. Homicide has never been a serious social issue in the United States compared with its actual impact. Why do we think the police alone can and should deal with a problem so much larger than one of law enforcement? We have a 200-year tradition of tolerating violence. London homicides may be up, but the rates—the level per capita—are insignificant for Americans.

Our loosely structured society with its individual freedoms has never considered homicide as a social problem belonging to all. Most Americans do not ask "for whom the bell tolls," especially with homicides, which happen more often to the poor and uninfluential. Murder is generally regarded as a crime against the individual, not against society. Yet, homicides send out rings of damage, scarring not only the victim's family but also neighborhoods, cities, and regions.

American individualism does not tie people in a tight web of concern and control. After all, we can move to better or at least different neighborhoods. The tradition of mobility is old. This is usually, and incorrectly, associated only with twentieth-century California and postwar suburbs. But twenty-five years ago, historians made the startling discovery that nineteenth-century America was highly transient, that small towns, farming regions, and big cities all had huge population turnovers every decade. "Churning," historians called it. Nineteenth-century cities had a tradition of moving day, when wagons, carts, and wheelbarrows jammed the streets as residents switched homes. This aspect of American liberty laid the groundwork for a social looseness that fertilized the field of violence.

From the individual or family point of view, leaving a bad neighborhood makes sense. From a social point of view, however, the consequences are unfortunate—especially because those who can't move are probably less able to fix whatever is broken about a neighborhood. Changing residence offers the hope of a better situation immediately; fixing a bad neighborhood seems hopeless for an individual.

Do these conditions explain why we have pockets of crime? In part they do, because the collective good—low violence rates—comes at too high a cost for individuals, families, and the larger social and political world. The investment required to make the United States as safe and reasonable as other Western nations is just too hard to accept, in particular because it does not resemble the things this country does so well. Our liberty, creativity, and looseness allow us to tolerate some bad consequences, as well as the many good ones.

Do these basic features of U.S. life fully explain the recent turn for the worse in Los Angeles and other, often dissimilar, cities? No. But they are reasons for the long-term crime problem in America. The prescription: Do what we think helps, but work, really work, for long-term solutions that may have an impact over succeeding generations.

6

THE VIOLENCE CONUNDRUM

Violent crime, homicide in particular, has been declining since 1992, both in large cities and across the country. Given that many of the underlying problems related to violence, such as a proliferation of highly efficient guns, have not gone away, this decline is nearly as surprising as it is welcome.

The national homicide rate has moved from a record high of 10.5 murders per 100,000 persons in 1993 to eight in 1995 (the most recent national data available from the FBI) and will probably be far lower for 1996 and 1997. In L.A. County, rates have been declining since 1992 and are now down to levels not seen since the mid-1970s. The exact timing and size of the downward shift differ from state to state and from city to city, making the phenomenon seem, on the one hand, to be local and, on the other, to be loosely national. But it can't be both. It is hard to see why Missouri, for example, should follow the pattern of New York or California. This good news has caused various experts and policy-makers to offer widely different explanations. They haven't yet debated the issue, perhaps because as long as rates decline, everyone is happy. But why do these experts disagree?

There are at least five reasonable explanations being offered for the decline. Each is, in many ways, intuitively satisfying. The explanations include recent changes in policing strategies emphasizing community policing; shifts in drug sales, especially crack, that make it less public and less likely to cause violence; subtle demographic decreases both in the numbers of young men and in their propensity to commit crimes; rising employment, which takes people into less risky lives; and increased imprisonment resulting from mandatory sentencing, such as California's "three strikes" law.

First published in the *Los Angeles Times,* November 30, 1997.

Yet, no one answer is definitive. There have been dramatic downturns before that defy sensible explanation. In late-nineteenth-century New York, for example, homicides declined at a time of corrupt and inefficient policing, terrible crowding and poverty, and when the likelihood of a murderer getting caught and going to prison was very low. At the time, few social observers realized their good fortune. Today, we look at Jacob Riis's famous slum photographs of that era, unaware that he portrayed poverty and chaos from a peaceful world, when the city's homicide rates were less than four per 100,000 through the 1890s. The still-unexplained low violence rates of that bursting city should caution anyone offering comprehensive theories today.

At the same time, the young were not nearly as violent as they are now. It is not that there were not young murderers then, for there were: boys of thirteen and younger stabbing or stoning each other to death. But the rates per age group were low.

During the twentieth century, the national homicide rate, as well as that of big cities like New York and Los Angeles, fell from the early years of the Depression through the early 1950s, when they flattened, then began the long increase that we hope has finally ended. Only a blurry message may be discerned in the big picture. After each major war—the Civil War, World Wars I and II—homicide rates declined. So much for the notion that war gets men's blood boiling. Cities have grown steadily since the nineteenth century, while homicide rates have gone both up and down. So it is not pure urbanization at fault. Capital punishment steadily increased from the nineteenth century to the Depression, then dropped, returning to popularity only recently. These rates, too, marched to a different drummer, simply because relatively few murderers are executed.

This historical background leads one to be cautious about easy explanations. It also creates tolerance for our current ignorance. Understanding personal violence, its ebbs and flows, is a complex challenge. But it is an urgent challenge, and one that is particularly American, not only because individuals suffer but because it hurts our economy.

Politicians, including presidents and many mayors, claim that community policing has led to the decline. The problem is, violent crimes have declined in cities without community policing. It is hard to argue that a change in policing in New York has reduced violence in Chicago. New York had no uniformed police in the early 1840s; homicide rates decreased for two years after the city got its first police, then seesawed back to new highs. The same thing happened in the mid-1850s, when the police went through a dramatic breakup and re-creation. Is it not possible that policing innovations came just as things had begun to change for other reasons?

Recent research by a group of social scientists associated with the National Consortium on Violence Research implies this might be the case. Working in several major cities, they discovered that the decrease in violence in these cities is for specific offenses, those related to crack. The drug now has a bad reputation; crack addicts are disdained by youth. At the same time, the crack markets have become less chaotic. Street-corner battles are no longer the cost of doing business. Just as with legal enterprises, the market shakeup has left a more orderly group of suppliers and buyers, who often work in less risky locations, using pagers and cell phones. Hence, the drop in drug-related crimes.

But there are other pretty good accounts for the decline in homicides, for example, a drop in the number of young males. Allan Abrahamse, at Rand Corporation, has identified a group of young offenders in California who account for a high proportion of violent offenses. Small changes in the numbers and actions of these young men can dramatically affect homicide rates. Nationally, the proportion of young males aged fifteen to twenty-four has declined slightly. However, the decline started at least two years before the drop in violence, and stopped two years ago [1995]. It is not purely demographics.

And what about unemployment and high rates of imprisonment? For some reason, these two ideas have taken on ideological shading, as though they are mutually exclusive. Just getting 140 potential L.A. County shooters into prison or a job would reduce homicide rates by 10 percent. Has this happened? Maybe, but we can hardly find out if someone would have murdered if they were not working, or were out of prison. So we cannot really test these hypotheses.

We have difficulty explaining homicides because they are relatively rare and because we have too many good explanations and too few actual tests of them. Careful research on homicide and personal violence is done by only a small number of people across the United States. It is characteristic of a field about which we don't know much to expect big solutions, big breakthroughs, and for the experts to never say, "I don't know." For homicide, a national problem as well as a local problem, the first step toward knowledge is to allow experts to say how much they do not know, to allow them to posit partial explanations, and then to be flexible in their policy applications.

Picking one explanation is not a good idea, yet. The systematic study of violence is young. Accepting that understanding may come slowly and with enormous effort is an important step toward knowledge. Meanwhile, expect a diverse range of accounts for the decline in violence, but ask for some quality research to back them up.

If we wish to harken back to the "good old days," we must be careful to say which ones. The mid-nineteenth century would be a bad choice. We would be appalled at the level of violence then. The 1890s would be better, or maybe the early 1950s. Let us hope that the next decade will usher in continually falling rates, and that we will consider reducing violence as a serious public goal and not just at election time.

7

Homicide over the Centuries

American violence is like a sore to which our worried attention keeps returning. No matter how we lick our wound, it fails to heal and we remain baffled. How, we cannot help but wonder, can a country so rich in many virtues, have this painful and harmful blemish? I return to this issue again and again. Here, I put a portion of our nation's past into the very long-term perspective. Usually the big overview provides an observer comfort: the thorns blur and the roses glow. Not so for violence, when even a giant step back in time reveals this persistent American problem.

As much as anyone, I search the data for good news, but it is difficult to find. One glimmer, and it is only a glimmer: violence rates do ebb and flow. This glimmer offers the place at which to begin fundamental inquiry: if we can find the reasons for the decline, perhaps we can turn to policy for pushing American violence at least into the same universe as the rest of the Western world. Note that I believe we can deal with this problem: that it is not caused by some sort of American fundamental flaw. At the same time, its persistence for two centuries suggests that the analysis and solutions may be slow in coming, and that we should truly work toward violence reduction over the next half century, not half decade.

Put briefly, reasonably consistent annual data about homicides were not systematically gathered and published prior to 1930, when the FBI began issuing its Uniform Crime Reports. There were vital statistics collected by individual states from about 1900, but these were incomplete. Recently, sociologist Doug-

First published in *The Crime Conundrum,* ed. Lawrence Friedman and George Fisher (Boulder, Colo.: Westview Press, 1997).

las Eckberg has made a significant breakthrough in correcting and reestimating these vital statistics, so that now we have the first even remotely believable national time series of homicides per capita available.[1] And Roger Lane's pioneering research on Philadelphia established estimates for the period 1839–1901, cumulated in seven-year intervals, which will probably prove to be prescient.[2]

In a project designed to move back systematically as far as possible, I have been assembling an annual homicide series on New York City probing back to the late eighteenth century.[3] It is desirable to go back even to the seventeenth century in order to facilitate comparison with England and Europe, where research has shown high medieval and somewhat lower early modern homicide rates.[4] New York City is an attractive study site because of its size, age, unity of city and county boundaries, and historically consistent political borders. There was only one major political boundary shift: in 1898 the city and county expanded from Manhattan to incorporate the formerly separate city of Brooklyn, as well as the Bronx, Staten Island, and Queens. The population denominator has been adjusted in my data series to capture this shift. The English takeover from the Dutch occurred in 1664, ensuring a long governance of the city under similar legal systems.

The further back in time, of course, the more likely the series is to be broken or fragmented or biased by unknown losses. Without developing the provenance of the New York City series in detail here, I can summarize its sources so that readers can be aware of the somewhat shifting sands on which it rests. FBI data suffice for the post-1930 years. For the era between the Civil War and 1930, the coroner's office published annual counts of homicides. As a check on the consistency of these data I have supplemented them for an eight-year period between 1866 and 1873 with individual cases. (And, as a further check, I have correlated 1882–1907 coroner counts with police arrests, yielding an R^2 of .90. This merely suggests that the direction of change charted by the two agencies is the same: the number of arrests was sometimes much more than the number of homicides.)

For the time between 1804 and 1866, I have used the coroner's individual reports and newspaper accounts. I have supplemented these with district attorney and police court papers, which extend back to the mid-1790s. The district attorney did originate some murder trial proceedings, but either most of these papers did not get preserved or most prosecutions occurred through the coroner. I have also supplemented and cross-checked the annual counts of these individual cases with annual counts published by the city inspector, who gathered causes of death from the city's cemeteries or perhaps from the coroner, and with the secretary of state's published counts of trials. (There is a loose but positive R^2 between convictions and my total count of homicides, 1800–1870: .36. No more than 26 percent of all homicides resulted in conviction; this observation is biased upward by the probability that I have an accurate count of convictions but an incomplete count of homicides, especially those generating little official action.)

Prior to the invention of the penny press in the late 1820s, newspapers did not seek out local noncommercial news, but the *New-York Weekly Museum* did on occasion report deaths, as did some of the other newspapers. In addition, I have used all published accounts of murders and murder trials as well as varied newspaper sources for the eighteenth century, including Benjamin Franklin's *Pennsylvania Gazette,* 1728–1765, available and searchable on CD-ROM. Dozens of additional and relatively thin sources have been explored, particularly for the eighteenth century, which is still frustratingly uneven.

There are obvious gaps: for instance, I have been unable to find a single homicide for the years 1790–1796. I suspect that this strange quiet is caused by a problem in sources. Similarly, but perhaps less surprisingly, the turbulent years of revolution and British occupation are very patchy; for this period a source problem is more predictable. The wars about which we know something clearly had an impact on crimes of violence; better data following the Revolution and the War of 1812 would be very informative. For this reason I have not graphed data prior to 1797.

The coroner's original records for the pre-1823 era dwindle, yet we know that there was a coroner. The district attorney and lower police courts have some cases unreported elsewhere, yet they do not contain the bulk of homicide cases I have found. The New York City Archives have all known district attorney, police court, and coroner's records. I have not yet found the right newspaper with chatty local news. The coroner's records become thin by the end of the nineteenth century, apparently containing only those cases where the killer was not prosecuted. Both the coroner and the district attorney prosecuted homicides until the early twentieth century.[5] At this point I have not yet used court records, mainly because it is preferable to use sources closer to the homicide.

And there are some tough definitional problems: infanticide, for instance. By the end of the eighteenth century, it appears that infanticide was seldom prosecuted. By the mid-nineteenth century, "dead infant found" was the laconic notice in police reports. Only when the death was so obviously infanticide that it could not be ignored did it appear as such in public notice. Contemporary culture is such that we might not classify infanticide as the same kind of thing as homicide. But at what age is infanticide no longer infanticide, but the murder of a child? One month? A year? Three years? While not a large category, these ambiguous infant deaths do on occasion push the statistics one way or another.

Equally frustrating, though for fewer sad reasons, are murders prosecuted in New York City but committed in the harbor or on ships bound in or out of port. I have excluded these from my count except when the ship was actually tied up in a slip. Again, as with infanticides, the number is not large. Self-defense and accidental killings are also definitionally tough; when the details are clear, I have made some judgments, disagreeing with a jury or two. But when the details are not clear, one risks including ambiguous cases: an occasional death caused by an unwitting street railway driver who felt the wrath of a jury unhappy with all street railway drivers has probably crept into the data reported here.

The population denominator has been taken from the U.S. census, supplemented for the period 1825–1875 by the New York state census. In addition, the city inspector reported the results of a census for 1805.[6] For intercensal years, I have interpolated linearly, except for years when certain events allow additional vital information to be incorporated (e.g., the cholera epidemics of 1795, 1798, 1832, 1849, and 1854, as well as the influenza epidemic of 1918). While such caution might seem to be excessive, it is probable that all counts have missed demographic surges that may have been important: for instance those before, during, and after wars, flight from fear of disease or civil disorder, and the like. In addition, though it is not reported here, my data analysis incorporates demographic shifts in age groups. Suffice it to say that such shifts, though real, do not affect basic interpretations.

Figure 7.1 displays the New York City homicide series as a bar graph, with the total U.S. homicide rate (from Eckberg and the FBI) as a line graph. One cannot help but notice first the tremendous increase in homicides starting in the late 1950s. This portion of the picture shows just how far the current decrease has to go to come anywhere near the turn-of-the-century or mid-twentieth-century levels.

Possibly the second feature of note is the changed relationship between the United States as a whole and New York City. Prior to 1958, New York City was safer than the United States as a whole. This dramatic change should give pause to anyone who theorizes that cities act as a cause or source of crime. From 1958 to the late 1960s, the city and the country as a whole were at least similar in their homicide rates. But after that, an astonishing departure occurred, and the city, like most other large cities, simply moved into a different category of violence.

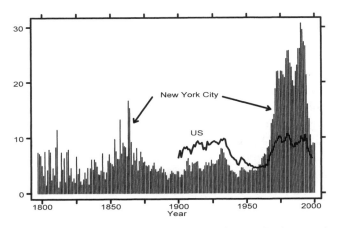

Figure 7.1 Homicides per 100,000: New York City (bars); United States (line). Source: Monkkonen data archived at ICPSR.

The twentieth century ends on a grim note, with U.S. cities plagued with a uniquely American kind of terrorism.

For the whole of the twentieth century, the New York and U.S. homicide rates, though on different trajectories, at least have crude parallelism in peaks and valleys. The Depression saw first a rise then a fall in homicides; World War I and World War II saw declines in homicides during the war followed by a slight move upward immediately after. Correlation between the two rates is .59: statistically significant and positive, but not the kind of relationship one would need to predict the future with any confidence.

The nineteenth century shows a good deal of episodic violence in the first half, with a Civil War era peak and a long decline thereafter. Several broad features of this pattern are worthy of comment. The second half of the nineteenth century saw enormous waves of immigration into New York City, resulting in poverty, crowding, and social turmoil. Yet homicides declined when virtually all social theory would have predicted the opposite. On the other hand, during the early nineteenth century homicide did increase and continued to increase after the years of heavy immigration beginning in the 1840s. But—and the point is important—the increase of the immigration years merely continued and established the trend.

What this short verbal skim through the data should make clear is that easy explanations do not work. And if they do not work, then any policy suggestions based on such explanations must be advanced with great caution.

One might turn to the relatively peaceful years of the 1830s, 1890s–1910s, or 1950s to ask what occurred then to achieve the peace. The demographic echo of war could have been a part of the peace, with the young male population of the city falling in the aftermath of the Civil War and World War II—except that the Civil War decline in young men was quickly wiped out in the late 1870s by immigrants. The correlation between homicides and young men per 100,000 over the two-century period is .42, which suggests that the relationship is not entirely spurious if also not very strong. The discovery that violence has demographic elements is neither new nor very useful, except for any corrective the demographic component offers to our understanding of trends. The homicide rate per 100,000 men aged sixteen to forty-five is so similar to that per 100,000 total population that we are left with the same broad outline.

This data series is the best one assembled for the United States, yet it leaves several questions in the air. We know, for instance, that rural white homicide rates in the 1870s were higher than those in New York City.[7] This confirms the picture of the U.S. homicide rate prior to the 1950s. But creating a consistent and reliable data series for rural areas presents even bigger challenges than for urban ones, so a careful over-time comparison of city and country awaits much more research.

At this point, awaiting more precise conclusions, one should draw at least two significant points from the long-term trend in New York City homicide:

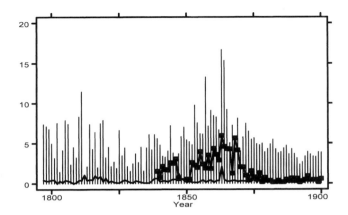

Figure 7.2 Homicides per 100,000: New York City (upper line); Liverpool (bars); London (lower line). Monkkonen data archived at ICPSR.

■ First, violence rates can change, and sometimes dramatically. It is worth considerable effort to find out what drives these changes, for this will then allow us to make intelligent policy choices.

■ Second, over this two-hundred-year period, New York's homicide rates always have exceeded those of London by a factor of at least five. On the other hand, the rates were matched for a few years in the mid-nineteenth century by those of Liverpool. (See Figure 7.2.) The comparison reminds us that the United States has a long way to go to achieve parity with England and that the divergence is quite well established. A tradition of personal violence as old as ours will probably take decades to combat. The answers will not come easily, nor will there be a simple solution. But the record of European nations shows that it is possible to live with less violence.

Our contemporary analysis of crime depends upon a shared retrospective understanding of what has preceded us. Unconsciously, we use our vision of the past to help frame the present. "Things," we think, are getting better, or, perhaps, they are getting worse. We probably project the future in a similar way, but are never so foolish as to put it in formal terms. If in the future our life in the United States is rocked by disaster, natural or social or political, then we will look back on our current discomforts as on a golden age. Obvious as such disasters are, few of us feel impelled to correct them, even though much retrospective ignorance is inherently correctable. The data reported upon here are being gathered in an effort to clear up one small area of common ignorance about violence.

NOTES

1. Douglas Lee Eckberg, "Estimates of Early 20th Century U.S. Homicide Rates: An Econometric Forecasting Approach," *Demography* 32, 1 (February 1995): 1–16.

2. Roger Lane, *Violent Death in the City: Suicide, Accident, and Murder in Nineteenth Century Philadelphia* (Cambridge: Harvard University Press, 1979).

3. Eric H. Monkkonen, "New York City Homicides: A Research Note," *Social Science History* 19, 2 (Summer 1995): 201–14.

4. Eric A. Johnson and Eric H. Monkkonen, *The Civilization of Crime: Violence in Town and Country Since the Middle Ages* (Urbana: University of Illinois Press, 1996), 6–7.

5. George P. LeBrun (as told to Edward D. Radin), *It's Time to Tell* (New York: Morrow, 1962).

6. Ira Rosenwaike, *Population History of New York City* (Syracuse: Syracuse University Press, 1972), 16–17.

7. Horace V. Redfield, *Homicide, North and South, Being a Comparative View of Crime Against the Person in Several Parts of the United States* (Philadelphia: J.B. Lippincott, 1880).

8

The American State from the Bottom Up: Of Homicides and Courts

Why is it that so few researchers on crime, crime control, and violence place it within a political context? From the creation of criminal law to its measurement and enforcement, the whole process requires political action. In this sense, it is inherently political. (Note that I do not want to invoke political as in partisan and ideology, although that does play an obvious role.) This blindness to the political is best demonstrated by the academic location of crime researchers, either in sociology or criminal justice or psychology or perhaps public health. Only the leading American thinker about these issues, James Q. Wilson, took up residence as a political scientist. (This is a suggestive, not a scientific statement.)

To say that crime is something social, not political, is to recognize its social context, but to miss something very basic: courts, legislatures, prosecutors, and the essential role of taxes in funding the apparatuses. This is not an insight as it is too obvious.

The following essay locates the long-lived American tradition of not convicting violent offenders, in this case, in New York City, who seem guilty enough to those of us on the outside of the courtrooms. Why have Americans for so long, with so many different reasons, not been able to punish the wrongdoers? And what does this show us about the complex underpinnings of our political structure?

First published in *Law & Society Review,* 24, no. 2 (1990). The research reported here was supported in part by a grant from the Academic Senate of the University of California at Los Angeles.

Sometimes the obvious poses a greater explanatory challenge than does the less visible. And sometimes what we think we already know is exactly what we should be endeavoring to understand. We know that in the United States most law-making and most legal activity occur at the state and local level. It is obvious that these things are rooted in a political structure that has only a loose relationship to social circumstance. Murder, a social and legal action, occurs in a legal/structural context of the known and the obvious. Hence we seek to understand it on the social and cultural level. Yet the initial results of my study of homicide in mid-nineteenth-century New York City raise some doubts about the "known" and "obvious," for such a small proportion of some eight hundred homicides ever went to court that we ought to wonder about the precise role of the legal system and the state.

Studies of courts and their actions over long periods have long assumed that courts index social behavior in the context of legal practice and legislation. The argument is that court outcomes mirror social actions, filtered by institutions (Friedman 1989b). As a result, for example, a quarrelsome society has more litigation than a quiescent one. The relationship of litigation to quarrels would be constant if procedures, laws, and the access to courts did not change, but because they do change, court outcomes are usually conceptualized as reflecting two processes, one social and the other institutional. Rather than abandon the idea that courts index society, however, I wish to argue that the two-part model, consisting of society on the one hand and legal institutions on the other, needs a third component: the local political economy. And to make this third component theoretically and historically meaningful, the political is best conceptualized as a portion of the complex American state.[1]

I. DYNAMICS OF THE LOCAL STATE IN THE NINETEENTH CENTURY: NEW SERVICES AND FISCAL CRISES

Between the Civil War and 1920, an organizational "revolution" reshaped the economic institutions of the United States. However, the state participated only partially in the sea change because, unlike other organizations, it was subject to a fiscally conservative, service-demanding electorate. As traced by Galambos (1983), this fundamental shift in the U.S. economy revolved around the nature of economic organization. The growth of the large corporation and its internal structure changed the way in which all large-scale economic activities were conducted. An extensive historiographical debate centers on the caused/causal nature of this change, along with the question of the impact on organizations of the military mobilization of the Civil War and attendant government expenditures. But within the debate, no one questions the actuality of the organizational transformation. Similar transformations affected the organization of governments, regulatory agencies, and rulemaking bodies, but unlike economic organizations, these bodies were subject to a fiscally conservative electorate that demanded services and parsimony. That is, their organizational and functional transformation took place within the constraint of an active political economy where the local public purse formed a direct link between voters and the state. In the aggregate, local governments controlled far greater fiscal resources than did states or the federal government, and governments used these resources to build complex institutional and physical infrastructures. But they did so with a stingy hand on the purse strings and a more liberal one on borrowing.

This revolution in economic organization affected state organization (including the local state) in three major ways. First, there was an uneven rationalization and centralization of its power (Skowronek 1982); some functions indeed became centralized and bureaucratized, while others did not. For example, interstate commerce acquired a centralized control bureaucracy, while building codes and policing remained local. The ideology of a republican, federal order forestalled the seemingly necessary centralizing of major functions or often crippled those that did centralize. Second, a service orientation became the permanent and "natural" mode of local government. Cities became providers of services in those situations where free riders made private provision dysfunctional (e.g., water supplies and sewerage). Though more pervasive and powerful than ever, the state grew less visible to its users, in part because it successfully became bureaucratized and efficient. Third, the local state had internalized its entrepreneurial and nonregulatory role: its job was to set the stage for economic growth. Inasmuch as such reform affected trial court business, the growth of regularized services stripped away functions. Probation and parole replaced petitions by judges and juries to governors for clemency or pardons. In such a low-profile, high-service state, the essentially confrontational, episodic, and externally driven system of court trials had no place. The invisibly efficient yet highly complex local state grew away from court trials as most cases became routinely administered. Trials became quaint, an Old World anachronism.

The aggregate outcomes of these conflicting demands and the larger changes in the structure and management of organizations were the overlapping local governmental hierarchies—including special districts (Diamond 1983), townships, cities, and counties—whose potential power was in turn limited by action from the next higher level of rulemakers. For example, as municipalities discovered and explored the creative use of their fiscal power to issue debt, state governments moved to limit the extent of the debt. It was in the interest of each municipality to borrow the most relative to other municipalities so as to attract people and industry: each strove to maximize its own debt for infrastructural development and economic incentives while simultaneously striving to lower the debt and economic advantages of competing municipalities. The consequence:

the organizationally complex, flexible, responsive, and powerful local state remained simultaneously self-limited by its own fiscal conservatism.

In its self-limiting nature, the local state had a powerful competitor: the federal government, which was equally self-limiting. This kept a broad spectrum of governmental activities local and made state and local governments more important than the federal government (Scheiber 1975; Campbell 1980). That is, policy-making, fiscal action, citizen participation, nonfiscal economic intervention, and legislative initiative and interpretation all took place at the local level. As Terrence McDonald has pointed out, this contradicts certain assumptions of the best recent studies of the American state, which focus on the federal government (McDonald 1986; Skowronek 1982). This focus on the national level may be applicable to the post–World War II era, but the basic question should not be, as it too often is, "Where did the national state come from?" Rather, the questions should be, "What has happened to the local state?" "How did the local state work?"[2]

Felony Courts, Homicides, and the State

The American state has developed on three parallel, independent, and sometimes inconsistent tracks: the national and state governments and local governments (counties, cities, towns, and various special districts).[3]

In this multilayered political system, felony courts have been a part of county government, although the laws, court structure, and procedural rules have been state-mandated. For homicides, county officials (coroners, prosecutors, jurors) and city officials (police and jailers) cooperate in arrest and punishment. For all these officials, the local political economy is of essential importance in making the presence of the state felt. Only local finance makes possible a thorough and careful state presence. When a felony occurs, only after local government has completed its work does the state step into the process. Yet the felony and its punishment are one of the critical arenas in which the state establishes its presence, legitimates itself, and protects its final power. Thus the attention it pays to felonies constitutes an essential part of the state's existence.

The local state's regulatory presence was built on seemingly trivial day-to-day matters and decisions. Local ordinances, ad hoc city council rulemaking, and concrete interpretations of the law from village, town, and county courts made the local state an important part of daily life. A steady stream of new legislation originated at the local level, and it may well be that state constitution making reflected local demands as well. Trial courts, too, opened a way for the local state to insert itself, or more accurately, to be pulled into, the lives of the populace. Litigation, among many other things, represents aggressive citizen usage of the state. And criminal prosecution often resulted from assertive complainants (Steinberg 1984).

Yet what we know about local courts has come from research designed to answer a different set of questions and to address a different research agenda. Local court studies have purposely conceptualized the court as telling us about society, or have asked what roles courts played in society. The records produced by courts have given us glimpses into otherwise unseen worlds; they will continue to do so. But we can also use the records produced by courts to provide us with primary, unfiltered information about the local state: they were and are about how the state works. From this point of view, then, courts do not index anything—they are the thing. From this point of view we can query courts to discover how the state works, how it routinely dealt with the nonroutine, how it defined itself behaviorally. And from this point of view, the division of courts in substantially different categories (criminal/civil) is of importance to the empirical analysis but sensible only if division is not concomitant with scholarly exclusion.

The business of criminal courts is the business of the state, by definition. Criminal violence, in Anglo-American law, has been the business of the state since the early Middle Ages. Its legal proscription, prosecution, and punishment machinery have been minor but persistent features of the state for so long that the popular mind associates the prosecution of criminals with the protection of society, not with the state (Hall 1935). And those historians who study criminal violence cannot help but focus on the episodic violent acts themselves, wondering about the people and the circumstances. Within the inherent drama of a violent narrative, the sorry survivors of a drunken brawl appearing in court seem to have little relationship to so grand a creature as the state. Yet, a careful consideration of the state and its reaction to or deliberate ignoring of episodic, personal violence is essential to finding any systematic, historical meaning in the drunken brawls, angry outbursts, and plain premeditated evil that together constitute homicides.

In the context of the peculiar local state and courts in the United States, murder constitutes a "hard case" for several reasons. It is episodic, irregular, often quite murky in specific circumstance, often dependent on the accidental conditions, and usually not a repeated series of events or a regular process—characteristics that do not lend themselves to monitoring, regulation, and bureaucratic management by the state. On the other hand, murders help generate a series of court outcomes so that the episodic behaviors underwrite a process. Of interest is the relationship of the process—trials—to the episodic behaviors—murders—for it is at this intersection that the state and the rough edges of society meet. I will argue that the trial proceedings give us information meriting a close textual analysis. Properly counted, such proceedings can serve as a measure of the state itself, an index to its busyness. But, on the other hand, this activity does not give us an accurate index to the proscribed behavior. Consequently, great care must be taken to make sure that the questions asked address issues extrinsic or intrinsic to the courts. That is, in the case of murder, do we ask about the nature of murder or about the nature of the state?

The feature of U.S. local state directly relevant to court studies is its dependence on voters for funding, including the supporting apparatus of courts, something that has escaped no politician's notice. The operational costs of the criminal justice system had to be kept low: a successful local political system had to operate without extracting much from taxpayers. Arresting felons was inexpensive; holding, prosecuting, and punishing them was not. A new courthouse could be financed by bonds and might attract new enterprise to a county; jailers drained local annual revenues. The local politics of fiscal constraint probably affected the entire criminal justice system unevenly: under close local scrutiny catchers of criminals are more likely to gain funding than are the punishers.

Criminal courts have been a relatively small part of the literature of court studies, with some exceptions (Friedman and Percival 1981; Monkkonen 1975). In his introduction to Laurent's study, Willard Hurst speculates that criminal legislation existed more as an "easy outlet for righteous indignation" than as a means of actually dealing with crime (Laurent 1959: xxiii). Thus in the real world with which the courts dealt, civil legislation affected civil courts more often than criminal legislation affected criminal courts. Hurst recognized that in the practical sense courts had little to do with defining criminal behavior. But the relative detachment of courts from more assertive involvement with criminal behavior may also reflect an important connection to the local political economy, namely, the consistent underfinancing of the local state. In contrast to civil courts where caseload depends heavily on the choices of litigants, criminal courts are only busy when other agents of local government, agents who are intimately tied to the local government's revenues, prosecutors, and police, are busy.

II. RECONSTRUCTING THE NINETEENTH-CENTURY COURT'S ROLE

When we look at homicide in nineteenth-century New York City, we find that courts were irrelevant to understanding murder, because they tried and convicted so few murderers. And if one were to continue to only consider the duality of court and behavior, then courts might well become only a footnote to the study of violence. But by keeping the triangle of state, local political economy, and social behavior as the conceptual map, one can begin to ask what murder can teach us about the growth and change of this whole tripart complex. Since the mid-nineteenth century, the United States has had the industrial world's highest homicide rates, a blemish on its historical record customarily ignored except in current discussions of crime. The rates may have declined from about 1850 to 1950, but they did not decline nearly so much as rates in Europe. The reasons are in some unknown part political, for Americans refused to implement the mechanisms to enforce their felony crime laws, proscriptions, and punishments. The American criminal justice system was remarkably similar in form to those of the rest of the Western world but not similar in substance. In 1850 the United States had far fewer police departments than did European countries, again reflecting the nature of the local state, for U.S. police were locally formed and funded. In 1850, about 5 percent of the United States was policed, as was about 50 percent of Britain; by 1870 the figures were about 20 percent and 100 percent (Monkkonen 1984a). In addition, American juries, especially coroners' juries, were reluctant to indict or convict. In New York City in the decades around the Civil War, between 10 and 25 percent of felony cases actually reaching trial resulted in some form of acquittal. Once tried and convicted, offenders still had a chance to avoid serving full sentences. Governors pardoned or commuted the sentences of about 10 percent of those convicted and sentenced, often yielding to the petitions of the same judges, prosecutors, and juries who had convicted the offender in the first place. For example, in 1856 New York's governor commuted five of a maximum possible twenty-one capital sentences to life. In the whole state, 1,205 of 2,215 felony indictments reached the trial stage in 1856; 844 resulted in conviction, while 323 resulted in acquittals (New York State, Secretary of State 1857).

In Table 8.1 I use data from my ongoing study of homicide in New York and London to sketch the pyramid of events from actual violent behavior to the final state-driven actions punishing "murder by death," as Benjamin Rush called executions. At the base of the pyramid are the actual number of homicides, an unknown figure; above it are those homicides I identified from newspaper accounts (determined by scanning for every day the *New York Times* and the sometimes published coroner's lists).[4] (Above the number of homicides should be those for which an indictment appeared, but the data cannot be reconstructed.) Above these are given the cases coming to trial. And above them the actual number of convictions. Above this number should be the sentences actually carried out, but again the data have not yet been reconstructed. Near the top of the pyramid are the punishments actually meted out and at the top the actual executions (almost always for offenses committed one to four years earlier). Ideally one would like to see such a pyramid constructed in time series so that executions are related to year of offense; the practical barriers to so doing—the basic difficulty in obtaining the information—make constructing estimates of all points extremely difficult and fragile.

In mid-nineteenth-century New York City, over 95 percent of the homicides resulted in an arrest, some in several. Often witnesses were confined as well. About 40 percent of known homicides came to trial; those for which I could actually find a sentence typically resulted in a two-year committal in prison; about one homicide in fifty resulted in an execution. The biases in these estimates are all toward undercounting homicides, and therefore the estimates of proportions convicted and sentenced are high, as those receiving no official attention were less likely to be in the newspaper. Charge or plea bargaining appears to have been common, in part because murder carried with it the death penalty, while manslaughter carried various shorter lengths of imprisonment.

Homicides occurring during brawls and drinking bouts inevitably carried minimal manslaughter charges. For example, a jury found Owen Kiernan guilty of beating his drinking partner to death with a cart rung, sentencing him to one year on a conviction for fourth-degree manslaughter. The same court on the same day put a forger away for fifteen years (*New York Times*, 23 November 1857). How long, or even if, either defendant actually served time is unclear, of course. Discovering the actual results of sentencing is very difficult. Even in the case of executions, the newspaper was more likely to note a death sentence than a death. The summary of the 1830–60 period in Valentine's *Manual*, which claimed that nineteen of forty-three capital punishments were actually carried out, is the most reliable-sounding statement I have found on this. Of the twenty-four capital offenders not hanged, thirteen were sentenced to life. The question then becomes, How long did they actually serve?

Table 8.1 Homicides in New York City, 1850–1869

Year	Homicides	Trials[a]	Convictions (N.Y. State)[b]	Executions
1850	19	4	25	0
1851	15	16	36	5
1852	24	10	24	1
1853	18	20	36	1
1854	7*	—	42	—
1855	38	10	28	0
1856	35	12	20	1
1857	86	19	36	2
1858	45	29	48	0
1859	49	19	36	0
1860	58	32	39	0
1861	43	25	58	1
1862	—	19	46	—
1863	47	19	43	0
1864	100	—	—	—
1865	55	2	—	1
1866	56	7	50	2
1867	55	14	—	3
1868	36	—	—	0
1869	45	—	—	0

Source: Compiled from search of *New York Times* and supplemented from Emerson (1941).
* Unverified.
[a] Listed as convictions in Valentine (1864), but probably all trials. 1865–67 from *New York Times*.
[b] Convictions for murder and manslaughter combined, from New York, Secretary of State (1905).

Although it is not explicitly clear that Owen Kiernan charge-bargained for his sentence, nine years later the *New York Times* editorialized against the plea-bargaining practice in an article titled "Murders Lightly Punished" (9 December 1866). Blaming the apparently regular bargaining on the "reprehensible indifference" of the district attorney's office, the article claimed:

> Instead of bringing a clear case of murder to trial, and doing all he can to
> convict the culprit, the acting representative of the District-Attorney is
> content to receive a plea of manslaughter in the lowest grade, and the
> murderer is sent to rusticate for a couple of years at Sing Sing in place of
> expatiating [*sic*] the offense on the gallows.

The most obvious conclusion to be drawn is that in nineteenth-century New York City, one could get away with murder: at least 50 percent and probably more than 75 percent of all murderers did. And those who did not escape punishment got off relatively lightly, serving mainly one or two years in prison with a 10 percent chance of pardon or commutation. Considering that most murderers were initially arrested, these figures should give pause to those of us who have mistaken a few highly publicized nineteenth-century hangings as somehow representing a stiff punishment regime (Kasserman 1986). Given the nearly universal twentieth-century opinion that homicide is the most serious crime, and given the public nature of most murders (all the homicide cases I have counted in this analysis were from news items), one can only conclude that the criminal courts of New York City simply were uninterested in prosecuting vigorously the most elemental criminal behavior. The poor funding of local crime control organizations and state-level punishment systems and the inability of local courts to mete out costly justice meant that the severe punishment regime in the United States existed only on paper.

III. CONNECTING THE FAILURE OF CRIMINAL JUSTICE TO THE POLITICAL ECONOMY

The study of trial courts over time helps us understand the nature of the American polity, and, in turn, the nature of the polity helps us reconsider the nature of trial court change. Any approach to New York City's criminal courts that examined only their business would have obscured their fundamental detachment from the world of homicidal violence.[5]

Considered in the context of historical change of the American state we have a framework within which to incorporate existing longitudinal studies of courts. A fiscal conservatism dominated the political economy. Costly revenue-funded activities were deemphasized. Activities that could be relatively well supported by fees or that represented legitimate debt funding went ahead, while any commitment to high operating costs got held back. Commitment to prison represented a high annual outlay, as might a serious felony prosecution. Civil courts could collect fees, but that was not always possible for felony courts. Thus court behavior could not mirror society; instead, it mirrored the state as mediated by a complex political economy, one relatively sensitive to voters. Applying this framework to the relationship of the court to homicides in New York suggests an active city government, one that reflected the local political economy. Police arrested most murderers; an active county and state government deliberately sided with the strong fiscal conservatism by dropping costly criminal prosecution of murderers. As an index of homicide in this period, courts prove to be terrible. But as an index to the American state, they are enlightening.

A multitude of studies from Laurent (1959) to Daniels (1986) provides us with the conceptual and empirical building blocks to structure several new questions about the local state. How active has the local state been? How can we measure this? Has there been variation or stability across time and region? Has there been a continual process of sluffing off the nonroutine when it becomes routine (e.g., divorce)? Has this routinization resulted in the building of state organizations at the local level virtually hidden from the dictates of any broader political consensus? In spite of any compelling legal mandate to do so, criminals have been prosecuted in a very similar manner across many legal systems. How can such a diverse patchwork of local governments end up acting in such amazingly copycat ways? Has the extraordinarily decentralized American system reflected a consensus, thus homogenizing its apparent local diversity?

No single study can answer all of these questions. But as an orienting device, focusing on political economy as a link between state and society will help empirical researchers attend to what they generally exclude. In so doing the promise that the research is additive and intellectually useful is greatly increased. For one of the latent problems in empirical longitudinal studies is that of moving beyond description. Since Francis Laurent's study (1959) of Chippewa County and the Massachusetts Superior Court project (Hindus et al. 1979) we have nearly two decades of research experience, but so far the results are disappointingly scattered and nonadditive. Of all aspects of longitudinal court-based studies, the one that has proved to be the most exciting is the litigation explosion (Galanter 1983a). It is exciting simply because the research addressed an unexamined assumption, turned it into a hypothesis, and then dramatically and counterintuitively rejected it. In order to create more exciting hypotheses, we must conceptually relocate court studies. A tripart scheme of the political economy, state, and society helps remind us where courts fit, provides us with cues we should take from other research hypotheses when we do our research, and helps us use the results of court-based research to address larger social science problems.

NOTES

1. For the sake of clarity, I capitalize "state" when it refers to the concept and leave it lower case when it refers to one of the fifty state governments.

2. One recent work on U.S. unemployment compensation, conducted within the paradigm of state studies, has an explicit research design focused on state governments, for the project recognizes that long before the federal government's activities in unemployment compensation, state governments had either implemented or tried to implement such programs. It is founded on the explicit understanding that "state-level processes were central to the shaping of U.S. public social provision" (Amenta et al. 1987: 140). State studies tend to conceptualize the state in terms of a centralized system. A federal, highly decentralized system such as that of the United States poses what may be a false problem, one which inheres in the concept of a state study: why is the system not centralized? To avoid such a false, or perhaps more accurately, premature question, Amenta et al. pose their problem as a comparison between nation states, thus facilitating their conceptualization without being trapped by the question of "Why no centralized unemployment compensation?"

3. The local governments, too, often have been wrongly conceptualized as powerless, essentially trivial, and purely dependent on state government, a conceptualization in conformance with their constitutional status. The result: a vast underestimation of the political (and economic) power of local government in the nineteenth and early twentieth centuries (Frug 1980). Recent work has shown convincingly that the formal nature of Dillon's Rule, which in the late nineteenth century articulated the dependent nature of all local government, had little impact on local government behavior. Teaford (1984) has analyzed legislation to show that in most cases, local governments and cities got exactly what they wanted from legislators. Partly because it was so intensely local, and partly because of electoral control over taxes, the local state has always been underfunded, thus fiscally constrained by its own taxpayers, not state governments. McDonald's (1987) study of San Francisco makes clear that the limitations of local government "imposed" by the state government were in fact done so at the request of local government. My work on finance, for instance, has shown that local finance was very much a local political tool (Monkkonen 1988; see also McDonald and Ward 1984).

4. Above this should be the numbers arrested. Here I omitted the data: when reported, the arrests often exceed known murders, probably due to multiple arrests in response to the same offense. Note that arrests do not include name lists, hence may not overlap with the newspaper and coroner's reports. In a newspaper-constructed data base, almost all of the mentioned homicides resulted in arrest.

5. Should we take this as evidence of an "autopoeitic" system, that is, a system that operates in relative independence from its environment (Teubner 1984)? Perhaps. The behavior of the state courts exhibited somewhat less annual variation than did the murder rates in New York City, suggesting that the court system had a more stable, internally coherent process while the homicide rates fluctuated more randomly. Regressions of New York City homicides and state-level convictions as pure functions of time also suggest that convictions had a slightly smoother linear drift (R^2 for the former is .05, the latter, .15). These statistics confirm to a very slight degree the independence of local criminal courts from actual crime. In that one can interpret R^2 as proportion of variance explained, one could interpret the statistics to mean that internal court processes accounted for 10 percent of the court's behavior. My sense is that the 10 percent of convictions for which simple linear drift accounts is an appropriate proportion of court behavior determined by "autopoeisis" and that the remainder comes from the external environment.

REFERENCES

Amenta, Edwin, Elisabeth S. Clemens, Jefren Olsen, Sunita Parika, and Theda Skocpol. 1987. "The political origins of unemployment insurance in five American states." In *Studies in American Political Development: An Annual* 2. New Haven: Yale University Press.

Ayers, Edward L. 1984. *Vengeance and Justice: Crime and Punishment in the Nineteenth Century American South.* New York: Oxford University Press.

Campbell, Ballard C. 1980. *Representative Democracy: Public Policy and Midwestern Legislatures in the Late Nineteenth Century.* Boston: Northeastern University Press.

Claggett, William, ed. Fall 1986. "Walter Dean Burnham and the dynamics of American politics." *Special Issue* 10, *Social Science History.*

Daniels, Steve. 1986. "Explaining case load dynamics: The use of evolutionary models." Law & Society annual meeting.

Diamond, Stephen. June 1983. "The death and transfiguration of benefit taxation: Special assessments in nineteenth-century America." *The Journal of Legal Studies* 12: 201–40.

Elazar, Daniel Judah. 1962. *The American Partnership: Intergovernmental Co-Operation in the Nineteenth-Century United States.* Chicago: University of Chicago Press.

Elias, Norbert. 1978–1982. *The Civilizing Process*, tr. Edmund Jephcott. 1st American ed. New York: Urizen Books.

Emerson, Haven. 1941. *Population, Births, Notifiable Diseases, and Deaths, Assembled for New York City, New York: 1866–1938.* New York: DeLamar Institute of Public Health.

Freidman, Lawrence, and Robert Percival. 1981. *The Roots of Justice: Crime and Punishment in Alameda County, California, 1870–1910.* Chapel Hill: University of North Carolina Press.

Frug, Gerald E. 1980. "The city as legal concept." *Harvard Law Review* 93: 1059–1154.

Galambos, John. 1982. "Technology, Political Economy and Professionalization: Central Themes of the Organizational Synthesis." *Business History Review:* 471–93.

Hindus, Michael S., Theodore M. Hammett, and Barbara M. Hobson. 1980. *The Files of the Massachusetts Superior Court, 1859–1959; An Analysis and a Plan for Action: A Report of the Massachusetts Judicial Records Committee of the Supreme Judicial Court, Boston, 1979.* Boston. G. K. Hall.

Jenkins, James Gilbert. 1864. *Life and Confessions of James Gilbert Jenkins: The Murderer of Eighteen Men.* Napa City, CA: Allen and Wood.

Kasserman, David Richard. 1986. *Fall River Outrage: Life, Murder, and Justice in Early Industrial New England.* Philadelphia: University of Pennsylvania Press.

Kelley, Robert. June 1987. "The westward movement, reconceived within a transatlantic framework." *Reviews in American History* 15:213–19.

Laurent, Francis W. 1959. *The Business of a Trial Court, 100 Years of Cases: A Census of the Actions and Special Proceedings in the Circuit Court for Chippewa County, Wisconsin, 1855–1954.* Madison: University of Wisconsin Press.

Gere, Edwin A. 1982. "Dillon's Rule and the Cooley doctrine: Reflections of the political culture." *Journal of Urban History* 8:271–291.

McDonald, Terrence J., 1987. "Building the impossible state: A polity centered approach to state building in America, 1820–1930." In John E. Jackson, ed., *Essays in American Institutions.* Ann Arbor.

———. 1987. *The Parameters of Urban Fiscal Policy: Socioeconomic Change, Political Culture and Fiscal Policy in San Francisco, 1860–1906.* Los Angeles: University of California Press.

McDonald, Terrance J., and Sally Ward. 1984. *The Politics of Urban Fiscal Policy.* Beverly Hills, CA: Sage Press.

Miller, Wilbur R. Spring 1986. "Police and the state: A comparative perspective." *American Bar Foundation Research Journal*, 339–348.

Millspaugh, Arthur C. 1936. *Local Democracy and Crime Control*. Washington, DC: Brookings Institute.

Monkkonen, Eric H. 1984. "The politics of municipal indebtedness and default, 1850–1936." In McDonald and Ward, 125–60.

———. 1988. *America Becomes Urban: The Development of US Cities & Towns, 1780–1980*. Los Angeles: University of California Press.

———. May 1984. "Why is the history of crime in the United States different from the history of crime in Britain?" International Conference on Violence in History, Maastricht.

New York. Secretary of State. 1857. *Report of the Secretary of State on the Criminal Statistics of the State of New York* (March 13, 1857). Senate Doc. No. 130.

———. 1905. *Annual Report on Statistics of Crime*. Table D, 99–159.

Palmer, Ian. 1985. "State theory and statutory authorities: points of convergence." *Sociology*. 19:523–40.

Pierson, Christopher. 1984. "Trend Report. New theories of state and civil society: recent developments in post-Marxist analysis of the state." *Sociology* 18:563–71.

Scheiber, Harry. 1975. "Federalism and the American economic order, 1789–1910." *Law & Society Review* 10:57–118.

Skocpol, Theda. 1987. "Social history and historical sociology: Contrasts and complementarities." " *Social Science History:* 17–30.

Skowronek, Stephen. 1982. *Building the New American State: The Expansion of National Administrative Capacities, 1877–1920*. New York: Cambridge University Press.

Steinberg, Allen. 1989. *The Transformation of Criminal Justice, Philadelphia, 1800–1880*. Chapel Hill: University of North Carolina Press.

Sylla, Richard. 1986. "The economics of state and local government sources and uses of funds in North Carolina, 1800–1977." *Research in Economic History*. JAI Press.

Taylor, W. B. 1985. "Between global process and local knowledge: An inquiry into early Latin American social history, 1500–1900." In Olivier Zunz, ed., *Reliving the Past: The Worlds of Social History*. Chapel Hill: University of North Carolina Press.

Teaford, Jon. 1979. *City and Suburb: The Political Fragmentation of Urban America, 1850–1970*. Baltimore: Johns Hopkins University Press.

———. 1984. *The Unheralded Triumph: City Government in America, 1870–1900*. Baltimore: Johns Hopkins University Press.

Teubner, Gunther. 1984. "Autopoesis in law and society: a rejoinder to Blankenburg." *Law & Society Review* 18:291–301.

Valentine, David T. 1864. *Manual of the Corporation of the City of New York, 1864*. New York, 104.

9

Racial Factors in New York City Homicides, 1800–1874

Usually race and crime receive scholarly attention when it comes to civil rights, to the excessive sentencing and poorer legal defense of people of color. Darnell Hawkins, editor of the book in which the following article appeared, challenged scholars to look at more aspects of race and crime. I was able to use the data collected for my book on New York City murders to directly address some issues of race and homicide in New York City. I say some, because most simple racial categorizations may elide as much as they reveal. Certainly in nineteenth-century New York, persons we now call "white" did not see themselves and were not seen that way. The Irish, in particular, had a separate racial category assigned to them. This makes the Irish very interesting from an analytic perspective, able to show us much about race as an identifier. At the same time, New York City's small African American community also stood apart, and both as victim and offender, needs a separate analysis.

In an era when the criminal justice system treats persons of color harshly, it may be difficult to imagine an earlier age, more racist than this one in most respects, which in general seemed less aggressive toward African Americans. Here, I think, is an important reminder: a nonattentive criminal justice apparatus is an even worse form of discrimination, a denial of social services to the poorest. Since most victims are of similar race and status as the offender, the ignoring of African American offenders in the nineteenth century was the denial of service to the African American community and a tolerance of violence toward black victims even higher than toward others.

First published in *Ethnicity, Race, and Crime: Perspectives across Time,* ed. Darnell T. Hawkins (Albany, N.Y.: SUNY Press, 1995), 99–120.

It is important to examine issues of race, ethnicity, and violence in a historical setting so that we may establish a perspective from which to view contemporary problems.[1] We may look back to a time when guns were rarer, when poverty was more widespread, and when racial discrimination was more intense, and ask what differences these made. There is more than an antiquarian interest that propels this quest: Gurr (1989) has surveyed a large body of research that indicates that our current high homicide rates and rates of other criminal violence are a relatively recent phenomenon. He shows how there is good evidence to beleive that homicide and violent crime rates have been declining since the Middle Ages. Some European scholars argue that there has been a more general transition over the past six hundred years from crimes of violence to theft (Soman 1980)—known as the *violence au vol* thesis.

Lane's research on Philadelphia suggests that these patterns were not the same for African Americans. After the Civil War, white homicide rates declined, while black homicide rates increased (1981, 1986, 1992). Lane shows how racial discrimination created what was a structurally different city for blacks, as opposed to the one for whites, including immigrants. He argues that these structural features account for the crime differences.

In particular, we can compare various newly arrived immigrants to African Americans. We know that African Americans faced increasing hostility from immigrants around the time of the Civil War and that all evidence points to their declining opportunities in the late 1850s (Hodges 1986).[2]

Although the data limitations frustrate fine-grained analyses, a historical analysis makes clear some of the differences between the nineteenth and twentieth centuries. These differences serve to remind us that broad historical change affects interpersonal behavior and conflict. That they are affected suggests that such patterns can continue to change, that a criminal offense sometimes considered to be beyond the reach of social control is not beyond the reach of social and historical circumstance. In some ways, the exact nuances of change are less significant than that there is change at all.

The data base used here, constructed for an ongoing quantitative study of homicide in New York City, provides us with an opportunity to examine race, ethnicity, and homicide in the nineteenth century. When possible, I will compare race and ethnic groups drawn as finely as possible, but as the discussion of the data explains, when the data seem too fragmentary, I then generalize to a more aggregated level.

SETTING

It is essential to understand some of the relevant features of nineteenth-century New York City even before describing the data. Though very important, New

York has never been a typical American city. In the first three quarters of the nineteenth century, it grew dramatically from a city of about sixty thousand to become a metropolis of over a million. This astonishing growth made it America's largest metropolis, with a polyglot immigrant population after 1840. Its early size alone makes the city worth studying, for while atypical, it was by any kind of definition, the major American metropolis.

Because most of the homicides analyzed below occurred after the 1830s—95 percent in the half century between 1834 and 1874—this description will focus on this mid-century period. By 1834, the city's population had reached a quarter million, but it would not be until the last years of the 1840s that the transforming demographic event occurred: the flood of immigration from Ireland and Germany. In 1850, the city reached a half million, and on the eve of the Civil War, over 800,000.

It may have had a foreign-born population as high as 20 percent in the 1820s, according to Rosenwaike (1972). In 1845, when the census began reporting birthplace tallies, the city had 135,000 foreign-born residents, about one-third of its population. By 1850 the figure had reached over a quarter million; in 1860 it grew again to well over a third of a million—almost one-half the city was foreign-born.

Yet for the city's African American population, there was a very different history—one of declension in size from 16,000 in 1840, to about 12,000 in 1860, and to perhaps less than 10,000 in 1865. New York State had abolished slavery by 1827. Thus, by mid-century, less than 2 percent of the city's population was black. This demographic trajectory, so different for the rest of the city's people, tells us much. Traditionally, African American men had worked on the city's docks, in its shipyards, and in various service occupations. The new immigrants competed vigorously, and sometimes violently, for these jobs.

This story had a tragic culmination in 1863, in the New York City draft riots. No matter how one interprets these riots, they always contain a base element of racism.[3] Triggered by the efforts to draft poor and immigrant workers, the city's white immigrant youth quickly turned their initial political protest into a race war against African Americans. A large but never reliably established number died—many victims of vicious public lynchings. Not too surprisingly, after the riots, the city's black population decreased even faster. Even though we can outline this demographic history of black New Yorkers, we cannot yet establish precise population measures, and it is clear that census enumerations might be highly inaccurate. Thus, constructing at risk denominators is extremely difficult.

The personal violence of the riots horrified New Yorkers. But personal violence had been an increasing feature of city life well before 1863. The estimated per capita homicide rate had been increasing for several decades, reaching heights that would not again be reached until 1970. This grim feature of the nation's largest metropolis went undiscussed in the nineteenth-century media.[4] Figure 9.1 establishes the increasing violence of New York City in the mid-nineteenth century.

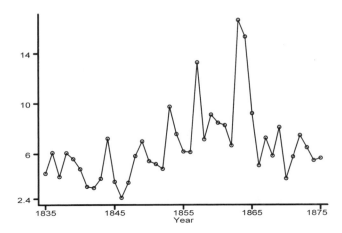

Figure 9.1 Homicides per 100,000, 1835–1875. *Source:* see text.

Data and Sources

The data consist of 1,559 murder cases. Ninety-five percent of these cases occurred after 1831 and before 1874. The small number (76) of pre-1831 cases are a result of fewer real homicides and more fragmentary sources. Variables include weapon, relationship of killer to victim, and subsequent outcomes affecting the killer—arrest to execution. For both killer and victim, variables include gender, age, and race or ethnicity. Seemingly obvious inferences have been avoided, which has created more missing variables: for instance, a person mentioned as a *youth* has not been assigned an age, or seemingly ethnic names have not been given an ethnic code. The reason for this seemingly excessive caution is that Lane's Philadelphia study used German names to indicate ethnicity, when it was equally possible that in Pennsylvania the person could have been fifth-generation American born. The one place I have made an interpretive leap is for some Irish-named people who were involved with other Irish born.

The data sources used here require detailed discussion, as their provenance suggests where the biases may lie. The data used for this study have been generated in the context of a long-term comparative study of annual homicide rates in New York, Liverpool, and London. Outside Massachusetts, nineteenth-century vital statistics for the United States are very poor. There are no *official* sources. The closest to such would be the coroner's reports, which begin with detailed annual reports in 1866. Even these annual reports are fugitive sources, and for this reason were gathered in a single place as a research project on mortality by medical researcher Haven Emerson (1941, 1955).

The coroner was required to investigate and call a jury to examine all non-natural deaths. These individual reports are available in the city archives. Prior to about 1823, they are fragmentary. Homicides comprise only a tiny part of these reports. After 1866, the summaries of these investigations were available in annual reports. The coroner's jury played a major role in determining how the deaths were reported. When the jury decided that the cause of death was not one man hitting another in a bar, but rather the fall to the floor or that the victim had a weak heart, the case would be tallied in the annual reports as an accidental death or as due to heart failure.

Juries were prone to do so in a society that still accepted physical violence between men as an ordinary part of social discourse. Few remember today that prior to his election to the presidency, Andrew Jackson had murdered one man in a gun fight, and that he had tried to murder others in violent attacks. In his day, these were understood as justified and exemplary of his manly virtues, virtually required because his honor and that of his wife had been slighted. In this world, gun murder could be interpreted as a duel; the beating nearly to death of a senator as a *caning*. Coroners' juries reflected their world, and as a result, they found no murder where juries today would.

To gather data on homicide, then, requires supplementing the coroners' reports. An initial check on the completeness of the 1866 homicide counts compared with those reported in the *New York Times* indicated some discrepancies, and further name comparisons have shown that for the pre-1870 years, the lists of homicide victims in the newspapers and in the coroner's records overlap but do not match completely. There was, in other words, an undercount by the coroner. The original manuscripts for the coroner are preserved in the New York City Archives in relatively complete form back to 1823, and sporadically for twenty-five years before that. The genealogist Kenneth Scott has transcribed essential details for all existent years prior to 1849 (1973, 1988, 1989, 1991).

Most of the data analyzed here have come from newspapers. After the 1820s and prior to the late 1870s, the press of New York City reported homicides with some vigor, if not with the constancy we might have wished. Typically there would be a notice of a fight or killing, which gave some detail of the event, the weapon, and the people involved. The media reported minor killings from elsewhere in the United States as well, giving some confidence that local events would not go unreported. In fact, the use of language tended to result in over-reporting: *fatal* or *mortal* did not mean that a person had died, only that it seemed like the person might die. All the killings reported here are those in which the newspaper report stated as a fact that the person was dead.

The newspapers of the day were particularly frustrating in the failure to follow stories that they had begun. Hundreds of reports involved a wounding where the conclusion was that the victim "surely will die." Did they die? We will never know because this conclusion often became a non sequitur. Similarly, dozens of stories about killings, and subsequent murderers' arrests, never drew to a close. Was there a trial? a conviction? Did those sentenced to die, die?

Using the newspapers is complicated by several other factors as well. By far the most consistent and reliable newspaper, the *New York Times,* began publication only in 1853. Compared to other papers, the *Times* exhibited less race bias than was typical for the era, in part because of its Republican leanings. For the era between the late 1820s and the 1850s, there are several newspapers that daily reported local news, like homicides: these included the *Daily-Tribune.* Prior to the mid-1820s, the reporting of what we call news was practically nonexistent. Newspapers served as means of financial communication for elites. Even so, careful searching has revealed homicide mentions do occur, and so my research continues to scan these early newspapers, including the *Commercial Advertiser, Evening Post,* and *Daily Citizen.*

Some supplemental information is available: for executions, a data set of all known executions in the United States was compiled by Watt Espy, so that for those few murderers executed, we are able to complete the stories (Espy 1987). Aggregate data on those convicted of murder are also available through state reports, so that we can compare numbers of homicides to numbers convicted, but this cannot be done by name, at least not yet.

There is with these data a question that has plagued all criminologists: unreported offenses.[5] While we know today that murders are the crime most often cleared by arrest, we are treading on more speculative ground in the past. For instance, far more people die accidentally than by murder. As a port city in an era when swimming was a rare skill and bathtubs even rarer, New York had hundreds of drownings every year. How many of those "found drowned" were victims of murder? Forensic science was nonexistent, so the person "found drowned" was almost never called a murder victim (Johnson 1994). Is it likely that hundreds of clever killers simply pushed their victims into the water, and that the data reported here only touch the dry-land killings? I hope not. What is known about the killings that did get reported lends substantial plausibility to this hope. Simply put, most killers knew their victims, did not try very hard at all to run away, and exhibited no wisdom or cleverness in their behavior. It is almost impossible to imagine that they would bother to lure a victim to the docks, especially when a fight and subsequent killing so seldom resulted in trial or punishment.

A more difficult issue remains the nonreporting of details of importance to us today: race, ethnicity, and age. For the analysis below, I have used differing assumptions, as appropriate, about the nature of missing information. In each case I make these clear and try to indicate how the biases might run. Moreover, the data reported on here should be regarded as those generated by a work in progress. Probably when the newspapers or coroner failed to note ethnicity, the person was most often native-born white. But this *most often* could still have been half the time, so that the undercount of other white ethnics could have been very high. Sometimes historians have been forced to guess at ethnicity by names, but

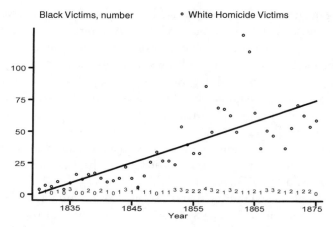

Figure 9.2 Counts of Homicides, 1830–1875. *Source:* see text.

I have avoided that here, except when there is a very strong contextual as well as textual probability that the person's ethnicity can be inferred. Such a case would occur when an Irish-named person was involved in a conflict with another, and the second person, in another article, was identified as Irish.

Trends—Fundamental Outlines

Although we cannot yet contrast the percapitized rates of black and nonblack homicides for lack of reliable population denominators, we can examine crude trends. Simply correlating the counts is not completely appropriate, because of the relative rarity of homicides. (Pearsonian correlation is .25, positive, but not very big.) Counts vary dramatically from one time period to another. For a small population, like the African Americans, many years may elapse between homicides. One or two missing observations can make the difference between a perceived crime wave and feelings of security. Therefore, I have used the regression lines to construct slopes.[6] These are not percapitized: the slopes are of actual counts. Given that the black population was steady or declining over these years, and the white population zooming upward, the scatter looks about right, especially for the fitful occasions of black homicides.

Race and Ethnicity

A question of initial interest is the nature of interracial homicides. These can give some insight into race relations and the nature of social relationships in nineteenth-century New York. It must be noted that even here relationships cannot be unambiguously inferred: a low level of interracial violence could simply be the result of high degrees of social segregation. Killer and victim races can first be examined under the assumption that all African American killers or victims were noted as such, while native-born whites, or persons who appeared to be, would likely go unnoted. Beginning with this least restrictive definition of race and ethnicity, Table 9.1 tabulates those identified as black versus all others, the assumption being that blacks would be more likely to be noted. Less than 4 percent of all killers or victims were black. The table shows that black victims were as likely to be killed by blacks as whites, while black killers were slightly more likely to kill blacks. This suggests some degree of racial motivation in the killings of blacks, dealt with further below.

In order to look more closely at ethnic and race relations between killer and victim, those victims and killers with ethnicity or race identified have been paired. Missing information reduces the total number of cases to 282 or about 20 percent of all killings. Table 9.2 displays the relationship: the diagonal shows that some ethnic/race pairing was common across the range of murders.

These figures can be interpreted several ways, but the most straightforward has to do with opportunity—killers and victims usually knew one another, were relatives, friends, workmates, or casual acquaintances. Even an interracial killing, the murder on October 20, 1844, of James Chapple (probably white) by Samuel Riley (black), is best understood this way: Chapple was a sailor and Riley the cook on board the docked brig the *Francis P. Beck.* The most clustered, the Irish, had

Table 9.1 Killer and Victim Races

Victim Race	Killer Race		
	White	Black	Total
White	1405	27	1432
Black	23	27	50
Total	1428	54	1482

Pearson chi2 = 373.7290 Pr = 0.000 likelihood-ratio chi2(1) = 126.8062 Pr = 0.000

Source: see text.

Table 9.2 Ethic and Race Identities

Victim's Ethnicity	Killer's Ethnicity						Total
	Black	U.S. White	Irish	German	Italian	Other	
Black	27	2	1	1	1	0	32
U.S. white	6	8	7	3	3	1	28
Irish	7	6	95	18	7	3	136
German	1	3	3	39	0	0	46
Italian	0	0	1	0	9	0	10
Other	3	4	7	9	1	6	30
Total	44	23	114	70	21	10	282

Pearson chi2(25) = 402.2995 Pr = 0.000

Source: see text.

83 percent of their victims from the same ethnic group, blacks had 61 percent from their group, Germans 56 percent, and Italians 42 percent. Irish killers and victims cluster strongly, suggesting their stronger degree of ethnic clustering. And, in this context, African Americans were no different from other sociocultural groups.

At-Risk Populations

While the data analyzed here include over a century of New York City's history, 1750–1874, three-fourths of the cases are for the two decades 1854–1874. During these years, the city's population grew from about 600,000 to just over a million. Its African American population, on the other hand, grew only slightly from 13,000 to about 14,000. If we take an imaginary population figure at the mid-point, about 800,000 and 13,500, we can contrast the homicides black and white in the ratio to populations—the black homicide rate equaling about twice the white one. (This ratio is based on the assumption that all black victims were reported as such, and that victims without racial identification were white.) By narrowing assumptions and defining the population at risk more appropriately, these figures may be refined.

The corresponding mid-point estimates of native-born whites, Irish, Germans, and Italians are 414,000, 160,000, 109,000, and 1000.[7] Assuming that native-borns were the least likely to be so noted in homicide reports, in contrast to the foreign-born and blacks, a crude ratio of homicides by group-at-risk setting native-born whites at 1, yields .8 for the Irish, .9 for the Germans, 2 for the African Americans, 15 for Italians, and .7 for all foreign-born.[8] The foreign-born ratio to the native-born white ratio is almost certainly a vast underestimate, the foreign-born white homicide victims simply not being noted in the sources. The best both sets of comparative at-risk estimates can give us is a sense that the black homicide rates probably ranged from 1.6 to 2 times the white homicide rate.

Even this range of estimates may need to be modified by the notion of population at risk, for homicide was both gender and age asymmetrical. Of the 1,397 nonblack victims where sex is mentioned, 78 percent were men; for blacks alone, the figure is 90 percent (for both killers and victims). Of the 555 victims where age is mentioned, 90 percent were between the ages of 17 and 50, 50 percent between 23 and 40; for 18 blacks alone, the figure is similar, 90 percent between the ages of 22 and 51, 50 percent between 26 and 40, although the low numbers of reported ages may bias these values.

The 1860 census of population reported age and sex distributions by race for New York County. Of the whites, 23.5 percent were males between 20 and 49; as contrasted with 23.3 percent of the black population. Yet one wonders about the believability of these data: by the 1910 census, 25.2 percent of the total white population were males between 20 and 49 years old, as compared to 30.9 percent of the black population. The 1910 age/sex distribution makes a notable difference: it alone would reduce the ratio of black to white homicides from 2 to 1.4. Changes of similar magnitude could occur for the other ratios. For the 1860 data, the question occurs of whether the decreasing population had been young men, or whether they had been miscounted. Recent studies suggest why the population counts might be biased. First, Margo Anderson's history of the U.S. Census establishes how volatile the issue of the black population was on the eve of the Civil War—especially the proportion of free versus enslaved blacks. Second, a recent issue of *Social Science History* devoted to the question of historical census undercounts shows that there were sometimes large count errors (Parkerson 1991). Third, the controversy over counting the very poor and racial minorities in recent censuses emphasizes how even today the proper enumeration of the poor is difficult (Anderson 1988).

Finally, Roger Lane's detailed study of *William Dorsey's Philadelphia* casts particular doubt on the 1860 census's accuracy in enumerating the African American population. Characterizing the census's enumeration in Philadelphia as "crudely unreliable," Lane argues that the census was a "barometer" of race relations, "an especially suspect enterprise from the black perspective." He points out that the northern city was a place for escapees to hide, that the Fugitive Slave Act certainly made free blacks afraid to give information to white officials, and public discussion of forced emigration to Africa added even more threat to any census. Lane shows, for example, that of twenty prominent black Philadelphians in 1870, six are missing from the census (Lane 1991: 59–60).

Given that the homicide rate is sensitive to how the population at risk is defined and measured, the demographic composition of the New York City African American population remains an important, unresolved, and perhaps even insoluble, issue.

Race and Weapons

Homicide notices often mentioned weapon type. Because their high cost and low quality no doubt cut down on their prevalence, guns were used far less often than today. The Civil War caused a step upward in the using of guns, though compared to today, guns were still relatively rare in homicides. Of the 1,323 cases with information on weapon, 18.7 percent were gun murders and 27 percent knife murders. Dividing these cases at 1861 gives 634 post-1861 cases; 25 percent were gun murders and 26 percent knife murders; the pre-1861 gun percentage drops to 13.

Race also made a difference in weapon use, as shown in Table 9.3. Twelve percent of black killers used guns, and 48 percent used knives. For whites the figures were 19 percent and 26 percent. Most interesting is the Civil War impact: prior to 1862, no black killers used a gun; all six incidents occurred after 1862. These differences suggest that blacks were less likely to own handguns, possibly due to cost.

Table 9.3 Race and Weapon

Weapon	Killer Race		
	White	Black	Total
Gun	241	6	247
Knife	328	24	352
Poison	33	0	33
Other	671	20	691
Total	1273	50	1323

Source: see text.

Race and Gender

As in the examination of race and age, our understanding of race and gender relations depends in some part on the population at risk. That is, should the gender ratio of the African American population differ dramatically from that of, say, the Germans, then this alone might account for differences in homicide.

Although there is no clear warrant to say so, I hypothesize that the African American population was more adult and more male than the white population. This would result in more black victims and killers being men. Interestingly, this was the case for victims but not for killers. For killers, the race/gender distributions were similar enough to show no statistical significance. For victims, the differences were statistically significant: 90 percent of the black victims were men, as opposed to 77 percent of the white victims (see Table 9.4). Given the small numbers of black victims with relevant information, this means that six more of the victims would have been women had the race differences not obtained.

Aside from the plausibility of differing but unmeasured at-risk populations, which would still leave unaccounted the differences between victims and killers, other possibilities can only be raised as questions. Were African American men more in public than women? Did their work on and near the docks put them at risk relative to African American women, who worked in safer locations? Did white men attack spouses and women companions more? Were there cultural differences in the tolerance of violence against women?

A cross-tabulation shows no statistically meaningful differences by killer's race and whether or not the victim was a spouse (see Table 9.5). But a comparison of noted ethnicity and race of men who killed women shows some apparent differences: 21 percent (10) of the victims of black offenders were women, as opposed to 39 percent (45) of Irish, 32 percent (24) of German, and 15 percent (3) of Italian. Note that all the cautions apply to interpreting these data: gender balance, the probable underreporting of ethnicity versus the probable higher reporting of race. The results nearly disappear when all killer-victim relationships are examined: 24 percent (296 of the 1,211 pairs where gender is positively

Table 9.4 Race and Gender

Victim Sex	Victim Race		
	White	Black	Total
Male	1044	43	1087
	78%	90%	78%
Female	304	5	309
	22%	10%	22%
Total	1348	48	1396
	100%	100%	100%

Pearson chi2(1) = 3.9603 Pr = 0.047
likelihood-ratio chi2(1) = 4.6544 Pr = 0.031

Killer Sex	Killer Race		
	White	Black	Total
Male	1116	46	1162
	94%	90%	94%
Female	74	5	79
	6%	10%	6%
Total	1190	51	1241
	100%	100%	100%

Pearson chi2(1) = 1.0547 Pr = 0.304
likelihood-ratio chi2(1) = 0.9204 Pr = 0.337

Source: see text.

known) of all killings were a man killing a woman. We are left with a conundrum—Was there in fact a cultural difference, did the apparently lesser degrees of femicide reflect demography and opportunity, or is the difference a consequence of poor reporting?

Racial Attacks

At least three killings of blacks could be identified in the media as having possible racial motivations. These exclude the dozens of racially motivated killings during the draft riot of 1863. One was in Brooklyn, which was not yet part of New York City, but a separate municipality, but I include it to supplement the descriptions. These three cases were identified by examining, where possible, the twenty-two cases where the victim was black and the killer was not identified as black. It is easy enough to guess that these cases are not representative, but I present them to give an idea of the information available.

An example from "Battle Row" in Brooklyn (hence one that does not enter the formal analysis here) in which race may have played a part is the August 25th murder of Charles H. Rodgers by a "rowdy white gang, without apparent cause of provocation" (*New York Times* 8-29-1866). This case typifies the interpretive

Table 9.5 Spousal Violence

Relationship	Killer's Noted Race or Ethnicity						
	U.S.	Black	French	British	Irish	(Irish?)	Total
Other	50	48	5	12	86	40	241
Spouse	3	8	2	1	40	12	66
Total	53	56	7	13	126	52	307

Victim	Male Killer's Noted Race or Ethnicity						
	U.S.	Black	French	British	Irish	(Irish?)	Total
Men	35	38	6	10	69	35	193
Women	12	10	1	1	45	14	83
Total	47	48	7	11	114	49	276

Source: see text.

difficulties encountered. Rodgers was stabbed in front of his house at 9 P.M. by one from the "skylarking group," which included Charles Kelly, Michael Quirk, Joseph Kelly, George Rampen, John Kennedy, and Frederick Miller. A witness stated that she heard the men say, "Show me the black s— of a b— who struck me and I will cut his d— guts out, or shoot him." Someone said, "There is the black s— of a b—; let's give it to him." The men were arrested. Had there been an earlier fight? Was this a race murder?

The first of the probable race murders in New York City took place on August 8, 1847, when an unknown person murdered a sailor named James Steele, who was returning to his barge. Although absolutely no mention is made of possible racial motives, one cannot help but wonder. Six years later, on December 22, 1853, James Crumsley murdered 29-year-old Edward Matthews. This happened when "a terrible conflict took place in the Fifth Ward, between a party of white men, who are of notorious character, and a gang of colored persons." This "riot" occurred after an African American had been assaulted by three of the white men and took shelter in a black oyster-and-liquor saloon run by Matthews, from whence a group of blacks returned to avenge his injuries. According to the paper, Matthews "was a sort of leader among the colored residents of the Fifth and Eighth Wards, in consideration of his pugilistic abilities" (*New York Times* 12-22-1853).

Ten years later, many race murders occurred during the draft riots. An article describing the arrest of John McAlister, a 40-year-old Irish laborer for the murder of a sailor, William Williams, indicates the nature of these murders. The tone of the article, entitled "Fiendish Murder of a Negro," captures the horrific incident. McAlister bashed in the head of Williams with a twenty-pound paving block in front of a crowd of "men, women and children, who coolly witnessed the fiendish act" (*New York Times* 8-1-1863). Police caught and arrested McAlister two weeks later.

In 1867 William Higgins and a gang of white men murdered Christian Bost-wick in Higgins's liquor store (*New York Times* 7-24-1867). Higgins testified that Bostwick, a cook on a coastal steamer, refused to leave the store, so he beat him. According to the article, Bostwick was well known among the "numerous colored population in the Eighth Ward." Police arrested Higgins.

All of these cases carry in common the elements of a racial attack. Typically, the killers were backed up by other white men, and typically the victims' noted occupations hint that there could have been latent conflicts over occupations involved. Since all the secondary literature for this era indicates how job "turf" formed an important part of antiblack aggression in northern cities, these incidents seem to support that notion. On the other hand, the high number of attacks that did not carry racial overtones requires that we be very cautious. In Table 9.1, above, the dichotomized race distribution of victims and killers contains little to support a strong pattern of race-motivated killings. Therefore, I conclude that race motivation played a secondary role in homicides. Yet in such a small black community, the impact of even a few unpredictable racial attacks must have been very deep. These occasional yet lethal attacks, followed by the awful events in the draft riot, imply that New York City's black residents always had to be alert to sudden attacks.

An Issue of Justice

The study of the role played by racial bias in the justice system is fraught with complexity, even in the present era. During the period under examination here, New York City changed from a slave to a nonslave to a fairly vigorous pro-Reconstruction political atmosphere. But ethnic and racial hostility ran high, and most New Yorkers were white, especially after the antiblack draft riots.

Immigrants, particularly the Irish and Germans, were more heavily involved in homicides than their numbers warrant, but as the city continued to fill with immigrants in the post–Civil War era, homicides per capita decreased.

The ways in which race mattered were complex and shifting, and my discussion here is based on the assumption that while ethnicity (and class) played a highly important role, the experience of blacks contrasted with all nonblacks is a fundamental starting point. Here the question is about treatment by the justice system: Were there differences in arrest, trial, and punishment of blacks and nonblacks?

The Appendix reports the results of logit analyses of the likelihood of arrest, trial, and execution for blacks versus all others. These analyses were done with two different assumptions about missing information: one, that cases with missing information on race or ethnicity should be dropped from the analysis, and two, that African Americans would be more likely to be noted than others, so that when unreported, a person's race was probably white.

Blacks had about the same likelihood of arrest and trial for homicides as non-blacks (see Appendix, Tables 9.6 and 9.7). It is possible that missing information about trials—quite common—biases these results, just as it is possible that there was an underreporting of murders by nonblacks. The data collection strategy for this research, using all suspicious deaths, whether or not called a homicide by a coroner's jury, was deliberately designed to overcome such events, however.

A precise analysis of the past is even more difficult, although one can guess that a society with fewer claims to evenhanded justice might have less to hide. Because we have good records on executions, it is possible to examine at least the outlines of the role race played in the heaviest and rarest punishment meted out to killers in nineteenth-century New York. For this portion of the analysis, the data on the beginning and end of the individual level processes are better than those on the middle. That is, the original counts of murder and any executions are more accurate than are arrests, trials, and sentences.

Nineteenth-century New Yorkers tended to be against capital punishment, in contrast to our perception of that era. Out of over 1,560 murderers, only 2 percent, 31, were executed for their crime. And the proportion being executed was diminishing over time—every year between 1800 and 1875 decreased the probability of execution by 3 percent. Even though a high proportion of arrests was made, there was erratic follow-up. Basically, it was easy to get away with murder, in part because when cases came to trial, juries were apt to give the offenders the benefit of the doubt. In a city filled with bars, rowdiness, and a good deal of physical violence, the all-important coroner's juries often placed themselves in the offender's situation and found the deaths to be accidental, the result of a friendly fight. Beginning in the decade of the 1820s, the loosely parallel relationship between executions and homicides ended—executions remaining at the same level, even as homicides spiraled upward. It is possible that this represents a measurement problem, that the further back in time, the more difficult the recovery of homicides with no punished killer.

The one exception to such leniency for capital offenses came for African American offenders, who were twice as likely to be hanged as their white compatriots. Surprisingly, the race of their victims did not seem to matter much, however. And even this clearly biased system allowed 90 percent of the black offenders (51 of 58) to escape the gallows. Executions became substantially less frequent every year (see Appendix for a fuller discussion).

CONCLUSION

There are several conclusions to be drawn from this probe, based on still fragmentary data. New York was a violent city, even if not as violent as today. Perhaps more important is what it was not: a city with violence coming from people of color. It was a violent city of principally white persons, many of them recent immigrants. Had guns been as prevalent as today, how much more violent would this city have been?

The rate at which homicides occurred fluctuated considerably through this period, but it is important to note that it often dropped as precipitously as it rose: immigrants did not necessarily produce violence, as though by some law of pressure cooking. Persons of color participated in this violent society. In the few specifically racial incidents, African Americans were the victims of racially motivated attacks. None of these incidents compared to the draft riots, of course, but they do illustrate that African Americans were in a dangerous city.

Finally, there are two broader implications to be drawn. First is a message of hope: rates of violence can come down, even if we cannot yet identify mechanisms causing that to happen. Second is a message about research: we can learn a great deal from the past that will help us think about the present, if we are willing to commit the energy to the task. It is worth doing. Coming to grips with contemporary crises as complicated and as ancient as interpersonal violence means coming to grips with a long human history.

APPENDIX

Logit Analyses of Increased Probability Racial Differences in Treatment of Murders

Below are various logit estimations predicting whether or not a killer was arrested, tried, and executed. They test various assumptions about missing information (concerning race) and about undiscovered homicides.

Table 9.6 estimates whether or not the killer's race affected probabilities of arrest, no assumptions about the killer's race being made. Because victims are not included in the equations, about 70 percent of the known homicides are used for the estimates. A coefficient of less than one for the killer's race indicates that being black reduced the probability of an event occurring, in this case arrest. Table 9.6 shows that race made little difference. Again, the assumption here is that the nearly four hundred missing observations made no difference. If we assume that all black killers were identified, then the first coefficients for Tables 9.6 and 9.7 become negative.

In Table 9.7 the effect of offender's race on the likelihood of being tried is examined: here the coefficient is positive, but as the standard error and the 95 percent confidence intervals both indicate, the amount greater than one is slight.

Table 9.8A is the first of several examining executions. Though infrequent as punishment, the existence of a separate data set on executions, in addition to the high probability of being reported, makes these data more complete and reliable than those on arrests and trials, where the possibility of an overlooked trial or arrest is much more likely. The separate data set is known as the Espy file, the results of years of work by Watt Espy, now archived at the Inter-university Con-

Table 9.6 Arrests (N = 1182 chi2(2) = 14.10 Pseudo R² = 0.0086)

Arrested	Coefficient	Standard Error	t	P>|t|	[95% Confidence Interval]	
Killer Black	.938	.2951	3.181	0.002	.3597	1.517
Year died	.0069	.0037	1.843	0.066	−.0004	.0142
Constant	−12.83	6.94	−1.848	0.065	−26.45	.790

Source: see text.

Table 9.7 Trials (N = 1182 chi2(2) = 15.23 Pseudo R² = 0.0159)

Tried	Coefficient	Standard Error	t	P>|t|	[95% Confidence Interval]	
Killer Black	1.192	.2942	4.054	0.000	.615	1.77
Year died	.0064	.0057	1.119	0.263	−.0048	.0176
Constant	−13.76	10.60	−1.298	0.195	−34.57	7.046

Source: see text.

sortium for Political and Social Research. This file contains all known executions in the United States, and for this project the New York series proved invaluable. Table 9.8A shows a coefficient of 2.36 with a more confidence-inspiring Chi2 than those in the two previous tables. The coefficient gives strong indication of the increased probability of execution for black offenders versus nonblacks. Note that the negative coefficient for the Year variable shows that the probability of execution, for all, was declining.

Table 9.8B relaxes the assumption that an offender's race cannot be inferred: instead, all persons not identified as black are assumed to be white. There are several instances where this is risky—those, for example, where a victim was found and there was never a hint of the murderer's identity. Note that the fit of this equation is not as good as that in Table 9.8A, but that the coefficients are very similar.

It seems that if the offender's race makes a difference in executions, then it is possible that the victim's race too would make a difference. Did the courts get even harsher for black defendants when the victims were not black? Table 9.8C brings the victim's race into the equation, again with the assumption that black victims, being more unusual, would also be more likely to be identified. Here, victims without ethnic or racial identification are coded as white. The coefficient for victim's race turns out to be nonsignificant, meaning that it did not affect the outcome.

In Table 9.8D, the assumption that nonidentified race means white is dropped, and the estimates are made only for that subset of cases (40 percent) where both persons have been identified. While the coefficient remains positive on the killer's race, that on the victim is nonsignificant, as in Table 9.8C.

Table 9.8A Executions (N = 1182 chi2(2) = 32.06 Pseudo R^2 = 0.1465)

Executed	Coefficient	Standard Error	t	P>|t|	[95% Confidence Interval]	
Killer Black	2.36	.4953	4.770	0.000	1.391	3.334
Year died	−.0387	.0088	−4.399	0.000	−.056	−.021
Constant	67.39	16.22	4.155	0.000	35.57	99.21

Source: see text.

Table 9.8B Executions Predicted by Offender's Race and Year, All Cases, Assumption That All Persons White Unless Otherwise Identified. (N = 1561 chi2(2) = 30.03 Pseudo R^2 = 0.099)

Executed	Coefficient	Standard Error	t	P>|t|	[95% Confidence Interval]	
Killer Black	2.021	.461	4.377	0.000	1.11	2.9279
Year died	−.0334	.007	−4.372	0.000	−.0484	−.0184
Constant	57.74	14.10	4.096	0.000	30.09	85.40

Source: see text.

Table 9.8C Executions Predicted by Both Offender's and Victim's Race and Year, All Cases, Assumption That All Persons White Unless Otherwise Identified. (N = 1561 chi2(3) = 30.11 Pseudo R^2 = 0.0989)

Executed	Coefficient	Standard Error	t	P>|t|	[95% Confidence Interval]	
Killer Black	2.1336	.594	3.591	0.000	.9680	3.299
Victim Black	−.2160	.748	−0.289	0.773	−1.684	1.252
Year died	−.03357	.0076	−4.390	0.000	−.0485	−.0185
Constant	58.05	14.11	4.114	0.000	30.37	85.73

Source: see text.

Table 9.8D Executions Predicted by Both Offender's and Victim's Race and Year, All Cases, *No* Assumptions That All Persons White Unless Otherwise Identified. (N = 675 chi2(3) = 23.12 Prob > Pseudo R^2 = 0.1192)

Executed	Coefficient	Standard Error	t	P>|t|	[95% Confidence Interval]	
Killer Black	1.888	.6537	2.889	0.004	.6048	3.172
Victim Black	−.242	.7946	−0.305	0.760	−1.802	1.317
Year died	.0302	.007	−3.856	0.000	−.0456	−.0148
Constant	52.31	14.4	3.620	0.000	23.94	80.68

Source: see text.

Finally, there is another feature that may affect patterns of missingness in the data: known homicides that my research assistants and I have not yet uncovered. As made clear earlier in this chapter, this project depends on the work of many different people, searching less and less rich sources. One aspect of the work, for instance, is establishing that zero homicide years are really zero—not exciting

Table 9.8E Executions Predicted by Both Offender's and Victim's Race and Year, All Cases, No Assumption That All Persons White Unless Otherwise Identified. Test of Impact of Latest Observation. (N = 674 chi2(3) = 24.01 Pseudo R^2 = 0.1239)

Executed	Coefficient	Standard Error	t	P>|t|	[95% Confidence Interval]	
Killer Black	1.904	.6528	2.918	0.004	.6228	3.186
Victim Black	−.1391	.7902	−.0176	0.860	−1.690	1.412
Year died	−.0312	.0079	−3.962	0.000	−.0468	−.015
Constant	54.18	14.53	3.729	0.000	25.65	82.72

Source: see text.

Table 9.8F Executions Predicted by Both Offender's and Victim's Race and Year, All Cases, Assumption That All Persons White Unless Otherwise Identified. Test of Impact of Latest Observation. (N = 1560 chi2(3) = 31.08 Pseudo R^2 = 0.1021)

Executed	Coefficient	Standard Error	t	P>|t|	[95% Confidence Interval]	
Killer Black	2.15	.5905	3.645	0.000	.9943	3.310
Victim Black	−.1154	.7398	−0.156	0.876	−1.566	1.335
Year died	.0345	.0076	−4.510	0.000	−.0495	−.0195
Constant	59.8	14.13	4.235	0.000	32.14	87.60

Source: see text.

research. In the intervening six months and approximately seven hundred research hours since the original logits were run, an additional homicide involving African Americans has been found: on December 28, 1801, a man named Haisty murdered Lewis Smith, upping to 59 the number of black offenders. Because of the Espy data set, we know that Haisty was not executed, and the news item indicates an arrest, but we know no more. Table 9.8E reestimates Table 9.8D, and Table 9.8F reestimates Table 9.8C. Table 9.8E makes a slight modification to the coefficients and fit of 9.8D, making the inferences from it slightly stronger. Table 9.8F has a similar resemblance to 9.8C, making the implications of its coefficients somewhat stronger.

NOTES

1. The research reported here has been supported by grants from the Academic Senate, University of California, Los Angeles. Many people have assisted in this project: graduate research assistants I wish to thank include Susan Meyer, Brian Griest, Sheila O'Hare, Tom Clark, Carol Winter, Rob Michaelson, and Matthew Lee. Elizabeth Stephenson and Martin Pawlicki of the Social Science Data Archives helped me with the Espy file. I wish to thank research assistants from the Student Research Program of the Honors College. These include Catharine Lamb, Sanjiv Rao, Gregg Doll, Cynthia Lum, Duyen Bui, Diane Kim, Sue Pak, Julie Jarboe, Serge Kogen, Tom Chung, Marcus Nenn, Colby Moldow, Mike Doyle, Cheryl

Feiner, Robbyn Wilkins, Barry Dewalt, Paige Anderson, Christa Welch, Andy Bodeau, Mike Doyle, Kenneth So, and Christine Statler.

2. Historians have long noted the irony of the situation of African Americans in northern cities prior to the ending of slavery: while free, and able to pursue their self-interests such as religion, northern blacks were systematically excluded from occupations open to them in the slave South. Frederick Douglass, for example, was unable to obtain work in northern shipyards as he had in Baltimore.

3. For the most recent work on the riots, see Bernstein (1990). His bibliographical essay, 341, summarizes the extensive literature on the riots.

4. I base this statement on the perusing of the *New York Times* and other materials. Only a handful of editorial comments on crime, with the exception of riots, ever appeared in print.

5. This discussion is built upon the extensive work by criminal justice historians that has focused on the kind and quality of information we have about the past. In particular the work of Roger Lane has helped us think about such frustrating problems.

6. Estimated by robust regression: black homicide slope = .033, nonblack homicide slope = 1.47. The latter changes to 1.81 for 1845 to 1874, a change visually apparent in the plotted actual numbers.

7. Note: I take the actual populations in 1865 here as Italians were not reported for 1855. These figures are not directly comparable to the mid-point estimates used above.

8. In all cases, these are for victims.

REFERENCES

Anderson, Margo J. 1988. *The American Census: A Social History.* New Haven: Yale University Press.

Bernstein, Iver. 1990. *The New York City Draft Riots: Their Significance for American Society and Politics in the Age of the Civil War.* New York: Oxford University Press.

Chudacoff, Howard P. 1989. *How Old Are You? Age Consciousness in American Culture.* Princeton: Princeton University Press.

Emerson, Haven, and Harriet E. Hughes. 1941. *Population, Births, Notifiable Diseases, and Deaths, Assembled for New York City, New York, 1866–1938, from Official Records.* New York: DeLamar Institute of Public Health, College of Physicians and Surgeons, Columbia University.

———. 1955. *Supplement 1936–1953 to Population, Births, Notifiable Diseases, and Deaths, Assembled for New York City, New York, 1866–1938, from Official Records.* New York: DeLamar Institute of Public Health, College of Physicians and Surgeons, Columbia University.

Espy, M. Watt. 1987. *Executions in the U.S., 1608–1987: [computer file, the Espy-file,* principal investigators, M. Watt Espy and John]. 1st ICPSR ed. Tuscaloosa, Ala.: John Ortiz Smykla (producer). Ann Arbor, Mich.: Inter-university Consortium for Political and Social Research (distributor).

Gurr, Ted R., ed. 1989. *Violence in America.* Newbury Park, Calif.: Sage Publications.

Hodges, Graham R. 1986. *New York City Cartmen, 1667–1850.* New York: New York University Press.

Johnson, Julie. 1994. "Coroners, Corruption, and the Politics of Death: Forensic Pathology in the United States." In Michael Clark and Catherine Crawford, eds., *Legal Medicine in History.* New York: Cambridge University Press.

Lane, Roger. 1979. *Violent Death in the City: Accident, Suicide and Homicide in Philadelphia, 1850–1900.* Cambridge: Harvard University Press.

———. 1986. *Roots of Violence in Black Philadelphia, 1860–1900.* Cambridge, Mass.: Harvard University Press.

———. 1991. *William Dorsey's Philadelphia and Ours.* New York: Oxford University Press.

Parkerson, Donald, ed. 1991. Special Issue on the Underenumeration of the US Census, 1850–1880. *Social Science History* (Winter) 15:4.

Rosenwaike, Ira. 1972. *Population History of New York City.* Syracuse: Syracuse University Press.

Scott, Kenneth. 1973. *Rivington's New York Newspaper: Excerpts from a Loyalist Press, 1773–1783.* New York Historical Society.

———. 1988–1989. "Early New York City Coroners' Reports." *The New York Genealogical and Biographical Record,* April 1988, 76–79; July 1988, 145–50; October 1988, 217–19; January 1989, 18–20; April 1989, 88–92.

———. 1989. *Coroners' Reports New York City, 1823–1842.* New York: New York Genealogical and Biographical Society.

———. 1991. *Coroners' Reports New York City, 1843–1849.* New York: New York Genealogical and Biographical Society.

Soman, Alfred. 1980. "Deviance and Criminal Justice in Western Europe, 1300–1800: An Essay in Structure." *Criminal Justice History* 1:1–28.

10

New York City Offender Ages: How Variable over Time?

We all know that homicides are the territory of the young, right? Wrong. This piece shows that youth homicides are a thing of the late twentieth century. It is a surprising finding, although it should not be. Some of the earlier data would have shown the same thing, and earlier scholarly wisdom would have as well. But, in the late twentieth century flood of violence, the newly youthful crowd of offenders became the norm and changed how we viewed young men.

It used to be that when violence researchers referred to the dangerous world of young men, such as in the violent frontier towns discussed by Roger McGrath and David Courtwright, they meant twenty- to forty-year-olds (Courtwright 1996; McGrath 1984). This essay helps clarify part of the unique nature of the late-twentieth-century violence boom: if the bulge in youth offenders continues, it suggests that a separate strategy for suppressing youth violence should be developed. As a nontraditional group, the violent youth may well respond to different controls and incentives. The targeting of weapons that appeal to youth, the development of separate diversion and prevention strategies, and the realization that violence is a problem that must be unpacked into disparate pieces, all flow from the age analysis here.

First published in *Homicide Studies* 3, 3, August 1999 © Sage Publications, Inc. This work has been supported by research grants from the National Science Foundation, the National Institute of Justice, and the Academic Senate of the University of California. In addition, 30 undergraduate volunteer research assistants have helped me by scanning nineteenth-century newspapers. For assistance with population data and with the contemporary literature, I wish to thank Alan Abrahamse, Richard Steckel, and Daniel Scott Smith. Catherine Fitch, Matt Sobek, and Steven Ruggles at the University of Minnesota helped me use the Integrated Public Use Microdata Series (IPUMS) data set. Kenneth Cobb, New York City Municipal Archives, has provided invaluable archival assistance.

Earlier work has established that there is a peakedness in all kinds of offending per age-specific population group but that this varies over time, offense type, gender, and place (Farrington 1986). Violent offender peak rates occur somewhat later than nonviolent rates, and women's often peak somewhat later than men's. Despite these variations, one can generalize that age-specific violent offending is ordinarily more likely within the younger segment of a population, somewhere between the late teens and mid-30s (Farrington 1986: 197). Several studies suggest that the maximum age rates for violent offending have become younger over time (Greenberg 1994: 370; Wolfgang 1958: 66, 72). One counterexample to this generalization is Farrington's (1986) data for England, which show an increased peak age rate for all male offending from 1938 to 1983, possibly an artifact of the inclusion of ages for all kinds of offenses.

By the late 1980s, the general public as well as criminologists and criminal justice personnel had become aware of the increase in dangerous young offenders. The rise of the young violent offender has brought up a whole range of troubling issues (Butterfield 1995). Whether one labels these younger groups as "super predators" (apparently first coined by DiIulio 1995), the incidence of younger offenders appears to be a significant shift (Fox 1995). Research on the late-twentieth-century period with the best data, which go back to 1976, the first year of the FBI's Supplementary Homicide Reports (SHR) with offender ages reported (Fox 1994), finds evidence of an increasingly younger age in high homicide offense rates from the 1970s through at least 1994 (Abrahamse 1997; Blumstein 1995; Blumstein & Rosenfeld 1998). By the late 1980s, young offenders, especially those in the teenage years, showed the highest rate of offending, and the age-rate curve peaked much more sharply than it did for the 1970s and early 1980s; this peak was probably more abrupt and at a younger age than for any known earlier period.

The research discussed here contrasts data on age-specific violent offending from the mid-nineteenth century through the late twentieth century in New York City. It also brings in supplemental evidence to raise further questions about the continued surge in youth offense rates.

DATA

As will be discussed, analyses of historical crime data present significant challenges. The offense level data used here are from two sources, the FBI's SHR series for 1976–1995 (pre-1976 SHR data report only victim's age) and a data set of New York City homicides from 1773 to 1874. To attain consistency across time, offenses with victims under five years of age are excluded, on the principle that these were erratically discovered and reported, particularly for the nineteenth century (Lane 1979: 90–101). Similarly, homicide here is defined as both manslaughter and murder, with justifiable homicide and abortion excluded (a woman dying during the course of abortion was deemed a homicide victim in New York prior to the early twentieth century).[1]

The choice of New York City assures a relatively reasonable across-time comparison. The city boundaries have only changed once, in 1898, when New York City incorporated the non-Manhattan cities such as Brooklyn. The reporting units—city and county coroner, district attorney, and police—have had consistent definitions of duties as far as homicides were concerned, the major shift occurring in the early twentieth century when the coroner's office lost its role as homicide prosecutor. For all of the era covered here, including the nineteenth century, the city was truly metropolitan, reaching a population of 1 million in the 1860s.

I use here the age of the first listed offender in all data sets. In 1993, for example, 16 percent of New York City homicides were committed by more than one person. In these, the offenders tended to be younger (mean age of 21 versus 29 for offenders in one-on-one offenses). For offenses with multiple listed offenders, the first listed offender was only slightly older than the second listed offender in 1993—21.6 versus 21.2 years old (not statistically significant, $n = 267$), so using the first offender age should not bias the results. There seem to have been fewer multiple offenders in the nineteenth century, with only 5 percent of all occurrences falling into this category. However, this may reflect efforts at the time to isolate exactly which person administered the fatal blow, particularly in barroom melees. Contemporary laws and policing practice tend to broaden the definition of offender to all who participate in the homicide.

The nineteenth-century data set consists of every identifiable homicide in New York City from the late eighteenth century to 1874. Ninety percent of the offender ages come from the years 1846–1874. All but a dozen cases with reported offender ages came from the period 1845–1874 and only two from before 1802.[2] Sources include newspapers, mainly the *New York Times* and *New York Tribune,* coroners' inquests (some of which are in the Superior or General Sessions court minutes), district attorney's (DA) papers, and published trial accounts (Monkkonen 1995, 1997). The inquests and DA papers are held by the New York City Municipal Archives; the inquests for 1823–1849 have been abstracted by Scott (1988, 1989a, 1989b, 1991). The complete data set contains 1,742 homicides, with information on both offender and victim. Age data are available for 21.4 percent ($n = 373$) of the offenders and 42 percent ($n = 732$) of the victims. This discrepancy is in large part because the coroners' inquests noted details about victims, not offenders. There is no evidence of systematic age omission.[3] When possible, missing ages have been supplemented from the manuscript U.S. censuses for 1840, 1850, 1860, and 1870, using CD indexes to household heads.[4] Because of the dominance of male offenders (only 25 offenders were female), this report focuses on trends in male rates.

Some nineteenth-century homicide reports mentioned only vaguely specified ages: "a lad" or a "boy" could mean anything from ages 9 to 19 (Chudacoff 1989:

9). At least six homicide offenders were such young men; however, they could not be found in the manuscript census and therefore have been excluded from the data. For the 1846 to 1874 period, the data are slightly more complete, with ages known on 24.7 percent of the offenders. As another test of possible bias in missing offender ages, I compared the means of the victim ages when the offender ages were also reported. The difference was not significant.[5] Contemporary homicide scholars will notice that some of these omissions echo today's data problems. The SHR, for example, include the ages of 68 percent of all first-listed offenders for the United States, 1976–1995, but only 41 percent for New York City.

What about the completeness of this nineteenth-century data set as a whole? Specifically, are there missing cases that would bias rates in a downward fashion? The one check on missing individual observations comes from annual counts done by the city inspector or later by the Department of Health. These other annual counts sometimes have a different number of homicides than what I have found. I suspect that overcounts in the comparison sources occurred due to the counting of accidental manslaughter, executions, and women who died during the course of abortions. An additional confounding definitional problem comes from infanticides and child murders; nineteenth-century New York officials tried hard not to notice these often tragic cases, and few were reported as such (Lane 1979: 90–101). Furthermore, undercounts in my individual level data set may have resulted from cases not reported or missed by me in newspapers and those missing from coroner and DA files. All told, comparing the total annual counts from other published sources to my individual-level data yields an estimate of 12 percent missing cases for the critical time period here, 1846 to 1874.

Population data for the denominators (1860 and 1990, each the closest decade to the weighted center year for each group) were drawn from the Integrated Public Use Microdata Series (IPUMS) Web site. These data, national random samples, are weighted, 1-in-500 for 1860 and 1-in-100 for 1990. They allow the construction of a precise population denominator for New York City for every age and each sex rather than for grouped ages. This advantage is offset by the subsequent age "heaping," the tendency of people to declare their age to the nearest zero or odd number. If age heaping were completely even across various sources, age rates would cancel out the effects, but that is not the case. Even the twentieth-century age rates show heaping; therefore, the plots here are smoothed. Offender age rates may be further refined to appropriate measures by selecting only male offenders and population denominators. The rates here are corrected by annualizing and inflating for missing age data.[6]

VIOLENT MALE OFFENDER AGE RATES

Calculated rates for the two different centuries are displayed in Figure 10.1; the plotted data are smoothed with a cubic spline (Goldstein 1992; Stata Corp.

1997). Not only is the twentieth-century curve much more peaked, but the peak year is much earlier than for the nineteenth century, about 20 now versus about 34 then. The nineteenth century had relatively high rates for older offenders, reflecting the sharp decline in older population numerators due to high mortality rates. Again, the actual counts here are small—3, 2, and 4, respectively (there were no 13-year-olds and 3 of age 14). This picure shows at least three similarities in the distributions. There are two peaks in both centuries, at about age twenty and in the mid-thirties. After the mid-thirties age group, homicide levels from the two distinct periods closely resemble one another, confirming the earlier hints that the ages of 13 to 33 provide the source of contemporary New York City's difference from the nineteenth century.

Overall, the picture presented by Figure 10.1 illustrates a sharp difference between nineteenth- and twentieth-century homicide offender age distributions. There is an enormous bulge in the contemporary younger offenders versus a relatively level rate of nineteenth-century offending that commenced at age ten, rose gradually to the mid-thirties, and persisted until late middle age—for all practical purposes, until the end of most active adult lives.

This finding is important but requires further confirmation and elaboration from different sites and time periods. It conforms with the data presented by Block and Christakos (1997) on Chicago, which implies a more level age rate of offending as recently as 1965. Furthermore, the results are similar to comparative data for France and Philadelphia that are displayed in Figure 10.2 and Table 10.1. The levels of homicide for France and Philadelphia are highly suspect, but

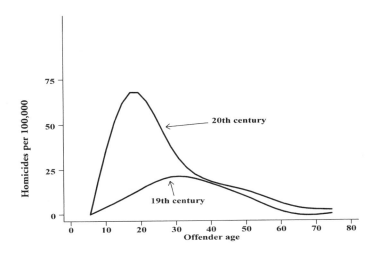

Figure 10.1 New York City Homicide Offender Age Rates (smoothed). *Source:* see text.

Table 10.1 Comparisons of Offender Ages and Age Rates

Place, Time	Peak Age Rate	Mean Age	Modal Age	Median Age
New York City, mid-19th century	35	30.0	20	27
France, 1887	32	—	—	—
United States, 1908–1912	—	—	20–29	—
Philadelphia, 1950	20–24	—	—	32
New York City, 1976–1995	20	28.3	20	25

Note: Durkheim gives two rates for France, one for unpremeditated (25–30), one for premeditated (30–40). I have given the mean.
Source: Durkheim (1951: 343); Hoffman (1925; cited in Wolfgang, 1958: 71); Wolfgang (1958: 66, 70).

I have not attempted to readjust from the original, because the purpose of the image is to show the shape of the age distribution.

Reflected in Table 10.1 is Wolfgang's (1958) discussion of earlier age-specific homicide rates, citing Durkheim's finding of peak homicide offender age rates in 1887 in France of 25 to 30, with "premeditated" murders higher at ages 30 to 40 (see Durkheim 1951: 343). In contrast, Wolfgang found a peak offending age rate of 20–24 in Philadelphia for 1948–1952 (1958: 66, 72). Wolfgang also found that for Philadelphia, 1948–1952, the number of known offenders—as opposed to age rates—peaked at age 20–24, then tapered off slightly through the next ten years (1958: 66).[7]

As a summary, one may characterize the reported age distributions of murder offenders in published studies as having a wide interquartile range with a median age at risk similar to the mean age, and the modal age quite younger. Prior to the late 1970s, "normal" homicide offenders used to be around age 30, with the peak offending years in the mid-20s to late 30s. The progressively younger peak age rate shown in the first column of Table 10.1 suggests that, like the results reported here, youthful offending has been increasing since the mid-nineteenth century.

The data shown in Table 10.1 are illustrated in Figure 10.2 where the shape of four homicide offender age rate distributions are compared—the two from New York City, Philadelphia in the 1950s, and late-nineteenth-century France.

Table 10.2 Indicators of Men at Risk to Participate in "Bachelor Subculture"

Year	Males 15–54 Not Born in New York State (%)	Males Unmarried or Not Living with Spouse, Not Born in New York State (%)
1880	19.0	7.0
1950	12.4	4.3
1990	14.3	8.5

Note: Pre-1880, marital status not coded in U.S. census.
Source: Ruggles & Sobek (1997).

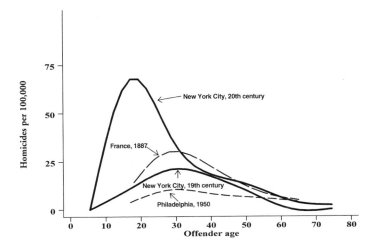

Figure 10.2 Comparative Homicide Offender Age Rates for New York City, Philadelphia, and France

The resulting plots show the distributions, smoothed with cubic splines, in their probable relationship to one another.

As shown in Figure 10.2, there is a relatively flat curve for the nineteenth century and a peaked curve for late-twentieth-century New York City. The data for France and Philadelphia add an interesting modification, for they show a flat curve resembling the nineteenth-century New York City distribution but with progressively younger maximums. The high peakedness of homicides in the last quarter of the twentieth century appears to be something that happened after 1950.

COMPARING OFFENDER AGES

Interestingly, when the larger population itself is ignored, the age distributions of known homicide offenders in New York City across two centuries show great similarity (that is, the offender age distribution ignoring the at-risk population adjustments). Unadjusted for population at risk, both means and standard deviations are similar. Male offenders had a mean age of 29.7 (27 median; 11.5 standard deviation) for the nineteenth century and a 28.1 mean age (24 median; 11.1 standard deviation) for the late twentieth century. Interquartile ranges are 21 to 36 and 20 to 33, respectively. The smaller standard deviation and narrower interquartile ranges for the twentieth century show slightly more compression around the mean compared to the nineteenth century but nothing like the age rate peak. In essence, very young offenders were relatively more numerous in the nineteenth century in terms of sheer numbers, but they were also a larger proportion of the overall population. The sharp difference in the age profile of offenders, therefore, is most evident in comparison of age-specific rates, not in the raw number of offenders.

DISCUSSION

A question to emerge from the findings reported here is why the nineteenth-century peak offending age came so much later than the twentieth century's. Could this mean that homicide in some peculiar way has more to do with the assemblage of older age groups semi-independent of the larger population? Some nineteenth-century evidence points toward a more comprehensive incorporation of young adults into "substitute" families when they had left their families of origin. Few people lived alone; children worked as apprentices and lived with families, and young adults and young marrieds boarded in homes. Could much longer-lasting family controls with the external employment of children and young adults have continued family ties and social control into middle age?

The results discussed here raise two issues. First, they establish that the current age distribution of urban male homicide offender rates is quite different from that of the nineteenth century. Second, they pose a question: Is the currently high rate of young age offending an anomaly, the signal of a long-term trend, or an incremental increase? The data in Table 10.1 suggest that lower age rate offending is new, but to establish more precisely when and how will require several more age rate distributions.

If the current situation is an anomaly, the explanatory task will be to show how the late twentieth century differs from other eras. If it is the beginning of a new trend, then the question will be to identify its components and causes.

There are several reasonable places to look for long-term explanations in the age structure of homicide. These include physiological and sociocultural changes in aging; changes in the family structure, particularly in its social control functions; and age-related changes in the cost, lethality, and cultural desirability of weapons.

A preliminary step toward identifying some basics is to refine even more the question of population at risk. The nineteenth century was, of course, very different from the late twentieth century. Mid-nineteenth-century New York City had a mean age of 24.6 for men and 23.9 for women, as opposed to 34.1 for men and 37.6 for women in 1990. Rather than looking at all males, one can theorize that males without family supervision or responsibilities, or without other community constraints, would be more likely to be offenders and victims. This is a version of the frontier hypothesis, most recently revived by Courtwright (1996) but long explored by historians from Schneider (1984) to Lane (1997). These historians typically argue that this "bachelor subculture" has structured the free time of young men and often played into increased violence. Perhaps the violence and confrontational masculinity was sometimes as lethal in the past as today; for example, McGrath's (1984) study of western mining towns and McKanna's (1997) work on several different western cities suggest high age-specific homicide rates. However, none of these researchers calculate age- and gender-specific rates.

Establishing the size of the bachelor subculture for New York City over a long time period is difficult due to changing census categories. However, two simple indicators are shown in Table 10.2: (a) the percentage of the total population who were males age 15 to 54, not born in New York State, and (b) the percentage not married or residing without a spouse, presumably a better (if less available) measure of bachelorhood. Ideally, the first row would be before 1860, not 1880, but prior to 1880, census enumerators did not code marital relationships. The available data show that New York City, when measured solely by male newcomers, probably had a diminishing population at risk to participate in the bachelor subculture from the mid-nineteenth century through the late 1950s. When this measure is modified by looking at those who were unmarried, a different at-risk population distribution appears, one that shows a recent increase in nonmarried men.

These data may help resolve a major puzzle. The median age of both New York City and the United States has been getting increasingly older since the early nineteenth century, with a deviation introduced by the baby boom, but violent crime has not followed such a steady trajectory. Therefore, the household status of the younger men merits greater attention. By focusing on the male population outside of the traditional control of families, we see that the at-risk population appears to have increased substantially.

The differences in age patterns in the risk of becoming an offender over this 150-year period suggest that there is an important research task—to more precisely identify age-at-risk rates across a variety of temporal and spatial settings. Age-at-risk rates are among the best tools we have to generate comparison data across seemingly impossible gaps in time and space. Answering the question of whether youthful offenders are an anomaly or a trend promises to help us focus on identifying unique temporal causes or longer-term demographic and social transformations that may account for this historical shift in patterns of homicide.

NOTES

1. See Spierenburg (1996: 69–76) for an excellent discussion of various homicide categorization schemes.

2. I continue to pursue missing data, so the final data set when archived will show marginally improved completeness. Only one missing source could make a dramatic difference, the ages of offenders as reported in jail registers. Unfortunately, the inmate register for the New York City Prison, or the Tombs as it was called at the time, cannot be found.

3. I report here three difference-of-means tests on offender ages to explore the possibility that the age data "missingness" is not random. Note that the missingness is not initially due to nonclearance but simply to the casual nature of nineteenth-century reporting. The first table examines the possibility that in some years some unknown event caused biased under-

	n	Mean Age	Standard Error	Standard Deviation	95% Confidence Interval
x	25	30.32	2.71	13.57	24.72–35.92
y	348	30.21	.62	11.65	28.98–31.44
Combined	373	30.22	.61	11.77	29.02–31.42
Difference			.11	2.44	−4.69– 4.91

Degrees of freedom = 371
Ho: mean (x) − mean (y) = diff = 0

Ha: diff 0	Ha: diff $\cong$ 0	Ha: diff $\not\subset$ 0
$t = 0.04$	$t = 0.04$	$t = 0.04$
$p < t = 0.52$	$p > \lvert t \rvert = 0.96$	$p > t = 0.48$

The second table compares adjacent high and low offender age reporting years, 1873 (x) with 48 percent reported and 1874 (y) with 69 percent reported, again using a two-sample t test with equal variances.

	n	Mean Age	Standard Error	Standard Deviation	95% Confidence Interval
x	15	31.9	2.92	11.3	25.64–38.16
y	26	35.6	1.99	10.13	31.51–39.70
Combined	41	34.25	1.65	10.59	30.90–37.59
Difference		−3.7	3.43		−10.63– 3.23

Degrees of freedom = 39
Ho: mean (x) − mean (y) = diff = 0

Ha: diff < 0	Ha: diff $\cong$ 0	Ha: diff > 0
$t = -1.08$	$t = -1.08$	$t = -1.08$
$p > = 0.14$	$p > \lvert t \rvert = 0.29$	$p > t = 0.86$

Finally, I tested all ages of those arrested $(n = 299)$ versus all ages of those not reported as arrested $(n = 74)$. None of these tests indicates that the offender ages were missing in a non-random pattern.

	n	Mean Age	Standard Error	Standard Deviation	95% Confidence Interval
Arrested	299	30.54	.70	12.12	29.16–31.92
Not arrested	74	28.88	1.19	10.21	26.51–31.25
Combined	373	30.21	.61	11.77	29.01–31.41
Difference		1.66	1.53		−1.34– 4.66

Degrees of freedom = 371
Ho: mean (x) − mean (y) = diff = 0

Ha: diff < 0	Ha: diff $\cong$ 0	Ha: diff > 0
$t = 1.09$	$t = 1.09$	$t = 1.09$
$p < t = 0.86$ $p > \lvert t \rvert = 0.28$		$p > t = 0.14$

reporting; to do this, the years with more completed reporting are compared to those with more fragmentary reporting. The strategy employed uses a two-sample *t*-test with equal variances, comparing years with more than 50 percent ages reported (x = 1803, 1809, 1820, 1873) versus all years with less reporting (y).

4. Theoretically, it is possible to fill in many missing age variables from manuscript census records, especially with CDs that index every head of household to the relevant page of the manuscript census. Marketed by Broderbund under the name Family Tree Maker®, these CDs index heads of households in the manuscript U.S. censuses for 1840 to 1870. However, three things frustate such efforts. First, nineteenth-century Americans (especially the poor) were highly mobile, with only about 50 percent of a community's population persisting from census to census (Knights 1991). Second, census undercounts were even more likely then than now to omit the poor (Adams and Kasakoff 1991; Parkerson 1991). Lane (1991), for instance, found highly inconsistent enumerations of Philadelphia's late-nineteenth-century African American population. Third, common naming patterns lead to impossible identification choices. As an illustration, 18 James Nolans were heads of households in New York City in 1870; their ages ranged from 16 to 51, and all but two were Irish. Which one of these men, if any, murdered Charles Wilson in 1870? (And, which Charles Wilson, of whom there were 23, did he murder?)

5. The test is as in the table below.

	n	Mean Age	Standard Error	Standard Deviation	95% Confidence Interval
x	230	30.33	.93	14.1	28.50–32.16
y	496	31.66	.59	13.22	30.49–32.83
Combined	726	31.24	.50	13.51	30.25–32.22
Difference		−1.33	1.08		−3.44– .78

Degrees of freedom = 724

Ha: diff < 0	Ha: diff ≅ 0	Ha: diff > 0
$t = -1.23$	$t = -1.23$	$t = -1.23$
$p < t = 0.11$	$p > \mid t \mid = 0.22$	$p > t = 0.89$

6. The data for each entire period are divided by the number of years in the period—the twentieth century by 19 years, the nineteenth century by 30. This collapses annual variation in favor of a mean rate. Inflating for missing variables (dividing the twentieth century by .41 and the nineteenth by .27) treats the missing variables as though they were randomly missing. This seems to be standard practice among those working with Supplementary Homicide Reports data.

7. Neither Wolfgang nor Durkheim analyzed patterns of missing data, though presumably their data had missing age variables.

REFERENCES

Abrahamse, A. F. 1997. "Demography and Youth Violence in California." In M. Riedel & J. Boulahanis, eds., *Lethal Violence: Proceedings of the 1995 Meeting of the Homicide Research Working Group*, 3–14. Washington, DC: U.S. Department of Justice.

Adams, J. W., and Kasakoff, A. B. 1991. "Estimates of Census Underenumeration Based on Genealogies." *Social Science History* 15: 527–43.

Block, C. R., and Christakos, A. 1997. "Firearm Availability and Firearm Homicide in

Chicago: A Work in Progress." In P. K. Lattimore & C. A. Nahabedian, eds., *The Nature of Homicide: Trends and Changes. Proceedings of the 1996 Meeting of the Homicide Research Working Group,* 184–89. Washington, DC: U.S. Department of Justice.

Blumstein, A. 1995. "Youth Violence, Guns, and the Illicit-Drug Industry." *Journal of Criminal Law and Criminology* 86: 10–36.

Blumstein, A., and Rosenfeld, R. 1998. "Explaining Recent Trends in U.S. Homicide Rates." *Journal of Criminal Law and Criminology* 88, no. 4; Fall: 1175–1216.

Butterfield, F. 1995. *All God's Children: The Basket Family and the American Tradition of Violence.* New York: Knopf.

Chudacoff, H. P. 1989. *How Old Are You? Age Consciousness in American Culture.* Princeton, NJ: Princeton University Press.

Courtwright, D. T. 1996. *Violent Land: Single Men and Social Disorder from the Frontier to the Inner City.* Cambridge, MA: Harvard University Press.

DiIulio, J. J., Jr. 1995, December 15. "Moral Poverty: The Coming of the Super-Predators Should Scare Us into Wanting to Get to the Root Causes of Crime a Lot Faster." *Chicago Tribune,* Sec. 1, p. 31.

Durkheim, E. 1951. *Suicide: A Study in Sociology.* J. A. Spaulding & G. Simpson, trans. Glencoe, IL: Free Press.

Farrington, D. P. 1986. "Age and Crime." In M. Tonry & N. Morris, eds., *Criminal Justice: An Annual Review of Research,* 7: 189–250. Chicago: University of Chicago Press.

Fox, J. A. 1994. *Uniform Crime Reports (United States): Supplementary Homicide Reports, 1976–1992* [Computer file]. ICPSR version. Boston: Northeastern University, College of Criminal Justice [producer]. Ann Arbor, MI: Inter-University Consortium for Political and Social Research [distributor]. Supplemented by updates from the ICPSR Web site (http://www.icpsr.umich.edu/study number 9028).

———. 1995, October 30. "The calm before the crime wave storm; the rate will soar as baby-boomers' children reach teenhood. We can invest in them now or build prisons later." *Los Angeles Times,* B5.

Goldstein, R. 1992. "Restricted Cubic Spline Functions." *Stata Technical Bulletin,* 10: 29–32.

Greenberg, D. F. 1994. "The Historical Variability of the Age Crime Relationship." *Journal of Quantitative Criminology* 10: 361–73.

Hoffman, F. L. 1925. *The Homicide Problem.* Newark, NJ: Prudential.

Knights, P. R. 1991. "Potholes in the Road of Improvement—Estimating Census Underenumeration by Longitudinal Tracing—United States Censuses, 1850–1880." *Social Science History* 15: 517–26.

Lane, R. 1979. *Violent Death in the City: Suicide, Accident, and Murder in 19th-Century Philadelphia.* Cambridge, MA: Harvard University Press.

———. 1991. *William Dorsey's Philadelphia and Ours: On the Past and Future of the Black City in America.* New York: Oxford University Press.

———. 1997. *Murder in America: A History.* Columbus: Ohio State University Press.

McGrath, R. D. 1984. *Gunfighters, Highwaymen, and Vigilantes: Violence on the Frontier.* Berkeley: University of California Press.

McKanna, C. V., Jr. 1997. *Homicide, Race, and Justice in the American West, 1880–1920.* Tucson: University of Arizona Press.

Monkkonen, E. H. 1995. "New York City Homicides: A Research Note." *Social Science History* 19: 201–214.

———. 1997. "Homicide over the Centuries." In L. Friedman & G. Fisher, eds., *The Crime Conundrum,* 1–7. Boulder, CO: Westview.

Parkerson, D. H. 1991. "Comments on the Underenumeration of the United States Census, 1850–1880." *Social Science History* 15: 509–15.

Ruggles, S., & Sobek, M. 1997. *Integrated Public Use Microdata Series: Version 2.0.* Minneapolis: Historical Census Projects, University of Minnesota. Available: http://www.ipums.umn.edu.

Schneider, J. C. 1984. "Tramping Workers, 1890–1920: A Subcultural View." In E. H. Monkkonen, ed., *Walking to Work: Tramps in America, 1790–1935,* 212–34. Lincoln: University of Nebraska Press.

Scott, K. 1988. "Early New York City Coroner's Reports." *New York Genealogical and Biographical Record* 119: 76–79, 145–150, 217–219.

———. 1989a. *Coroners' Reports New York City, 1823–1842.* New York: New York Genealogical and Biographical Society.

———. 1989b. "Early New York City Coroners' Reports." *New York Genealogical and Biographical Record* 120: 18–20, 89–92.

———. 1991. *Coroner's Reports New York City, 1843–1849.* New York: New York Genealogical and Biographical Society.

Spierenburg, P. 1996. "Long-Term Trends in Homicide: Theoretical Reflections and Dutch Evidence, Fifteenth to Twentieth Centuries." In E. A. Johnson and E. H. Monkkonen, eds., *The Civilization of Crime: Violence in Town and Country since the Middle Ages,* 63–105. Urbana: University of Illinois Press.

Stata Corp. 1997. *Stata Statistical Software: Release 5.0* (Vol. 2, G-O). College Station, TX: Author.

Wolfgang, M. E. 1958. *Patterns in Criminal Homicide.* Philadelphia: University of Pennsylvania Press.

■ PART III:
POLICE

Serious historical scholarship about the police dates from the work of James Richardson and Roger Lane in the mid-1960s. Writing what would have been institutional histories fifty years earlier, they used the perspective of the new social history to look at broad issues in policing, issues that are just as alive today. Clearly influenced by national events—crime control and corruption, police brutality and reform, politics and finance, riots and repression—their work touched on all these themes. Since then a wealth of police research has emerged, and it continues to proliferate. It would be easy to fill a year-long graduate seminar with intense reading just on American police. If there were police training equivalent to military training—a sort of West Point of policing—there probably would be seminars for police theorists to learn from the past, as military theorists do.

The essays here represent the tip of a large iceberg then, one iceberg in a field. Readers should know that my position on police history is that much is to be gained by gleaning from the quantitative trail left by the past and that police must be always understood in a historical and bureaucratic context extending well beyond the confines of the station house. Obvious as this sounds, the very localism of the police departments affects the historiography, so that creating a picture beyond events remains extraordinarily difficult.

11

The Dynamics of Police Behavior:
A Data Reanalysis

In theory, the good thing about data and data analysis is that the analysis can be redone, errors can be discovered, and old conclusions can be amended and approved. In practice, few scholars wish to rehash someone else's work. Who wants to spend valuable research time merely confirming a previous point, especially one made by someone else? Even rejecting previous work is not as interesting or as important as proposing a new analysis or idea. (This is in part the source of "publication bias," the tendency for only positive results to be published in journals.)

It was sheer good fortune that I was able to profitably reanalyze some of my own previously published and analyzed data. Because the Statistics Department at UCLA asks its dissertation writers to work with other scholars, I was able to have Catrien Bijleveld work with me on arrest data that had been an important part of my book *Police in Urban America.*

Using a technique now sometimes called correspondence analysis, her work refined and clarified some of what I had either missed or not understood in my previous analytic efforts. At least two important clarifications emerged from this collaboration: first, the homicide arrest rates that had seemed unrelated to anything in my earlier analysis turned out to relate to other measures of crime; and second, the analysis clearly identified a turning point, 1894, in the relationship of police size to activity, confirming that policing really did change in the last decade of the nineteenth century.

Perhaps the most interesting question this article raises, however, is what else other historians and I have missed. Typically, historians expend enormous

First published in *Historical Methods* 23, no. 3 (Winter 1991).

effort gathering information, data, and then are relatively brief in their manipulation of this hard-earned information. Few of us seek external statistical help, especially when authorship becomes raised to a joint level. There are good reasons for this conservatism: joint-authored efforts may escape the understanding of each author, so that there is a loss of control for both. A bad choice in the team member means a flawed analysis. And the final paper may be difficult for any single person to evaluate.

On the other hand, the likelihood may well be that the thousands of quantitative studies done in the past four decades have unmined ore in them, just waiting for an imaginative reanalysis.

The history of uniformed police in the United States poses far more complex data analysis problems than may at first be expected. Prior to the middle of the nineteenth century, a night watch and day constabulary, derived directly from the Anglo-Saxon tradition, caught criminals, served warrants, and acted as agents of the court system. The constables earned their incomes from fees; the night watch, ostensibly volunteers, were paid substitutes for those sensible citizens who wished to sleep at home. On occasion vilified as inefficient, this responsive, decentralized, and nonbureaucratic form of policing served large cities of up to three-fourths of a million people before the modern, uniformed police so familiar today replaced it.

In the first half of the nineteenth century, when reformers introduced these uniformed civil police to the United States, they explicitly modeled them on the Metropolitan Police of London, but with one very large difference. The reformers who admired the English police could not change the United States Constitution, which reserved much power to the states. Nor could the reformers have impact on the dozens of state constitutions, which in turn delegated police power and responsibility to local governments. Unlike the more comprehensive and more centralized English system that served as their model, local governments, from the beginning, created and paid police in the United States. Consequently, the police never had jurisdiction or funding beyond their individual localities. This meant that local taxpayers, who paid for them and observed them in their daily rounds, also cared very much about the existence, size, activities, and costs of the police. Local responsibility and control also account for the great variety in kinds and quality of policing today in the United States, for no consistent oversight organizations or standards existed.

In spite of their local origins, local funding, and the diverse circumstances of their creation, the police did have broad commonalities from city to city for the simple reason that no cities were highly innovative. Ironically, the decentralized, local power fostered parallel, similar local structures, even without central coordination. To the best of their abilities, cities mimicked each other, copying police uniforms, legal foundations, and organizational shapes. The criminal offenses for which police arrested people, offenses against state laws and local ordinances, were classified almost identically in the formal annual reports published by each city, and police activities beyond crime control served everywhere as catchalls of services, such as dispensing welfare, inspecting boilers, catching loose dogs, or returning lost children (Monkkonen 1979). Therefore, one may build on these similarities across independent jurisdictions to create a broad, generally urban perspective. The highly similar categorical activities of the police can be aggregated over many cities and analyzed to discover law enforcement practices within these categories.[1] And analyzing these aggregated data, in turn, can address fundamental historical questions about policing and, to a somewhat lesser extent, about crime and about the local governments that created and supported the police.

For instance, did cities introduce the police in response to rising crime? This question assumes the functional crime-control model. Or were police introduced to control the increasingly diverse and numerous European immigrants in cities? This presumes a social-control model. Or did law enforcers get introduced in response to urban riots and persist because of their unanticipated and varied utility, which assumes a crisis model? One way to begin to unravel these distinct propositions is to look carefully at measures of what the police did. The best measures available for the analyst are those accounting devices used with great consistency by police, numbers of arrests. In addition to these counts, we also have a measure of another, now forgotten police activity, housing the homeless, "lodgers," an obligation of police that was shunted off to municipal welfare agencies in the 1920s. The annual number of "lodgers" reflected the total nightly count of persons given some form of overnight shelter, a service that ranged in quality from a place on a cement floor to a clean bunk and breakfast in the morning (Monkkonen 1981).

DATA REANALYSIS IN HISTORICAL RESEARCH

Although data collection and archiving represent major investments of the historian's time, data reanalysis has a slender tradition in historical writing. Even though historians value careful empirical work, such care has seldom extended to the reworking of old data. This is primarily because the craft's research training emphasizes the use of new sources and the presentation of new material as opposed to reworking familiar territory with newer techniques. "Original research," in practice, means the exploitation of material previously unused by historians. Reanalysis of existing material, already developed by another historian into a part of a coherent analysis or story, is viewed implicitly, and unfortunately, as secondary, noncreative work. (For two rare but important recent examples of significant data reanalysis, see Kousser, Galenson, and Cox 1982, and

Horan 1985.) And, quite often, reanalysis has appeared to involve purely destructive criticism without offering new and positive interpretations. Some of the early criticisms surrounding Robert Fogel and Stanley Engerman's *Time on the Cross* (1974) depended on their sharing their data, a task involving considerable attention and energy, all for the purpose of testing the original conclusions. Though such criticism is very important, all too often the consequences are too bifurcated. What should be refining reanalyses ends by being seen as accept/reject reductions. A spirit of qualification, modification, and new interpretation has never gained a foothold in the profession.

In the case of quantitative history, the lack of a tradition of reanalysis represents a loss to the research community, in part because new statistical techniques are often invented and introduced specifically to correct the previously known but unmanageable shortcomings of earlier techniques. The struggles that the original researcher went through a decade ago in doing an analysis have often been made unnecessary, and, in the process, better, more powerful tools have been invented. Even when major portions of original interpretations still stand after scrutiny through better statistics, the new techniques may bring added insights and new subtleties to established tales. Finally, researchers owe it to themselves to do the best job possible, and data reanalysis should be a natural extension of the original task.

The new technique for longitudinal reduced rank regression analysis, or state space analysis, employed here offers the possibility of modeling more complex multivariate relationships than other, more traditional techniques. Here we contrast the results of the new technique with several multiple regression analyses conducted earlier. Conceptually speaking, in the original analyses, several one-dimensional, cross-sectional processes were modeled; in this analysis, we model one multidimensional, dynamic process. The data reanalysis does not overturn the earlier results. It does demonstrate that expected, yet unconfirmed, relations between the variables were in fact present, though not discernible with regression: contrary to the original regressions, in the longitudinal reduced rank regression, the variable homicide arrests play a substantive role. In addition, the longitudinal reduced rank regression analysis points out an unanticipated relationship: one group of arrest rates, for felony crimes, varies independently from the structure of policing.

ORIGINAL ANALYSIS OF ARREST RATES

Three models guided the regression-based analysis in the original research. All stipulated that the size of police departments (POLICE) and the numbers of the most visible crime of personal violence, homicide (HOMICIDE ARRESTS), would act as independent variables. The measurement of police department size is unproblematic. Although homicide arrests can only be considered a coarse indicator of actual homicides, it at least may be conceptualized as independent of pure police initiative. These two variables were modeled as driving three conceptually different dependent variables in separate equations. Three conceptual arenas of police control activities—criminality, public order, and welfare—were indexed by arrests for serious crimes (CRIME ARRESTS), arrests for public order offenses, such as drunkenness (ORDER ARRESTS), and number of overnight lodgers taken in by the police (LODGERS).

Originally, each of these three models was estimated in a regression using first differences (that is, the present year's value minus the previous year's value). First differences mirrored the assumption that the change from year to year, rather than absolute yearly values, characterized the relationship between the variables. Not coincidentally, this is an established, if crude, way of data transformation to account for a serially correlated error term and subsequent biased estimates of the coefficients (Rao and Miller 1971: 71). In the original estimates of these three models, a dummy variable was used to determine that a shift in the slopes of the regression lines occurred at the midpoint of the series, about 1890.

The original analysis suggested several important relationships in each model. It appeared that crime arrest rates and lodging were determined by sizes of police departments. However, one part of the original hypothesis proved disappointingly insignificant. The hypothetical reason to include the homicide arrest variable was based on the knowledge that homicides are known to be overwhelmingly cleared by arrest today. If one assumed this to be true in the nineteenth century, then homicide arrests might be taken as a reasonable index of all homicides, something not true of any other arrest figure, where arrests could not possibly be constructed as having isomorphic relations to the actual criminal behavior. More to the point, as homicide is the most serious and visible crime of violence, the homicide arrest rate could be taken as an index of demand for police action, on the assumption that large numbers of homicides would produce police action on other fronts that were actually more open to police action, that is, arrests for public order offenses and for felony crimes. In other words, one could predict that in a time of many homicides the police would be under pressure to squelch or reduce all crime. Thus the poor performance of the homicide variable in the original regressions led to two equally plausible conclusions: either (1) the hypothesized relationship of homicide arrests to other aspects of police behavior was not correct or (2) the arrests were a poor indicator of actual homicides. As the data were originally collected to find out about police behavior, losing the homicide indicator was merely disappointing and did not detract from the main thrust of the work. More recent work suggests that the homicide arrest variable began in about 1910 to capture the influence of accidental homicide by automobile (Lane 1989). Furthermore, ongoing work on homicide in New York confirms that in the 1850s and 1860s, there was a close fit between homicide arrests and actual homicides (Monkkonen 1989). Homicide arrests were good indicators down to 1910, but, as tested with the regressions, their relationship to other aspects of police behavior seems to have been wrongly conceptualized.

Although historical data are often in series, accounting for the time dependency in such series is no easy matter. The simplest and most understandable way is to do as was done with these data originally, to use first differences. From the historian's point of view, this procedure mirrors an understanding of a short-term process: what varies is the change from the previous year; a pure annual repetition is not variation. While close to true for city budgets (McDonald 1986), this assumption is clearly an inadequate way of thinking about things such as murders, each of which is a unique social outcome, although most people would assume that no change in homicide rates from the previous year represents some sort of social regularity or equilibrium. To capture the annual lack of change is as important as to capture the change, and there are several time series techniques that work at this problem. For those accustomed to regression analysis, all require new ways of thinking about modeling relationships. The state space analysis technique used here is particularly attractive to historians for several reasons. First, it allows the capture of more than one time dimension process; in other words, the researcher does not have to assume that simply one dynamic process constitutes the relationship between the dependent and the independent variables. Second, several "dependent" variables can be modeled simultaneously. Third, a changing relationship(s) through time may be discovered in vector plots (explained below), rather than by staring at variable plots or by manipulating dummy variables, both of which are somewhat ad hoc procedures. In application, as will be shown below, the state space technique is both powerful and subtle, in that it highlights and confirms the earlier, regression-based substantive conclusions but, more important, highlights previously unseen relationships.

LINEAR DYNAMIC SYSTEMS ANALYSIS

In the ordinary linear regression situation we observe independent, or input, variables (x) and a dependent, or output, variable (y), all measured at N observation points. The independent variables are believed to be the causes of the dependent variable, and, in that sense, the two kinds of variables play an asymmetric role. The consecutive observations are assumed to be *independent,* that is, x_1 influences y_1, x_2 influences y_2, but there is no influence of x_1 on x_2 or on y_2. Another important aspect of this model is *stationarity,* that is, the influence of x_1 on y_1 is the same as that of x_2 on y_2, and so on. A geometric representation of the linear regression model appears in Figure 11.1.

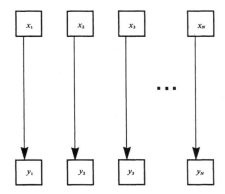

Figure 11.1 Geometric Representation of the Linear Regression Model

More complicated models emerge when the influence of the x on the y is mediated by an unobserved, or latent, variable z, with x determining z, and z determining y. Such models are called reduced rank regression models, MIMIC models, or errors-in-variables models. Often there are several dependent variables; the number of orthogonal dimensions of the latent state z is generally chosen to be lower than that of the x, and in that sense z *filters* the relationship between x and y. The latent variable is often called the (latent) state, and its dimensionality the (latent) state space. A geometric representation of this model appears in Figure 11.2.

When the measurements of x and y have been obtained at consecutive points in time, the independence assumption is usually not tenable. A dynamic version of the reduced rank regression model emerges by modeling dependencies

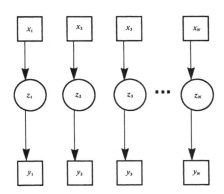

Figure 11.2 Geometric Representation of the Reduced Rank Regression Model

between the values of the latent state. Such models are known as longitudinal reduced rank regression models, state space models, or linear dynamic systems (Bijleveld 1989; O'Connell 1984). See Figure 11.3 for a geometric representation.

In the linear dynamic system, the latent variable z plays a crucial role. It serves as an intermediary between the independent and dependent variables, filtering the dependence of y on the x variables. Second, it functions as a *memory* of the system. The latent state z follows a Markov-type time dependency, which implies that z_{t-1} influences z_t, z_t influences z_{t+1}, etc., but no influence of z_t on z_{t+k} ($k > 1$) is accommodated. Thus, those past occurrences that are relevant for the future must be incorporated by the present. In that sense, the latent state also filters the past, retaining that information that can improve predictions of present and future.

In the following, vectors are denoted by boldface, lowercase characters. If we have measured k input variables and m output variables, and if we model p latent state variables, the state space model can be written in formula as follows:

$\mathbf{z_t} = \mathbf{F}\mathbf{z_{t-1}} + \mathbf{G}\mathbf{x_t}$ (system equation)

$\mathbf{y_t} = \mathbf{H}\mathbf{z_t}$ (measurement equation)

with $\mathbf{x_t}$ the $k \times 1$ vector of input values at timepoint t, $\mathbf{y_t}$ the $m \times 1$ vector of output values at timepoint t, $\mathbf{z_t}$ the $p \times 1$ vector of values of the latent state at timepoint t, and $\mathbf{F}$, $\mathbf{G}$, and $\mathbf{H}$ transition matrices of dimensions $p \times p$, $p \times k$, and $m \times p$, respectively.

The state space model is fitted with an iterative alternating least squares algorithm[2] that computes least squares optimal solutions for the transition matrices, given starting values for the latent states; least squares optimal solutions for the latent states, given these transition matrices; new least squares optimal solutions for the transition matrices, given these latent states; etc. At each iteration, a normalized least squares fit that varies between 0 and 1 is computed, and when this

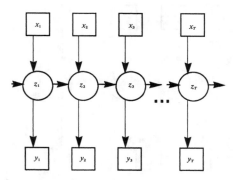

Figure 11.3 Geometric Representation of the Linear Dynamic System

has converged according to a convergence criterion, the analysis results can be interpreted.

As in factor analysis, this is done by interpreting the latent state variables through the correlations of the variables with these states. The scores of the time-points on the latent state variables can be plotted in a configuration of two or more dimensions. Also, by drawing in as vectors the correlations of the variables with the respective latent state variables, we can explore the relationships between input and output variables, and between variables and timepoints. For interpreting such a plot, the relative positioning of variables toward each other and the relative positioning of years toward the variables, rather than the actual values of the correlations of the variables or of the timepoints' state space scores, are of interest. Variables that point in the same direction measure approximately the same thing. The farther apart the vectors of variables are, the less these variables have in common; when vectors of variables are at right angles, variables are said to be independent. Vectors that point in the opposite direction measure the opposite, or the same thing in the opposite way.

For a more extensive discussion of linear dynamic systems analysis, see Bijleveld (1989). For mathematical and numerical details of the algorithm, see Bijleveld and De Leeuw (1991), and, for an application on historical data, see Ouweneel and Bijleveld (1989).

ONE-DIMENSIONAL LINEAR DYNAMIC SYSTEMS ANALYSIS

Let us recapitulate more formally our research questions. We are investigating the relations between the five variables, POLICE, HOMICIDE ARRESTS, LODGERS, ORDER ARRESTS, and CRIME ARRESTS. We suppose that the variables POLICE and HOMICIDE ARRESTS influence LODGERS, ORDER ARRESTS, and CRIME ARRESTS. In our model, POLICE and HOMICIDE ARRESTS are thus considered as the independent variables, and LODGERS, ORDER ARRESTS, and CRIME ARRESTS as the dependent variables. Second, we are dealing with data that have been collected on a yearly basis, and we suppose that there is a time dependency in the measurements.

To start with, we analyzed the relations between the five variables—POLICE, HOMICIDE ARRESTS, LODGERS, ORDER ARRESTS, and CRIME ARRESTS—allowing for one dimension of the estimated state. The model we analyzed is represented geometrically in Figure 11.4.

Setting the convergence criterion at .00005 (the difference in fit between consecutive iterations), the algorithm converged fairly quickly (in 17 iterations) to a normalized fit of .624. The correlations of the input and output variables with the latent state space scores appear in Table 11.1.

Both POLICE and HOMICIDE ARRESTS correlate positively, though not very strongly, with the state. LODGERS and ORDER ARRESTS both correlate negatively

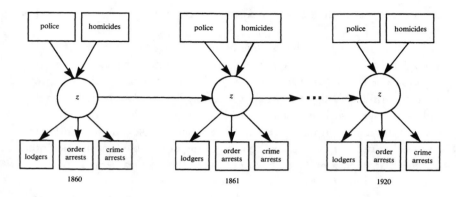

Figure 11.4 Geometric Representation of the Linear Dynamic Model of Relations between POLICE, HOMICIDE ARRESTS, LODGERS, ORDER ARRESTS, and CRIME ARRESTS Variables

and strongly with the latent state. The correlation of CRIME ARRESTS with the state is negative but weak; it seems as though CRIME ARRESTS takes only a minor part in the interrelatedness of the other variables and may even play a somewhat independent role. These findings can be explained by supposing that not one but several processes might in reality play a role in the interrelatedness of our variables. Thus our second procedure was to reanalyze the data with a two-dimensional state variable.

Table 11.1 Linear Dynamic Systems Analysis Solution with One-Dimensional State

	Latent state
POLICE	.686
HOMICIDE ARRESTS	.535
LODGERS	−.903
ORDER ARRESTS	−.803
CRIME ARRESTS	−.353

Table 11.2 Linear Dynamic Systems Analysis Solution with Two-Dimensional State

	Dimension 1	Dimension 2
POLICE	.707	−.170
HOMICIDE ARRESTS	.892	.267
LODGERS	−.856	.339
ORDER ARRESTS	−.810	.331
CRIME ARRESTS	.249	.933

TWO-DIMENSIONAL LINEAR DYNAMIC SYSTEMS ANALYSIS

A two-dimensional latent state space was modeled, again setting the convergence criterion at .00005. This time the algorithm took longer to converge (55 iterations); the normalized fit improved to .876. The correlations of the input and output variables with the orthogonal dimensions of the latent states are shown in Table 11.2.

Comparing the solutions with a one- and a two-dimensional state, we see that the correlations of POLICE and HOMICIDE ARRESTS with the first dimension have increased nicely. The correlations of LODGERS and ORDER ARRESTS with the first dimension have changed only superficially, and the correlation of CRIME ARRESTS has changed sign and dropped even farther. On the second dimension, none of the independent variables has a sizable correlation with the state, and the correlations of LODGERS and ORDER ARRESTS with this dimension are also relatively unimportant; the variable CRIME ARRESTS, however, seems to be the sole representative of this dimension. Judging from the correlations only, it appears as if the provisional conclusions from the one-dimensional analysis are underlined by the two-dimensional analysis.

In order to interpret and explore this solution more thoroughly, we have drawn a picture of the state space scores (that is, the scores of the years on the two state variables that we estimated) and the correlations of all five original variables with the two state variables (Figure 11.5).[3]

Interpreting the arrows in the picture first, we see that higher numbers of policemen are related to lower incidence of lodgers and order arrests, and vice versa. The number of crime arrests seems to follow an independent course, weakly related only to the homicide variable. This is illustrated by the almost right angle between CRIME ARRESTS and ORDER ARRESTS, LODGERS and POLICE. The number of murders occupies an intermediary position, as its vector is placed in between the vectors of POLICE and CRIME ARRESTS; HOMICIDE ARRESTS is the only variable that is related to the number of crime arrests, and is simultaneously related to the numbers of policemen, lodgers, and order arrests.

The first cluster, 1860–1879, has relatively high numbers of lodgers and order arrests, low numbers of policemen, low numbers of murder arrests, and rather high but decreasing numbers of crime arrests. This corresponds to the period of early policing labeled in the previous analyses as "class control." The second cluster of years, 1880–1897, is characterized by generally low numbers of crime arrests, a still low but increasing number of murders, below average but increasing numbers of policemen, and decreasing numbers of lodgers and order arrests. This period is the end of "class control" policing and the transition to a modern crime control model, which continues through the last two periods. The third cluster of years, 1898–1913, is characterized by low but rising numbers of crime arrests, slowly increasing numbers of murders, somewhat high but stable numbers of

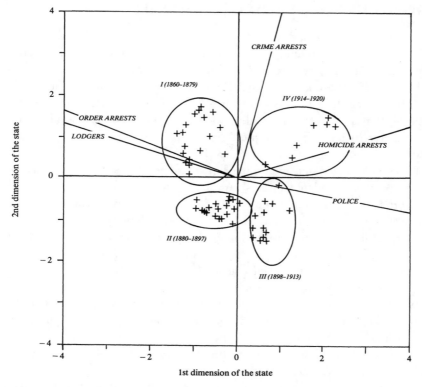

Figure 11.5 Correlations of the Variables with the Dimensions of the Latent State Space and Scores of the Years on the Dimensions of the Latent State Space

policemen, and low numbers of lodgers and order arrests. In the fourth period, from 1913–14 onward, the numbers of murders and crime arrests both rise sharply, accompanied by a more slowly growing police force and low and steadily decreasing numbers of lodgers and order arrests.

Finally, in Figure 11.5, the horizontal axis, which stands for the first dimension of the state, and the vertical axis, which stands for the second dimension of the state, might somewhat tentatively be interpreted as *control* and *criminality* dimensions, respectively. Increased control (POLICE) causes lowered numbers of order arrests and lodgers. Increased numbers of murders accompany decreased numbers of lodgers and order arrests. Increased control seems to correlate with increased homicide, too. This confirms the original hypothesis that rising numbers of murders should lead to an extension of the police force, which was rejected by the original regressions. Increased numbers of criminality arrests are caused by increased numbers of murders, rather than by a larger police force.

On the whole, however, criminality seems to follow an independent course, influenced only marginally by any other variable.

Turning from the original variables, we can examine in more detail the state space scores as plotted against time (Figures 11.6 and 11.7). The developments over the years 1860–1920 can be summarized briefly as follows. On the first dimension, control, there is a steady trend away from large numbers of lodgers, crime arrests, and a small police force, and toward small numbers of lodgers and crime arrests and an increased police force. Simultaneously, on the second

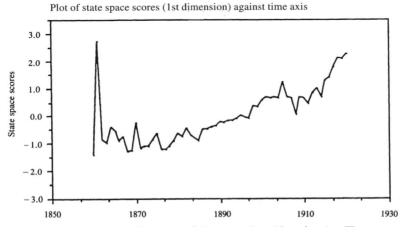

Plot of state space scores (1st dimension) against time axis

Figure 11.6 Scores on the First Dimension of the Latent State Plotted against Time

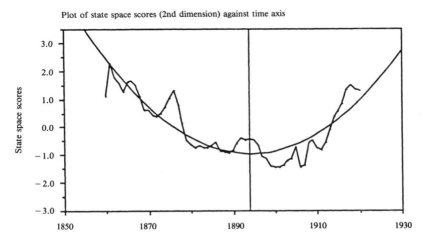

Plot of state space scores (2nd dimension) against time axis

Figure 11.7 Scores on the Second Dimension of the Latent State Plotted against Time

dimension, criminality, high numbers of crime arrests and considerable numbers of murders swing down toward small numbers of both, and then back up again toward high numbers of murders and crime arrests. This upward swing begins in about 1894,[4] corresponding to the Progressive Era reform of policing, as well as to an apparent shift in criminal behavior.

CONCLUSION

This application of a more powerful and newer statistical technique demonstrates that in data analysis, better approaches can yield far more informative results. The possibility of rejecting earlier results is, of course, always latent in such an adventure. But most reported quantitative research in history has been buttressed by other forms of evidence and analysis, as well as historiographic and contextual information, so that incorporating a data misreading giving nonsensical results would have been unlikely anyway. Thus Type I errors—accepting as true false hypotheses—are not as probable in historical research as Type II errors—rejecting as false hypotheses that are true. And in this case, that is what had happened. Because it had been a small part of the whole project, such a (premature) rejection was not dramatic, but from the point of view of the original researcher, it was disappointing. Thus, to be able to return to an original proposition, that homicides, and police responses to them, positively affected the broader spectrum of felony arrests, is indeed exciting. And, the relative independence of the z_2, the "criminality dimension," from police force size suggests an additional research orientation that is not exclusively focused on police behavior but rather tries to locate measures that affect only crime. And this, even more than the modification of the original research conclusions, demonstrates another reason why historians should continue to press for data reanalysis using better methods.

NOTES

1. Problems of methods and sources make collecting and analyzing even these most consistent policing data difficult. Sources are on occasion missing. Moreover, the organization and effectiveness of departments varied from place to place. From the data collection point of view, we can be grateful that the police were very unimaginative in counting what they did, so that the counts from various cities were usually reported in the same way. Because each city had its own police, these counts have not ever been systematically collected. The data for this analysis were compiled from the annual reports of the police departments of the twenty-three largest cities in the United States, that is, all cities over 50,000 in 1880. The data are archived at the Inter-university Consortium for Political and Social Research. For further data details, see Monkkonen (1981, 69–71, Appendix B). These data, in order to overcome lapses in reporting, have been reduced to aggregated, percapitized observations on all cities reporting in any given year. Thus, as used here, the data are in rates by year.

2. The program for longitudinal reduced rank regression analysis is available from C. Bijleveld, Dept. of Statistics, NIPG-TNO, P.O. Box 124, 2300 AC Leiden.

3. In Figure 11.5, each plotted point represents a year, but there are too many points to label each in the picture. To facilitate interpretation, we have marked clusters of years.

4. We fitted a quadratic function to the curve (R^2 =.779) in Figure 11.7. Its minimum occurred at 1894. It is not surprising that in the dynamic analysis the shift point is somewhat later than in former regressions, as in the dynamic analysis the modeled time dependency allows former occurrences to have a continued influence through time.

REFERENCES

Bijleveld, C. C. J. H. 1989. *Exploratory Linear Dynamic Systems Analysis.* Leiden: DSWO Press.

Bijleveld, C. C. J. H., and J. De Leeuw. 1991. "Fitting Longitudinal Reduced Rank Regression Models by Alternating Least Squares." *Psychometrika* 56: 433–47.

Fogel, R. W., and S. L. Engerman. 1974. *Time on the Cross: The Economic Origins of American Negro Slavery.* Boston: Little, Brown.

Horan, P. M. 1985. "Occupational Mobility and Historical Social Structure." *Social Science History* 9:25–48.

Kousser, J. M., D. W. Galenson, and G. W. Cox. 1982. "Log-Linear Contingency Tables: An Introduction for Historians." *Historical Methods* 15:152–69.

Lane, R. 1989. "On the Social Meaning of Homicidal Trends in America." In *Violence in America,* edited by T. R. Gurr. Beverly Hills: Sage.

McDonald, T. J. 1986. *The Parameters of Urban Fiscal Policy: Socioeconomic Change, Political Culture and Fiscal Policy in San Francisco, 1850–1906.* Berkeley: University of California Press.

Monkkonen, E. H. 1979. "Municipal Reports as an Indicator Source: The Nineteenth-Century Police." *Historical Methods* 12:57–65.

———. 1981. *Police in Urban America, 1860–1920.* New York: Cambridge University Press.

———. 1989. "Diverging Homicide Rates: England and the United States, 1850–1875." In *Violence in America,* edited by T. R. Gurr. Beverly Hills: Sage.

O'Connell, P. E. 1984. "Kalman Filtering." In *Handbook of Applicable Mathematics VI: Statistics B,* edited by W. Ledermann. Chichester: Wiley.

Ouweneel, A., and C. C. J. H. Bijleveld. 1989. "The Economic Cycle in Bourbon Central Mexico: A Critique of the Recaudación del diezmo líquido en pesos." *Hispanic American Historical Review* 69:480–530.

Rao, P., and R. L. Miller. 1971. *Applied Econometrics.* Belmont, Calif.: Wadsworth.

12

Crossing The (Blue) Line:
The Problem With Commissions

Police corruption is nearly as old as policing. The current scandal ["Ramparts" became public in the late 1990s] roiling the Los Angeles Police Department, though it may have some slightly different twists, is not unique. There is even a historic pattern in the public response to such scandals: the hope that a commission of esteemed notables can investigate the incidents and cure the problem.

There have been two kinds of police corruption. The first, and ultimately the worse, is between the police and the political process, in which cops influence elections and political parties control access to police jobs. Police, in turn, look the other way at electoral misbehavior. This sort of corruption strikes at the core of democratic political systems but describes the situations in many nineteenth- and early-twentieth-century U.S. cities, where political corruption was a major problem.

The LAPD Ramparts crisis is an example of the second type of corruption: between police and criminal offenders, not their victims. Police officers allegedly victimized gang members, some of whom may have been criminal offenders. Prosecuting gang members is difficult, because their victims are often other gang members. They are reluctant witnesses, afraid of reprisals and perhaps as opposed to the police as to other gangsters. So police may fabricate evidence or lie in court—in New York City, in the 1990s, police officers called it "testilying." A bad practice that began with ends justifying means can turn into corruption for profit instead of corruption for crime control.

First published in the *Los Angeles Times* (September 26, 1999). This article is co-authored by Catrien Bijleveld.

In general, this second kind of corruption depends on the nature of vice, which has no complaining victims or outside parties to participate in the relationship between police and offenders. When a police officer arrests a person for prostitution or selling drugs, credibility is on the officer's side, making it easy for the officer to lie and difficult for the offender to complain: Whom is the jury going to believe? If the "victims" of vice, dope dealers' or prostitutes' customers, were willing to complain and testify, vice control would be easier and the police would be in a poor position to lie.

New York City has been visible as a leader in many things good and bad. The tight connection between the police and the Tammany Hall political machine lingered into the twentieth century. Political parties arranged for men to get policing jobs, ensuring their allegiance. Starting in the mid-nineteenth century, the link involved both vice and politics. Here's how it worked: police officers collected payoffs from illegal vice or after-hours operations, in turn ignoring or going easy on illegal activities. Some of the money went into the political parties, some made officers rich. By the 1890s, there were officers like Alexander "Clubber" Williams, who policed the vice district in New York City. On a policeman's salary, he managed to acquire an estate in Connecticut and a steam launch.

When public awareness of scandal comes to a boil, there is a traditionally accepted response: create a commission to investigate. Composed of important people, commissions meet for a discrete purpose, take witness testimony, issue reports, and disband. Los Angeles has had many, most recently the Christopher Commission in 1991. But the problem with these ad hoc groups is that they have little clout unless their recommendations are followed up by legislative action.

Why so little impact, given the prestige and expertise they command? Because the commissions are not stakeholders in the process; they do not live with the consequences of their recommendations. Their careers are not on the line, nor do they have continuing involvement.

Historically, two investigative commissions achieved particular notoriety. The first was prompted by a city so corrupt that no agency had the power and independence to investigate its police: the 1894 Lexow committee of New York State, which investigated police corruption in New York City. This investigation, while looking into real problems, was motivated by a Republican legislature seeking to gain control of Democratic New York City. This does not diminish the commission's portrait of police corruption: how politicians used police to extract money from vice and to keep control of the polls. The police had become a direct part of the machinery used by political parties to stay in power. Though the Democrats lost the mayor's office historian James Richardson concludes the resulting reforms were "not very impressive."

The second important committee was the 1929 Wickersham Commission, which examined crime and criminal justice in the nation. Initiated during President Herbert Hoover's administration, the commission produced a high-quality fourteen-volume report. One volume dealt with police corruption, abuse and torture of prisoners (euphemistically called the "third degree"). Its title gets the point across: "Report on Lawlessness in Law Enforcement." But by the time of its publication in 1931, the country was in the Great Depression, which distracted the nation's attention from its criminal-justice system.

The morals of this commission's story: One, what happens after an event can completely alter its meaning and impact, and, two, police reform has frustrated some of the nation's best minds.

Somewhat earlier than the national Wickersham Commission, the Crime Commission of Los Angeles tried to clean up L.A.'s corrupt police department by hiring Berkeley's August Vollmer as a reform chief in 1923. All too effective, he lasted only one year. Vollmer attempted to apply the best "scientific" thinking to policing by convening a conference of police executives and university professors. The effort resulted in a report that, according to Joseph G. Woods, was the only such report since 1897 that the City Council filed and refused to publish. Published by Woods fifty years later, the report revealed that the LAPD's racism, intolerance, and ineffectiveness mirrored that of the larger society. Woods concludes that in "1924, August Vollmer was too advanced for Los Angeles, or any other American city. Police reform stopped when he left." The report contained Vollmer's recommendations for reorganizing the police. It is now best read as an example of how difficult it is to get much useful thinking about policing.

In the 1930s, L.A. officers were linked to the corrupt Mayor Frank L. Shaw in a manner similar to their counterparts in New York, with one major exception. Control of the electoral process was no longer operative. But Depression Los Angeles saw severe police corruption. The postwar reforms initiated by Chief William H. Parker were significant, creating a department that prided itself on its lack of political corruption. It is important to remember it has remained free of this taint.

Just because there is a pattern to police corruption does not mean there is a standard way to deal with it. Exhortation, investigation, better training, and higher standards are all good ideas. But the fundamental fact is, police are in an odd situation: for the most part, they are not independently trained professionals, like doctors or lawyers, yet they have enormous power and responsibility. (The highly rated Los Angeles Police Academy is a seven-month program.) They are asked to make difficult decisions. Even in the best of times, there is not an exact guide to behavior for police officers, so individual discretion adds up to hard-to-control outcomes.

By the end of the twentieth century, the United States had achieved honest electoral processes, free from police influence. This is an important gain. But it is not enough. The often troubled relation between police and the public remains. Vice, as most police managers know, is always a potential source of officer misbehavior and corruption. Police abuse of individuals when there are no outside witnesses is hard to monitor. No one solution can be relied on. Police problems may be predictable, but solutions are not. Oversight agencies, whether internal or external, can help, but cannot substitute for internal demands for fairness, honesty, and quality.

On the other hand, as with similar organizations, schools, for example, the tone is set at the top. Police executives can demand quality, but if those who hire chiefs and control budgets do not make this clear, the city has little reason to expect it. If the city's message is, "Stop the gangs, we don't care how," then it has to accept responsibility for its agents.

Commissions, whether internal or external, are better than complacency. One hundred years after the first such commission, and the modest shakeup it caused, it is hard to believe any oversight investigation can produce lasting structural change. Different versions of old problems constantly emerge. This should not cause us to disparage the work that will go into investigating and trying to fix the current crisis, but it should serve as a cautionary tale. Policing change comes with difficulty, that we know for sure.

13

Policing in the United States, 1930–1972

The history of postwar policing has just begun, and it will be an enormous challenge to get the outlines of the picture right. Perhaps Samuel Walker has put the most effort into this. But no one has begun to weave together the complete picture: the growth of multiple federal bureaucracies, the state-level professionalization efforts, the sweep of privatization, the impact of federal money for training, the increase in wages for police officers. (On private policing, see David Sklansky, "Private Police," *UCLA Law Review,* 1991). Federal agencies like the FBI have evolved from relative backwaters of white male competence towards a carefully educated and racially diverse professional group. Civil rights law enforcement has clearly cramped the style of police departments, which are probably behaving much better than when no one but their victims cared.

The study of professionalizing the U.S. police hinges, at first, on the vision of a handful of well-known police reformers. In retrospect, their goals look simple. But, at the time, their efforts to bring policing into a bureaucratic mode were herculean. This essay emphasizes the effects of American federalism in shaping a patchwork of police agencies. Lest one conclude that police departments in the United States all look as good as on *Cops*, where high-tech equipment and in-car videos abound, one should read Alec Wilkins on *Midnights, A Year with the Wellfleet Police* (1982), an account of small-city policing.

If there is a pattern to contemporary history research and writing, it follows two parallel tracks, one examining the origins and foundations of critical failures and problems, like police violence, the other telling the stories of individuals who

First published in *The State, Police and Society* (Brussels: Editions Complex, 1997).

seem at the time to be major players. Thus we have a few biographies of people like J. Edgar Hoover or analyses of police and their race control, such as Edward J. Escobar's outstanding *Race, Police, and the Making of a Political Identity: Mexican Americans and the Los Angeles Police Department, 1900–1945* (1999). The next stage, which I try to launch in this essay, is to start building an overview picture, linking together the relevant organizations and individuals, asking big questions and at the same time posing problems that will lead scholars to the right sets of archives and primary sources.

Here, I argue that the peculiar American history of a federal system, with the parallel growth of local and federal agencies, sets a stage for all American criminal justice and that any history must first attend to this unusual system.

One must understand the general political structure of the United States prior to interpreting twentieth-century U.S. policing. This framework alone helps explain why there are more than 17,000 state and local law enforcement agencies in the United States.[1] It accounts for much of the variation in American police departments from city to city, especially before the war. It gives a background in which to place regional differences, for some departments were efficient and well run, while others were corrupt, brutal, and incompetent; some were well funded and carefully professional, while others were poor and struggling. Often these differences obtained in adjacent municipalities, reflecting differing tax bases.

After the Revolution, the government structure created by the new United States was based on the best political thought of the eighteenth century, overlaid on the customary English colonial government. Local government—which included policing—received little attention at the founding. It was relegated to the enormous and vague area of the Tenth Amendment: "The powers not delegated to the United States by the Constitution, nor prohibited by it to the States, are reserved to the States respectively, or to the people." Thus, under the U.S. Constitution, local government is a matter left up to the states. Each state may create and authorize the form of local government it wishes. Theoretically, a state could have no local government. Typically, each state delegates local authority to counties, and the counties enforce the state's criminal laws. County prosecutors try the accused in county courts, county jails hold defendants, and county sheriffs manage the whole thing. And for the most part, city police actually arrest the offenders. The revenue for each unit derives from local taxes. This governance mode descended directly from the English Middle Ages.

In the Middle Ages, cities were special creations of the monarch, who granted the right to exist to individual cities with a written document enumerating the city's special privileges—a charter. Each city had a different charter, unique to its circumstances and privileges. In the English colonies, the same format obtained.

And in neither was there a police force. There was a system of constables and a volunteer night watch: the constables did all sorts of work for all courts—civil and criminal—and the watch patrolled the city or town at night, under the guidance of a constable. A victim of a crime could go to court and make an accusation, or could pay a constable to arrest someone or try to solve a burglary, again for a fee. The burden of crime control was on the community and the victims.

England began to change this in the 1830s, Parliament creating a template for local governments, including a police force. Local governments had autonomy over local decisions, but their structure and their tax system were all mandated by Parliament, as was the police system. When Canada became unified in the late 1860s, it followed this model. Because the United States had been independent for over a half century, its government remained structured on the best eighteenth-century principles. And since the few American cities were small corporate oligarchies and the constable watch seemed adequate, their omission didn't really concern anybody until well after the chance for change. Instead, when they began to grow, American cities got corporate charters vaguely descended from the medieval cities but also vaguely similar to those of the burgeoning for-profit private corporation.

When U.S. cities created uniformed police, in the 1850s and 60s, they thought they were copying the English, but of course, the copy stopped at the uniform. Most cities and towns asked for state legislation enabling their police: they did not have to if they did not want to. Occasionally, some states imposed a police system on a city, but they did so out of partisan political rivalry rather than civic concern. It is for these historical reasons that the United States today has such complex law enforcement agencies, and this is why there are such differences between police departments. This is why police officers have their careers tied to one city, for there are no such things as transfers. This is why Los Angeles County has more than eighty-six cities, many of which have their own police departments; this is why the second largest policing agency in Los Angeles is actually the Sheriff's Department, which contracts policing to some cities. And it is why San Francisco, which unified its city and county governments long ago, has only one police department.

In the years since World War II there has been convergence in police departments in the sense of standards, structures, and rules. In part this has occurred because the number of corrupt political machines has declined. Such machines thrived on autonomy from outside control, and they used their police to control voting, as a place to hand out political rewards, and as an agency to allow illegal business to operate. These police departments could hardly be expected to professionalize. But convergence came for other reasons, too. The writings of police reformers became guidebooks on how to organize and run police departments, and even the most idiosyncratic departments could turn to these handbooks, rather than be endlessly creative. By the end of the thirties, reform writing was effectively channeled through urban professional organizations, which increased and broadened its impact.

Because police departments are creatures of local government, concerns about their organization and administration most often came from city governments. In 1938, the International City Managers' Association published the first edition of its series on municipal administration, one volume of which was *Municipal Police Administration*. This was revised by O. W. Wilson and Theo Hall in 1943.[2] Wilson was by then a professor of Police Administration at the University of California, Berkeley; he had been chief in Wichita, Kansas (population just over 110,000). Hall was chief of the Wilmette, Illinois, police (population less than 20,000). While such manuals might not immediately affect big-city police, or those under heavy political control, they did go out to the thousands of small cities, especially those that were run by city managers. In essence, the book and its varied revisions over the next fifty years provided an easily accessible blueprint for bureaucratic rationality.

The FBI also had something to do with convergence: in 1935 it began offering classes to local police officers through the National Police Academy. The number attending was tiny, growing slowly after the War. There is some indication that J. Edgar Hoover's obsession with communism may have influenced the academy's programs; this would have affected the "Red Squads" in local policing but not have made much difference to police professionalism. The big jump in academy attendance came in 1972, just after Hoover's death,[3] when a new campus dedicated to teaching local police departments was opened in Quantico, Virginia. Graduating about a thousand students a year after this date, the academy would affect fewer than one in five hundred local police officers. One such school alone cannot account for convergence in policing, yet it can be understood as an index to this convergence. When future FBI director William Webster addressed the 112th class of the National Academy in 1978, he articulated the notion of standards that went far beyond localism: "You will set the standard for integrity, competence, dedication, and professionalism among public servants. The public's attitudes about law, government, and public justice will in large measure be determined by the professional manner in which you meet your responsibilities."[4]

In the postwar era U.S. policing changed dramatically. Many of the changes came as a result of extensive lobbying and writing efforts by police leaders and reformers like August Vollmer, O. W. Wilson, and others in the pre-war police professionalism movement. These reformers did not head large federal commissions or other central agencies, nor did they need to. Their local experiences qualified them to be experts, and there really were no national leaders to turn to. Policing in the United States has remained a profoundly local activity; consequently change comes from many different sources, internally through influential police professionals as well as externally through larger social changes. Most police departments have similar organizational rules because they copy each other, not because they must. Yet not all changes in policing came from prominent reform leaders; probably more came as a result of the decline of urban political machines, the expansion of civil rights, urban growth, and underlying demographic shifts. Reform changes did not address the underlying tensions in policing. These tensions—group conflict, often but not only centered on race, and urban fiscal crises—came from the urban world outside policing.

In addition, there has been a slow numerical and fiscal growth of federal level police (which include the border patrol) in the mix of all law enforcement, in part the result of an increase in federally defined crimes, such as racketeering and some drug crime. This is reflected in the data in Figure 13.1.

POLICE PROFESSIONALISM

Police professionalism has been a fundamental reform goal within police organizations since the early twentieth century. Professionalism can cover issues from simple safety planning so that officers don't get killed in car accidents to complex management of large organizations. It can mean community policing, research on forms of patrolling, or spying. And it depends ultimately on a body of special knowledge. In the early twentieth century, these reforms were called "scientific policing," the chief proponents of which were August Vollmer, Richard Sylvester of the Washington, D.C., police and the International Association of Chiefs of Police, and the various scholars and members of the crime-

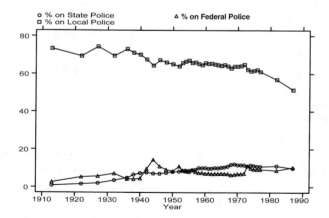

Figure 13.1 Proportions of total police expenditures by level of government. *Source*: compiled from *Historical Statistics of the United States* (1975) and various *Statistical Abstracts*, all from the U.S. Bureau of the Census

control community who all communicated through the pages of the *Journal of Criminal Law and Criminology* which began publication in 1909.[5]

Vollmer was the major figure in the reform of U.S. policing.[6] His primary practical experience came from the reforms he introduced as chief of the Berkeley police. He had been elected Town Marshal in 1905, supervising a force of three nonuniformed officers. Vollmer achieved publicity first in local and later in national newspapers, wrote extensively in professional journals, and published several well-respected books. He used his connections with the University of California, where he occasionally taught police science, to gain intellectual credibility. Vollmer's innovations included a counseling clinic with a psychiatric social worker, Elisabeth Lossing, and an aggressive policing policy which emphasized intervention in personal affairs and prevention through methods prescribed by the latest thinking of the mental hygiene movement. The most recent scholarship on Vollmer denies his supposed genius without denigrating his considerable achievements: "Rather than an original thinker, Vollmer's strengths lay in finding ingenious practical applications of ideas he borrowed from others, in carefully supervising the implementation of a wide variety of technical and procedural innovations, and, perhaps, most important, in maintaining high personal involvement and exercising decisive leadership in community affairs that impinged on police functions."[7]

Vollmer's new and generous vision of policing was all directed toward crime prevention—his interventionist social-work orientation, his genuine sympathy for and stern guidance of troubled people. Many of these changes reflected the Progressive Era's belief in efficiency, and many of the ideas have a kinship with other changes Progressive Era reformers had been pushing for two decades. Nevertheless, Vollmer's credibility with other police officers—he was one of them, after all—and the very concreteness of his reform ideas made him an enduring figure in American police practice.

Not too surprisingly, even Vollmer often could not reform corrupt police departments. For example, the Crime Commission of Los Angeles tried to clean up its corrupt city government by hiring Vollmer as a reform chief in 1923, but there he lasted only one year. During his short tenure he attempted to bring the best "scientific" thinking to the police by convening a conference of police executives and university professors. The effort resulted in an anuual report, which, according to Joseph G. Woods, was the only such report since 1897 that the city council filed and refused to publish. Published fifty years later, this report reveals that the Los Angeles Police Department's racism, intolerance, and ineffectiveness really mirrored that of the larger society. Woods concludes that in "1924, August Vollmer was too advanced for Los Angeles or any other American city. Police reform stopped when he left. . . ." One can conclude that many ideas of the time were close to crackpot.[8] The report, with the exception of Vollmer's practical recommendations for reorganizing the police, contained a hodgepodge of ideas, and is now best read as an example of how difficult it has been to obtain much useful thinking about policing.

For instance, American cities had seen sporadic riots before, but police had never really learned to cope with them. During World War II, when vicious race riots in several cities took the lives of both African Americans and Mexican Americans, the police not only failed to control the riots but were in many cases part of the problem. Thurgood Marshall compared the Detroit police to the Gestapo. Indeed, some police officers saw the riots as providing fuel for Nazi anti-American propaganda.[9] In Milwaukee in 1944 police chief Joseph Kluchesky did earn a national reputation for his race relations training program. In the same year, the International City Manager Association published a manual on police relations with minority groups that became widely used throughout the United States. Samuel Walker found twenty-two cities adopting some race relations training between 1943 and 1950 (to be sure, in some cities this involved little more than a two-hour lecture). However, the relatively small number of urban riots after World War II until the 1960s never really tested the effectiveness of these programs or their companion anti-riot strategies, leaving the police with untested and feebly implemented programs when the urban riots of the 1960s began.[10]

After Chief Vollmer's era, another Californian, who was also chief in a small city, Orlando Wilson of Wichita, Kansas, became the major shaper of policing.[11] More practical than Vollmer, Wilson wrote prolifically, producing both technical and popular articles, and many manuals, including the widely used textbook *Police Planning* (Springfield, Ill.: Thomas, 1952), which went through multiple editions. Essentially a how-to book, it is written with all the passion of a car repair manual, focusing on issues like filing systems and inventory control. While Vollmer had sought to engage the police in their larger social role, Wilson worked out the details of roll call.[12]

During Wilson's nine-year tenure, the Wichita police force was transformed, against all odds, from being a source for national articles on police corruption and brutality to a showcase for European police reformers. On his first day, for instance, Wilson noted that the door to the booking room had been painted red, clearly in order to hide blood spatters from police beatings. He ordered it painted white immediately, and began dropping into the station and to beats at odd hours. Wilson's very success at controlling corruption was ultimately his undoing, and local politicians forced him out in order to return to a more corrupt and vice-tolerant era. His success and failures both illustrate the strength and weakness of decentralized police: local bias and corruption may create an unjust system of police, even though such decentralizing of power would also resist any unitary, top-down takeover.

From his post in Wichita, Wilson went back to California to become Berkeley's first professor of Police Administration and dean of its School of Criminology. During World War II he insisted on entering the military, and became active in Italy and Germany in reorganizing the civil police (his master plan for Germany was published as a *Public Safety Manual*). Wilson's career capped his long efforts to professionalize police, and his final success was to become the reform chief of Chicago from 1960 to 1967, bringing some temporary respectability to one of the nation's least respected police departments.

Wilson's writings and actual reform activities focused on tight administration, careful record keeping, and evaluation of practices. He never trusted rank-and-file police officers and planned on constant monitoring of their activities. Politically conservative, he promoted women and minorities as a part of what he saw as better police work, not as a part of any social vision.

Given his exemplary career, it comes as a shock to discover that FBI Director J. Edgar Hoover clearly disliked and actually shunned Wilson. In an incident well known in professional circles, Hoover blackballed the vote that would have given Wilson an International Association of Chiefs of Police award, ordered the FBI not to cooperate with his efforts to fight organized crime in Chicago, and on at least one social occasion left the room when Wilson jovially proposed that they learn to cooperate. Was it because Wilson actually wrote his own material? Because in the 1930s Wilson had written that policing in the United States should always be local?[13] Because he was truly honest? Because he met and cooperated with Martin Luther King Jr.? This issue is more than personality, for Wilson was clearly just the kind of police leader whom the FBI should have supported. Hoover's enmity may well have set back American crime-control efforts for decades.

In the era of national television, some policing actions were exposed to public scrutiny in ways that have made reformers' claims much more persuasive. The Little Rock police attained considerable notoriety in 1957 and 1958 for their morally repugnant refusal to protect black children in the school integration crisis. Such outrages as these, exposed in the national media, helped gain public support for stronger federal standards in all areas of law enforcement. But, as an earlier era of reformers had recognized, the distinction between local and national control of police has never guaranteed quality or justice. Bad policing, whether in Little Rock or Los Angeles, reminds us that local control can be prejudicial; the FBI's record on civil rights similarly reminds us that national control does not always assure fairness.

THE DECLINE OF URBAN POLITICAL MACHINES

The expansion of civil rights concerns over excessive police violence focused on the "third degree" prior to World War II. Starting in the 1920s, ad hoc commissions investigating the police criticized them for beating and torturing accused offenders while in custody. Historian Wilbur Miller argues that since their formation in the 1850s, U.S. police had seen themselves as administering "street justice," as opposed to British police, who saw themselves as representatives of the constitution, on the streets. And who can doubt the meaning of New York Police Inspector "Clubber" Williams's claim that "there is more authority in the end of a policeman's night stick than in a Supreme Court decision?" Yet, in spite of ample evidence that the police beat people in public, the early-twentieth-century concern was with their abuse of prisoners in custody. This in part came about because the death of a prisoner in custody is more clearly the fault of the custodians than is the death of a person in public, about whom an argument can always be made about police self-defense.

The NAACP began challenging police beatings of blacks after the war. In New York NAACP exposés of police brutality in 1949 prompted the mayor to form an investigative commission.[14] In 1954, *Brown v. Board of Education,* while it had nothing to do with policing, showed the readiness of the U.S. Supreme Court to recognize racial discrimination exercised by local governments—in this case schools. Beatings, hidden and public, were in some ways eclipsed in the 1970s, when shootings by police officers seem to have increased.

Yet, police beatings did not end, and in the early 1990s once again they bloodied the nation's conscience. The widely televised attack by Los Angeles Police Department officers on Rodney King touched the American conscience in 1991. Later, in 1992, another televised beating, this one live, of a truck driver by rioters, again caused Los Angeles pain and anguish. Both King and the truck driver survived, though neither would completely recover. Why do these images remain while those of murder victims fade? In part, because living but damaged victims can remind us again and again, but also in part because if we watch a beating, we see and feel the blows, and the prolonging tells us again and again how cruel and painful and needless it is. When the violence comes under the color of the state, or when it represents a gross failure of the state, the responsibility moves from the individual to the collectivity.

Because of an unusual doctoral dissertation, we may gain a special glimpse into policing in the immediate postwar era. William A. Westley, a young graduate student in sociology at the University of Chicago, spent the year 1950 interviewing police officers in the Gary, Indiana, police department, during which he made some chilling discoveries. The resulting dissertation was not published as a book until twenty years later. This delay says much: in the 1950s, crime, police, and especially police violence were not on the national intellectual agenda; twenty years later these issues were very much to the fore.

Westley's book remains a remarkable document for several reasons.[15] First, it gives us an understanding of an occupational group that is very visible but usually quite misunderstood. Second, Westley's attention to structural tensions between the police and the public, which he sensitively analyzed as issues of respect and self-worth, still applies with the same cogency more than forty years after his findings. Third, Westley's observations about the conflict between police professionalism, corruption, and politics have proved to be far more prescient than anyone might have guessed. And fourth, his attention to police uses of violence against African Americans—or anyone perceived by the police as being tough or likely to go unpunished—highlighted issues that, in 1950, had not yet begun to enter public discourse.

The police world sketched by Westley bears no resemblance to that of the *Dragnet* television series popular at the time for a simple reason, one made clear by Westley's analysis of the world of the uniformed police officers:[16] the police had become an occupational subculture separated from the larger public by a code of silence. In part this culture occurs in any organizational setting, but it has been particularly strong for police officers from the beginning. On patrol, a young officer quickly learns that backups must be absolutely reliable: in the daily work routine, a partner's dependability is more important than anything else. The code of silence is an essential part of this daily routine. The work culture of "us against them" further enforcing this code of silence probably had existed much earlier. In the 1880s, for instance, a "policeman's wife" wrote about how her whole family was "ostracized" by the neighbors because of his job.[17] In more recent years, as the police job became subject to civil service rules and as retirement after twenty years became the customary reward for maintaining organizational unity, there was an additional very powerful incentive to reinforce the code. Getting a fellow officer disciplined could affect the job security and retirement benefits of all.

Of the fifteen officers Westley interviewed intensively, eleven said that they would not report other police officers for theft. One officer told Westley:

> I wouldn't turn a policeman in for anything short of murder. When I think that I have seventeen years to go on the force before I get my pension and having those fellows look at me that way I wouldn't turn any man in. I have made a buck in my time from the speeders and even if I saw a policeman breaking into a store I'd run the other way. I'd never see him.[18]

Tied as the code of silence is to the career prospects as well as daily life of the police officer, the likelihood that *Dragnet* or any stories like it would give a "true" view of the police world was remote, to say the least. Throughout his book, Westley documents a police fear of internal informants, of "stool pigeons," which runs so deeply as to give the job a sense of constant stress and tension, of a latent internal violence. An individual police officer's self-worth, daily life, and actual job were always dangling by the thread of other officers' trust, and their distrust

163

could at any moment release the thread and plummet their unhappy coworkers into joblessness, insecurity, and even physical danger.

In part the code of silence derived from and grew in contrast to the police view of the public. The police officer's relationship with the public results in a self-definition as victim. Police contacts with speeders who try to evade their guilt; with courts where plea bargains are normal practice; "with juvenile delinquents, when he [the police officer] sees the public as demanding action on the crimes they commit but at the same time refusing to incarcerate them . . . from this experience there grows a definition of the public as selfish, and of himself as a victim of injustice."[19]

In his "Preface" written twenty years later, Westley made a striking point that had only been implicit in the book. The city he had investigated had a police department whose chief was closely tied to corrupt city politics. Police officers had to be careful not to upset politicians, and their cynical view of the public resulted in part from very real corruption. They were linked to the political system in a way that professionalizers like O. W. Wilson and his successor in Los Angeles, Chief William Parker, were successfully trying to break. Westley suggested that ending such corrupt relationships might have the dangerous consequence of isolating the police even further, given the inherent nature of their relationship to the public. Professionalization might cause the police "to draw away from the public, to resist public control and accountability. . . . Under extraordinary strains and threats they can become exceptionally brutal and withdrawn."[20] Such a prediction seems to describe exactly the position in which the Los Angeles Police Department found itself by the late 1980s. The Christopher Commission, investigating it in the aftermath of the televised beating of Rodney King, described the biggest impediment to its investigation of the LAPD as "the officer's unwritten code of silence: an officer does not provide adverse information against a fellow officer."[21]

Finally, Westley's research project, which he intended to focus on the occupational subculture of policing, documented the depth of racial contempt held by many police officers. Racial contempt was as much a part of the police subculture as were the occupational code of silence, the police feeling of victimization by the public, and the inherent problems of professionalization versus political corruption. Older police officers taught rookies to treat middle-class people differently from the poor, from central city blacks, from sex offenders, and from "wise guys." The middle class, while a part of the group that wrongly victimized police, could be treated with words. So too could middle-class blacks not from Gary's poorest ghetto. But for African Americans from that neighborhood, the rule was to use violence to achieve respect.

One white officer told Westley, "the colored people understand one thing. The policeman is the law and he is going to treat you rough and that's the way you have to treat them. . . . If you don't treat them rough they will sit right on top of your head."[22] Throughout his study period Westley encountered different versions of this statement, but they all made the same point. The police officer must establish the relationship with blacks by the use of violence and intimidation; failure to do so would result in disrespect.

Violence in the initial relationships with blacks was justified by the officers' prior biases. Violence in relationship to whites had to be justified by cues. Said an officer,

> Usually you can judge a man who will give you some trouble though. If there is any resistance you should go all out on him. You shouldn't do it in the street though. Wait until you get in the squad car, because even if you are in the right and a guy takes a poke at you, just when you are hitting back somebody's just likely to come around the corner and what they will say is that you are beating the guy with your club.[23]

These police officers in postwar Gary embodied the larger society's tensions and conflicts. Most were white men for whom policing represented an occupational choice over blue-collar work in the steel mills. The job's merit—regular pay and retirement after twenty years—came at high personal and moral costs. Officers worked six days a week; they lived in a world of secrecy and self-repression. According to Westley, the police officer, in spite of the justifications about using violence, "carries a residue of guilt about his own behavior and insecurity about his own self-esteem."[24] Reflecting their own sense of degradation, 70 percent of the police officers he interviewed did not want their sons to become officers.

Of course, in the half century since Westley conducted his research, some aspects of policing have changed, most notably training and recruitment practices.

First, we no longer write about police*men*, because so many police officers are women. There were women in policing in the 1940s, too, but there were far fewer and they were often assigned to "suitable" tasks—dealing with women offenders and juveniles and seldom doing beat or patrol work. Interestingly, some of the concept of policing as a "man's job" came from outside of the police departments, for several official statements made by the Gary Police Department explicitly refer to men and women.

Second, a much greater proportion of police officers are of racial minorities. Again, as with the inclusion of women, the change has not been absolute but one of proportions. African American police officers existed even in the late nineteenth century (Detroit had at least one black officer in 1883, while New Orleans actually had a sizeable number of black police officers prior to the 1880s). By the time of World War I, both Chicago and New York had many black officers. But, as with women, these officers could not expect to rise far in the ranks nor even earn the same pay as the whites. The role of the black police offi-cer has never been easy, though probably few now have to endure the treatment accorded to Samuel Battle of the New York Police Department, when other offi-cers shunned him with silence for two lonely years, from 1911 to 1912. Battle went on to rise through the ranks and ended a distinguished public service career vol-unteering with the YMCA, NAACP, and National Urban League until his death in 1966.[25] The changes in opportunities for minorities accelerated dramatically after World War II for many reasons, from the civil rights movement to the occu-pational chances that the army opened to black soldiers.

Edward D. Williams's autobiography showed one example of this process.[26] Born in 1921 in Newark, he served in the navy (which was still segregated), and after the war returned to his truck driving job. In 1953, a white police officer he knew suggested that he join the police department, stressing its security and pen-sion. Williams also thought of the job as one offering community recognition, and he realized that he knew at least one black sergeant, suggesting the hint of mobility. Then he talked to a black policewoman he knew, who also encouraged him. The elements of job security, prestige, and a chance for advancement all drew him in. These aspects of policing are often ignored by the public, and they deserve to be stressed more often.

Police spying and the fears of its subversive effects on society have been pres-ent in Anglo-American society since the Fielding brothers began their efforts to create a police system in eighteenth-century England. Their efforts met resis-tance in part because of fear that the police would trample on traditional Eng-lish liberties, spying for political purposes as did the police in France. The ten-sion between the legitimate duty of police to discover clandestine wrongdoers and the rights of citizens to pursue freely their interests is inherent in democra-tic societies. Or so most people have thought. It is hard to imagine, but crusty English squires in the mid-eighteenth century were so opposed to police as to say that they would accept a few more murders rather than have a policed soci-ety. As late as 1812, English writers opposed a central police force as "a system of tyranny."[27]

In the 1970s the work of Michel Foucault and Michael Ignatieff challenged this notion. Both developed the idea that in the eighteenth century, Western soci-ety changed, with power becoming exercised through constant bureaucratic sur-veillance of people's lives. Ignatieff used the model prison designed by Jeremy Bentham, the panopticon, to symbolize this new world. Foucault's writings have had enormous influence in some literary and historical circles, so that now it is quite common for college students to learn about the idea of the surveillance soci-ety. The fear of spying—of an invasion of privacy, of the "gaze" of oppressive power agencies, of conspiracy—touches upon a long-standing and common idea in the United States, so that while college students have the fear articulated via

Foucault, others get a version of the same thing from ultraconservative radio talk shows. In essence, today the intellectual avant garde and the popular ultra right come together on a vision drawn from two-hundred-and-fifty-year-old fears.

Objectively, of course, mass society, especially in the United States, is far *less* intrusive upon privacy than were smaller-scale and less mobile earlier societies. Although mobility and poor communication hampered the accurate identification of migrants in the eighteenth and nineteenth centuries, neighborhood surveillance was still both more possible and more common. In the cases of most serial murderers, Americans discover how little surveillance there actually is in contemporary society. Serial murderers like John Wayne Gacy, who killed and buried thirty-three boys in his Chicago house between 1972 and 1979, or Jeffrey Dahmer, who tortured and murdered at least seventeen boys, are able to kill so many for such a long time precisely because they can so easily escape the gaze of neighbors, family, and, in particular, judicial officials. Gacy, after all, was married, had been arrested before, and at least on one occasion had police come to his house investigating screams. In spite of electronic monitoring of credit cards and the like, most Americans live as anonymously as they wish in large cities, where police interventions are rare and brief.

In the most recent historical examination of U.S. police spying, Frank J. Donner traces "Red Squads"—nicknames earned in the "Red Scare" in the twenties—through urban police departments and state police right down to the present.[28] Special police spy units began in the nineteenth century, usually in anti-labor operations and occasionally deliberately stirring up trouble. Although the evidence is only suggestive, Donner cites the Haymarket (1886) bombing in Chicago as an example of police operating as agents provocateurs. In the post-war era, Chicago (which he calls "The National Capital of Police Repression"), New York, Philadelphia, Los Angeles, Detroit, Baltimore, Birmingham, New Haven, and Washington, D.C., all had police spy units. In the 1960s, the CIA Training Branch trained forty departments in espionage techniques, a relationship the CIA supposedly severed in the early 1970s.[29]

The LAPD under chiefs Parker and Ed Davis had an active Intelligence Division that infiltrated "subversive" groups. Parker, much favored by the ultraconservative John Birch Society, followed later by Davis and Darryl Gates, promoted a spying operation that gained humiliating (but not terminal) publicity when it videotaped a city council meeting attended by anti-nuclear protesters in 1978.[30] Donner's work shows how there is a long series of police spying activities that have served to undermine civil liberties.

Yet, the case against police spying is not quite as clear as it may first appear: when police intelligence units penetrate terrorist groups, racist hate groups, or organized criminal conspiracies, their work is seen quite favorably. Gary Marx, no police apologist, comes to the measured conclusion in his study, *Undercover,* that police espionage is essential to police work, and that substantive control and avoidance of politically motivated infringement of liberty must be enforced, even though this is a difficult compromise.[31]

It is easy to think that our policed and spied-upon age, with its electronic surveillance, somehow invades more into private lives and behavior than was the case a long time ago. This is true if we think only of the formal units of government as the invasive spies; but as historians of early modern village life have shown, that life was based upon neighbor watching neighbor, with bullies exerting lasting influence, and with the local community maintained by ruthless exclusion of the unwanted and persecution of the different. This is not to say that it couldn't happen, for we see from the example of the former East Germany how police spying can infiltrate and poison a whole society, but for the United States and its less than efficient police bureaucracies, such concerns should be placed in perspective.

Brutality and incompetence are much bigger problems for American policing. Neither is as easily handled as we might wish and both have strong self-reinforcing linkages. The idea of street justice, that the mistreatment administered by a police officer is the only justice, gets reinforced by a criminal justice system that seems slow, erratic, and unfair.[32] And because we cannot monitor every officer-citizen interaction, because this is a society with surprisingly loose surveillance mechanisms, controlling police wrongdoing is very difficult.

Improving policing is also difficult because of the work culture, for in a risky environment even a bad situation may seem preferable to uncertain change.[33] And the public debate tends to be so oversimplified that policy positions never reflect the subtlety and insight which the police deserve. So, tradition continues to govern policing, with crises rather than clear thinking the driving force.

NOTES

1. Kathleen Maguire and Ann L. Pastore, eds., *Source Book of Criminal Justice Statistics—1994* (Washington, DC: U.S. Department of Justice, Bureau of Justice Statistics, 1995), Table 1.32.

2. The International City Managers' Association, *Municipal Police Administration,* revised edition (Chicago: The International City Managers' Association, 1943).

3. Wilson and his nemesis Hoover both died in 1972.

4. Stephen D. Gladis, "The FBI National Academy's First 50 Years," *FBI Law Enforcement Bulletin* (July 1985): 9.

5. David R. Johnson, *American Law Enforcement: A History* (Saint Louis: Forum Press, 1982), 70.

6. He was not, however, the first police chief reformer; Chief Fred Kohler, in Cleveland, for instance, introduced many policing reforms such as the "Golden Rule" for drunks (officers took them home instead of arresting them).

7. Julia Liss and Steven Schlossman, "The Contours of Crime Control in August Vollmer's Berkeley," *Research in Law, Deviance and Social Control* 6 (1984): 81.

8. Joseph G. Woods, "Introduction," Los Angeles Police Department, *Law Enforcement in Los Angeles: Los Angeles Police Department (August Vollmer, Chief) Annual Report, 1924* (New York: Arno Press, 1974).

9. Samuel Walker, "The Origins of the American Police-Community Relations Movement: The 1940s," *Criminal Justice History: An International Annual* 1 (1980): 231.

10. Ibid., 236–38, 242.

11. For a thorough biography, see William J. Bopp, *"O. W.": O. W. Wilson and the Search for a Police Profession* (Port Washington, N.Y.: Kennikat Press, 1977).

12. For instance, he introduced so-called "roll-call training" in 1930; Bopp, *"O. W.,"* 46.

13. Ibid., 56.

14. James I. Alexander, *Blue Coats, Black Skin: The Black Experience in the New York City Police Department Since 1891* (Hicksville, N.Y.: Exposition Press, 1978), 56.

15. William A. Westley, *Violence and the Police: A Sociological Study of Law, Custom, and Morality* (Cambridge: MIT Press, 1970).

16. Were Chief Parker around to comment, he would say, of course, that the big difference was due to the fact that the Los Angeles Police Department was not corrupt, as was the Gary department.

17. Mrs. Andrea Marie Kornmann, *Our Police . . . By a Policeman's Wife* (New York, 1887).

18. Westley, *Violence and the Police,* 115.

19. Ibid., 106–107.

20. Ibid., xvii.

21. Independent Commission on the Los Angeles Police Department, *Report of the Independent Commission on the Los Angeles Police Department* (Los Angeles: The Commission, 1991), xx.

22. Westley, *Violence and the Police,* 124. The same officer indicated that the NAACP had had an impact on police violence when he continued: "It's different on the south side now, from what it used to be. You can't beat on colored folks like you used to. They are bringing cases to the courts and that has softened it down a lot."

23. Ibid.

24. Ibid., 146.

25. Alexander, *Blue Coats, Black Skin,* 33–34.

26. Edward D. Williams, *The First Black Captain* (New York: Vantage Press, 1974); Alexander, *Blue Coats, Black Skin;* University of California, Los Angeles, Center for Afro-American Studies, *The Police and the Black Community* [sound recording] / Mrs. Roberta Reddick (Los Angeles: Regents of U.C., 1971); Homer F. Broome, *LAPD's Black History, 1886–1976* (Norwalk, Calif.: Stockton Trade Press, Inc., 1977); W. Martin Dulaney, *Black Police in America* (Bloomington: Indiana University Press, 1996).

27. James Richardson, *The New York Police* (New York: Oxford University Press, 1970), 24.

28. Frank J. Donner, *Protectors of Privilege: Red Squads and Police Repression in Urban America* (Berkeley: University of California Press, 1990).

29. Ibid., 87.

30. Ibid., 272.

31. Gary T. Marx, *Undercover: Police Surveillance in America* (Berkeley: University of California Press, 1988).

32. As in the transmission in the late 1980s from a LAPD officer:

"We got a burglar tonight, who was cold 6c and had nine thousand dollars warrant . . . you want any help just holler."

"No: I'm just going to shoot him."

(*Report of the Independent Commission,* 53).

33. See, for example, a recent article in *The Police Chief* by Robert L. Ortiz and Marilyn B. Peterson, "Police Culture: A Roadblock to Change in Law Enforcement" (August 1994), 68–71, which explores how the organizational culture of policing continues to impede change.

14

History of Urban Police

American police, created for a wide variety of "municipal housekeeping" tasks, have continued to be organizations with oddly shaped purposes. Crime control, it would appear, is their basic function. Yet, the messy reality the police encounter on the streets—their uniformed visibility making them the representatives of the city to everyone with a need—keep their functions far from clean and orderly. They deal with the sick, the injured, the angry, the lost. And often the trivial nature of their activities creates a crisis in perception: how can a group designed to catch criminals end up in such ambiguous, fractious, and messy situations?

American police grew in per capita strength from the mid-nineteenth century until the first decade of the twentieth, when they reached their present strength. Not until the end of the nineteenth century did they begin to focus more narrowly on crime control; in so doing they diminished their varied range of social services, which included the overnight housing of thousands of homeless people. The broad range of police activities and their complex relationship to cities in their formative era have made them the subject of increasing historical research.

I offer a contemporary example: a Los Angeles Police Department training officer, Greg Dossey, specializes in instructing in physical confrontation techniques. This would seem to be an easily understood area, but what he discovered after analyzing a sample of police-offender conflicts is that in a large proportion

First published in M. Tonry and N. Morris, eds., *Modern Policing,* vol. 15 of *Crime and Justice: An Annual Review of Research* (Chicago: University of Chicago Press, 1992), 547–80. A revised version was published as "The Urban Police in the United States," in Clive Emsley and Louis Knafla, eds., *Crime History and History of Crime* (New York: Greenwood Press, 1996), 201–28.

of cases police officers end up struggling on the ground with the offender. So, in a kind of revolution in training, he began to focus on what to do when rolling around on the dirt and pavement with a kicking, biting, and noisy opponent (*Los Angeles Times*, December 13, 1998). This undignified example serves to remind us that the Dick Tracy image still inheres for most of us, including police officers, and when messy reality intrudes, we reject it as an aberration.

The even bigger messy reality is that police, from their beginnings, confront untidy, ambiguous situations. My example of importance: who would design a publicly funded organization to return lost children to their parents? Not crime victims, no public danger, unlikely to cause fires or accidents, and not in need of medical assistance, lost children immediately became a policing duty once the police hit the streets in uniform. Many other unforeseen police duties moved on to new city government agencies, but some, like lost children, remain.

Historians working in the field of American crime and justice have produced a massive body of scholarship, a recent selected collection of articles alone consuming over seven thousand pages over sixteen bound volumes.[1] A significant portion of this work deals with the police as opposed to a more holistic view of the criminal justice system, or, alternatively, of the whole city government. The police have attracted the historian's attention for many reasons, ranging from simple curiosity to questions about urbanization, crime control, and the history of society. Although no one concept or paradigm has guided this research, the result has been a rich and valuable set of empirical studies.

A decade ago Roger Lane published in *Crime and Justice* a synthetic article on urban policing that newer work expands upon in several different directions.[2] This essay follows the directions of the new research, emphasizing areas where substantive gains have been made. The intention here is to examine the areas where there is new knowledge, rather than to write a completely new history of policing. That task grows ever more complex, especially for the years after World War I. Historians have, for the most part, concentrated on the earlier years for several reasons. First, the history of the nineteenth-century United States has captured intense research excitement in many fields, and the police have given historians an avenue of investigation with a unique perspective. Second, in most periodizations of U.S. history, the Progressive Era, closed by World War I, culminates in many of the principles and issues that undergird the major intellectual, social, and political developments of the remainder of the twentieth century. Finally, modern social science has much better documented the post–World War II era, so that the challenge of historical recovery and analysis has not been as great for more recent historical events.

The new studies have deepened our understanding of the origins of the police, their functional roles, their relationship to criminal behavior and public order, police organizations as employers as well as controllers of labor, the police professionalization movement, the complex and unique situating of police in the larger political order, and the growth and change of nonurban police—private and federal, in particular. In addition, we now have a fuller picture of police as they became regular components of the urban service sector and essential participants in the criminal justice system.

Parts I and II of this essay summarize my book on the police, supplementing its research and analysis with other new and relevant work.[3] Part I stresses the social and political innovation represented in policing, while Part II emphasizes that the fundamental aspect of U.S. policing as a component of local government has made police a part of urban services. The essay then turns to new research publications focusing on police as employers (III. A.), and police relations with organized labor (III. B.). Part IV turns to those issues in police reform that have attracted historical research, while Part V focuses on policy issues in the context of a federal political system. The conclusion delineates future research needs and directions.

I. POLICE AS AN INNOVATION

Police are relative newcomers to the Anglo-American criminal justice system. The Constitution does not mention them. Early city charters do not mention them either, for the simple reason that as we know them, police had not been invented. Instead, cities had loosely organized night watches and constables who worked for the courts, supplemented by the private prosecution of offenders through lower-level courts.[4] The night watch and day constable, dating from the Middle Ages, were familiar comic figures in Shakespeare's plays, and were not replaced until the 1820s when London police were reorganized by Robert Peel. The police precedent for the United States, as is well known, came from the Metropolitan Police of London (1829). Peel used his military experience in Ireland to create a social-control organization midway between a military and a civil force.[5] The new police solved both tactical and political problems: they were cheaper than a military force; they created less resentment; and they were more responsive to civil authorities.[6]

Constables were responsible to civil and criminal courts. They supported themselves by fees that came from serving warrants and civil papers and arresting offenders. The victim of an offense had to seek a constable and pay for his actions. Ferdinand's study of Boston showed that a few constables often took the initiative in making drunk arrests, apparently to make a continuous income.[7] The fees for catching an offender or for restitution could often be higher than the value of a stolen object, but Steinberg's new work suggests that these fees were no deterrent to many poor people using the criminal justice system. His work also shows that the constables could be sidestepped, victims going directly to local aldermanic courts.

Night watch did just that: they were to raise the hue and cry in case of an offense or to sound an alarm for a fire. The usual criticism of them was that they slept, used their noisy rattles to warn off potential offenders, and ran from real danger. The *New York Gazette* asserted that the watch were a "Parcel of idle, drunken, vigilant Snorers, who never quelled any nocturnal Tumult in their lives; but would, perhaps, be as ready to join in a Burglary as any Thief in Christendom."[8] These criticisms are difficult to evaluate, but they do suggest that the night watch, who were either citizens doing required volunteer service or, more likely, their paid substitutes, were not in any way a serious crime-fighting organization.

There are four important innovative features of the new police as created in the United States. First, the new police had a hierarchial organization, with a command and communications structure resembling the military. This gave them an ordered and centralized hierarchy with an immediate communication superiority to all other urban organizations as well as the preceding constable watch system. Even without an electronic communications system (call boxes or police telegraphs first, then the telephone which came a little later in the nineteenth century), the simple chain of command meant that a citizen could report an offense to an officer who would in turn relay the information to headquarters, which could then distribute the information back down the line. While no doubt the system operated with less than perfect precision, the traditional constable watch system was even less efficient. Haller's work on Chicago shows that after 1930, centralization increased further, especially with the introduction of radio cars, and the local station house decreased in importance.[9] Since under the pre-police constable watch system the constables had gained their incomes from fees, the structural incentive encouraged them to follow up promising (that is, high fee-generating) leads themselves.

Second, increasing functional differentiation in revised city governments located the police under the executive rather than judicial branch—previous constables and watch had been part of the lower courts.* As a part of the mayor's executive office, the police were no longer general factotums for courts, which freed them from civil court activities. This shift had to accompany the abandonment of fees for service, for civil fees had been a part of the constabulary incomes.[10] This shift also sent the American police down a different developmental path from the English police, who remain much more active and involved in preparing and prosecuting criminal cases than do their American

---

* It is necessary to caution that this distinction overdraws the notion of executive, legislative, and judicial, for aldermen held courts. See Edwin C. Surrency, "The Evolution of an Urban Judicial System: The Philadelphia Story, 1683–1968," *American Journal of Legal History* 17 (1974): 95–123.

counterparts. It also ensured a structural antagonism between the courts, prosecuting attorneys, and the police as the divide in responsibilities took on greater ideological content in the twentieth century. This antagonism, usually characterized as an aspect of adversarial justice, was not at all intended and sets the United States off from other nations.

Third, the uniforms made the police visible, hence accessible to all, whether neighbors or strangers, and this essentially made them the first and for a long time only officials easily seen by the public. Uniforming, an integral part of their new organizational model, generated consternation and some amusing anecdotes for police historians. At first the uniforms were mocked by commentators and shunned by police officers. Called "popinjays" in Boston, ridiculed as "expensive and fantastical" in New York, derided as "livery" in Chicago, and refused by an officer in Philadelphia as "derogatory to my feelings as an American," uniforms were a difficult part of the transformation.[11] Americans valued greatly their freedom to wear what they pleased. Previously, only soldiers and servants of the wealthy had been seen on the streets in such outfits. But the uniforms instantly increased citizen access to patrol officers, now visible for the first time. This visibility, for instance, combined with a centralized communication system, accounted for the sudden turn to the police by parents of lost children; prior to the police, they had had to conduct frantic, random community searches.[12] In addition, uniformed officers were easier for their superiors to find and control.

Fourth, the police were conceived to be active: this entailed patrol (expected to discover and prevent), regular salaries and lines in the city budget, and free prosecution of criminal offenders. Conceptualized as bringing regular and more effective crime prevention to the city, this new activity contrasted with the constables' specifically responsive, fee-based work. City officials hoped that regular patrol would prevent crime by scaring would-be offenders. If successful, of course, then fees for catching offenders would no longer be a fair way of paying for police services. So the new police had to have regular salaries, to be a part of the city budget. An unexpected consequence of this was free prosecution of offenders; no longer did a victim have to calculate the value of a stolen pair of boots before calling a constable. Steinberg's research in the Philadelphia Aldermanic court records suggests that people may have been quite willing to pay a fee to prosecute neighbors: he argues that one reason for creating the Philadelphia police was to stop frivolous private prosecution.[*] And the regularity of the salaries made the police jobs more attractive; hence their almost immediate seizure as political plums to be handed out by the political party gaining the mayor's position. From this then developed the use of police in political control,

---

[*] To be sure, the reporting of offenses and liabilities; witnesses were on occasion still locked up.

police officers sometimes deterring voters and generally working for a partisan control of the ballot boxes.[13] This, in turn, meant that as immigrant voting machines grew, immigrants had access to these city jobs early on; the image of the Irish cop had a genuine basis in reality, even in cities like New Orleans.

Steinberg's important work on Philadelphia shows that prior to the police, a vigorous system of private prosecution had kept the aldermen and mayor busy adjudicating minor criminal offenses. He argues that this system, though corrupt, kept the citizenry in easy and constant contact with the law, and that the police for their first two decades mainly pursued arrests for public order offenses, the petty larcenies and assaults being handled by these lower and more neighborhood courts. His book adds an additional dimension to what local criminal justice looked like prior to the police, revising the work on the constable watch by Ferdinand, who emphasized their inefficiency and unsystematic entrepreneurialism. It raises new sets of complex questions for further analysis in the history of crime control and policing, in its argument that the police deliberately, albeit slowly, eroded the vigorous involvement of the urban poor and laboring classes in the justice system. That is, regular patrol by salaried officers in theory reduced corruption, increased the availability of the police for consistent service, and removed the opportunity for frivolous complaints and prosecution by those with the money to pay fees. Did the modern police in fact decrease crime control and make the justice system less easily accessible?

Steinberg's work depends in part on a scholarly find, the fragmentary logs of three aldermen. Apparently, almost all of the numerous aldermen kept no written records, which means that a more systematic comparison than he has essayed will depend on historians discovering new records. Nevertheless, until Steinberg's book, no historian even had the idea of looking for such materials, and his work opens an exciting new set of questions. In addition to such logs, police historians have already uncovered a rich lode of systematic sources.[14] These include detailed annual reports, internal records, less regularly preserved blotters (the daily log of station activities), and, for the nineteenth century, detailed newspaper accounts. Most police departments have written histories which vary widely in quality and coverage.[15] In addition to these specifically police-oriented sources, there are records produced by courts, coroners, and carceral institutions. Most of these are manuscripts, but state governments produced annual summaries of court, prison, and jail activities. In addition, the federal censuses have interesting data, rendered difficult to use by its inconsistency from decade to decade.

II. POLICE AS AN URBAN SERVICE

The new kind of police came as costly service innovations to American cities, stingy city governments often resisting the transition specifically because of their new claim on city budgets.[16] Uniformed police spread across the United States to most cities in the three decades between 1850 and 1880. It sometimes seemed that local incidents, most typically riots, "caused" a city to change its police to the modern form. But in general, a city's rank size in the U.S. city system determined the order of police adoption, the spread of police innovation following a diffusion curve typical for all sorts of innovations.[17] Some historians have argued that police were created in response to rising crime, but there is little empirical evidence to support this: most social scientists now assume that the long-run trends in crime have been downward.[18] More to the point, those creating police would have had little way of detecting rising crime. Riots had long been a part of American urban life, and historians have been able to describe in considerable detail the political ends of riots as conscious social forms.[19] New York City, for instance, had major nineteenth-century riots in 1806, 1826, 1834, 1837, 1849, 1855, 1857, 1863, 1870, 1874, and 1900.[20] At best, one could say that the creation of the police reflected a growing intolerance for riots and disorder, rather than a response to an increase. Gallman has shown that this was the case for Philadelphia, a city with a long tradition of rioting, where, he argues, citizens no longer accepted public outbursts.[21]

The police grew in per capita strength from around 1.3 per thousand in the 1860s, stabilizing at 2 per thousand in 1908, still around the current ratio. Examined more carefully, the data suggest two eras of growth, the first up to about 1890, when police became permanent fixtures of city government, and the second the decade of the 1890s when they again and finally expanded in strength. As a reciprocal to the increasing number of police per capita, the proportion of patrol officers fell from around 95 percent to about 75 percent by 1920. Toward the end of the nineteenth century, the actual patrol hours may have declined also, for not only did the proportion of patrol officers decrease, but the two-shift system (12 hours on, 12 off) yielded to the more humane three-shift system in this era.[22] Certainly, the twentieth century saw declining patrol hours per officer. Watts, using more precise data for the St. Louis police department, has estimated police hours available for patrol since 1900, accounting for vacation and work week changes. He concludes that since the nineteenth century, police have consistently declined in the hours per officer on the street, as one might expect given the general decrease in the length of the working day. Using hours worked in 1958–1962 as a base, police worked about 80 percent more at the end of the nineteenth century, about 20 percent more between 1907 and World War II, and about 10 percent less after 1962.[23] At least for time allotted to patrol, police presence began declining within four decades after their introduction to cities.

Once in place, city police almost immediately began doing things unexpected by their original creators, whose expectations were more along the lines of crime prevention. Along with arresting offenders, the police took in tramps, returned lost children by the thousands,, shot stray dogs, enforced sanitation laws, inspected boilers, took annual censuses, and performed myriad other small tasks. Their unique communications organization and street presence virtually forced them to become city servants as well as crime-control officers. Simultaneous with a pull toward urban service came a surprising inability to fulfill other crime-related functions, most notably riot control and catching of offenders whose crimes crossed many local government districts (e.g., thieves on railroads), and unpredictability in controlling strikes, police sometimes siding with strikers (e.g., Homestead). Fogelson shows that urban elites created armories in response to strikes and riots beginning in the post–Civil War era, signaling their clear recognition that police skills did not include anti-riot mobilization.[24] Or, as the contributor to the *Cyclopedia of American Government* stated: "Labor riots, particularly against strike breakers, sometimes have the sympathy of the police."[25]

From very early on police did something for which they had not been created: they dispensed forms of welfare in response to the pressing demands of citizens. It is important to be clear about this particular transformation: in the mid-nineteenth century, all welfare was a local responsibility. The federal government took no such responsibility until the early twentieth century. State governments accepted limited responsibility for the blind and mentally ill and juveniles in need of reform.[26] County governments accepted responsibility for paupers, a group confined to the severely disabled, the old and infirm, and pregnant destitute women.[27] City governments took on all others, from orphans to the homeless. Police departments were the front line of encounter for a good many of such needy people. Station houses contained separate dorm-type rooms to house overnight "lodgers." Each city varied in what it provided, but the accommodations were primitive and limited to a few nights. A police officer recorded each person's name and sometimes rather detailed information (age, place of birth, occupation, "whither from," and destination). Such police service did not go unnoticed, either by the poor or by city officials.

Toward the end of the nineteenth century and into the 1920s, many reformers worked to dismantle station house lodging. Jacob Riis, in his autobiography, complained bitterly about his and his dog's maltreatment by the police when he stayed in stations in New York City and Camden, New Jersey, after his arrival in the United States in the 1870s.[28] Later his bitterness fused with the critique of police commissioners like Theodore Roosevelt, who argued that the presence of tramps was degrading and threatened police officers with contagious diseases.[*] At the same time other reformers in major Eastern cities worried about the con-

---

[*] Jay S. Berman, *Police Administration and Progressive Reform: Theodore Roosevelt as Police Commissioner of New York* (New York: Greenwood Press, 1987), in telling the story of Roosevelt's career as New York City Police Commissioner, captures nicely this transition and its linkage to the larger program of the progressive movement, rationalization, efficiency, and an end to corruption.

sequences of the indiscriminate giving of overnight lodging. This, they argued, did nothing to reform the bad habits of the poor: scientific charity should not be indiscriminate. Instead they encouraged cities to substitute for police lodging municipal lodging houses, requiring delousing and work from the overnight lodgers. Such reforms carried through at least in Boston and New York, much to the unhappiness of the lodgers who preferred dirty but no-strings-attached shelter. By the 1920s, police were out of the lodging business, and only rarely have social welfare histories shown an awareness of this important role taken on by the police.

It seems almost natural to ask today why this simple police activity should have been allowed to disappear, especially since there is no evidence suggesting that the police themselves complained. But in the context of the original impetus behind their creation, crime control, and the changing focus of their range of activities, the disappearance of lodging makes more sense. Social welfare reformers, and some police chiefs, began to differentiate the components of the "dangerous class," and tramps became, to them, the unemployed rather than dangerous. After the 1890s, police really did focus more and more on crime control. So did the other loose components of the criminal justice system: Friedman and Percival, in their study of Alameda County, California, show that in this period "criminal justice shifted away from amateurs and part-timers toward full-time crime handlers."[29]

Other tests confirm the change in police focus from broad welfare as well as crime control to more concentration on crime control; for instance, correlation in most major cities between arrests for criminal offenses (as opposed to public order offenses) and numbers of police per capita increased after 1890. A recent analysis of arrests for murder, other felony crimes, lodgers, and police strength in the twenty largest U.S. cities more precisely confirms 1894 as the turning point, the moment when police began to respond more directly to crimes of violence—measured by murder arrests. At the same time, they focused their attention on other felony crimes, continuing to sluff off their burden of housing homeless lodgers and even reducing the numbers of people arrested for order misdemeanors.[30]

The narrowing focus of police on crime in turn came with a new set of external pressures including demands for efficiency, for honesty, and for crime control. Coordination of departments began at the modest scale of sharing information. The Police Chiefs Union, founded in 1893 (to become the IACP [International Association of Chiefs of Police]), started a modest bureau of identification at some point in the 1890s. Their efforts did not meet with success because of the nature of the federal system: voluntary contributions from city police departments could not provide an adequate or consistent funding base for this national activity. Not until a president with experience in local policing, Theodore Roosevelt, were police leaders to see the creation of the Federal Bureau of Identification, some twenty years later.[31] A range of local changes paralleled these fledgling national coordinating efforts.

In this context, the question of the police and public order gains new significance. Miller argued that compared to their British predecessors, the new police in the United States envisioned their role as keepers of public order, dispensing summary justice immediately, on the street.[32] Police organizations had high turnover on the job, in part because of their nature as political plums in cities with rapid regime transitions and in part because high residential mobility characterized all of urban America. Turnover ensured that police professionalization issues never mattered for the nineteenth-century officer. And for the whole police organization, the keeping of lodgers had no logical role conflict with arresting drunks and felons: all of these activities involved control of what was then called the "dangerous class." The cessation of control of the "dangerous class" came with the first reforms of police corruption in the 1890s, followed by new emphases on investigative techniques like fingerprinting (around 1905), and with the slow change of the job from political plum to career occupation. By the end of World War I, police were in the business of crime control: other city- or state-run agencies had taken over their former non–crime control activities.

It should be noted here that the dating of the turn to crime control here is based on police behavior; additional evidence suggests that over the decades of the early twentieth century, the crime-control model became more explicitly drawn. Douthit, for instance, presents evidence that in the 1920s and 1930s, an effort to create a professional police brought with it an even more refined focus on crime control which excluded all other forms of social conflict. In the mid-1920s the concept of a "war against crime" was popularized by businessman Mark Prentiss, who wrote in the popular magazine *Current Opinion*, as somewhat more serious work was being conducted by crime commissions or crime surveys in twenty-four states.[33] President Coolidge's National Crime Commission (1925) brought national attention to the movement; President Hoover created a better-known National Commission on Law Observance and Enforcement, usually referred to as the Wickersham Commission, which published fourteen reports and had research conducted by such experts as August Vollmer, Zechariah Chafee Jr., Newton Baker, Edith Abbott, Mary Van Kleeck, Sam B. Warner, Miriam Van Watters, Clifford Shaw, and Henry Mackay.[34] These national commissions and the high publicity earned by J. Edgar Hoover marked an image-setting finale to the much longer swing of the police mission to crime control.

Not all scholars agree with the 1890s dating of the transition to a crime-control model for the police. In a debate over policing practice and public order arrests, Watts has argued that crime control–oriented policing was not finalized until the 1940s, an argument based on internal documents as well as quantitative evidence from the St. Louis police.[35] On the other hand, Wertsch, in a close documentary analysis of the Des Moines police department, argues for a change in the 1920s; a "methodological change in policing that drew its attention away from public disorder offenses toward the more urgent task of protecting lives and property."[36] Therefore, while there is agreement that a shift from order control to crime control did in fact occur, the precise timing remains disputed. Several factors probably affected this transition and its city-to-city variability, just as several factors affected the initial adoption of uniformed police. More precise examination may well establish a parallel: an early but longer-lasting transition, say, from 1890 to 1920, in those large cities with both progressive reform movements on many fronts and with innovative police departments, with a later but quicker transition in smaller cities.

A declining per capita rate of arrests for drunkenness offenses may also have resulted solely from this shift in emphasis, although there is strong, if contested, evidence suggesting that drinking itself has been in a long decline since the mid-nineteenth century (Watts 1983; Wertsch 1987).[37] For instance, the complexity of the topic and the question of policy is most dramatically illustrated by the articulated policy change in the Cleveland police in 1908. Under Chief Fred Kohler, the police adopted the "golden rule" in 1908, assisting drunks home or ignoring them. As the seventh largest U.S. city, Cleveland was often looked to as a model for reform.[*] Arrests for drunkenness offenses plummeted from 18,743 in 1906 to a low of 909 in 1912, the most visible impact being between 1907 and 1908 when the arrests fell by 80 percent. Patrol officers arrested about thirty-seven per year in 1906 and less than two per year in 1912. But this dramatic policy change simply followed on a more complex trend in Cleveland: arrest rates for drunkenness had fallen from as early as 1873 until the mid-1890s, and the peak in 1906 was the result of a decade of increased aggressiveness. Kohler's policy could actually be interpreted as a return to an established pattern. Thus a probable scenario, one linking policy to public behavior, is that for decades more decorous behavior had begun to prevail on the city streets, the long nineteenth-century campaign against excessive drinking slowly spreading its influence. In the larger context of growing urban order and political progressivism, the police themselves shifted toward a crime-control orientation, and simultaneously reconsidered the effectiveness of arresting drunks. Kohler also called his "golden rule" "common sense," so for the drinking world, nonarrests were a golden rule while for temperance advocates they were just common sense.

Whether or not public behavior became less disorderly, it is very clear that the policing of drunkenness had been in a long downswing prior to the movement in

---

[*] Note that although Cleveland's arrest trends are not typical of most cities, it is included here for its observed policy shift and to exemplify how Progressive Era reforms moved the police toward the goal of crime control.

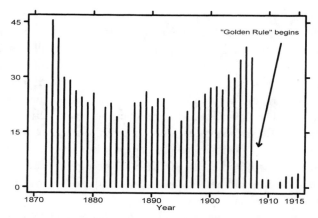

Figure 14.1 Cleveland Drunk Arrests per Thousand, 1872–1915. Source: Monkkonen, *Police in Urban America* (1981).

the 1970s to decriminalize public drunkenness. And when the question of drunkenness is considered in the context of public order, more broadly defined, the notion of a shift in police action from order maintenance to crime control remains a major argument from the past decade's research. It should still be considered as a hypothesis worth more systematic exploration. At least one pair of scholars is doing this. A project by Weinberger and Reinke has been designed to compare two industrial locations, Manchester, England, and Wuppertal, Germany, for the period 1890–1930.[38] Based on the American work and on work for England which argues that urban policing had aggressively reduced criminal offenses until the 1890s, they seek to further expand and make more precise the relationship between police, public order, and issues of social welfare. They have already found important differences from the American experience and evidence that suggests that the shift away from welfare concerns may not have occurred until after World War I. In Britain police orientation toward class control was "self-evident."[39] In Germany, the police explicitly focused on controlling worker politics and unions, and at the same time separate health and sanitary police were created to implement growing expertise in these fields.[40]

III. A. POLICE AS EMPLOYERS

In the United States, through their organizational tie to the mayor's office and to local partisan politics, police have been important as employers of some immigrant groups, most notably the Irish. This held true even for southern cities; in 1850, over one-third of New Orleans' police force had been born in Ireland (as opposed to about one-fourth of the city population).[41] Rousey quotes northern visitor Frederick Law Olmstead's encounter with a police officer in New Orleans in 1854:

when Olmstead asked him for directions, "a policeman, with the richest Irish brogue, directed me back to the St. Charles."[42] Nativist politicians purged the police of most of their immigrant officers in the late 1850s, but by 1870 the Irish were back in the department. Summarizing the experience of seventeen southern cities, Rousey discovered that Vicksburg and Memphis both had 50 percent of their officers born in Ireland as late as 1880 (if children of immigrants were included, this proportion would probably have been much higher). He concludes that "a large Irish role in southern urban policing was the rule" for most of the nineteenth century.[43]

Several recent studies by Watts analyze police hiring practices in St. Louis in great detail, using personnel data that include persons not hired. The results of his work provide a unique source of information on twentieth-century police departments. Between 1917 and 1969, one-third of St. Louis's recruits had had a previous local arrest record. The median age of recruits, around thirty at the beginning of the twentieth century, dropped slowly as policing changed from a job, typically one of several in a man's life, to a career.[44]

As the twentieth century began, even a heavily German city like St. Louis had an Irish police force: only a slight 3 percent of its population had been born in Ireland as contrasted to one-third of its police force. Of more importance, at the turn of the century the total ethnic composition of police, fire, and watch reflected the immigrant heritage of the city, three-fourths of whom were immigrants or children of immigrants, a figure somewhat less than that for Milwaukee, New York, or Chicago.[45]

At the turn of the century 6 percent of St. Louis's population was black; its police department appointed its first two black police officers in 1901. Watts points out that Democrats controlled the police department, and that virtually all of the city's black voters were Republicans, which suggests that politics combined with racial exclusion.[46] A Republican governor in 1920 admitted fifteen black officers to the department, and in the immediate post–World War II era, when black voters shifted to the Democratic Party, 10 percent of all new recruits were black. Watts argues that many changes in the racial and ethnic composition of the St. Louis police in the twentieth century were actually not the result of reform, but of larger "societal changes," such as the black shift to Democratic politics.[47]

Probably the most significant result to come from Watts's intense analysis of the individual career patterns of police officers is his discovery that over the course of the twentieth century, "no truly 'typical' pattern ever emerged."[48] The average tenure of police officers varied highly at the beginning of the century, and continued to vary through the 1970s. Moreover, actual individual careers belied the seemingly clear structural reforms and the appearance of a transformation of the police from a relatively simple and unpredictable internal structure to a highly structured and rationalized bureaucracy. His conclusion that the "police in St.

Louis failed to establish a uniform, coherent career pattern for its members" provides a cautionary note to the strong impression most scholars carry of the police as a Weberian bureaucracy in the process of professionalization.

III. B. POLICE AND LABOR

Police control of labor in the United States has been much less direct and open than in Germany, and the recent historiography reflects a surprisingly ambiguous though still incomplete picture, one tied in large part to issues in private policing. In spite of notorious incidents, like the Memorial Day Massacre in Chicago in 1937, when police killed demonstrating workers, most recent labor history does not paint a completely anti-labor picture of American police and organized labor. In fact, until the defeat of striking police officers in Boston in 1919 ended police unionization efforts for almost a half century, police themselves were often a part of the American labor movement.[49] One of the best-known labor historians, Herbert Gutman, pointed out that police sometimes sided with striking workers.[50] Usually this occurred in smaller cities where police budgets depended on taxes paid by workers. Additionally, in small cities, police officers were often related directly to strikers or were literally from the same labor pool. And finally, in small cities, labor parties often gained considerable political power: Terrence V. Powderly, the founder of the Knights of Labor, also gained the mayor's seat of Scranton, a town racked with anti-labor violence (not by the police). According to Walker, as far as the police were concerned, "Powderly resembled his predecessors," making the police a part of his political machine and trying to get the city council to enlarge the force.[51] In larger cities, police officers did not know or were not related to strikers, so at least the personal element of police/labor amicability was missing.

By far the most systematic and wide-ranging examination of police-labor relations, however, has not come from labor historians but from a police historian, Sidney Harring.[52] In a study of Great Lakes cities, he has identified strong anti-union bias of the police in Buffalo, Chicago, and Milwaukee (under a socialist government). He argues vigorously that the police in these and other cities acted as shock troops for local capitalists, pacifying and controlling local labor under the dictate of local businessmen. In Chicago, for instance, Harring has identified extensive strikebreaking activities by the city police, especially after 1910. Though his evidence for Chicago is very persuasive, it is less so for other cities where his arguments remain widely disputed and highly controversial. For instance, in Chicago in 1905, in Oshkosh in 1898, and in Akron in 1913, police "weakness" failed to curb strikes, and either private guards or the militia intervened.[53] But until further systematic research is completed, Harring's stands as the best study of police and labor to date.[54]

In one of the most famous labor disputes in the United States, the lockout in Homestead, Pennsylvania, local police sided with the locked-out workers;

Carnegie's plant officials had to hire nearly four hundred Pinkerton agents to support them. The agents attacked the strikers from barges in the river; three agents and ten strikers were killed. This incident highlights two long traditions: one that the police have local political ties by virtue of their local funding, and, two, that their responsiveness to local circumstances created an opportunity for private enterprise, the private police.

In a careful institutional history of the Pinkerton National Detective Agency, Frank Morn has provided a badly needed narrative history of the most visible and oldest form of private policing, the detective. Morn shows how this famous agency quickly moved from "detection to protection," becoming a "private army of capitalism." He argues that "railroad expansion [in the 1850s] quickly exposed the weaknesses of police work in a country enamored of federalism."[55] Once a train left a city, it had no police protection; on a long-distance trip it passed through many small police regions. Pinkerton capitalized on this gap in governance, in the railroad industry first, "testing" employee honesty (e.g., theft by conductors), as trains rolled across the countryside. Later his business expanded to capture similar opportunities in other industries, and began to include strikebreaking in instances where neither local police nor militia could or would provide assistance. In all situations, the private sector either filled in governmental interstices or took on possibly illegal activities. (For instance, employee testing involving "sting"-like operations where Pinkerton agents tried to bribe conductors to let them ride without tickets; they then filed reports to the companies who fired corruptible conductors. Did the Pinkerton operatives in fact blackmail or extort money on occasion?)

Reviewing Morn's book, Jeffreys-Jones observes that it is "the first serious monograph on private detective agencies."[56] Jeffreys-Jones clarifies how Allan Pinkerton's pro-labor radicalism was also anti-strike and anti-communitarian; how in the United States he could be a reformer yet also work against all labor violence. Moreover, Jeffreys-Jones sets a research agenda for more work to be done in the history of private detective agencies as part of the history of private policing, including divorce work and family law, with a suggestion of new primary sources. This brief but important essay, then, provides the starting point for the next round of historical research.

Yet the role of such private armies did not pass unscrutinized. The Homestead incident shocked the nation and prompted a federal investigation which resulted in no federal legislation but in widespread anti-detective legislation in many states.[57] The irony of the Pinkerton agency's anti-labor reputation came from Allan Pinkerton's widely publicized pro-labor radicalism which had forced him to leave Scotland in the 1840s. The company was embarrassed by the Homestead fiasco, and actually did little strike work for ten years after it. However, anti-labor activity could include more than strikebreaking, and by the 1930s the company was a leader in the industrial espionage field, with over one thousand operatives in all major unions. Again the focus of an embarrassing federal investigation and exposé, the Pinkerton agency left these activities by 1940, slowly moving into the private security business.[58]

Private police like the Pinkerton and Burns Agencies gained their economic advantage by moving across political regions, using means of dubious legality and working only for the monied. But they were not the only private police, for another form of non–municipally controlled police has been present in American cities since the 1890s: privately employed off-duty police officers and, more important, public officers appointed and employed solely by private organizations. Reed's work on Detroit has shown how these officers, their commissions issued by the police department, grew in numbers as crime (indicated by the homicide rate) and population increased while the percapitized police budget decreased. About a fourth of these officers were employed by other municipal agencies and about two-thirds were employed by businesses; in essence, businesses hiring these officers simply eliminated the services of detective agencies. Reed also has evidence that the police department was "reluctant" to let the police be used in strikes and that these privately employed police may have been business's response to the official aversion to strikebreaking.[59]

Recent work on a famous teamsters strike in Minneapolis in 1934 supports Reed's insights. The so-called Citizen's Alliance was in fact a group of businessmen vigilantes who supplemented the police in the strike. Formed in 1917 to keep Minneapolis open shop, it successfully "eliminated the political threat of the WPNPL [Municipal Nonpartisan League of the Minneapolis trade unions] and the NPL [Nonpartisan League], deunionized the Minneapolis police, maintained an effective intelligence service, and helped establish a Highway Patrol and a Bureau of Criminal Apprehension headed by men it could trust."[60] Its political clout and credibility ended when its members tried to drive and guard trucks to keep goods flowing in the strike; armed with clubs and guns, they actually got into armed conflict with the strikers where their amateurish aggression resulted in deaths. After this misadventure, one in which the governor intervened on the side of the strikers, the Citizen's Alliance did not disband, but instead hired para-police to do investigative and patrol work. In essence, this private group used force of dubious legality to supplement the legitimate police when they were unwilling to step over the bounds of legitimate action.

IV. REFORMING POLICE

Often police have overstepped bounds of legitimate action, and corruption has been a persistent problem in U.S. policing. The Lexow Commission (1894, of the New York state legislature), gained national prominence during its investigation of the New York City police and subsequent exposé of corruption; subsequent investigative reforms occurred in other large cities for the next three decades.[61] Sherman has observed that waves of scandal and reform have run in twenty-year cycles since 1894 and the Lexow Committee's investigation of New York City police corruption. He argues that "virtually every urban police department in the United States has experienced both organized corruption and a major scandal over that corruption."[62] Reforms following scandal, he contends, have often been successful, but control of scandal, like control of crime itself, is hampered by fundamental freedoms. As opposed to most crime, however, scandal arises under fairly predictable conditions, usually surrounding vice operations. Historians have shown the long connection of police corruption with prostitution and drugs (including alcohol when illegal).[63] The potential for scandal is made most clear in those episodes when cities tried, for health reasons, to regulate prostitution without legalizing it. By the turn of the century, local political machines depended on these semi-legitimate vice districts, the bribes from vice entrepreneurs funding the machines. (In some cases, elected non-machine governments depended on the revenues from such fines, for example, the small city of East Grand Forks, Minnesota, in the pre–World War I era.)[64] Since the 1960s, federal investigations of police corruption have reduced the ability of local vice entrepreneurs to control police (Haller 1990).

Earlier, police historians had envisioned the first decades of the twentieth century as the dawn of scientific policing, a notion associated with Berkeley's famous chief August Vollmer, Richard Sylvester of Washington, D.C., and the IACP, and the serious communication among scholars and various segments of the crime-control community through the pages of the *Journal of Criminal Law* and *Criminology* which began publication in 1909.[65] Yet recent work has made this clean, Progressive Era picture more complex. For instance, as Watts's work has shown, the emergence of a more professional police force did not result in more orderly career paths for St. Louis police officers, implying that the bureaucracy did not have the organizational rationality earlier observers had envisioned.[66]

Nor did shedding by police of service activities and focus on crime-related arrests conform to the professional picture being painted by prominent police officers like August Vollmer. Vollmer, elected Town Marshal of Berkeley in 1905, where he supervised a force of three nonuniformed officers, soon became famous and influential. He achieved publicity in local and national newspapers, wrote extensively in both the professional journals, and published several well-respected books. His innovations included a counseling clinic with a psychiatric social worker, Elisabeth Lossing, and an aggressive policing policy which emphasized intervention in personal affairs and prevention through methods prescribed by the latest ideas of the mental hygiene movement. The most recent scholarship on Vollmer denies his widely acclaimed genius without denigrating his considerable achievements: "Rather than an original thinker, Vollmer's strengths lay in finding ingenious practical applications of ideas he borrowed from others, in carefully supervising the implementation of a wide variety of technical and procedural innovations, and, perhaps, most importantly, in maintaining high personal involvement and exercising decisive leadership in community affairs that impinged on police functions."[67]

It is important to see the shift Vollmer represented and advocated as not directly countering the narrowing police function, nor as a return to the multiservice police of the nineteenth century. All his intervention and social-work orientation, his genuine sympathy for and stern guidance of troubled people, was directed toward the end of crime prevention. Earlier, police had taken in the homeless as a sort of municipal housekeeping, which was in fact technically implied by the legal notion of "police power," meaning the power of a state or its local governments to literally do housekeeping, from cleaning streets to creating an orderly public arena.[68] Vollmer's new and generous vision of policing was all oriented toward the prevention of individual criminal actions.

This same vision enabled police to respond in new ways to old problems. During World War II, vicious race riots in several cities took the lives of African Americans and Mexican Americans. More to the point, the police not only failed to control the riots but were in many cases part of the problem. Thurgood Marshall compared the Detroit police to the Gestapo; some police officers saw the riots as providing fuel for Nazi anti-American propaganda.[69] From these experiences, Milwaukee police chief Joseph Kluchesky earned a national reputation for his race relations training program in Milwaukee in 1944. In the same year, the International City Manager Association published a manual on police relations with minority groups that became widely used throughout the United States. Walker found twenty-two cities adopting some race relations training between 1943 and 1950 (to be sure, in some cities this involved little more than a two-hour lecture). However, the lack of urban riots after World War II until the 1960s never really tested the effectiveness of these programs or their companion anti-riot strategies, leaving the police with untested and feebly implemented programs when the urban riots of the 1960s began.[70]

While much has been written about the urban riots and the civil rights movement, no historian has yet tackled these episodes and the police roles in them in a systematic way. For instance, the Little Rock police attained considerable notoriety in 1957 and 1958 for their morally repugnant refusal to protect black children in the school integration crisis. Did such outrages as these, exposed on national television, prompt public support for stronger federal standards in all areas of law enforcement? Did the question of racial fairness make an impact in other cities which did not gain media attention? Atlanta marketed itself as the "city too busy to hate" at the very same time; did other urban boosters strive to make their cities and police fairer for latent economic incentives? And in the 1960s, did the impact of seeing riots on national television have an equal if different impact?[71]

V. FEDERAL-LOCAL POLICY ISSUES

As these visible urban problems in which the police were inextricably involved gained public attention, scholars turned to researching local police departments. The work of the 1960s and 1970s focused intensely on local aspects of policing, on detailed studies of individual police departments, and on questions of the social side of policing.[72] Implicit in all this was the recognition that policing in the United States was an activity done by local governments. Historians ignored issues of larger political entities in order to assess the details of the actual local systems. But now some historians whose earlier work began in the arena of the local have turned toward these other issues relating to the nature of the federal system and policing. In so doing they bring their sensitivity to the all too often ignored importance of the local and its imbeddedness in the federal. The significance of their work is in its clear comprehension of the high visibility of federal levels of policing, but of federal policing's relatively small scope compared to the local. This work represents only a beginning. The working out of the appropriate theoretical context has only begun.[73] The work of Athan Theoharis has focused on the issues of "intelligence and legality" and the long conflict they represent within the FBI mission.[74] Alix has published a unique study on a single criminal offense, kidnapping, which includes an examination of the federalization of this crime and its incorporation into the purview of the FBI.[75] But most work on the FBI has not considered the context of policing or the nature of criminal law in the United States; and, as a result, it is too often journalistic, attending to particular aspects without relating them to any larger context, or deals with abuses, in particular FBI abuses of power.

Miller's work represents a pioneering approach to federal law enforcement.[76] Examining the issue of collecting federal revenue on alcohol production in the South, he highlights both the scope and limits of this early form of federal policing. While he draws no explicit comparison with current drug enforcement today, the contemporary comparison with the too often romanticized illegal production of the nineteenth-century drug of choice, liquor, is obvious. The revenue collectors were sometimes corrupt; moonshiners often resisted violently, killing ten revenue collectors between July 1877 and June 1878. There was also internal violence in the moonshine business; after 1879, federal troops accompanied revenue collectors; people in rural communities, often women, did not all approve of the illegal liquor and secretly informed to the revenue collectors. The question of moonshine, Miller makes clear, is the question of state penetration into illegal business, just as it is today with nonalcohol drugs. Successful federal efforts were characterized by consistent and fair prosecution, a system of fines and suspended sentences which could be revoked if the defendant resumed illegal alcohol production. By the end of the nineteenth century, popular support for moonshine had dramatically eroded because of the consistent and judicious federal effort, so that moonshiners were often denounced as "gangs of lazy, bad men . . . of general worthlessness."[77] While for Miller the important contrast in the research is with federal failure to enforce civil rights, he might well have made the contrast with current efforts on drug enforcement.

One hopes that further work on federal policing will supplement Miller's work so that we may begin to understand the nature of policing across the American social and political landscape. His central argument is perhaps of more interest to historians and political scientists than to those in the criminal justice fields: the historiography that emphasizes the failure of Reconstruction to protect black citizens in the South "overlooks the internal revenue system, a product of the Civil War that became a permanent element of expanded national authority."[78] This insight suggests that "expanded national authority" and policing do have an important connecting link: federal laws are enforced through a wide variety of organizations, and too often writers attend only to the FBI as a unique institution. One hopes that Miller's recentering of thinking about national law enforcement by highlighting a forgotten aspect of national policing will provoke other historians into looking at other federal policing systems— the park police, for instance, as examined by Mackintosh in an internal history which does not link this agency to the broader context of police history, or the police of Washington, D. C., who, in spite of their federal mandate, have a past quite like that of other cities.[79]

David R. Johnson's work on federal policing (1995) combines two approaches, one emphasizing a federal crime, counterfeiting, and the other focused on large bureaucracies and state building. He argues that the "fitful" and "obscure" process behind the creation of a federal police followed from the creation of federal authority over currency during the Civil War.[80] Subtly using currency and counterfeiting as his topic, Johnson directly relates the question of state building to the chasing of counterfeiters, showing how the creation of a nation state required a strong currency, which in turn boosted the creation of a small national police. He details how both criminals and federal agents operated in a local and highly irregular manner. Traub, writing on the use of rewards in the West, has evidence that both local governments and U.S. marshals, reporting directly to the attorney general, used rewards as an attempt to compensate people for catching, and often killing, known offenders. He argues that rewards were a rational way to communicate and provide crime control in lieu of an efficiently organized state, although he notes that the system encouraged murder rather than trials.[81] Unlike

Johnson, he neither links his analysis to theoretical questions surrounding local and federal policing nor to state building, clearly the essential missing element in the Western United States.[82]

Uchida's work on the early FBI clarifies its origins in the Bureau of Investigation, begun by President Roosevelt in 1908. He provides a clear bridge to local policing by showing how this federal organization was begun by a politician expert in the ways and limitations of city police from his term as New York City police commissioner. Roosevelt mandated that the Bureau of Investigation initiate criminal investigations for crimes spreading beyond local felonies, beginning with political land frauds. While not explicitly understood as a structural problem related to the federal system, Roosevelt's agency indeed focused on those felonies simply beyond the scope of local police. Rather than seeing Roosevelt's actions as purely politically motivated, one might instead draw a comparison with progressive reformers in the late nineteenth and early twentieth centuries, who, Jeffreys-Jones contended, exaggerated the amount and fear of labor violence in order to accomplish their electoral and legislative goals.[83] In other words, reformers exaggerated fears to accomplish somewhat different ends.

Some of this recent police history has raised policy issues that cut across other features of local governments and services. Police, like schools, provide labor intensive services which do not seem to be easily replaced by technology. Greater bureaucratic complexity has not broken down tasks to simple elements easily performed by machines and such does not seem to be a realistic expectation. Local governments have the potential of doing some things much better (e.g.., traffic control), but policing and schooling do not have such rosy futures. Perhaps this is one reason why they both remain at the center of controversy: the jobs get no easier and the bureaucracies no more efficient with the passage of time and the growth of expertise. Equally important, the efficiency of these labor intensive services seems to have an inverse relationship to city size: at some size, the bigger the city, the more costly and perhaps less efficient the service, whether school or police.[84]

The history of police raises some difficult theoretical questions about urban government and has unclear implications for policing. Paul Peterson, in *City Limits*, argues that policing is an "allocational" function of city government, meaning that it is neutral vis-à-vis increasing or decreasing the city's long-run expectations for revenue.[85] As the history of the police makes clear, their functional change over time renders Peterson's analysis problematic, while at the same time making his overall model even more useful. In the nineteenth century, police clearly performed part of the city's welfare or distributional function. As the police shifted to a crime-control emphasis, they became essential to the city's promotional functions in that they helped provide a safer environment for urban economic activities.

Following Peterson's larger argument, that distributional activities migrate to the highest—that is, geographically most capacious—level of government, while promotional activities stay at the lowest—that is, the smallest geographical units—of government, then his theory could help describe and explain why policing changed from broad class control to more narrow crime control. Given the historic limitations of U.S. policing to small locales and the strong tradition prohibiting the creation of a state or national police system as in Europe, the police came under steady pressure to change what they did. As distributional actors, cities were under competitive constraints to spend less on welfare services, including those accomplished by the police, while at the same time they were under pressure to attract revenue-enhancing activities by providing crime-free environments. The fixed location of American police would then account for their turn to crime control and away from welfare in contrast to the continued welfare and broader service orientation (class control) of European police. This constraint would also help account for the relatively low amount of development of crime control–oriented policing at the state and federal level in spite of tremendous political and social pressure to have more effective crime control. Crime control, then, would not migrate to the national level until local revenue enhancing disappeared, an unlikely scenario given the long history of local government. If one can imagine an international scenario in which the United States will have to make itself crime free to attract investment, then crime control might move to broader levels of government.

CONCLUSION: FUTURE RESEARCH NEEDS

The research of the past decade has given scholars a much deeper context and much greater empirical knowledge in which to understand current policing. As Lane's essay of 1980 synthesizes the pioneering generation of police historians, this essay builds on the maturing field. This generation has had the advantage of a growing body of research and a broad spectrum of theoretical perspectives, from the Marxism of Harring to the interdisciplinary approach of Schneider. It has been much more synthetic than that of the pioneering generation. My overview and history in 1981 pulled information from dozens of late-nineteenth- and early-twentieth-century local police histories. In addition, it and the articles of Watts introduced new levels of statistics to the field. Friedman and Percival's study of Alameda County (1981) looked at the whole criminal justice system—police, the courts, law, lawyers, offenders, jails, the media. Schneider's work on Detroit (1980) mapped arrests, police distribution, and tied the social and economic geography of the city to the nineteenth-century development of its police and crime. And Emsley published the first scholarly history of policing in Europe and England, enabling American scholars to begin to appreciate more deeply the complex differences between North America and Europe.[86]

This new stage of sophistication was matched on another level, too. On the international scene, a loose affiliation of scholars known as the Dutch Group had put together international scholarly conferences on crime history. Organizing a larger meeting in conjunction with the seventh International Economic History Congress in Edinburgh in 1978, this group created a new more formal organization and publication, the *International Association for the History of Crime and Criminal Justice Newsletter*.[87] Published by the Fondation de la Maison des Sciences de l'Homme in Paris, the *Newsletter* began the complex task of coordinating and informing researchers about the varied and rich research being conducted around the world in criminal justice history.[88] The work of this group introduced Americans to the historical sociology of Norbert Elias, whose generous theoretical approach underwrites much of the contemporary European scholarship. In the United States in 1980, the journal *Criminal Justice History* appeared; an annual, it publishes international scholarship and with its first issue established itself as a serious scholarly journal.

The research developments discussed in this essay suggest a diverse research agenda. For instance, Steinberg raises a two-pronged challenge, first to find sources that will permit the documentation of pre-police modes of criminal justice. He has found fragmentary evidence on aldermen's courts. We need similar sources on church courts; Kasserman has documented the Methodists' exclusion of a young woman for prostitution, while Waldrep has systematic evidence on church trials and county court trials for a rural county in late-nineteenth-century Kentucky.[89] He argues that a decline in church trials preceded a rise in felony court prosecutions. Similar work also must be done in labor union court records. Garlock, for instance, has documented the Knights of Labor courts in the late nineteenth century, showing that the expulsions mainly were for offenses having to do with union affairs, but that the court structure of the union was specifically designed as a fairer alternative to the existing police and judicial machinery. He quotes Terrence Powderly: "They [workingmen] have long perceived that at the hands of advocates, justices and police, they get an immense amount of *law*, but no *justice*."[90] Finally, excellent recent studies of vigilantism and crime show the need for further systematic work on the power of the state and crime control.[91]

We also need comparable, systematic research on the constable watch system. These are all essential if we are to understand the transition to the police and a formal, state-run justice system. Steinberg argues that in many ways the quantity as well as quality of local crime control decreased after the introduction of the police. This is a challenging assertion, and should attract the research efforts of historians.

The work of Loftin and McDowell provides a model for research design in historical studies.[92] Constructing a long (fifty-year) data series of police behavior and expenditures, and paying careful attention to the population denominator, they reexamine the role of expenditures on policing in Detroit. While they find a weak relationship between expenditures and apprehension rates, the article is of more importance for its demonstration of the feasibility of long time series. Its research design is clearly generalizable to other cities, and it should provide a beginning orientation for future research.

How do police relate to issues of public order, from misdemeanors to riots? In spite of all the research, there has yet to be a research design capable of convincingly testing counterfactuals, that is, asking what would cities have been (or be) like without the police. Schneider has systematically examined the relationship of police to riots in the mid-nineteenth century, looking as well at cities where there were no riots (he argues that Detroit Germans and Irish had residential and journey-to-work patterns that minimized the friction causing riots in other cities) (1980). No historian has examined twentieth-century riots and police in such a systematic way. If urban rioting declined with the introduction of policing, did this reflect effective riot control, the consequence of a visible control mechanism, or an independent increase in urban order? The late-nineteenth-century decline in violent crimes and in accidental deaths suggests the latter, but the project specifically designed to test these alternatives has yet to be conducted.[93]

We still need to know far more about the police themselves. Were nonurban police and private police so active in labor control that the local police could remain relatively absent? What has been the impact of police training and civil service rules (Johnson 1981)? Did the slow change in police technology indicate a resistance to innovation detrimental to crime control? Did the transition from more generalized class surveillance and control to crime control wipe out an important urban welfare service? The question of productivity in a labor intensive service like policing (and also teaching school) implicitly plagues most analyses; little has been done to estimate the contributions of technological change to productivity and then to estimate the total changes in policing.

The question of police and order has special significance for southern cities, where the work of Rousey on New Orleans suggests a very different development path from the North's. Rousey has also shown how New Orleans in the second half of the nineteenth century was far more violent than northern cities. This extended to the police, often with disastrous results. In the period 1863–1890, police officers more often shot bystanders than did civilian shooters; in addition, police officers were more likely to be killed by fellow officers than by civilians.[94] In an unpublished article, Rousey shows how the police of New Orleans were essentially a military force, patrolling the city primarily to control slaves.[95] It is not yet clear whether we should even call the "city guard" police, for with their swords, armory, and uniforms, they more greatly represented a European-style urban military; indeed, they were at first called, in 1805, the Gendarmerie. The New Orleans police were demilitarized later in the century, and the post–Civil War police represented the city's first modern police system. The contrast between the South and the North in the pre–Civil War era suggests that an unfree society cannot support a modern police system. Systematic comparison of both organization and behavior can make clearer these regional differences, and in the process show how the issues of liberty, partisan politics, and the legitimacy of the state directly affect policing. Thus further opportunities for police history go in several directions, from policy to urban political theory to fundamental issues of democracy and liberty.[96]

NOTES

1. Eric H. Monkkonen, *Crime and Justice in American History* (Westport, CT: Meckler Publishing, 1990).

2. Roger Lane, "Urban Police and Crime in Nineteenth-Century America," *Crime and Justice: An Annual Review* 2 (1980): 1–44.

3. Eric H. Monkkonen, *Police in Urban America, 1860–1920* (New York: Cambridge University Press, 1981); see also Monkkonen, "From Cop History to Social History: The Significance of the Police in American History," *Journal of Social History* 15 (1982): 575–91.

4. Allen Steinberg, *The Transformation of Criminal Justice: Philadelphia, 1800–1880* (Chapel Hill: University of North Carolina Press, 1989).

5. Stanley H. Palmer, *Police and Protest in England and Ireland, 1780–1850* (New York: Cambridge University Press, 1988).

6. Wilbur R. Miller, *Cops and Bobbies: Police Authority in New York and London, 1830–1870* (Chicago: University of Chicago Press, 1976).

7. Theodore N. Ferdinand, "Criminality, the Courts, and the Constabulary in Boston, 1702–1967," *Journal of Research in Crime and Delinquency* 17 (1980): 190–208.

8. Quoted in Arthur E. Peterson and George W. Edwards, *New York as an Eighteenth Century Municipality;* 2nd ed. (Port Washington, NY: Friedman, 1967), 324.

9. Mark H. Haller, "Civic Reformers and Police Leadership: Chicago, 1905–1935," in Harlan Hahn, ed., *Police in Urban Society* (Beverly Hills: Sage, 1970), 39–56; "Historical Roots of Police Behavior: Chicago, 1890–1925," *Law & Society Review* 10 (1976): 303–23.

10. Steinberg, *Transformation,* 1989.

11. Roger Lane, *Policing the City: Boston, 1822–1905* (Cambridge: Harvard University Press, 1967), 105; James F. Richardson, *The New York Police: Colonial Times to 1901* (New York: Oxford University Press, 1970), 65; David R. Johnson, "The Search for an Urban Discipline: Police Reform as a Response to Crime in American Cities, 1800–1875," Ph.D. diss., Univ. of Chicago, 1972, published as *Policing the Urban Underworld: The Impact of Crime on the Development of the American Police, 1800–1885* (Philadelphia: Temple University Press, 1979), 172–76.

12. Monkkonen, *Police,* 109–28.

13. Laylon W. Jordan, "Police and Politics: Charleston in the Gilded Age, 1880–1900," *South Carolina History Magazine* 81 (1980): 35–50.

14. Eric H. Monkkonen, "The Quantitative Historical Study of Crime and Criminal Justice in the United States," in James Inciardi and Charles Faupel, eds., *History and Crime: Implications for Contemporary Criminal Justice Policy* (Beverly Hills: Sage, 1980), 53–73; tr. in M. Rehbinder and M. Killias, eds., *Rechtsgeschichte, Rechtssoziologie und Historische Kriminologie*

(Berlin: Duncker & Humblot, 1985), 169–94; "Municipal Reports as an Indicator Source: The Nineteenth-Century Police," *Historical Methods* 12 (1979): 57–65.

15. See Monkkonen, *Police*, 164–68, for a bibliography.

16. John C. Schneider, *Detroit and the Problem of Order, 1830–1880: A Geography of Crime, Riot, and Policing* (Lincoln: University of Nebraska Press, 1980).

17. Monkkonen, *Police*, 49–64.

18. For the response argument, see Bobby L. Blackburn, "Oklahoma Law Enforcement since 1803," unpublished Ph.D. diss., Oklahoma State University, 1979; Felix Rippy, "Crime and the Beginnings of the Muncie Police Force," *Indiana Social Studies Quarterly* 38 (1985): 5–18; see Ted R. Gurr, "Historical Trends in Violent Crime: Europe and the United States," for the other argument, in Gurr, ed., *Violence in America: Volume 1: The History of Crime* (Beverly Hills: Sage, 1989), 21–54.

19. Paul A. Gilje, *The Road to Mobocracy: Popular Disorder in New York City, 1763–1834* (Chapel Hill: University of North Carolina Press, 1987).

20. Monkkonen, *Police*, 196.

21. James M. Gallman, "Preserving the Peace: Order and Disorder in Civil War Pennsylvania," *Pennsylvania History* 55 (1988): 201–15.

22. Monkkonen, *Police*, 144–45.

23. Eugene J. Watts, "Police Priorities in Twentieth-Century St. Louis," *Journal of Social History* 14 (1981): 671, n. 15. (Watts 1981b, p. 99)

24. Robert Fogelson, *America's Armories: Architecture, Society and Public Order* (Cambridge, Mass.: Harvard University Press, 1989).

25. Andrew C. McLaughlin and Albert B. Hart, *Cyclopedia of American Government* (New York: Appleton, 1914), 3: 584.

26. Barbara M. Brenzel, *Daughters of the State: A Social Portrait of the First Reform School for Girls in North America, 1856–1905* (Cambridge: MIT Press, 1983); Ellen Dwyer, *Homes for the Mad: Life Inside Two Nineteenth-Century Asylums* (New Brunswick, N.J.: Rutgers University Press, 1987); Steven Schlossman, *Love and the American Delinquent: The Theory and Practice of "Progressive" Juvenile Justice* (Chicago: University of Chicago, 1977).

27. Michael B. Katz, *In the Shadow of the Poorhouse: A Social History of Welfare in America* (New York: Basic, 1986); Joan Underhill Hannon, "The Generosity of Antebellum Poor Relief," *Journal of Economic History* 44 (1984): 810–21; idem, "Poverty in the Antebellum Northeast: The View from New York State's Poor Relief Rolls," *Journal of Economic History* 44 (1984): 1019–31.

28. Jacob Riis, cited in Monkkonen, *Police*, 92.

29. Lawrence M. Friedman and Robert V. Percival, *Roots of Justice: Crime and Punishment in Alameda County, California, 1870–1910* (Chapel Hill: University of North Carolina Press, 1981), 194.

30. Eric H. Monkkonen and Catrien Bijleveld, "Cross-sectional and Dynamic Analyses of the Concomitants of Police Behavior," *Historical Methods* (1991): 16–24.

31. Donald C. Dilworth, *Identification Wanted: Development of the American Criminal Identification System, 1893–1943* (Gaithersburg, MD: IACP, 1977); Graig D. Uchida, "Policing the Politicians: Theodore Roosevelt and the Origins of the F.B.I." (paper presented at the Academy of Criminal Justice Sciences annual meeting, San Antonio, 1983).

32. Miller, *Cops and Bobbies*; see also Friedman and Percival, *Roots of Justice*, 80–81.

33. Nathan Douthit, "Police Professionalism and the War against Crime in the United States, 1920s-1930s," in George L. Mosse, ed., *Police Forces in History* (Beverly Hills: Sage, 1975), 318–19.

34. Samuel Walker, *Popular Justice* (New York: Oxford University Press, 1981), 173–75; National Archives 1936.

35. Eugene J. Watts, "Police Response to Crime and Disorder in Twentieth Century St. Louis," *Journal of American History* 70 (1983): 352, 357.

36. Douglas Wertsch, "The Evolution of the Des Moines Police Department," *Annals of Iowa* 48 (1987): 448; see also Eugene Watts, "Police Priorities in Twentieth Century St. Louis," *Journal of Social History* 14 (1981): 658.

37. Eric Monkkonen, "A Disorderly People? Urban Order in Nineteenth- and Twentieth-Century America," *Journal of American History* 68 (1981): 539–59; William J. Rorabaugh, *The Alcoholic Republic: An American Tradition* (New York: Oxford University Press, 1979); Jack S. Blocker Jr., *American Temperance Movements: Cycles of Reform* (Boston: Twayne, 1989); Eric H. Monkkonen, "Toward an Understanding of Urbanisation: Drunk Arrests in Los Angeles," *Pacific Historical Review* 50 (1981): 234–44.

38. Herbert Reinke and Barbara Weinberger, eds., *Policing Western Europe, 1850–1940: Politics, Professionalization, and Public Order* (Westport, Conn.: Meckler Publishing, 1990).

39. V.A.C. Gatrell, in Gatrell, Geoffrey Parker and Bruce Lenman, eds., *Crime and the Law: The Social History of Crime in Western Europe since 1500* (London: Europa, 1980).

40. Barbara Weinberger and Herbert Reinke, "A Diminishing Function: A Comparative Account of Policing the City," *Policing and Society* (1991), pt. 1, 14, pt. 2, 8–9.

41. Dennis Rousey, "Hibernian Leatherheads: Irish Cops in New Orleans, 1830–1860," *Journal of Urban History* 10 (1983): 62.

42. Ibid., 61.

43. Ibid., 80.

44. Eugene J. Watts, "St. Louis Police Recruits in the Nineteenth Century," *Criminology* 19 (1981): 82, 84.

45. Watts, "St. Louis Police Recruits," 100, 99. See also Robert Fogelson, *Big City Police* (Cambridge: Harvard University Press, 1977).

46. Eugene J. Watts, "Blue and Black: Afro-American Police Officers in Twentieth Century St. Louis," *Journal of Urban History* 7 (1981): 131–68; Watts, "St. Louis Police Recruits," 105–106.

47. Watts, "St. Louis Police Recruits," 107, 109; Watts, "Patterns of Promotion: The St. Louis Police Department, 1899–1975," *Social Science History* 6 (1982): 233–58, also demonstrates in an analysis of promotion practices that the only meaningful variable for promotion is seniority.

48. Eugene J. Watts, "Continuity and Change in Police Careers: A Case Study of the St. Louis Police Department," *Journal of Police Science and Administration* 2 (1983): 224.

49. Samuel Walker, *Popular Justice* (New York: Oxford University Press, 1980), 166–69.

50. Herbert G. Gutman, *Work, Culture, and Society in Industrializing America*, "Part IV. Local Behavior and Patterns of Labor Discontent in Gilded Age America" (New York: New Viewpoints, 1977), 293–343; Bruce C. Johnson, "Taking Care of Labor: The Police in American Politics," *Theory and Society* 3 (1976): 89–117.

51. Samuel Walker, "The Police and the Community: Scranton, Pennsylvania, 1866–1884, A Test Case," *American Studies* 19 (1978): 79–90.

52. Sidney Harring, *Policing a Class Society: Police and Labor in Buffalo, Chicago, and Milwaukee* (New Brunswick: Rutgers University Press, 1982).

53. Ibid., 125–31.

54. Richard J. Terrill, review of Harring in *Criminal Justice History: An International Annual* 7 (1986): 206–207; Roger Lane, review of Harring, in *Journal of American History* 71

(1984): 650–51; for a new look at police and labor, see Thomas Clark, "Police and Labor in California, 1870–1930," Ph.D. diss., UCLA, 1993.

55. Frank Morn, *"The Eye That Never Sleeps": A History of the Pinkerton National Detective Agency* (Bloomington: Indiana University Press, 1982), 24.

56. Rhodri Jeffreys-Jones, "The Defictionalization of the American Private Detective," *Journal of American Studies* 17 (1983): 266.

57. Morn, *"The Eye,"* 91–109.

58. Ibid., 187, 192.

59. Rebecca Reed, "Private Employees/Public Badges: 'Additional Patrolmen' in the Policing of Detroit," paper read at the Social Science History Association annual meeting (St. Louis, 1986) 5, 10, 11.

60. William Millikan, "Maintaining 'Law and Order': The Minneapolis Citizen's Alliance in the 1920s," *Minnesota History* 51 (1989): 219–33.

61. Jay S. Berman, *Police Administration and Progressive Reform: Theodore Roosevelt as Police Commissioner of New York* (New York: Greenwood Press, 1987), 23–29.

62. Lawrence W. Sherman, *Scandal and Reform: Controlling Police Corruption* (Berkeley: University of California Press, 1978), xxiii.

63. Joel Best, "Keeping the Peace in St. Paul: Crime, Vice, and Police Work, 1869–1874," *Minnesota History* 47 (1981): 240–48; Clare McKanna, "Hold Back the Tide: Vice Control in San Diego," *Pacific History* 28 (1984): 54–64; Mark H. Haller, "Illegal Enterprise: A Theoretical and Historical Interpretation," *Criminology* 28 (1990): 207–35.

64. Stephen G. Sylvester, "Avenues for Ladies Only: The Soiled Doves of East Grand Forks, 1887–1915," *Minnesota History* 51 (1989): 291–312.

65. David R. Johnson, *American Law Enforcement: A History* (St. Louis: Forum Press, 1982), 70.

66. Watts 1983b

67. Julia Liss and Steven Schlossman, "The Contours of Crime Control in August Vollmer's Berkeley," *Research in Law, Deviance and Social Control* 6 (1984): 81.

68. Eric H. Monkkonen, "Regional Dimensions of Tramping," in Monkkonen, ed., *Walking to Work: Tramps in America, 1790–1935* (Lincoln: University of Nebraska Press, 1984), 189–211.

69. Samuel Walker, "The Origins of the American Police-Community Relations Movement: The 1940s," *Criminal Justice History: An International Annual* 1 (1980): 231.

70. Ibid., 236–38, 242.

71. Hubert Williams and Patrick V. Murphy, "The Evolving Strategy of Police: A Minority View," *Perspectives on Policing,* No. 13 (1990).

72. George L. Kelling and James K. Stewart, "The Evolution of Contemporary Policing," in William A. Geller, ed., *Local Government Police Management* (Washington: International City Management Association, 1991).

73. Wilbur R. Miller, "Police and the State: A Comparative Perspective," *American Bar Foundation Research Journal* (1986): 339–48.

74. Athan G. Theoharis, *Spying on Americans: Political Surveillance from Hoover to the Huston Plan* (Philadelphia: Temple University Press, 1978); Theoharis, "The Presidency and the Federal Bureau of Investigation: The Conflict of Intelligence and Legality," *Criminal Justice History* 2 (1981): 131–60.

75. Ernest K. Alix, *Ransom Kidnapping in America, 1874–1974: The Creation of a Capital Crime* (Carbondale: Southern Illinois University Press, 1978).

76. Wilbur R. Miller, "The Revenue: Federal Law Enforcement in the Mountain South, 1870–1900," *Journal of Southern History* 55 (1989): 195–216.

77. Ibid., 201, 206–208, 212.

78. Ibid., 196.

79. Barry Mackintosh, *United States Park Police: A History* (Washington, DC: USGPO, 1985); n.a., *A Statutory History of the United States Capital Police Force, Ninety-ninth Congress, first session* (Washington, D.C.: USGPO, 1985).

80. David R. Johnson, *Illegal Tender: Counterfeiting and the Secret Service in Nineteenth-Century America* (Washington, D.C.: Smithsonian Institute Press, 1995).

81. Stuart H. Traub, "Rewards, Bounty Hunting and Criminal Justice in the West: 1865–1900," *Western Historical Quarterly* 19 (1988): 299.

82. For the best description of local violence in the West, see Roger McGrath's study of mining towns, *Gunfighters, Highwaymen, and Vigilantes: Violence on the California Frontier* (Berkeley: University of California Press, 1985).

83. Rhodri Jeffreys-Jones, *Violence and Reform in American History* (New York: New Viewpoints, 1978).

84. Eric Monkkonen, "The Organized Response to Crime in the Nineteenth and Early Twentieth Centuries," *Journal of Interdisciplinary History* 14 (1983): 113–28.

85. Paul Peterson, *City Limits* (Chicago: University of Chicago Press, 1981).

86. Clive Emsley, *Policing and Its Context, 1750–1870* (London: Macmillan, 1983).

87. IAHCCJ *Newsletter* 1 (1979): 4.

88. Eric H. Monkkonen, "The History of Crime and Criminal Justice after Twenty-five Years," *Criminal Justice History* 5 (1984): 161–65.

89. Christopher Waldrep, "'So Much Sin': The Decline of Religious Discipline and the 'Tidal Wave of Crime,'" *Journal of Social History* 23 (1990): 535–52.

90. Jonathan Garlock, "The Knights of Labor Courts: A Case Study of Popular Justice," in Richard Abel, ed, *The Politics of Informal Justice* (New York: Academic Press, 1982), 29.

91. Larry D. Ball, "Military Posses: The Territorial Militia in Civil Law Enforcement in New Mexico Territory, 1877–1883," *New Mexico History Review* 55 (1980): 47–69; Phillip J. Ethington, "Vigilantes and the Police: The Creation of a Professional Police Bureaucracy, 1847–1900," *Journal of Social History* 21 (1987): 197–227; Craig B. Little and Christopher Sheffield, "Frontiers and Criminal Justice: English Prosecution Societies and American Vigilantism in the Eighteenth and Nineteenth Centuries," *American Sociological Review* 48 (1983): 796–808; Roger McGrath, *Gunfighters*.

92. Colin Loftin and David McDowell, "Conflict, Crime and Budgetary Constraint: Police Strength in Detroit, 1927–1976," in Terrence McDonald and Sally Ward, eds., *The Politics of Urban Fiscal Policy* (Beverly Hills: Sage, 1984), 101–124.

93. Roger Lane, *Violent Death in the City: Suicide, Homicide, and Accidental Death in Philadelphia* (Cambridge: Harvard University Press, 1979).

94. Dennis C. Rousey, "Cops and Guns: Police Use of Deadly Force in Nineteenth-Century New Orleans," *American Journal of Legal History* 28 (1984): 57.

95. Dennis Rousey, "Out of the Orbit of Mars: Demilitarizing the New Orleans Police, 1805–1836" (unpublished manuscript).

96. I wish to thank the participants at the conference on Modern Policing (Washington, D.C., 1990) for their extensive and useful comments. In addition, Mark Haller has helped me rethink many issues posed here and I thank him.

■ PART IV:

CITIES AND CRIME

There is ample evidence to demonstrate that cities themselves are not crimenogenic, that the urban condition does not lead inexorably to deviance and personal violence. City walls were to keep the troublemakers out, not in.

Nevertheless, cities at the turn to the twenty-first century are the locus of much crime, and in the United States, cities are also the center of that most visible anticrime agency, the police. Not only are contemporary cities more dangerous than smaller rural places, but the crime in them is more visible. A forest with brigands still looks good; drunken bandits carousing in the woods will attract no notice. But urban disorder, especially when the disorderly are poor people who act out in public rather than indoors, has a special character. Public places, with disorderly or threatening people present, lose their liberty in a sense, particularly for the weak or vulnerable. Consequently, public crime and disorder result in places dominated by young males; in the last third of the twentieth century, this has driven public urban life to the private sector, shopping malls in particular.

Even if cities are not crime incubators, they have become the places for crime, and the quality of present-day American urban life has been diminished sharply as a result.

15

The Power of "Excuse Me"

As good manners moved from the court to countryside, violence steadily
declined for five centuries. Will a dose of old-fashioned etiquette make cities
less dangerous today?

Mayor Rudolph W. Giuliani of New York City wants schools to teach civility
and all citizens to behave less rudely. No doubt, before his campaign ends, this
will all come back to haunt him, especially if he loses his temper. As for civility
on the city's streets, there is no way to go but up. Yet, Giuliani will probably be
criticized by those who say manners are trivial compared with the big issues.

Surprisingly, the mayor has history on his side, especially if we consider the
big sweep of Western civilization. Anger control and violent responses are culturally and historically determined. In his unusual two-volume book *The Civilizing Process,* sociologist Norbert Elias was the first to link the rise of manners
and the rise of the state. His ideas seemed preposterous: could his study of such
things as one use of the fork really be serious?

Elias tied table manners, body posture, and small bits of daily behavior to
the rise of centralized monarchies and, ultimately, the bureaucratic state. He
showed how apparently different realms—kings and table manners—attached
together. For example, rather than stab meat from the center of the table with
their own knife, those at court learned to take turns and use a fork. The king's
power at court required an orderly crowd who could pay attention and not turn
a meal into a grab fest. Taking turns required patience and self-restraint. It still
does. The power of the state began to shape the most basic human actions.

First published in the *Los Angeles Times,* March 8, 1998.

This issue is still urgent. Stateless societies are usually violent ones, whether frontiers, cities in disarray, or nations in collapse.

Many historians and sociologists now believe that the long history of manners in Western society, and the growth of the state indirectly propelling them, help account for a five-century decline in personal violence. The analysis goes like this: in the fourteenth and fifteenth centuries, monarchs took control of their courtiers by insisting on some simple rules of behavior at court. Don't hit. Eat with the fork, not with the knife (reduces violent fights at high table). Self-control, even in the way one greeted another or stood in a group, began at court. Hence: the word "courtesy." Thus began the slow spread of manners from court to countryside.

If this is correct, it suggests that stronger states would have less violence, and cities less than rural areas. This is exactly what historians of medieval crime have found. Lower rates of violence began in cities and spread to the countryside, both in England and on the Continent. Overall, bloody interpersonal violence declined from its high point in the Middle Ages as people began to depend on each other's predictable, nonviolent responses.

Rules of etiquette made courtly social relations less impulsive, and impulse is what usually led to violence. Impulse control, on the other hand, led to order. Am I the only one with the impulse to shoot a rude driver? Where did I learn to control such impulses? From an early age, we teach children to sit properly, not to interrupt, to take turns: This is how we learned impulse control. Courtiers learned these rules, too.

Manners can be imitated, and change can ripple through a society with often unexpected consequences. The medieval courtiers elaborating polite forms of greetings and early writers of etiquette manuals were not trying to reduce impulsive violence among peasants. *Romeo and Juliet* reminds us that personal violence once accompanied elite behavior.

If we all used Miss Manners as our guide to human relations, wouldn't we be better off? It is indeed true that rude interactions can lead to violence. Cut someone off on the freeway (a key late-twentieth-century form of rudeness), and they may shoot you. Presumably, if the shooters were never cut off, they wouldn't shoot. Or if they had a Miss Manners–trained response to slights, they might politely flash their lights and leave it be.

Imagine if every police-citizen interaction were governed by etiquette: the noncriminal would go away less offended and maybe even bad guys would learn how to treat others. Nice manners don't cost much and lower tensions between strangers as much as between friends.

The problem is that if Elias and the historians who have followed his lead are correct, manners are deeper than a few surface rules. They take centuries to permeate society. Indeed, manners go deep and shape an individual's self-concept, just as they go wide and relate to all members of a social system. Manners are both a consequence and a cause. The "civilizing process" reduced violence over a four-hundred-year period, not overnight.

And there certainly are some strong arguments against good manners, especially in America. Our nation has an ingrained suspicion that manners mask and deceive. We have a long-held demand for authenticity: we hate hypocrites and dissemblers.

This search for authenticity was evident in the nineteenth century. Mark Twain made us see the moral superiority of Huck Finn and Jim, both bereft of the Victorian veneer of good manners. Huck apologized for his honesty and authenticity. He felt bad that he couldn't live up to the hypocritical rules and superficial politeness of the do-gooders trying to save him.

Today, schools of pop psychologists teach us how to declare our true feelings, how to overcome the false smiles implied in courteous behavior.

Another problem is that the content of good manners makes a huge difference. Following social rules can lead as surely toward violence as away from it. In the late nineteenth century, some of the highest murder rates in the United States were probably among the most polite Americans: white Southerners. The gloss of good behavior could turn a simple slight into a deadly confrontation.

One of the most infamous bludgeonings in U.S. history did not occur at Florence or Normandy but on the floor of the U.S. Senate, in 1856, when Senator Preston Brooks of South Carolina beat Senator Charles Sumner of Massachusetts unconscious with the metal end of his cane. Brooks came up behind Sumner, who was seated at his desk, and attacked without warning. This all followed prescribed rules of gentlemanly behavior, for in an anti-slavery speech, Sumner had insulted Brooks's uncle in such a way that a duel was not called for. Sumner was an invalid for three years.

Slights and insults can be turned into murder if the rules of etiquette guide them that way. In *All God's Children,* Fox Butterfield relates how Senator Strom Thurmond's father, the South Carolina state prosecutor, shot a drunken salesman who walked into his office. He had called Thurmond a "scoundrel" and, according to etiquette, that insult merited a lethal comeback. No wonder Southerners were polite to one another. The fragile veneer of good manners overlaid weak, almost nonexistent states that depended on the slaveholders' violence for stability. No etiquette could fix that.

Contrast this southern code of manners to the infamously blunt, laconic, and unfriendly Yankee. Randolph Roth, the leading historian of New England violence for the nineteenth and early twentieth centuries, has had to work hard to explain why this region has so little violence. He has too few murders to study. One wouldn't turn to New England for etiquette lessons but, on the other hand, no one will kill you if you say the wrong thing.

Apparently, these regional differences are more than stereotypes. Psychologists Robert Nisbett and Dov Cohn have done a fascinating experiment with college students, comparing the reactions and testosterone levels of young men subjected to unexpected and unreasonably rude behavior. Those from the South have a rise in testosterone and anger levels, while those from the North laugh off the intrusion. Could these culturally ingrained ways of dealing with anger and slights explain why Georgia had a white murder rate nearly three times that of Massachusetts in 1995?

So the expectation that polite and predictable behavior—"after you," "I'm sorry," "pass the salt, please," "you're welcome"—will give social interactions the sanity, tolerance, and safety that everyone wants has some flaws. Courtesy must reflect an individual's inner self or the superficial veneer can lead one down the path to bloody confrontation. We have to actually mean, "Excuse me."

Giuliani's idea is a good one—and cheap, too. If New York's mayor succeeds, we can hope that having tried civility, everyone will like it and keep at it. But for this to happen, mayors and council members everywhere will have to mind their manners, to provide a solid government presence so we can see them. That may lead, over the long term, to the good behavior that can make all lives more pleasant, less stressful, and safer.

16

Nineteenth-Century Institutions: Dealing with the Urban "Underclass"

American cities created a wide range of ad hoc responses to the social problems that they made visible. From free medical care to public baths to orphanages, individuals, groups, and governments dotted the urban landscape with buildings to help the needy. We have forgotten many of these, and many, when remembered, are remembered only in a negative way. Orphanages, for example, have been the lightning rod of ideology and blame; yet the historians who study them discover places softer, more reliable, and less vicious than we now imagine. They also discover a long-gone world, where the physical and organizational structures dealt with the consequences of poverty, unemployment, and lack of social security and welfare provision now taken for granted.

For example, orphanages had a large proportion of "half orphans," meaning children with one parent. This category has disappeared with the rise of various welfare services, foster parenting, and simple, high real incomes for the poor. Or, public baths: a great idea, but the easier solution was a rising real income which made indoor plumbing common.

This essay emphasizes the creativity that this landscape represented and points out some of its advantages: highly visible, this architecturally ordered welfare system was probably much easier for the illiterate and non-English-

First published in Michael Katz, ed., *The "Underclass" Debate* (Princeton, N.J.: Princeton University Press, 1992). I wish to thank Robert Fogelson, Joan Waugh, Bruce Schulman, Sanford Jacoby, Julie Szende, Robin Einhorn, Daniel Scott Smith, and Thomas C. Clark for their comments and suggestions. Also, I wish to thank Michael Katz and the members of the SSRC staff and study group on the history of the underclass for their comments and suggestions. And in particular, I wish to thank Bruce C. Bellingham for his extensive remarks.

speaking populace, especially when contrasted to the bureaucratic nightmare of modern welfare.

*   *   *

Forty thousand vagrant children . . . in the dens and stews of the city . . . are driven from their vile homes to pick rags and cinders, collect bones, and steal. As they grow up they swell the ranks of the dangerous classes. To rescue them . . . they are made clean, are clad comfortably, and learn to sing the sweet songs about the Savior and the better land. They owe their deliverance from disgrace and shame to the outstretched arms of these Missions.[1]

We have lost many of the nineteenth century's institutions that dealt with the urban poor. It was a world at once cruel and ineffective, rich and complex. It locked blind children in the same room with deranged criminals. It tolerated starvation.[2] Yet it could be simple, direct, and unbound by rules. It located non-bureaucratic custodial child care right where parents needed it, gave out overnight lodging to the homeless in each police precinct station house, offered the poor free baths.

This world differed most dramatically from ours in the face it presented: a very visible face of large, well-made buildings, buildings of which the most prominent city dwellers were proud. On the one hand, the faith that social reformers placed in these buildings and their programs to us seems astonishingly naive, on occasion cruel. Their physical layouts deliberately forced the poor into inappropriate molds, splitting up families, mixing the criminal with the abandoned, and somehow expecting the internal lockstep discipline to translate to social change. Almost as soon as they were built, almshouses and reform institutions became targets of crusading reformers, who exposed their internal cruelties and inadequacies.

Yet on the other hand, these efforts challenge us, for our predecessors took pride in their ways of dealing with social inequality. And few Americans today would point to their welfare system with pride. In addition, there may have been an unplanned advantage to this system of aid and control, for it emanated from easily identified buildings scattered across the landscape. Their visibility and location made them an accessible part of a community in a way that we have lost.[3]

Historians have overlooked the most striking difference between the nineteenth and twentieth centuries' worlds of urban poverty. That we have done so is itself testimony to the nature of the transformation: in looking back at a very different world, we are able only to look for what we can understand, for the familiar. We have not looked at the physical manifestation of that world, at the literally thousands of poorhouses, dispensaries, orphanages, police stations, jails, settlement houses, Magdalene houses, lodging houses, wayfarers' homes, and kindred institutions, all showing their imposing facades to city dwellers.

These facades—"handsome buildings," as their builders termed them—formed an integral part of nineteenth-century cities, cities whose architectural features could be absorbed at a much slower and more intimate pace than can most of today's cities. In contrast with today, the social-welfare and social-control apparatus of the nineteenth century was visible, comprehensible, and physically accessible in a way that we can no longer imagine; it is no wonder that historians have themselves neglected this.

Although we have forgotten the complex and varied nineteenth-century institutions that dealt with the urban underclass, their heritage is still invisibly with us.[4] We have built our current systems either directly from them or in direct rejection of them: in either case, history governs our policies with a heavy hand. The nineteenth-century beginnings and subsequent transformations of these institutions have been of significant importance in shaping the way in which we deal with the urban underclass today. Institutions that deal with the urban underclass can be grasped only by locating them in the context of their historical transformations.

If there is a pattern to this institutional tangle of branches and stems, it is that of a shift from a few kinds of organizations dealing with many kinds of people to many kinds of organizations dealing with narrower ranges of people. This long shift has resulted in the confusing welter of organizations today, but the underlying logic has been to narrow the kinds of problem people any one organziation treats. The consequence, from the individual's viewpoint, is a complex bureaucratic world: from the bureaucratic viewpoint, the outcome has been a narrowing of particular function and a more specific kind of treatment or aid regime.

More to the point, this institutional world of the nineteenth century differed from ours in a way somewhat difficult to comprehend: it was much more physically visible. Today cultural historians talk about "reading" buildings, by which they mean that the visual and spatial and material aspects of buildings can supply a communicative discourse to the properly accelerated "reader." That was precisely what happened in the nineteenth century, when the poor and needy could easily "read" the buildings about them. What they read led them directly to help. The difference with our day is dramatic: then a tramp on the brink of starvation could ask, "Where is the police station?" or "Where is the poorhouse?" and expect to walk or be carried there. Today, as Joel Handler and others have amply documented, even the simplest emergency aid requires that the needy person find a General Relief office of the county welfare system, which in turn will give the person vouchers for meals and housing. The difference now is that the physical location is a low-visibility office building that gives only pieces of paper. Nineteenth-century places of aid were highly visible, in fact, were often architectural high points, and directly gave aid, then and there (see Figure 16.1). It takes an able person to be needy today.[5]

209

An abbreviated description of police functions can give a sense of this transition from the nineteenth century to the twentieth. At the time of the Civil War, a police department consisted of uniformed police officers but had no detectives. In addition to accommodating patrol and arrest activities, the station house had separate rooms to house the homeless overnight, and the patrol officers also reported dangerous boilers and overflowing sewers, rounded up stray animals and lost children. By the 1890s, police matrons tended the children and also oversaw the women lodgers. Separate divisions of the city's bureaucracy treated the roving animals, the sewers, and boilers. Policing of crime had grown more complex, with detectives now in charge of investigating serious offenses, bicycle patrols aggressively chasing down offenders, and a telegraph system allowing officers to contact the station houses. In another twenty years, the lodgers were gone from the station houses, and police chiefs had a professional organization. While the police organization was more complex, it covered far fewer functions, and each of the discarded activities now had a separate bureaucracy.

Figure 16.1 Tramps Being Booked for Lodging or Vagrancy, Hartford, 1895. This photo, from the rich collection of tramp scholar John J. McCook, shows men whose names are being entered on the police "blotter." McCook's interest was in what caused tramping: he was one of the first to proclaim that it had its roots in unemployment. The men pictured here were laborers, cooks, and former saloon keepers. They wear many layers of clothing. By April, when this picture was taken, most tramps no longer stayed in police stations but slept in other, less restrictive shelters, in this case, a local barn. *Source:* J. J. McCook. Photographer, Mr. Wadsworth. (Courtesy Butler-McCook Homestead Corporation, Antiquarian and Landmark Society, Inc.)

PAYING FOR THE POOR

"But," says the objector, "this would cost something." So do our houses of correction, police courts, and jails. . . . Is it not more humane and wise to *prevent* crime than to *punish* it?[6]

From the colonial period, the welfare structure of U.S. cities inherited a tradition of blending the public and the private. There had always been a willingness to allow private groups or individuals to accomplish public responsibilities. Thus budgets show monies or in-kind payments to individuals for taking care of the sick poor or the invalid, or to large institutions for that part of the program taking care of a public obligation. Although local taxes, mainly on property, provided the funding for the operating costs of local institutions, circumstances varied considerably from place to place. The cash outlays can be relatively well documented, for they were the most visible form of public tax accounting and were usually required by law. But variation and ambiguity occurred with other important forms of local support. The picture is least ambiguous for schools, which, by the early decades of the nineteenth century, had become "public" in our contemporary sense of blending both "ownership" and "control." The Northwest Ordinance (1795) set aside public lands for schools, county buildings, and welfare-related institutions, thus establishing a template for the future.[7]

Most states, either through legislation or their constitutions, enabled local governments to care for the poor and to catch and punish criminals by using land as an asset, with construction and operating costs coming from taxation. Cities often followed the same model, introducing even more variety and freely mixing private and public funding and land subsidies. For instance, by 1841, New York City spent 3 percent of its teaching budget for instruction in private orphan asylums and granted them buildings and grounds.[8] Until 1935, a viable alternative to the model of local public support for local public and private institutions did not really exist. In an ironic twist of enduring significance, the United States, under its very modern Constitution, continued to operate a local welfare system based on the Elizabethan Poor Law, rather than on the much less localist New Poor Law of 1832, simply because the Revolution had come prior to parliamentary modernization.[9]

URBAN INSTITUTIONS

Uniformity in the states relative to public charity does not exist. Each state has evolved its system, or rather a lack of a system, by a slow process.[10]

Nineteenth-century cities inherited from the colonial era two institutional forms dealing with those who would soon be called the "dangerous class"—the criminal justice system of constables and jails, and the relief system, including the almshouse in bigger cities or straightforward outdoor relief in smaller ones.[11] This limited array of institutions reflected in part the more intimate scale of colonial society but also the more attenuated colonial state.

The period from 1830 to 1890 saw vigorous institution building on the local level by private and public groups. Chronologically, these included orphanages, various institutions for women, police departments, newsboys' lodging houses, armories, settlement houses, and an early social-work system. Structurally, the shift was to move the institutions and institutional funding away from the local to the state and federal: this was an uneven and incomplete shift, so that traces of the local remain in the federal.

After 1890, the urban locus of reform activity began to shift to the county and, more especially, to the states. Urban variety and inconsistency frustrated reformers who wished to use higher levels of government to ensure more rational bureaucracies and more consistent institutional forms. Thus the period from 1890 to 1930 was one of increased rationalization and coordination as the multiple organizations were gathered into state and county governments.[12]

Almost all local revenues came from property taxes, and home owners defaulted on tax payments in the Depression. Shortages of cash and credit exacerbated this revenue problem for cities, over three thousand of which went into default after the banks temporarily closed in the Bank Holiday of 1933. Compounding the stress already felt by relief organizations, the Depression's tax crisis caused the near fiscal collapse of most state and local organizations. By the third decade of the twentieth century, the previous century's heavy programmatic emphasis on infrastructure already had begun to shift toward experts, bureaucracies, and intensive treatments involving "outdoor relief." Thus the fiscal crisis precipitously capped a longer underlying transition away from local welfare, moving the United States permanently into the era of the nation-state. Although police remained tied to local government through this crisis, they were affected too: the FBI actually created the Uniform Crime Reports in 1930, possibly the single most centralizing action on local police to date.[13]

This dense web of buildings and land dedicated to helping or reforming the poor, from the poor farms on the outskirts of nearly every county seat to the rooms set aside for lodgers in police stations, gave a physical and symbolic presence to the local state that we have a hard time imagining now. Their monumental quality has been interpreted by many historians as representing the intimidating force of the state. My interpretation differs for several reasons. First, as illustrated by Rothman, who wished to contrast the cottagelike earlier buildings with the post-1830 buildings, any actual scaling of figures in the foreground to the pictured buildings in the background demonstrates that in all cases the artists dramatically exaggerated building sizes, giving them fifteen-foot doors and preposterous external dimensions.[14] This exaggeration suggests that both the early buildings as well as later ones were often pictured as grand achievements of local government.

We know about the appearance of mid-nineteenth-century institutions because they appeared so often in the promotional/descriptive/historical local literary genre so popular in the late nineteenth century. The boosters who wrote this literature about a city or region tried to give positive assessments in order to attract people and business. Odd as it may sound now, a handsome new poorhouse qualified as one of a city's positive features. For example, Jacob H. Studer's *Columbus, Ohio: Its History, Resources, and Progress* (1873), a typical boosterish history and promotional book, includes with the engravings of the city's markets, parks, commercial blocks, churches, schools, banks and the architect's rendering of the new poorhouse (Franklin County Infirmary—today, the Alum Creek Manor). Studer narrates a brief history of the institution, details the purchase of a new tract by the county commissioners just outside the Columbus city limits for seventeen thousand dollars, and elaborates on the plans for this impressive structure. He represents the building to impress the outside world with Columbus's achievements, not to terrify the poorhouse's inmates. These buildings are still with us, usually transformed by additions, facelifts, and new, friendlier names (see Figure 16.2).

OUTDOOR RELIEF AND ALMSHOUSES

> Needless burdens are imposed on the public by indiscriminate giving to the poor, or a possible perversion of the fund to other purposes than those contemplated by the law.[15]

Smaller cities and towns often relied upon outdoor relief in the colonial period. One must be careful in drawing too precisely the distinction between indoor and outdoor relief, for poor farms and almshouses sometimes, counter to their rules, gave outdoor relief. Moreover, city size or degree of urbanization did not prove determinative of relief forms, for by the end of the nineteenth century, many southern rural counties had their poor farms. Outdoor relief was more fiscally visible than relief administered through fixed real property: city and village accounting called for the listing of cash and in-kind payments. In addition, corrupt municipal politicians could funnel outdoor relief to party supporters (of course, they could funnel jobs in the institutions to party supporters, too).

This inherent visibility helps account for a turn away from the principle of outdoor relief, for it appeared every month, quarter, and year as a drain on the cash resources of local government. Why not change the people taking these payments rather than continually fund them? The underlying notion became one

Figure 16.2 View of Columbus Poor House, about Two Miles from the State Capitol. By this time, the poorhouses in Ohio had been officially renamed infirmaries, capturing the reality that so many inmates were ill as well as poor. This institution's replacement, Alum Creek Manor, is now the county nursing home. This view of the new building is included in local publisher Jacob Studer's promotional *Columbus, Ohio: Its History, Resources, and Progress* (1873). The end papers of the book included advertisements for local businesses—including insurance, coal, and railroad companies—suggesting the pride the city elite took in its institutions, including those of the poor.

of malleable individuals passing on to their children their inadequacies; once cured, their social defects would be eliminated and the problem eradicated for ever. The response became poorhouses. Starting in the 1830s, state governments began to rewrite (or write for the first time) laws covering the poor, mandating that every county have a poor farm.[16] States just writing their constitutions at the time included such features in their new governments.[17] Thus the responsibility shifted from the town to the county. For approximately one hundred years, then, the county poorhouse was the single broadest and most inclusive institution for the poor.

The poorhouse, as ubiquitous in local government's political landscape as the courthouse, stood at once as a dread symbol of the life of the unsupported and unattached and, simultaneously, as a place for reform. Outdoor relief was suspect throughout the nineteenth century, whether because it could be subverted for corrupt partisan political purposes or because it could be imagined as an income supplement going unearned. In an era and nation with a firm political commitment to education, such an analysis could make ground: the control possible in the poorhouse offered a location for such mechanisms of change. Thus the factory model of the poorhouse, which tried to reap a profit from the labor of the inmates, and the individual reform or educational approach of the early nineteenth century provided a positive alternative to constant local budget drains. And the principal urban institution dealing with the poor—straightforward relief—suffered continual ideological and fiscal attack throughout the nineteenth century. When charity reformer groups such as the Charity Organization Societies argued for a reform of the whole diverse welfare system, so that a thorough scrubbing of society of its inadequate could be accomplished, they usually identified outdoor relief as a problem, leaving some form of indoor relief as a solution.[18]

Whether called poor farms, infirmaries, or almshouses, these institutions sheltered a variety of dependent people for long periods of time, while often dispensing outdoor relief or temporary overnight shelter.[19] Although these institutions were not intended for the "undeserving poor," for instance, prostitutes and thieves, they often ended up aiding such people. They took in those without personal resources or family members able or willing to help. And on occasion, from the eighteenth to the nineteenth centuries, judges sentenced criminal offenders to the poorhouse, an action reformers often complained about.[20]

In essence, the apparently specialized institutions actually served multiple functions, in part because there were so few structures of any kind to which governments had access. (This is why city market houses sometimes contained a jail cell.) Thus their functional capacity was partially related to their buildings, their infrastructure, but also to their mechanism for funneling aid or punishment on an ad hoc basis.

On occasion, cities tried to reform as well as to warehouse, which in practice usually meant setting the inmates to work. Boston began as early as 1702 "To sett and keep the poor people and Ill persons at work" in the almshouse.[21] Later, the Boston Workhouse (1739), followed by a "Manufactory" (1750), kept the poor spinning and weaving. New York City inaugurated its workhouse in 1736; Philadelphia, its "bettering house" in 1766.[22] They were all modeled on the much earlier workhouses in Amsterdam, where the women spun and the men rasped wood into ship-caulking material.[23] These factories for the poor dated back to the sixteenth century in Europe, and their introduction to North America represented no uniquely American spirit of reform or repression.

By 1827, the Boston poorhouse was formally known as the House of Industry; its genuine industriousness may be sensed by what the residents actually did. Of its 408 inmates, 28 percent were children and 29 percent were too sick to work; nearly 60 percent, in other words, could not be asked to work. Twenty-five percent of the able men picked oakum (that is, picked apart tarred rope to create a sticky, fibrous mass which could be used for caulking ships) or did unskilled labor, and 30 percent of the women spun or worked in the kitchen. The remainder worked at various other tasks. The oakum pickers produced forty dollars a year apiece in oakum, not nearly so much as the nearly one hundred dollars per year of farm products generated per worker.[24]

The end to the poorhouse can be dated with some precision to 1935, the middle of the Depression, a time when one might expect the poorhouses to have been bulging.[25] By 1935, many of the children, the insane, and the retarded were no longer in poorhouses, which contained principally the poor aged. The federal Old Age Assistance Program of 1935, part of the Social Security Act, began to give direct monthly grants to needy persons over sixty-five who did not live in public institutions. Counties acted quickly to establish welfare boards to administer the funds. In some states, as the old moved out of poorhouses, other destitutes moved in. "Governors may tell the world that they have 'abolished' the 'poorhouse' when they sign old age assistance bills, but a small cash pension, which cannot buy medical and nursing care, does not answer the need of hundreds of aged persons today."[26] In Minnesota, for example, some counties sold their poorhouses, while others leased theirs to private individuals. In this way, the county retained control. The change in ownership patterns then brought about new names: the Dodge County poor farm became the Fairview Rest Home.[27]

Many of the issues, patterns, and problems associated with the almshouse paradigm have persisted until today, and it is very difficult to study them without a sense that nothing has changed. But, indeed, there have been significant alterations. The perception of outdoor relief, the granting of assistance to people in their own homes, slowly shifted from that of a vice which nineteenth-century policy tried to eliminate to that of a virtue in the Progressive Era. In other words, in the mid-nineteenth century, reformers thought that aid to the poor had to be given in an institutional setting where the poor, as captains of their own fates, could be taught new ways of living. As the analysis of poverty changed, reformers challenged the institutional reform mission; by the early twentieth century, preservation of the nuclear family became the reform goal. The sad practice of lumping together all sorts of people in need has diminished with the provision of broader aid to the elderly and the ill. On the other hand, the sense in the nineteenth century that the very poor and dependent somehow trapped their children into repeating their lives has come back as a major social belief. In the nineteenth century, this outcome was understood as a result of mixing different kinds of people in the almshouses. Later in the nineteenth and well into the twentieth century, the notion that genetic patterns propagated the poor and criminal gave seemingly scientific grounds for separating different kinds of needy people: promiscuous "mixing" could lead to more genetically defective children.[28] Thus, from the visible evidence confronting almshouse managers— that is, people of inappropriate kinds and conditions grouped in forced social arrangements—a simple explanation for a range of human ills began. The almshouse and its mutations functioned then to provide an explanation as well as accommodation.

An important exception to the mixing of people in the poorhouse was race: fragmentary evidence suggests that early in the nineteenth century, poorhouse officials racially segregated occupants, occasionally defining Irish as a race.[29] In the post–Civil War South, blacks appear to have been excluded from state institutions except in the most desperate situations. Jails were segregated, and cities in which police did take black lodgers, kept separate facilities.[30] From the point of view of African Americans, racial segregation might have been preferable to what appears to have been simple exclusion in many locations. In the post-bellum South, for instance, poorhouse occupants appear to have been mainly white, which clearly indicates that poor, disabled, or very sick black people were simply excluded from even the minimal aid of the poorhouse.[31] This exclusion raises several as yet unresearched questions about social structure and institutional intervention: What was the regional pattern of black exclusion from state institutions? What were the differential impacts of this exclusion, comparing, for instance, blacks and the Irish or, later in the nineteenth century, other very poor white groups? Did the "indiscriminate" mixing of children with derelicts in poorhouses harm them more than the black children's exclusion from all aid?

HOSPITALS AND DISPENSARIES

> In our best communities, the almshouse today is recognized as an infirmary and hospital.[32]

If the poorhouse is no longer a visible part of the urban scene, the hospital, in particular the hospital for the urban poor, still is. It may in fact be the one exception to the greater trend away from large institutional settings. Illness has always been a constant and dangerous companion of the poor. For families paying rent by the week and buying food daily, illness and disease were more instantly threatening than unemployment. Narratives of the lives of the poor are always punctuated by episodes of illness.[33]

While the big-city hospital did very often provide the place of last resort for the nineteenth-century urban poor, they were far more likely to seek treatment at the poorhouse (or infirmary) or dispensaries.[34] Intended to be the major form of medical care for the "industrious poor," dispensaries treated a vast range of ailments.[35] An institution originating in England and Europe, the dispensary spread across the United States from the late eighteenth century onward, declining in favor of the hospital outpatient clinic only in the early twentieth century. Again, these institutions were highly visible urban establishments, dispersed throughout larger cities in prominent if smaller buildings. Unlike the publicly funded hospitals, early dispensaries were formed with a combination of private and public monies. In 1830, for example, the New York City Dispensary had 40 percent city funding.[36] They were quite dispersed throughout the city by the late nineteenth century; New York City had 29 (1874) and Philadelphia 33 (1877), but an exact account has been elusive thus far (see Figure 16.3).[37]

From our point of view, the dispensary, in particular one that emphasized preventative medicine, seems like a logical and reasonable way to get health care to the poor at a point prior to the person's need for hospitalization.[38] The demise of the dispensary and its replacement by the large central hospital with an emergency room providing almost all treatment for the urban poor came about in the first decades of the twentieth century. The shift had very little to do with the medical needs of the poor. Instead, the nature of the medical profession allocated prestige and research principally to doctors practicing in large hospitals. Medical training, too, spliced its need for students' patients (the poor) with the location of research in the central hospital: the outcome—medical care for the poor at one place in most cities, the emergency room of the central training hospital.

BATHS

Three years ago the Amelia Street School introduced a bath tub.[39]

The poor in cities had neither bathtubs nor hot water, and the New York Association for Improving the Condition of the Poor had as early as 1852 built the People's Bathing and Washing Establishment. It closed nine years later, no doubt because the Lower East Side residents could not afford to use it. Bathing, that is, in swimming pools, came to American cities between 1865 and 1885, with public baths for the purpose of cleanliness not arriving until the 1890s. Public baths, another imported idea, spread across U.S. cities in the early twentieth century. As cleanliness became a virtue in the mid-nineteenth century, access came to be seen as an access to virtue. Like other reform institutions, the baths were in elegant-looking buildings, buildings that belied their rather humble purposes. New York State in 1895 required all cities with a population over 50,000 to provide free public baths.[40] Of course, they disappeared as rising real incomes turned into plumbing and bathtubs in the mid-twentieth century. More than providing cleanliness, however, public baths may have actually accomplished a significant life-saving purpose by making it unnecessary for poor city residents to bathe in rivers and harbors.[41]

JAILS

It is universally agreed by students of penology that the county jail system of the United States is bad.[42]

Figure 16.3 View of New York City's Central Dispensary. Appearing in the *Manual of the Corporation of the City of New York* for 1870, the descriptive paragraph which followed explained that "a large portion of the Dispensary district is thickly covered with a shanty population, and these unfortunate people are, as a rule, extremely poor and improvident; so that should the head of the family be taken sick, the entire household at once suffer for the very necessaries of life. . . . It is undoubtedly not only a matter of charity to the unfortunate, but also wise political economy, to restore such people to health as soon as possible" (371). The numerous views in the *Manual* suggest that those institutions designed for "fallen" women were more modest in their facades and lacked signage.

Probably the most famous jail of the nineteenth century was New York City's Tombs Prison, so named because of its Egyptian revival architecture. Its popular name—"The Tombs"—says all that need be said about the U.S. jail, for people put there were and are less likely to be targeted for programmatic attention than are people in almost any other institutional setting. We must keep in mind that prior to the creation of separate institutions, jails held the insane (as they do once again), that police handled a range of welfare activities, and that prostitute reform involved family counseling and child care. Just as the scope of the orphanage included juvenile offenders, so jails took in orphans.

Jails have never aroused the same ideological contestation that poorhouses did, for they had been purposely built to punish and detain, not to shelter and reform. Local governments designed city and county jails to house those accused of crimes, offenders serving short sentences for non-felony crimes, witnesses who might bolt, persons lacking sufficient self-control to be put in the poor-house (the insane), and, after the creation of the uniformed police, occasional tramps. Even today, jails stil serve no ostensible punishment, reform, or treatment goal. As long as the inmates do not die and do appear at the correct place at the correct time, jails are considered functional. Always and still administered by local governments, jails continue to have a deservedly terrible reputation. This derives from their purpose: custody and mild punishment.

For as long as outside observers have visited them, jails have been over-crowded and have mixed the seriously deviant with nondeviant people. (Empty jails do not get reported or commented on, as they are never newsworthy.) In essence, jails cannot work well: they hold people against their will, including those who may not deserve to be there. In administering the jail, local government has a thankless task, and its response has never been satisfactory. Jails have slowly narrowed their inmate mix by removing children, the insane, the sick, the homeless, witnesses to crimes, and otherwise dependent, noncriminal populations. Yet even this may be changing: recent reports of jails holding more mentally ill than other institutions do have appeared in the media.[43]

It is of interest and importance that of all local institutions dealing with the underclass, jails were least affected by the Depression and New Deal programs. Only more recently have the combined efforts of the federal government and inmate lawsuits begun to seriously challenge these known jail deficiencies. Regular federal surveys of jail suicides, for instance, have highlighted inadequate prisoner protection, especially for juveniles. Even this way of measuring jail treatment—by its lack of violence—highlights the peculiarly custodial and neutral role of jails.

Although jails organizationally belong more often to the county than to the city, physically and functionally they are tied to the police, a city organization. For about a fifty-year period, 1870–1920, there was an intermediary functional and physical institution between the two, the police station lodging house. Now gone and forgotten, this institution filled an important service gap, taking in the destitute for overnight shelter. But the proper context for understanding lodging is that of the police.

THE POLICE

Why not create an efficient police?[44]

Of course, the major institution interacting with the poor and criminal offenders was and still is the police. The nature and quality of the police and the structure of their public interaction have changed dramatically over the past two centuries. The United States is unique in its form of independent yet highly dependent local government, and the police are a key part of this political organization. City governments are creatures of state government; they are a privilege created by state constitutions and laws, with no status beyond that. The police organizations of the United States were copied from the London Metropolitan Police (1829), itself modeled on the Royal Irish Constabulary. The police were created for multiple reasons, but the principal resistance to their initial creation came from stingy city councils, for the system that they replaced took no tax dollars, but ran on fees. This system, referred to as the *constable watch system,* echoed directly early medieval police. The night watch was essentially a guard service; the constables arrested people, served warrants, and performed other tasks for courts, civil and criminal.

Lack of systematic patrol and policing led many urban dwellers to use lower criminal courts and justices of the peace to prosecute criminal offenders.[45] In these ward-based courts, crimes and misdemeanors were prosecuted on the initiative of the victims. Evidence suggests that the volume of prosecutions was considerably greater than in the subsequent police system. Of particular significance is evidence that the police were introduced, among other reasons, to reduce the numbers of privately originated criminal prosecutions, in part because some of the cases were frivolous and corrupt, and in part because there were just too many of them.

Originators of the new police specifically designed them to be preventative, to stop crime before it happened. Uniforms made them more visible to the public and to their supervising officers. Introduced with some fits and starts (New York City's police did not stay a consistent organization until after 1853), police departments spread to most major cities by the 1880s. They were not expected to do the other non-crime-related activities that they immediately took on, however. Almost instantly they were taking lost children to the station houses, checking for open sewers and roving livestock, and putting up homeless wanderers and tramps overnight. While women did not appear on patrol until the very end of the nineteenth century, they were quickly hired to be matrons in the rooms for lost children and in the dormitory rooms for women "lodgers," and even to help reform "vicious" women and girls.[46] Patently unrelated to crime control, police station-house lodging became a massive activity in every city with a police department.

The police deserve special attention in order to highlight their role in housing the homeless, referred to in the nineteenth and early twentieth centuries as "lodgers." Lodging came under external criticism at the end of the nineteenth century because of its very nature: short term, with no questions asked. Like outdoor relief, lodging seemed to many Progressive Era reformers to accomplish the antithesis of quality aid: it made no demands on those lodged, taught them no moral or fiscal lessons, and made it possible for the lazy to survive. As a substitute, urban reformers created municipal lodging houses, which provided overnight beds but for a price—delousing and chemical disinfectant baths and usually a "work test," which involved chopping wood or breaking up rocks. Because the wood-lot tasks took place in the early morning, the tramps who depended on getting to early morning hiring points for day laborers avoided the municipal lodging houses, preferring to sleep outdoors or to try to get in at police stations. As police slowly went out of the lodging business after 1900, this service essentially disappeared, unless it was picked up by other private organizations like the Salvation Army. By the crisis of the Great Depression, most cities, when faced with thousands of homeless people, were at a loss, typically turning to armories for housing. New York even used its armories for daytime shelter in 1934. Robert Fogelson points out the irony of using for shelter a "structure designed to intimidate the 'dangerous classes,' not to accommodate them."[47]

Any analysis of the police must locate them in their city-government context. The police chief reports to the mayor; the city council determines their budget; property taxes provide the revenue. Police deal with offenders more than any other criminal justice organization does. But unlike most other organizations dealing with poor people or offenders, police do not have a long-term responsibility toward individuals; they deal with them only prior to and including their arrest, but not afterward. In addition, potentially violent force underlies police actions. Consequently, police/individual relationships are asymmetric and tense. The communities that need and want the police the most are usually at the same time the most hostile. The police are visible and accessible symbols of bad news. They represent the state in an inevitably distasteful and conflicted way.

As an additional constraint, policing remains labor intensive, with few technological substitutes to increase productivity, and stressful. Police are primarily present at the actual point of crisis, of failure, of victimization. But in any policy considerations, we must continue to include the police, to comprehend the particular constraints upon their role, to reconsider their historic role and presence in poor communities, and to think creatively about using them as a positive social force.

OTHER DEPENDENCY-DRIVEN INSTITUTIONS

At a Place called "Long Island Farms," not far from the city of New York, there are 1200 once abandoned children, who were picked up in the vilest portions of that great metropolis, and are now supported and educated at the public expense. . . . Ohio takes criminal parents and locks them in jail, while the children wander about the streets, sleep under carts, in door yards and haylofts, and furnish themselves the means of sustenance by theft.[48]

The process of separating the dissimilar groups of people in poorhouses began to accelerate in the early nineteenth century with orphanages leading the way.[49] As in the case of the poorhouse and other forms of care and control, the orphanage had a long tradition in Europe, where the institution accomplished a broad range of functions, everything from providing the church with young recruits to supporting children of the urban bourgeoisie, as in the Amsterdam Burgerweeshuis.[50] Folks identifies the first public orphanage in the United States as that established by the city of Charleston in 1794.[51] Private orphanages predated this considerably; one was established in New Orleans in 1729, followed by one in Savannah in 1738.

From their beginning, orphanages tended to specialize, by religion, race, and ethnic origins. This specialization reflected the wishes of parents as much as it reflected social fissures. We have a sense of parents' wishes through the "half-orphanages," institutions that took in the children of poor one-parent families, and that often specialized by religion and ethnicity.[52] Parents often employed orphanages as strategic resources, leaving their children during times of economic stress, sometimes returning to reclaim the whole family.[53] Other times, they might leave one or two of their children in institutions in times of family need, removing them when they could.[54] Valentine's *Manual* for New York City (1864) lists the following orphanages, which indicates the institutional range of orphanage client populations: the Female Roman Catholic Orphan Asylum, the Roman Catholic Orphan Asylum for Boys, the Orphan Asylum, Orphan's Home Asylum, Protestant Half-Orphan Asylum, Leake and Watt's Orphan House and School, the House of Refuge, the New York Infirmary for Indigent Women and Children. (The Colored Orphan Asylum had been burned by this time, but it also had received some city subsidies, including its land.)

The outdoor relief equivalent of the orphanage was indenture, and in all probability, more children were indentured than housed in orphanages until perhaps the post–Civil War era. Related to indenture were the "orphan trains," which rounded up street children from the 1850s until the early twentieth century, sending them to rural areas in the West, where families shopped for them.[55] Cities also saw this marketing of children: in Boston until 1940, orphanage workers took children from parish to parish for church services, afterward lining them up for inspection by potential adopting families.[56]

The reform of almshouses contributed to the pressure on orphanages and foster homes; New York passed the first law forbidding the housing of children in almshouses in 1875, and other states followed suit. By 1910, when the data become most reliable, there were 1,151 orphanages in the United States, about 90 percent of which were private but that typically had considerable support from public sources.[57]

The disappearance of the orphanage followed state legislation creating "mothers' pensions" and New Deal legislation augmenting the state efforts. Illinois created the first such program to aid mothers in 1911, and by 1921 forty states had similar programs.[58] These programs supported poor mothers and sometimes fathers, and in turn kept them from being forced to give up their children as half-orphans. An additional factor in the decline came from a parallel decrease in family size and the number of children at risk; a parent's death in a large family put children at risk of entering an orphanage.[59] This decline in children at risk for the orphanage preceded the baby boom, which theoretically should have produced a similar orphan boom. But with declining institutional support, these orphans of the baby boom must have gone to adoptive and foster parents. The scenario is not well documented. For instance, the usual source for such information, *The Historical Statistics of the United States,* has no data on orphans or orphanages, and there is only one scholarly book on the subject, Holloran's *Boston's Wayward Children,* which for all its unique detail does not supply a time series. Figure 16.4 reproduces the best historical data.[60] These data make clear the trajectory of the orphanage as an institution, expanding until the New Deal, then virtually disappearing. Only very recently has there been the hint of a reversal, as forms of the orphanage return, one oriented toward children too old and independent to be placed in foster homes but too young to live on their own, and the other more of a group home.[61]

In the second half of the twentieth century, the foster home has replaced the orphanage. Foster homes represent, first, the rejection of the large institution as a preferred setting for child rearing.[62] Second, they substitute private care largely invisible to outside public scrutiny for the more visible treatment afforded by publicly funded institutions. The current crisis in foster care points to the dilemmas resulting from this transition. The foster-care system depends on a coordinating bureaucracy and a financial arrangement that in some ways resembles an older tradition of a private/public mix. The orphanage's near disappearance reflects the transition from a visible and accessible urban institution to an invisible bureaucracy. Did the presence of orphanages across the urban landscape make a meaningful, positive difference to urban life that we have not yet discovered?

NEWSBOYS' LODGING HOUSES

> The attention of the poor boys [to speeches by Judge Kirtland and Mssrs. Roosevelt and Howe at the Boys' Lodging House] who find a temporary home here is marked, evidencing that those gentlemen who take so kindly an interest in them are not laboring in vain.[63]

The newsboys' lodging houses were dormitories with plain furniture, open bunks, lockers, a clerk, and rounds of speech-making visitors. Their residents:

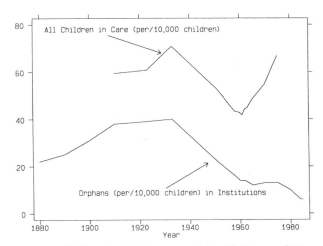

Figure 16.4 Children in Orphanages and in All Forms of Care, 1880–1985. *Source:* See note 60.

young boys who supported themselves by the "street trades."[64] For us in the twenty-first century, it is difficult to imagine the newsboys' lodging house, which starkly symbolizes the harshness of nineteenth-century urban life. The first, started in New York City in 1853, was, in fact, located on the third story of the *Sun* newspaper building. These institutions were charitable but not free dorms for boys who supported themselves. Their label, *newsboys* (or, alternatively, *street arabs*), indicates that they became common and visible with the introduction of the penny press in the 1830s. This new media depended on constant street sales; thus the boys and the press needed one another. The term *newsboy* was generic for children who slept in doorways and supported themselves by shining shoes, doing odd jobs, and selling the many daily newspapers.[65] What has been written about them is all cheerful and bright: plucky lads socializing around the warm stove in the evening and leading adventurous lives on the streets. But one fact should give us pause: Horatio Alger Jr., who gave us the quintessential and brilliant portrait of a newsboy in *Ragged Dick* (1868), had been evicted from his pastorate for sexually abusing young boys.[66] We have no idea about what went on in these or in other institutions that never showed a rent in their Victorian screen of sentimentality, and it may well be that Alger was an exception and no longer a child abuser when he worked in an institutional setting.[67]

We might use the newsboys' lodging house as a reminder: the second half of the nineteenth century permitted large numbers of children to live as self-supporting individuals, representing them as boy heroes through literary and journalistic portrayals.[68] Newsboys and their lodging houses served as transitional institutions between the orphanage and the streets; they were viable in an age that offered jobs to children. But they should serve to remind us of the shocking lack of social responsibility that obtained in our cities less than a century ago.

WAYFARERS' HOMES

All vagabondage has its origin in neglected childhood.[69]

Religious and charitable organizations created a range of institutions to deal with "little wanderers," which I cluster in this section. Like the newsboys' lodging houses, they took in children who were not in their families. Their creators had mixed humanitarian and social motives: rescuing children and preventing future criminality and poverty. Gender segregated, these included several organizations designed to prevent girls from becoming prostitutes or to reform the still malleable young prostitute, and yet others to deal with young boys, either the homeless or the young criminal offender. These homes were often local and usually specialized by race and religion. State governments also created a few such institutions, for instance, the Minnesota State Public School for Dependent and Neglected Children (1886), and the federal government funded state-level agencies for children of war veterans. The "Michigan system" removed all neglected children from poorhouses, providing a widely copied model for the centralized, nonlocal state care (including indenturing and foster-home placement) of children.[70] These institutions differed somewhat from the prototypical New York House of Refuge (1825), the first U.S. reform school for child offenders. The intent was the same, however: on the one hand rescuing children and on the other preventing their future criminality.[71]

All these institutions aimed at children administered heavy doses of moral teaching (and denominational preaching). The newsboys' lodging house taught the ethic of hard work and saving, encouraging the boys to build up individual bank accounts held by the superintendent. Thrift, usually aimed at keeping the boys out of the thriving street culture described by Stansell (1987), would bring them security; the lodging houses deliberately served dinner when popular theaters opened to keep the boys away from this costly entertainment. The theme of thrift echoed into the twentieth century as settlement houses (and schools) created similar banks. Their innovative significance has been overlooked, but working people had no access to savings banks, so the various "Penny Provident" funds actually were a new resource for the poor.

A related emphasis on order, both in daily routine and visual presentation, permeated this class of institutions. Photographs usually showed before-and-after pictures: the contrast the viewer was supposed to notice was in the disheveled, dark, and dirty clothes versus the white, starched, and somehow angelic clothes. Often the same institutional reports containing these images also printed the daily institutional schedule; again, in it, reformers made their message clear—order in presentation and daily activity. The contrast with what seemed to be the urban poor's daily life—a physically disordered environment and unpredictable, apparently impulsive, daily (and nightly) activities—was deliberate and dramatic. Since the early Middle Ages, the spread of the state has socialized people to become more orderly, less impulsive, and more predictable in social interactions. Some theorize that this emphasis on order, especially in the public schools, had a "civilizing" effect on urban immigrants, training them for the factory and indirectly suppressing opportunistic and random crime.[72] This broad similarity in internal organization and goals across varied child-saving institutions mirrored schooling, both public schools and Sunday schools, and we may conclude that for all the institutional variety, there was remarkable internal consistency in the institutional experiences of "at-risk" children in the nineteenth and early twentieth centuries.

Perhaps the most innovative of the child-saving institutions were the "junior republics," begun in the 1890s. They modeled themselves on republican virtues and on republican social and political organization in order to shelter and shape children. These institutions deliberately rejected the distinctions between delinquency and dependency: "any difference between the youthful criminal and the homeless youth was deceptive."[73] Yet in their goals and organizations, the best of these raised a new problem: did they really want to reproduce the larger society that had victimized the children? Ashby concludes that this question troubled them deeply, leading one reformer in 1926 to question "whether society, as it is, is worth reproducing."[74]

These histories reveal that while we have a long distance to go on care for children, it is quite easy to forget just how bad things were until very recently. For instance, a glance at Minehan's Depression classic, *Boy and Girl Tramps of America,* can serve to remind us that thousands of ten-year-old children in the Depression roamed the country looking for food. Some estimates run as high as 1.25 million homeless children.[75] There must be many seventy-year-olds today who spent a childhood of insecurity and desperation in their daily struggle to survive.

MAGDALENE HOUSES

> We have satisfactorily ascertained the fact that the numbers of females in this city, who abandon themselves to prostitution is not less than TEN THOUSAND!!!!! [which works out to about one woman in five][76]

Magdalene Houses deserve special attention for their role in actively dealing with prostitutes.[77] American Magdalene homes originated in mid-eighteenth-century England, where philanthropic homes at once protected and imprisoned fallen women.[78] In Boston, the City Missionary Society in 1822 founded the Penitent Females' Refuge, theoretically taking women who wished to escape prostitution. Hobson found evidence that no more than one inmate in six applied voluntarily and that most were informally sentenced or forced into the institution. In addition, she found that most ran away rather than formally asked for permission to leave. In any case, the institution was intended to shelter and reform its inmates in a more homelike setting than a jail or poorhouse—and the women got white bread instead of brown, as in the poorhouse.[79] Only slightly later, a similar Catholic institution came to American cities. Administered by the Sisters of the Good Shepherd, a French order, and called the House of the Good Shepherd, it occupied a similar niche in many American cities. The earliest included Louisville (1842), Philadelphia (1856), New York (1857), Chicago (1858), and Boston and six other cities by the end of the Civil War.[80] In the second half of the nineteenth century, Protestant homes grew with the urban West, where women activists "rescued" Chinese prostitutes, women running from polygamous marriages, and Native American women.[81]

These homes could accommodate a relatively small number of long-term occupants; there were also those designed for more short-term stays, such as the Temporary Home for Fallen Women in Boston, founded in 1844. Hobson found that while the Penitent Females' Refuge had an inmate population of about twenty, the Temporary Home took in one hundred to four hundred women per year and also ran a boardinghouse.[82] In both, the women were young, between fifteen and twenty-five, and in "various stages of delinquency." While in the short-term institution, women were not trained for domestic service as they were in the long-term institution, but only sewed themselves nice new clothes for their departure. The designers of these institutions consciously intended them to prevent participation in crime and vice, by both the inmates and their children, born and unborn. The *Prisoner's Friend* in 1850 cited a New York City police chief: "What fearful fruit will the seeds of sin, thus early sown, bring forth in womanhood?"[83] By targeting mothers, reformers hoped to stop the production of potential criminals. The same question ultimately was to trouble many leaders in the quintessential and most visible urban reform movement: the settlement house.

SETTLEMENT HOUSES AND THE "INSTITUTIONAL CHURCH"

> The typical settlement is one which provides neutral territory traversing all the lines of racial and religious freedom.[84]

In the last decade of the nineteenth century, as reformers philosophically opposed institutional, or indoor, relief, urban social reform took on several new aspects. The reformers themselves moved into institutions, while those they aided stayed outside. This resulted in part from simple city geographical growth: middle-class and wealthy people no longer lived near or came into daily contact with the very poor. The rowdy boys of the nineteenth century who threw snowballs at gentlemen's tall hats or sold pencils door to door moved out of the middle-class vision.[85] But the socially and structurally significant churches remained in the central city, so that by 1880, churches whose name began with "First" had their elite congregations travel in from afar; the neighbors were usually poor and often Catholic. Sometimes ministers and parishioners cared; from them came the "Social Gospel" movement, which used the large church structures as a base for social programs. A parallel movement came with an English innovation that captured the imagination of a larger body of American social activists: the settlement house. Almost like colonial outposts of the middle class in the slums, these institutions housed mainly nonresidential activities that broadly constituted what we now call social work.[86] Programs in these buildings took features of the preexisting children's institutions, such as the banks, the moral entertainments, and music, and added to them an extensive variety of educational, social-activist, and counseling types of activity.[87]

Though not nearly so well off as the white churches, black churches also launched programs dealing with the plight of the urban poor. Rather than build programs within one church, they often cooperated with other churches to create programs. In late-nineteenth-century Philadelphia, for instance, the Women's Union Christian Association (founded in 1873) aided the destitute with "job placement, guidance, day care and groceries."[88] Lane argues that such reform efforts helped unite black Philadelphians across church and social class lines.

It is important to note that the settlement house, like other urban institutions, had a solid physical presence. Hull House, the best known, started in a large house of relatively recent construction and expanded its infrastructural base to a much larger building complex over the years. Across most U.S. cities, settlement houses either purchased or built their presence in the slum or in working-class districts of cities.[89] Many of the approximately four hundred still stand. Their architectural history is yet to be written, for these structures were examples of sophisticated programmatic design.

From their settlement-house base camps, reformers launched programs for social and individual reform and change. While historians have detailed settlement-house histories, calling them, in Davis's memorable phrase, "spearheads of reform," they have yet to evaluate their many and varied programs.[90] This may never be possible, because the settlements had a physical as well as programmatic presence. William J. Wilson has made a two-part argument concerning the lack of role models in very poor neighborhoods today; his argument about the exit of working-class people is most widely noted, but the second part may be more relevant, the exit of institutions.[91] This is because after the 1950s, most social programs became purely bureaucratic: outdoor relief, in nineteenth-century parlance. Settlement houses, orphanages, and various houses of refuge have all disappeared from the landscape of the slum. Dealing with modern institutions of criminal justice or welfare often takes on a Kafkaesque quality, even for the mentally and physically able, because they are complex bureaucracies that require organizational skills and a high degree of literacy to navigate.[92]

Even the large original churches with their institutional programs have now left. Like settlement houses, the large churches had exerted a physical and programmatic presence in the slum. Settlement houses were almost exclusively Protestant, which enabled them to dovetail ideologically and culturally with programs of the reform-oriented Protestant churches. But after the 1920s, the large old Protestant churches became less of a reform presence in their neighborhoods, as did settlement houses. Catholic churches proved the exception, and through them some exceptionally important programs of reform and intervention were enacted.[93]

CONCLUSION

For some urban poor, institutional presence made a tremendous difference, and for others, it made none whatsoever. For the tramp Bill Aspinwall, life in the 1890s was a daily struggle to survive, literally on the very margins of the more stable world. Paying train passengers cheered his efforts to hang on to their car's smokestack; he reflected on the tramping worker's marginality as "somewhat exciting, but not pleasant, ennobling nor remunerative."[94] But he proudly avoided the kinds of institutions I have discussed above, carefully distinguishing himself from that class of tramps that would use such institutions. Aspinwall argued that only a small portion of tramping workers corresponded to what we call the underclass, a group for which most tramps had "no use": "They are composed of ex-convicts, Jail Birds, and Regular Dead Beats. . . . It is [this] Class that . . . patronizes the Poor Houses, Jails, &c."[95]

In the remarkable letters of Maimie Pinzer, we do have a chance to see the impact of a reform institution. In 1899, when she was fourteen, her mother and uncle, working with a city magistrate, had her put in a Magdalene Home, which she described as "a mild sort of reform school for girls who had gone astray," for one year.[96] In her hundreds of pages of letters, this experience merited only one short paragraph, allowing us little more than the assessment that as an institutional experience, she found it neither terrible nor scary.

The specific forms of institutions described here have not always survived—the police lodging rooms, the newsboys' lodging houses—most often because other, less-specific forms of aid have alleviated the original symptoms. Young children, for instance, can live at home and not need to be self-supporting because of Aid to Families with Dependent Children. And for most children, the result is a vastly better and more humane life.

But is it possible that we have also lost some valuable features of institutional life? We know that on occasion these institutions actually seemed to accomplish their ends: perhaps when they helped people achieve regularity and follow rules, they really helped some people to gain an ability to order their daily lives. In our efforts to help the nuclear family be the center of caring, we have perhaps turned too far away from one alternative form and in so doing stigmatized it and the people it has helped. In a sense, we continue today with a radical individualism, which tries to be sensitive to individual differences and then rejects institutional variety. Thus we have built a welfare state that is more comprehensive than its nineteenth-century predecessor but that is in its own way so bureaucratic as to lose all flexibility and responsiveness.

We have something to learn from our predecessors about our welfare and crime-control systems. They were proud of what they did, perhaps out of naïveté. If we were to value our own public commitments, we might also regain some of that pride, and we might be able to see our difficult social responsibilities in another light. If we were to value our professional, social, and political expenditures the way that our predecessors did, we might work at improving the public sector. We may no longer need the imposing public buildings that we once had, but we do need to value the public sector in order to make it work better. Such pride need not preclude serious criticism and evaluation. Indeed, a part of responsibility would be to seek out criticism and work to make a better civic response. Such pride would help us conceptualize the organizational and bureaucratic responses to need as a part of our civic obligation, an obligation which we should accept openly and positively as that of a mature society.

APPENDIX: RESEARCH TASKS

The increasing number of historians working on histories related to the welfare, social-control institutions and the people with which they deal suggests that there is little need to urge more of all kinds of research. But there are a few key areas that may be overlooked, and in which serious work is very much needed so that we may continue to augment our understanding of both the past and present.

First, serious efforts at constructing data series are essential. These include data on the number of and people in or served by various institutions, including the number and kinds of institutions themselves.

Second, we need an accounting of social expenditures that includes local, state, and federal governments plus private organizations, infrastructural costs, opportunity costs (in addition to lost taxes; this includes the opportunity costs represented by women and members of religious orders who worked for dramatically lower salaries because of a restricted labor market). Both of these efforts must be at a standard that would result in new data series for the *Historical Statistics of the United States*.

Third, we need imitations of Schlossman and Sedlak's evaluation of a Catholic-church-based program, Clifford Shaw's Chicago Area Project, which operated from the 1930s until 1959, and was a long crime-reduction project that embodied many of the most popular early-twentieth-century reform theories.[97] A neighborhood-based project launched out of a church, it incorporated active interventions into the lives of children and families. In their work, Schlossman and Sedlak conclude that the project had important and, at the time, ignored successes. Now, twenty-five years after Shaw's own self-critical evaluation of his project, the question for social programs has become, What works? Reevaluating previous histories becomes a significant way to evaluate policy.

Finally, there is a significant theoretical problem: the transition from yesterday's local systems to today's national/local mix, once adequately measured, then needs to be recast in the context of the Peterson thesis, which shows how transfer payments migrate to levels of government that deter bidding while promotional expenditures remain local and market oriented.[98] This thesis, which makes complete sense of the current scene, appears to contradict the actual trajectory of the institution-building period of the American state. Only careful research and reanalysis will resolve this contradiction: so doing will lead to new analyses of proper governmental roles in policy for the underclass. And along the way, we may find a great deal to learn from our predecessors' successes and failures.

NOTES

1. Elizabeth Oakes Smith, *The Newsboy* (New York: Derby, 1854), 208.

2. For instance, police found Isabella Grant dead of apparent starvation in a rear room at 312 West 28th Street. Lying on a pile of straw, she had no furniture or material resources. Her daughter Kate, nine, had been out all day begging ("Subterranean Civilization," *National Police Gazette*, November 21, 1863).

3. I wish not to exaggerate: some poor farms were actually farms, hence on the outskirts of any town or city, two or three miles away.

4. I am uncomfortable with any one term to designate the various groups of people and behaviors we indicate with the word *underclass*. Our nineteenth-century predecessors called them the "dangerous class," the "perishing class," or, much more usefully, the "defective, delinquent, and dependent classes." The terminology poses practical problems in its inexactitude, which becomes apparent when grouping various specialized institutions. Those which took in prostitutes or juvenile delinquents clearly dealt with the kind of people of interest here, but the all-purpose poorhouse (or poor farm, or almshouse, or infirmary) literally took in the

whole range of defective, delinquent, and dependent people. It is very difficult to refer to the group found in a poorhouse—a foundling, a tramp with frozen feet, a pregnant destitute woman, a dying old man, and a delinquent "half-orphan"—all as the dangerous class or the underclass.

The phrase *dangerous class,* which appeared in the United States in the 1840s and in England slightly earlier, preceded the word *underclass,* although one could argue that the nineteenth-century concepts of the "deserving" and the "undeserving" poor also divide the poor into two groups, the latter corresponding to the underclass. The "dangerous" or "under" class corresponds as a concept to what Marx called the *Lumpenproletariat,* a group he was careful to identify as a class enemy of the proletariat. The transliteration of *underclass* also appears in a similar usage in the eighteenth century in Germany; see Norbert Finzsch, *Obrigkeit und Unterschichten: Zur Geschichte der Rheinischen Unterschichten Gegen Ende des. 18 und zu Beginn des 19. Jahrhunderts* (Stuttgart: Franz Steiner Verlag, 1990).

In all varieties of the term, the fundamental notion is that this class is an enemy or at least a threat to society.

5. For a poignant example, see Joel Handler, "The Transformation of Aid to Families with Dependent Children: The Family Support Act in Historical Context," *New York University Review of Law and Social Change* 16 (1987): 457–533, esp. 529–33.

6. G. W. Quinby, *The Gallows, the Prison, and the Poor-House* (Cincinnati, Ohio: G. W. Quinby, 1856), 252–53.

7. "Local governmental responsibility, family responsibility, and legal settlement—the three principles expressed in the English Poor Law—were transplanted some 250 years later to a new Midwestern American territory" (Ethel McClure, *More than a Roof: The Development of Minnesota Poor Farms and Homes for the Aged* [St. Paul: Minnesota Historical Society, 1968], 7). Sophonisba P. Breckenridge, *The Illinois Poor Law and Its Adminstration* (Chicago: University of Chicago Press, 1939), 9–13, discusses the Northwest Territory's welfare provision of 1795.

8. For example, the city had granted twenty lots to the Association for the Benefit of Colored Orphans by 1843 (later burned by a mob in the Draft Riot of 1863). Report of New York City Commissioners of School Money, in *Documents of the Board of Aldermen,* vol. 9, document no. 8 (New York: Charles King, 1843), 70–71. Across the country, such "free" lands, real property confiscated or purchased from Native American people, when turned to local public uses, should have been calculated into the revenues and expenditures in several ways. First, the land's value should have been calculated as its "opportunity cost," or the income it would have generated had it been rented. Second, the lost property tax was important, because property tax was the major source of local revenues. The latter was never calculated, and the former only when a locale actually purchased property and paid a mortgage (which was usually only for the buildings). This aspect of nineteenth-century institutions confounds measurement efforts, for nowhere in city budgets do we find an estimate of the annual opportunity costs these structures represent, and as a result, recent econometric analyses are downwardly biased. Nor do more recent studies or accounts of welfare or criminal-justice expenditures calculate these opportunity costs. Many locales opted to convert their set-aside lands into cash, thus lowering their opportunity costs except for that land upon which the untaxed structures actually sat. As the years passed, these structures and their lands appreciated considerably, so that by 1890, the real property infrastructure represented a large but as yet unmeasured opportunity cost for local governments.

9. For a summary of the New Poor Law, see Derek Fraser, *The Evolution of the British Welfare State: A History of Social Policy since the Industrial Revolution* (London: Macmillan, 1984).

10. C. L. Stonaker, "Report of Committee on County and Municipal Institutions," in *Proceedings of the National Conference of Charities and Corrections* (Boston: Press of Fred J. Heer; n.d.), 375.

11. See Carl Bridenbaugh, *Cities in the Wilderness: Urban Life in America, 1625–1742* (New York: Ronald Press, 1938), for extensive colonial detail.

12. See Peter C. Seixas, "'Shifting Sands Beneath the State': Unemployment, the Labor Market, and the Local Community, 1893–1922" (Ph.D. diss., University of California at Los Angeles, 1988), for a discussion of local, state, and federal government welfare structures.

13. Samuel Walker, *Popular Justice: A History of American Criminal Justice* (New York: Oxford University Press, 1980), 186.

14. David Rothman, *The Discovery of the Asylum* (Boston: Little, Brown, 1971), 37.

15. *Seventh Annual Report of the Board of [Ohio] State Charities* (Columbus, 1883), 43.

16. A late entry, Texas legislated poorhouses in 1869, requiring inmates to take a pauper's oath, which took the paupers' citizens' rights, similar to the restrictions placed on felons. Most were in rural counties. See Debbie M. Cottrell, "The County Poor Farm System in Texas," *Southwestern Historical Quarterly* 93 (1989): 169–90.

17. When not in the state constitutions, this local obligation appeared in city charters. For instance, in "an Act to Incorporate the City of Alton," sec. 9. "The common council shall provide for, and take care of all paupers within the limits of said city; and to accomplish this object, they shall have the exclusive right, power and authority to license and tax all ferries, taverns, merchants, auctioneers, parlayers, grocers, vendors of spirituous liquors and wines, . . . public houses of entertainment, theatrical and other shows" (*Laws of the State of Illinois* [Vandalia: William Walters, 1837], 21). When revised twenty-two years later, the charter incorporated children of the "dangerous class": "To authorize and direct the taking up and providing for the safe keeping and education, for such periods of time as may be deemed expedient, all children who are destitute of parental care and left to wander about, and growing up in mendicancy, ignorance, idleness and vice" (*Laws of the State of Illinois* [Springfield: Bailhache and Baker, 1859], chap. 5, sec. 46, p. 51). One might call this the Huck Finn Law.

18. Michael Katz, *In the Shadow of the Poorhouse: The Social History of Welfare in America* (New York: Basic Books, 1986); Joan Waugh, "Unsentimental Reformer: Josephine Shaw Lowell and the Rise and Fall of the Scientific Charity Movement" (Ph.D. diss., University of California at Los Angeles, 1992).

19. Dorothea L. Dix campaigned against keeping the insane in poorhouses and jails. In her *Memorial: To the Legislature of Massachusetts* (Boston: Monroe and Francis, 1843), she describes visiting lunatics in jails and almshouses throughout Massachusetts. These people were from very poor families and were chained or locked up in pens or cages like wild animals; typically, only a slightly more able pauper cared for them. On Concord, better known to us for its transcendentalists, she noted: "A woman from the hospital in a cage in the almshouse. In the jail several, decently cared for in general, but not properly placed in a prison. Violent, noisy, unmanageable most of the time" (5). She also notes how the insane were often auctioned by towns, the bidding for the lowest cost to the town (23).

20. Arthur E. Peterson and George W. Edwards, *New York as an Eighteenth Century Municipality* (1917; reprint, Port Washington, N.Y.: Friedman, 1967), 298–99. For instance, New York City built a municipal poorhouse in 1736, which functioned as an almshouse, a place for "Beggars, Servants running away or otherwise misbehaving themselves, Trespassers, Rogues, Vagabonds, poor persons refusing to work," and, in addition, employed a public whipper and served as a site of corporal punishment for criminal offenders. This building actually preceded the first separate city jail, which the city built twenty-three years later, in

1759, and which attracted travelers' attention as a fine prison. Its replacement, built in 1775, was considered the "most imposing public building erected on Manhattan Island during the colonial period" (303).

21. Bridenbaugh, *Cities in the Wilderness,* 234.

22. Gary B. Nash, "The Failure of Female Factory Labor in Colonial Boston," *Labor History* 20 (1979): 165–88; idem, "Poverty and Poor Relief in Pre-Revolutionary Philadelphia," *William and Mary Quarterly* 33 (1976): 3–30; Peterson and Edwards, *New York as an Eighteenth Century Municipality,* 98, 99.

23. Peter Speirenburg, "From Amsterdam to Auburn: An Explanation for the Rise of the Prison in Seventeenth-Century Holland and Nineteenth-Century America," *Journal of Social History* 20 (1987): 439–61.

24. Calculated from David Rothman, ed., *Poverty U.S.A.: The Historical Record. The Almshouse Experience, Collected Reports* (New York: Arno, 1973), 34–36.

25. The marginal location of these institutions and the marginal social status of their inmates have made what was once a network of structures and reams of internal records vulnerable to neglect and destruction. Cottrell, "The County Poor Farm System," discusses the results of a systematic identification and preservation effort in Texas. She concludes that in the next decade "most remaining physical evidence of poor farms will vanish," and that with the disappearance of the written records, poor farms will become "a completely invisible part of the state's past" (189). For a similar story of erasure, see Steven R. Hoffbeck, "'Remember the Poor' (*Galatians* 2:10): Poor Farms in Vermont," *Vermont History* 57 (1989): 226–40.

26. Quoted in McClure, *More than a Roof,* 165, from Helen G. Tyson, "The Poorhouse Persists," *Survey Monthly* 74 (March 1938): 76.

27. McClure, *More than a Roof,* 166-67.

28. Richard Louis Dugdale, *The Jukes: A Study in Crime, Pauperism, Disease, and Heredity* (New York: Putnam's, 1877).

29. Rothman, *Discovery of the Asylum,* 8, 14.

30. Gilles Vandal, "The Nineteenth Century Municipal Response to the Problem of Poverty: New Orleans Free Lodgers, 1850–1890, as a Case Study," *Journal of Urban History* 19 (1992): 30–59, citing the *Picayune,* December 19, 1866, December 17, 1867, March 13, 1875.

31. Booker T. Washington used this example of obvious discrimination to argue that rural blacks relied on families for aid rather than on the state, and that "in our ordinary southern communities we look upon it as a disgrace for an individual to be permitted to be taken from that community to any kind of an institution for dependents" ("Destitute Colored Children of the South," *Proceedings of the Conference on the Care of Dependent Children Held at Washington, D.C., January 25, 26, 1909* [Washington, D.C.: 1909), 114–17, cited in Robert H. Bremner, ed., *Children and Youth in America: A Documentary History,* vol. 2 [Cambridge: Harvard University Press, 1971], 301). Exclusion of blacks from welfare continued well into the twentieth century. Police intimidated Houston blacks in relief lines; see Randy J. Sparks, "'Heavenly Houston' or 'Hellish Houston'? Black Unemployment and Relief Efforts, 1929–1936," *Southern Studies* 25 (1986): 358–59.

32. Stonaker, "Report of Committee on County and Municipal Institutions," 376.

33. Michael Katz, *Poverty and Policy in American History* (New York: Academic Press, 1983); Ruth Rosen and Sue Davidson, eds., *The Maimie Papers* (Old Westbury, N.Y.: Feminist Press, 1977).

34. Charles E. Rosenberg, "Social Class and Medical Care in America: The Rise and Fall of the Dispensary," *Journal of the History of Medicine* 29 (1974): 32–54; and *The Care of Strangers: The Rise of America's Hospital System* (New York: Basic Books, 1987), 5, 419.

35. Charles E. Rosenberg, *Caring for the Working Man: The Rise and Fall of the Dispensary. An Anthology of Sources* (New York: Garland Publishing, 1989), 58.

36. Ibid., 51.

37. Ibid. has an excellent short introduction; see also David Rosner, *A Once Charitable Enterprise: Hospitals and Health Care in Brooklyn and New York, 1885–1915* (New York: Cambridge University Press, 1982), 217, n. 1.

38. See on this point, George Rosen, "The First Neighborhood Health Center Movement: Its Rise and Fall," *American Journal of Public Health* 61 (1971): 1620–27.

39. Dana W. Bartlett, *The Better City: A Sociological Study of a Modern City* (Los Angeles: Neuner, 1907), 90.

40. Marilyn T. Williams, *Washing "The Great Unwashed": Public Baths in Urban America, 1840–1920* (Columbus: Ohio State University Press, 1991), 16; Frank D. Watson, "Public Baths," in Andrew C. McLaughlin and Albert B. Hart, eds., *Cyclopedia of American Government* (1942; reprint, Gloucester, Mass.: Peter Smith, 1963), 122–23.

41. The high rate of nineteenth-century drownings has puzzled many historians, and rather than seeking an explanation in swimming skills, we might instead turn to the rise of the bathtub and public bath. Roger Lane, *Violent Death in the City: Suicide, Accident and Murder in Philadelphia* (Cambridge: Harvard University Press, 1979), 36, 48–51, has shown that for Philadelphia, the rate of drowning peaked between 1850 and 1885, then slowly began to decline by the 1890s.

42. Hastings H. Hart, "County Jails," in McLaughlin and Hart, *Cyclopedia of American Government,* 497.

43. E. Fuller Torrey, "The Madness of Deinstitutionalization," asserts that 15 percent of the Los Angeles County Jail population is mentally ill, more people than are in state institutions for the mentally ill (*Los Angeles Times Book Review,* September 9, 1990).

44. James Bryce, *The American Commonwealth* (New York: Macmillan, 1895), 2:568.

45. Allen Steinberg, *The Transformation of Criminal Justice: Philadelphia, 1800–1880* (Chapel Hill: University of North Carolina Press, 1989), has unearthed the most detailed evidence of the activity in these lower criminal courts in his study of Philadelphia's aldermen's courts.

46. A movement "mothered" and paid for by the Women's Christian Temperance Union since 1876, in Portland, Maine. See Sarah W. Devoll, "The Results of the Employment of a Police Matron in the City of Portland, Maine," *Proceedings of the National Conference of Charities and Corrections* (1881), 309–17.

47. Robert M. Fogelson, *America's Armories: Architecture, Society, and Public Order* (Cambridge: Harvard University Press, 1989), 231.

48. Quinby, *The Gallows, the Prison, and the Poor-House,* 246, 256.

49. See for the best recent analysis, Bruce Bellingham, "Waifs and Strays: History of Childhood, Abandonment and the Circulation of Children between Households in the Mid-Nineteenth Century," in Peter Mandler, ed., *The Uses of Charity: The Poor on Relief in the Nineteenth-Century Metropolis* (Philadelphia: University of Pennsylvania Press, 1990).

50. John Boswell, *The Kindness of Strangers: The Abandonment of Children in Western Europe from Late Antiquity to the Renaissance* (New York: Pantheon, 1988); Ann McCants, "The Burgerweeshuis" (Ph.D. diss., University of California, Berkeley, 1991).

51. Homer Folks, *The Care of Destitute, Neglected, and Delinquent Children* (New York: Macmillan, 1902), 7–11.

52. Note how the terminological focus has changed from "half-orphans" in the nineteenth century to "single-parent families" in the twentieth. This shift suggests the nineteenth-century concern with the child as individual, the twentieth century with the family unit. None

of the following discussion of the orphanage should be taken to imply that orphanages dealt only with children of the underclass. But what should be kept in mind is that these institutions were available to all children, so by definition represent a resource and institutional intervention in the lives of dependent children, including those of the underclass.

53. See Peter C. Holloran, *Boston's Wayward Children: Social Services for Homeless Children, 1830–1930* (Rutherford, N.J.: Fairleigh Dickinson University Press, 1989), who details the interactions between parents and orphanages in a way that shows a variety of family interactions with the orphanage. See also Judith Ann Dulberger, "Refuge or Repressor: The Role of the Orphan Asylum in the Lives of Poor Children and Their Families in Late-Nineteenth-Century America" (Ph.D. diss., Carnegie Mellon University, 1988), who argues that "poor families used nineteenth-century institutions to meet their needs and advance their interests" (ii).

54. In a curious confirmation of these tendencies, for example, Louis Armstrong went into the New Orleans Colored Waifs Home (1913) after being caught for shooting a revolver on New Year's Eve when he was thirteen. Both of his parents were alive but separated. He spent a year and a half there, where he learned the bugle and cornet and joined their band.

55. Charles L. Brace, *The Dangerous Classes of New York and Twenty Years' Work among Them* (New York: Wynkoop and Hallenbeck, 1872).

56. Holloran, *Boston's Wayward Children*, 1989, 103–4.

57. Bremner et al., eds., *Children and Youth in America* 2:1523, 284.

58. Grace Abbott, *The Child and the State* (Chicago: University of Chicago Press, 1938), 2:229–34, cited in Bremner et al., *Children and Youth in America* 2:384–85.

59. Marshall B. Jones, "Crisis of the American Orphanage, 1931–1940," *Social Service Review* 63 (1989): 613–29, argues that the financial crisis of the Depression, rather than the dynamics I have described, triggered the demise of the orphanage. In essence, the New Deal welfare legislation substituted other forms of cash support for orphanages in a structural shift parallel to that ending the poorhouse.

60. Data sources: for 1960–85, *Statistical Abstract of the United States* (Washington, D.C.: Government Printing Office, 1986), 366, taken from Social Security Administration's unpublished data; for 1910–60, Martin Wolins and Irving Piliavin, *Institution or Foster Family: A Century of Debate* (New York: Child Welfare League, 1964), 37; for 1880–1900, Folks, *Care of Destitute Children*, 195–96, from Frederick H. Wines, *Tenth U.S. Census: The Defective, Dependent, and Delinquent Classes* (Washington, D.C.: Government Printing Office, 1888); *Eleventh U.S. Census: Crime, Pauperism, and Benevolence* (Washington, D.C.: Government Printing Office, 1895); population, *Historical Statistics of the United States: From Colonial Times to the Present* (Washington, D.C.: Government Printing Office, 1977), 10; Seth Low, "Foster Care of Children: Major National Trends and Prospects" (Washington, D.C.: Dept. of Health, Education and Welfare, Welfare Administration, Children's Bureau, 1966).

61. For an argument in favor of the orphanage, see Lois G. Forer, *Unequal Protection: Women, Children, and the Elderly in Court* (New York: Norton, 1991). See also Penelope Lemov, "Return of the Orphanage," *Governing* (May 1991): 31–35, cited in Liz Westerfield, "Children by Order and System: The Making of a Separate Children's Institution in Philadelphia, 1820" (Unpublished paper, University of California at Los Angeles, 1991).

62. Jack Patten, *The Children's Institution* (Berkeley, Calif.: McCutchan, 1968).

63. *New York Times*, January 9, 1871.

64. See David Nasaw, *Children of the City: At Work and at Play* (New York: Oxford University Press, 1985), appendix, 207–8, for an excellent list of primary sources on "newsboy studies." Bruce Bellingham, "The 'Unspeakable Blessing': Street Children, Reform Rhetoric and Misery in Early Industrial Capitalism," *Politics and Society* 12 (1983): 303–30.

65. John Morrow, *The Newsboy: A Voice from the Newsboys* (New York: Published for the benefit of the author by John Morrow, 1860), xii.

66. Gary Scharnhorst with Jack Bales, *The Lost Life of Horatio Alger, Jr.* (Bloomington: Indiana University Press, 1985), dismisses the claim that Alger lived at the Newsboys' Lodging House. The point here is that benevolent institutions did not have protection as a goal.

67. Albert Wilson, *These Were the Children* (Menlo Park, Calif.: Wilson, 1963); Wilson visited his former (and hostile) orphanage supervisor and reports his shock at discovering that her room was filled with pictures of nude girls.

68. See, for an early example of the boy hero genre, Morrow, *The Newsboy.*

69. LeRoy Ashby, *Saving the Waifs: Reformers and Dependent Children, 1890–1917* (Philadelphia: Temple University Press, 1984), 48, quoting the words of Victor Hugo favored by child reformers.

70. Homer Folks, "Municipal Charities in the United States," *Proceedings of the National Conference of Charities and Corrections* (Boston: National Conference of Charities and Corrections, 1898), 113–84; and Folks, *Care of Destitute Children.* The New York State Senate committee of 1857 discussed twenty-six state-funded orphanages, containing 2,816 children in 1857; arguing that children in poorhouses were "much more pitiable" than those in orphanages, it recommended their removal to orphanages (Gerald Grob, *The State and Public Welfare in Nineteenth-Century America: Five Investigations* [New York: Arno, 1976], 10).

71. Holloran, *Boston's Wayward Children*, has an astonishingly complete survey of these institutions for Boston; Linda Gordon, *Heroes of Their Own Lives: The Politics and History of Family Violence in Boston, 1880–1960* (New York: Viking, 1988), follows the interventions of one Society for the Prevention of Cruelty to Children for several decades, also in Boston; while Barbara M. Hobson, *Uneasy Virtue: The Politics of Prostitution and the American Reform Tradition* (New York: Basic Books, 1987), works out from Boston, tracing a longer history of those organizations dealing with prostitutes. This recent research carries on a tradition of concern about abandoned or abused children that began in the 1830s and has not diminished since, in spite of the recent "discovery" of child abuse in its varied forms.

72. This is the now-classic argument of Norbert Elias, *The Civilizing Process,* trans. Edmund Jephcott (New York: Urizen Books, 1978–82). Lane, *Violent Death in the City,* uses this notion to account for the decline in late-nineteenth-century urban crime.

73. Ashby, *Saving the Waifs,* 133.

74. Ibid., 212.

75. Jones, "Crisis of the American Orphanage," 625.

76. Christine Stansell, *City of Women: Sex and Class in New York, 1789–1860* (Urbana: University of Illinois Press, 1986), 172, quoting John McDowall, *Magdalene Facts* [first annual report of the Magdalene Society] (New York, 1832).

77. These institutions designed to reform women should be distinguished from those which appeared a bit later in the century, and which simply provided a place to say. For instance, in 1873 "The Fraternals, a band of young men connected with the Church of the Strangers," created the "Free dormitory for women" a "stone's throw from Washington Square" in New York City. In December 1873, it lodged 124 women (*New York Times,* February 1, 1874).

78. For the details, see Hobson, *Uneasy Virtue.*

79. Ibid., 120.

80. Holloran, *Boston's Wayward Children,* 127.

81. See Peggy Pascoe, *Relations of Rescue: The Search for Female Moral Authority in the American West, 1874–1939* (New York: Oxford, 1990).

82. Hobson, *Uneasy Virtue,* 118–30.

83. Ibid., 125.

84. Ruth Hutchinson Crocker, *Social Work and Social Order: The Settlement Movement in Two Industrial Cities, 1889–1930* (Chicago and Urbana: University of Illinois Press, 1992), 66, quoting Robert Woods and Albert Kennedy, *The Handbook of Settlements* (New York: Charities Publication Committee, 1911), v.

85. Elizabeth Oakes Smith met the boy she wrote about as he sold her newspapers at her window (*The Newsboy* [New York: Derby, 1854], 5).

86. See Allan F. Davis, *Spearheads for Reform: The Social Settlements and the Progressive Movement, 1890–1914* (New Brunswick, N.J.: Rutgers University Press, 1984); Clarke A. Chambers, *Seedtime of Reform: American Social Service and Social Action, 1918–1933* (Minneapolis: University of Minnesota Press, 1963).

87. See for the classic description, Jane Addams, *Twenty Years at Hull House* (New York: Macmillan, 1910).

88. Roger Lane, *William Dorsey's Philadelphia and Ours* (New York: Oxford University Press, 1991), 296. See also Ralph E. Luker, "Missions, Institutional Churches, and Settlement Houses: The Black Experience, 1885–1910," *Journal of Negro History* 69 (1984 [published 1989]): 101–13.

89. Ruth H. Crocker, *Social Work and Social Order,* discusses location of settlement houses in the context of race, detailing at least one occasion when a house moved away from an African American neighborhood. This study explicitly compares white and African American settlement houses in Gary and Indianapolis.

90. Davis, *Spearheads for Reform.*

91. William J. Wilson, Introduction to *The "Underclass" Debate: Views from History,* ed. Michael B. Katz, 1993.

92. See Joel Handler, "The Transformation of Aid to Families with Dependent Children: The Family Support Act in Historical Context," *New York University Review of Law and Social Change* 16 (1987): 457–533, app. 2, 529–33. Dulberger, "Refuge or Repressor?" working with letters children wrote back to the superintendent of the Albany Orphan Asylum, cites at least two instances where they ask for or comment on views of the asylum buildings. Rather than finding it oppressing, one boy seemed proud of its size—"almost as big as a City, well not quite" (291–92).

93. See the appendix on research needs for an example of research on such a church-based effort.

94. From a letter to reformer John J. McCook. Quoted in Roger A. Bruns, *Knights of the Road: A Hobo History* (New York: Methuen, 1980), 66.

95. Quoted in Bruns, *Knights of the Road,* 64–65.

96. Rosen and Davidson, *The Maimie Papers,* 196.

97. Steven Schlossman and Michael Sedlak, *The Chicago Area Project Revisited* (Santa Monica, Calif.: Rand, 1983).

98. Paul Peterson, *City Limits* (Chicago: University of Chicago Press, 1981).

17

A Disorderly People? Urban Order in Nineteenth- and Twentieth-Century America

I have never been able to find credible evidence that cities cause social problems, and I have been fighting this idea my whole life. You would think I was some sort of Jane Jacobs/Richard Sennett city-loving, suburb-hating person, fighting a quixotic scholarly defense of the city. So, to set the record straight, I like orderly safe societies, in city, suburb, and the country. It is a sin that poor people get off Greyhound buses in city centers to scenes of disorder, danger, and despair.

For the United States to get to the situation of safety, order, and hope, a correct understanding of the basic problem is essential, thus getting rid of urban essentialism becomes important.

If we think that downtown bus stations are dangerous because that is the nature of the city, the essence of urbanism, then we will never take the many concrete steps needed to make them as safe as they should be.

The pro–urban disorder argument, or at least, sentiment, is that from urban detritus, conflict, and contrast come invention, creativity, and insight. This is deeply wrong, I suspect. It is more that persons who have benefited from order, or who have overcome disorder in their own lives, can find the new in urban disorder. And, to take the extreme argument, if by sanitizing our cities so that the powerless as well as the powerful could lead safe lives we lost something, let's say some creative edge, that loss might be worth taking.

Historians have characterized American cities as violent, noisy, chaotic, and disorderly.[1] This description accords well with the writings of contemporaries who

First published in *The Journal of American History,* vol. 68 no. 3 (December 1981). A research grant from the UCLA Academic Senate supported this research.

loved the city, like Walt Whitman who saw it as disorderly or, in his phrase, "brawling, lusty." Stephen Crane seconded this image in *Maggie,* with his portrayal of children fighting, adults fighting, and a general air of brutal self-expression. And Mark Twain lent his support to this image by commenting in *Innocents Abroad* on the quiet and civility of European cities. The order of the Paris train depot amazed him: "There was no frantic crowding and jostling, no shouting and swearing, and no swaggering intrusion of services by rowdy hackmen."[2] Examples of contemporary perceptions of public disorder in American cities could be expanded considerably, but to do so would do more to enlarge our knowledge of urban observers than to deepen our understanding of public disorder.

The most common forms of criminal behavior can serve as a conceptual device with which to examine the relationship of social structure and cultural values to public disorder. This essay focuses on urban society through the "lens" of drunk and disorderly conduct, behavior that, when done in public, leaves one liable to criminal arrest even though there is no particular victim. Cities are peculiarly suited to an analysis of public order because they are characterized by relatively intense use of public space by people of all classes.[3] Moreover, the "publicness" of urban disorderly behavior made it, by definition, open to observation, unlike most other criminal behavior. At the same time that the legal definition of disorderly behavior into various categories of misdemeanor made policing agents responsible for producing arrests without the requirement of complaining victims and with rather simple rules of evidence, the threat or actuality of arrests was more annoying than awesome to offenders. Thus, one reason to use the unimportant offense of drunken or disorderly conduct as an indicator of order is because of its very property of being unimportant.[4]

Can we learn from arrest rates? In order to know about "real" offenses, would we not need to consider those unobserved by police, those where for some reasons police did not make an arrest, and those where police made false arrests? Cases where police acted but did not arrest might be called harassment rates. Criminologists romantically refer to the incidence rate of "real" crime as the "dark figure." In the past five years, the federal government has begun to investigate this figure, using what are called victimization surveys to discover how many people actually have been victims of criminal offenses every year. But in the case of the behavior with which we are concerned here, drunken and disorderly conduct in public, such surveys would be an irrational measure. Nor would self-reporting studies help—presumably, one might have been disorderly and unaware of it. So, for a study of public disorder, getting the "dark figure" might well be impossible. Arrest rates do not so much index some other form of behavior as index a complete universe of social interaction. Hence criminologist Thorsten Sellin's dictum to use statistics as close as possible to the crime might have been, in this special case, nearly accomplished.[5]

What, given perfect information, would we wish to know about disorder in public to be able to measure its change over time? First, we would like to have precise behavioral standards: definitions of disorderly conduct that an outsider could readily apply. Second, we would like to know how evenly and consistently these standards had been applied; this would tell us whether or not we could trust enforcement activity as a measure. Third, we would need to know the deterrent effect of enforcement; we can reason that the deterrent effect of enforcement for public behavior is relatively greater than the deterrent effect for criminal offenses with victims.[6] Fourth and most unattainable, we would need some sort of yardstick of people's daily (or nightly) behavior in public. If, in an imaginary world, we could account for these four, the first three would explain much of the fourth, and what we could not explain we could define as behavior that came from broader social and cultural antagonisms, conflicts, and normative differences. Usually, and too glibly, historians assume that a category of police-prosecuted behavior like drunk and disorderly conduct presents primarily this latter category—the different and conflicting cultural norms of, let us say, recent European immigrants and native-born Protestant Americans. We should be skeptical of this assumption until it can be demonstrated. To do otherwise is to accept wholly the native-born elite perspective with a very slightly shifted value judgment.

Instead of these imaginary, perfect measures, we can, at best, find arrest rates. We can survey the legal standards for situations where arrests made for disorderly conduct or drunkenness came to an appellate court, but we can know neither the precise local behavioral standards for disorderly behavior nor the varying perceptions of what constituted disorderly behavior.

Let us first consider a nineteenth-century police officer's decision to arrest and take into custody a drunk or disorderly person, examining the differences between the nineteenth century and the mid-twentieth century. Prior to the last two decades of the nineteenth century, one of the most difficult parts of the arrest process, from both the officer's and arrestee's perspective, was the period between the arrest and booking in the station house. Before a city had both an electronic communications system and a wagon to haul in the arrested person, the officer and the arrestee had to walk or take public transportation to the station house. Even toward the end of the century, after most cities obtained some form of electronic communication, the officer and the arrestee had to walk to a call box, signal in the request, and wait for a horse-drawn wagon to come from the station house. Until the wagon arrived, the officer and the arrestee were, at best, alone; more often, they were surrounded by curious onlookers or, worse for the officer, the arrestee's friends. In all cases the arrest involved physical contact and struggle in public: the officer had to be sure of his ability to control the arrestee. When successfully accomplished, the process of getting to the station house had all the elements of what sociologist Harold Garfinkel has called a "degradation ceremony."[7] Clearly, the public nature of the arrest gave it a symbolic impact that the relatively quick arrest and removal of a person in a radio car lacks.[8] Thus, the annual arrest rates between 1860 and 1970 index events with different public and private impact; the pre-1930 data index public arrests and domination events, the post–World War II data refer to a world of radio cars and quick removal from the public arena.

Disorderly conduct was and still is a catchall offense category that could be used to arrest anyone for behavior of many types. An incentive to use the category exists in those situations where the police think a person has violated the law but know that evidence, witnesses, or proof will be difficult. The misdemeanor charge gets the offender off the street, inflicts some punishment, and avoids the difficulty of a felony court trial. For instance, disorderly-conduct charges are often used in situations where riot charges might be considered more appropriate, but more difficult to prove. Or, to avoid worry about the complainant's testimony, disorderly conduct might be charged rather than simple assault. In these examples the offender has violated the law, and the police can take punitive action quickly, easily, and with technical certitude. That the charge does not produce a pure index of public disorder for future historians is of no matter.

One must not be misled, however, by the large permissible scope of disorderly-conduct arrests into thinking that the category simply conceals a whole range of other offenses. On the contrary, because of the large numbers of arrests made within this category, these masked charges probably constitute a negligible proportion of the whole. This is partly why the offense works well as a methodological catchall for historians and a behavioral catchall for the police. In fact, drunkenness and disorderly offenses composed over half of the total of urban arrests in the period to 1920. By the 1970s the proportion had declined to about one-fourth of all arrests. The large number of these arrests has another methodological advantage: the rates, when plotted, exhibit a high degree of stability. When only a few events make up the numerator of a plotted series, the variation from year to year can be confusingly high, but with the kind of data analyzed here, both the trend and the deviation from it have a high degree of reliability, both statistical and interpretive. Figure 17.1 shows trends of the combined arrest rates for urban drunken and disorderly conduct from 1860 to 1977. It should be noted at the outset that the data come from two different sources: the data before 1950 from the annual police reports of the major cities, the post-1950 data from the *Uniform Crime Reports for the United States* of the Federal Bureau of Investigation. The overall decline in per capita arrests for public misbehavior since the onset of the Civil War to the present is without question the most striking feature of the data. It seems clear from this trend that, as arrest categories, drunkenness and disorderly conduct continue to diminish and may be destined to virtually disappear.[9]

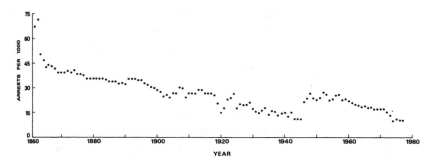

Figure 17.1 Arrests for Drunkenness and Disorderly Conduct per 1,000 Population, Urban Data, 1860–1977*
*Data for 1860–1920 include arrests for "suspicion" and vagrancy, as well as for drunkenness, disorderly conduct, drunk and disorderly, and breach of peace. Data for 1861–1919 are smoothed with a three-year running average.
Source: 1860–1920 data are from annual reports of police for the twenty-three largest cities for which data were available, as listed in Table 17.1, with the actual years for which data could be gathered noted under the heading *Period*. 1920–1950 data are from the annual reports of police for the fourteen cities listed in Table 17.3. Post-1950 data are from U.S. Department of Justice, Federal Bureau of Investigation, *Uniform Crime Reports for the United States,* for cities over 2,500 persons. Note that while inconsistent with the earlier data, the post-1950 data are dominated by large cities.

An event in this arrest series almost equal in drama and importance to the overall decline of the past century is the spectacular burst in drunk and disorderly conduct arrests which occurred between 1945 and 1946. The obvious cause of this jump in arrests, followed by an eight-year period of high arrests which equaled the 1905–1918 era, appears to have been demobilization subsequent to World War II. We can speculate that three consequences attendant upon the end of World War II contributed to the leap in arrest activities: the increased numbers in arrest-prone age groups (young men), the return to work of younger police officers, and the increased post-Prohibition consumption of alcohol.

The downward arrest trend allows several inferences of broader implication than the simple, and important, observation that police have for over a century been making fewer and fewer catchall arrests. Given that the prime mover in creating these data was the police, we can only speculate about the probable social meanings of the trends, stepping further away with each level of speculation from confident and precise measures. It is valuable to do so. First, the trend represents a lagged, out-of-focus mirror of social perceptions of unacceptable public disorder. On one level, the police enforce laws that loosely reflect the dominant society's consensus. But this police-enforced perception lags slightly behind changes in the larger society's perceptions because of bureaucratic inertia; so arrests for disorderly conduct give only a loose behavioral measure of this larger set of perceptual definitions. If the society thought it saw an unacceptable

244

increase in street disorder, then police could be expected to act on this perception by making more arrests. Given the vague wording of the statutes, an increased production of arrests would represent no vast distortion of legal precedents. But, in fact, this did not occur. The data demonstrate a clear downward trend. At this first and least interpretative level of speculation we must infer that national urban perceptions, as expressed through the police, included a stable trend in disorder in the streets or a decline in the demand for enforcement of order. (See appendix.) This interpretation of the arrest trend runs counter to many, if not all, historical works dealing with the perceptions of urban disorder, where the research inevitably focuses on statements that indicate both a perception of rising urban disorder and increasing demands for order.[10]

This first speculation—that public perceptions of the level of street disorder declined—does not claim that disorder actually did decline. As John C. Schneider has pointed out, spatial differentiation of cities made a difference in demands on police for order arrests, suggesting that the continued trend toward spatial segregation has contributed to rising perceptions of order.[11] We can also read the trend as indicative of a decline in police initiative in making arrests. That is, police made fewer and fewer arrests per officer as well as per capita for offenses where the action usually depended on the police officer's initiative.[12] Possibly an increase in rules governing police conduct coupled with the growing complexity of the arrest process enhanced the incentives not to arrest. In addition, police officers may have begun to opt either for no action or for informal action—verbal harassment, beating, and so forth—but no evidence implies that such choices increased or decreased. Most certainly, however, the data indicate a decline in officer-initiated arrests.

With rising perceptions of public order and the decline in police initiation of arrests, what remains in the trend may be a measure of the actual incidence of disorderly and drunken public behavior. (See appendix for a discussion of alcohol consumption.) Unfortunately, the first two components of the trend cannot be removed from the data to arrive at a true estimate of this last component. We cannot, in fact, absolutely know the direction of any of the three components; all we know is that at least one and possibly all three are downward. That only one is downward, so strongly that it masks two upward trends, seems unlikely, but it is a logical possibility. More probable, however, is that all three trends are in fact downward, which means that the actual incidence of disorderly conduct in public decreased. While this decline is a speculative inference, it is an inference based on some empirical evidence as opposed to previous discussions of public order.[13] If anything, the biases in the data should have distorted the trend in an upward direction, making the actual downward direction seem all the more reliable.

A closer examination of the arrest trend shows that the Civil War years had a high degree of public disorder in spite of the aggressive draft policy that removed just those people one would expect to produce drunken and disorderly behavior. The decrease in disorder as the war continued does indicate the war's attrition of revelers. Nevertheless, the sharp postwar decline suggests that, more than just affecting the population mix present in cities, the war also fostered a loosening of social norms. Yet this did not happen during the Spanish-American War nor World War I. The Civil War was, in fact, an exception, and the other small bursts of disorderly and drunken conduct came during depressions—1873, the early 1890s, 1907, and 1912–1913.

The relationship between the Civil War disorder and these other smaller bursts may have been more direct than is readily apparent. All of these cataclysms—internal war, unemployment, and depression—moved fifteen- to forty-five-year-old males out of their homes, communities, and jobs. Homeless men in the nineteenth and early twentieth centuries represented a visible threat. Whether called tramps, migrant workers, or a bachelor subculture, this group of men congregated in particular parts of town. They had a social life that of necessity centered around saloons and boardinghouses, presenting a visible contrast to the nuclear family, the model of urban stability. Forced migration and temporary homelessness moved these men into public places, making their behavior more at risk for observation and arrest. Not only were they in fact more disorderly in public than the norm, their numerical preponderance during war and depression challenged the basic social arrangement—the nuclear family—in an already stressful period. After all, where were the age-equivalent women for these men? Unmarried, at their parents' homes, or at work? Some, if not many, of these men were fathers. What about their families? Who supported them?[14] The tramp or discharged soldier was more than just a potential criminal; he represented a deeply disrupted social order, a society without the stable nuclear family.[15]

The social perturbations that the bursts in drunken and disorderly conduct represented came not from violent internal disruption, but from temporal events that caused age- and gender-specific population movements. This is not to minimize the severity of individual suffering caused, for instance, by the massive unemployment of the depression of 1873. It does specify and clarify the kind of social event that created visible differences, which in turn created more drunken and disorderly conduct in public and great fear of a deeper social disorder. This explanation does not assert that family, work, and the military functioned as social-control institutions, keeping fifteen- to forty-five-year-old men treading the straight and narrow. The point is that the nuclear family, jobs, and the military located men in private space, thus removing them from risk of observation and arrest, as well as from opportunity for drunken and disorderly conduct.

During and after World War I this set of relationships between unemployment, war, and public disorder changed. Unlike previous depressions, the Great

Depression did not see a clear burst in drunk and disorderly-conduct arrests, and only one of the World War II years, 1942, experienced anything that could be called a rise in order arrests. Most significant, of course, the rise in arrests after World War II was a new event, a pattern absent from the Civil War, Spanish-American War, and World War I. The Great Depression's low level of public disorder partly reflects the relatively greater severity of this depression over previous ones. More than this, however, it reflects the increased privatization of urban life, the decline in intensity of street life attendant on suburbanization and the automobile. While the walking city had begun to disappear by the mid-nineteenth century, for the poor and those who tended to be at risk for drunk and disorderly-conduct arrests, cities were still walking cities until World War I. But the advent of cheap transportation—the privatization of commuting for an increasing proportion of workers who used the automobile—emptied city streets of both those who might have been arrested for drunk and disorderly conduct and the public who demanded decorous behavior. The Great Depression, after all, saw many of the poor moving by private transportation in search of jobs, something that had never happened in depressions before. The end of World War II, on the other hand, saw an increase of leisure time, relative propserity, and a short-term shortage of automobiles. Cities that had for generations been experiencing less and less public disorder were suddenly confronted with more disorder and reacted repressively. Public-order arrest rates temporarily soared and then resumed, at a high level, the longer downward historical trend.

What about national Prohibition? John Burnham has shown that it effectively began with war legislation in 1917, that it saw a period of successful enforcement with a deterrent effect from 1919 to 1922, and that the period from 1925 to 1927 was one of widespread violation. As Prohibition raised the risk of liquor distribution and therefore the cost of drinking, it cut down on working-class drinking the most—by at least 50 percent, Burnham estimates. Thus it should have cut down on those public drunks most at risk to be arrested. The arrest data in Figure 17.1 reflect just that, with a decided low point in arrests in 1920. Earlier research has already made this point, but only in the context of data from a decade on each side of 1920.[16] We can now see that the decline would have come about anyway, given the long-term historic trend, perhaps in a dozen years, perhaps in twenty-five years, certainly by the mid-1970s. Prohibition served to hasten a process at least a half century old.

The arrest trends discussed thus far have been national, which means that many different cities have been aggregated and treated as one. This procedure can be justified on methodological grounds because some individual cities had idiosyncratic reporting years or political regimes; further, the aggregation smooths out irregularities in the data and tends to distribute the errors randomly.[17] Nevertheless, the examination of particular cities can show us whether or not national trends had local meaning. For twenty-three cities, Table 17.1 tabulates the slopes of the drunk and disorderly-conduct arrest trends for the period from the Civil War to the end of World War I.

Nine cities conformed closely with the national trend. New York, Philadelphia, Chicago, Cincinnati, Cleveland, Washington, Newark, Milwaukee, and Providence all had declining arrest rates for drunk and disorderly conduct from the Civil War era through World War I and subsequent national Prohibition. Only two cities clearly conflicted with the national pattern: San Francisco and Louisville showed consistent increases in arrest rates over the period. Eight cities displayed no consistent trends over the whole period: Boston, St. Louis, Baltimore, Buffalo, Detroit, Richmond, New Haven, and Lowell had arrest rates that drifted erratically. Four cities had too little or too scattered data to allow generalizations about the whole period: these include Brooklyn, New Orleans, Rochester, and Pittsburgh. Of these twenty-three cities, eight developed an interesting, short-run pattern: from about the turn of the century until national

Table 17.1 Trends in Arrest Rates for Drunkenness and Disorderly Conduct for Individual Cities, 1860–1920: Slope, Significance, and Period Reported

City	Slope	Significance	Period
New York City	−.79	.001	1860–1916
Philadelphia	−.26	.001	1860–1920
Brooklyn	−.09	n.s.	1860–1896
Chicago	−.46	.001	1870–1920
Boston	.16	n.s.	1860–1920
St. Louis	−.03	n.s.	1866–1919
Baltimore	−.03	n.s.	1864–1920
Cincinnati	−.10	.002	1864–1916
San Francisco	.16	.044	1862–1912
New Orleans	.36	.018	1891–1915
Cleveland	−.43	.001	1872–1915
Buffalo	0	n.s.	1872–1920
Washington	−1.42	.001	1862–1920
Newark	−.43	.001	1870–1920
Louisville	.23	.012	1870–1915
Detroit	−.08	.09	1862–1918
Milwaukee	−.10	.001	1868–1920
Providence	−.22	.04	1863–1915
Rochester	−.23	.07	1877, 1902–1918
Pittsburgh	.62	.004	1888–1915
Richmond	−.04	n.s.	1873–1920
New Haven	−.03	n.s.	1863–1920
Lowell	.09	.09	1862–1920

Source: Annual reports of city police departments or annual mayor's reports. This list is ranked by city size in 1880.

Prohibition, Boston, Cincinnati, New Orleans, Buffalo, Louisville, Detroit, Pittsburgh, and New Haven showed an increase in arrests.

The cities that did not conform to national trends can be categorized in several more ways (see appendix). Four cities stand isolated: Buffalo, St. Louis, San Francisco, and Louisville. San Francisco saw the longest consistent increase in drunk and disorderly-conduct arrest rates, a trend broken only in 1875 and more dramatically by the 1906 earthquake. Buffalo experienced a rather steady increase for the years 1877–1901.[18] And St. Louis, except for peaks in the early 1870s and in the first decade of the twentieth century, maintained remarkable stability in arrest rates from the end of the Civil War to 1905. Another subgroup of five cities showed marked peaks in their arrest trends in the decade of the 1890s: these include Detroit, Baltimore, Richmond, New Haven, and Lowell. For this subgroup, arrest rates seem to chart city politics to a greater degree than do the arrest rates for the whole group of major American cities and thus conform to some of historians' earlier views on policing, urban immigrants, disorder, and political response. Thus, for this subgroup of five cities, the arrests followed increased immigration, rising until the late nineteenth century when machine politics responded to immigrant demands and subsequent arrest rates declined. In the early decades of the twentieth century it further appears that the Progressive, good-government scrutiny of policing in Detroit, Baltimore, and New Haven drove the arrest rates upward until the intervention of national Prohibition.

The cities that vary from the dominant pattern illustrate the danger in only examining national trends. They also expose the potential shortcomings of case studies that have not employed some means of examining larger patterns. If one chose, for instance, to examine drunk and disorderly-conduct arrests in Louisville, Buffalo, or San Francisco only, one would be analyzing idiosyncratic cities and adopting explanatory strategies that might be inappropriate for generalization to other places. For these three cities, interesting in their contrasts to most large cities, a comparative analysis would be most appropriate.[19] Within the subgroup of five cities that deviated from the national trend—Detroit, Baltimore, Richmond, New Haven, and Lowell—three cities—Detroit, Baltimore, and New Haven—display arrest patterns that current historiography might have predicted. Public-order arrests rose with increased immigration, declined when machines responsive to immigrants came to power, and rose again when anti-immigrant Progressive machines asserted themselves in the early twentieth century. Finally, we must note that within the group of cities that provided the statistical basis for the overall decline are individual places that can fuel almost any argument, although, of course, the greatest number of cities exhibited parallel downward trends.

This examination of individual cities supports and constrains the earlier conclusions of this essay. Some, but not all, cities mirror the national trend.

Overall, arrests for public-order offenses as well as the actual amount of disorder in public have declined from the Civil War era until recent times. The meaning of the experiences of cities with conflicting trends is not fully clear, for while we can reasonably infer that a decline in arrests indexes a decline in offenses, we cannot so easily infer the opposite.[20] Still, given the general dominance of this trend since the growth of the industrial city, one might well speculate that the trend will continue, that public order will increasingly become the mode, and that drunken and disorderly behavior will become an insignificant aspect of urban life. Furthermore, good fortune and success will probably come to policy makers who try to eradicate such forms of disorder, for it appears that no matter what they do, order will increase.

Historians have dealt with the perceptions of urban disorder that echo in the primary literature down through the Progressive Era in four ways. One emphasizes ethnocultural and class conflict. Another focuses on changing standards and demands for control and use of urban space. A third looks at the phenomenon of urbanization. And a fourth considers the problem in terms of the rise and decline in Victorianism. While these four different conceptual and explanatory schemes overlap and tend to subsume one another, their arguments are of great importance in helping to conceptualize the problem of American urban disorder.

In the most common way of accounting for disorder, analysis rests on the expectation that ethnic, cultural, or class conflict in urban places could only be directly controlled or repressed through the formal application of legal sanctions reflecting the demands of the dominant group. The definition of dominant group depends, of course, on the historian's definition of conflict. In the case of ethnic conflict, the dominant group was usually native-born whites; for cultural conflict, the dominant group was usually Protestants; and for class conflict, the dominant group was the bourgeoisie. While these are overlapping definitions, the analysis of one usually precludes the other two. Thus, Progressive urban reformers have been seen as motivated by fear of immigrants, Catholics, or the working class. Each interpretation has similarities with the others. All, for instance, stress that the dominant group has a less expressive mode of public behavior than the subordinate group, and these behavioral differences account for the focus of the dominant group on rowdy public behavior. The assumption is that the subordinate groups, in fact, sanction behavior in public that is different from the dominant group's.[21]

A second scheme for analyzing disorder argues that changes in the uses of urban space lay at the heart of changed demands for public order, a position persuasively put forth by Schneider.[22] He shows how in the last half of the nineteenth century changed residential and commercial locations in Detroit created a more socially differentiated use of public space, especially in the downtown.

This made visible the rise of a "bachelor subculture," whose behavioral norms conflicted with those of the middle- and upper-level families; consequently, demands for policing of public behavior increased. This accounts for apparent changes in perceptions of and demands for order by placing all parties in a changing spatial context. Thus, the first issue to resolve, if we adhere to Schneider's analysis, relates to the spatial use of the city. And even if we do not follow his lead, we should keep in mind his point that disorderly conduct occurs in a spatially structured environment.

The third conceptual framework within which to examine urban disorder comes from a long line of discussion about the negative social consequences of urban life. According to proponents of this argument, urban life alienates people from traditional cultural values and social control norms, causing deviant, socially disruptive, and even violent behavior.[23] This notion has come under heavy attack in the past decade, with new evidence showing clearly that urbanization as a social force can no longer be seriously considered as a cause of criminal or deviant behavior.[24] At least one historian, Roger Lane, has made the counterargument that cities, especially large ones, had a moderating effect on disorder and violence. Lane asserts that the rise of large-scale workplaces, public education, and other organizations in nineteenth-century cities helped people to get along with one another, to resolve conflicts less violently than previously, and, in general, to make more orderly places in which to live.[25] Therefore, while some observers may wish to hold to the belief that the social effects of urban life create deviance, disorder, and violence, the recently developed evidence runs contrary to this view. Instead, current thinking suggests that we should expect either no causal links or a negative relationship between urban growth or size and indexes of deviance, disorder, and violence. Given this suggestion and the notion of competition for urban space, we have two conceptual frameworks that predict different outcomes for the nineteenth and twentieth centuries, the spatial-competition model of Schneider predicting a temporary rise in disorder arrests and Lane's model predicting a decline.

A fourth conceptual framework, the delineation of which is still emerging, promises to have applicability to problems in social history, including urban disorder, at least through the early decades of the twentieth century. This is the Victorian synthesis.[26] Most clearly articulated for the study of women's history, the Victorian synthesis holds promise for several reasons. It avoids the awkward political periodization of the nineteenth and early twentieth centuries, a periodization that is not very useful for organizing many aspects of social history and one that in some cases has subtly pushed historians to try to account for phenomena within the wrong time constraints.[27] The implied periodization of the Victorian synthesis, roughly from 1840 to 1920, accords well with many important features of American urban development, extending from early incorporation movements to the decade when most urban features had assumed their present institutional arrangements. In addition, the Victorian synthesis suggests that a certain unity, if not hegemony, in public behavioral values and norms obtained at least down to World War I. It implies that by the transitional era marked by World War I we should find changes both in disorderly behavior and in the norms of orderly behavior. This view tends to subsume the Lane thesis that nineteenth-century cities moderated the behavior of their inhabitants; it attributes the moderating effects to an even larger causal context, including a transatlantic bourgeois ideology, the expansion of industrial capitalism, and new behavioral expectations and definitions of gender roles. Finally, the Victorian synthesis suggests that disorderly behavior would have followed a certain trajectory of empirical incidence: a decline as hegemony became established; perhaps, but not so certainly, a rise as the hegemony declined. The prediction of a twentieth-century increase in disorder is problematic, for the decline of Victorianism does not necessarily mean a decline in all of its values and norms. If disorderly conduct had not risen in the 1920s, for instance, we could conclude that this specific set of values and the social means of informal implementation had persisted.

Each of the four conceptual frameworks described here applies more to the nineteenth than to the twentieth century, and each carries certain predictive expectations. As pointed out in the discussion of the Victorian synthesis, some predictions do not refute the others, but several do. We can summarize the predictions of each position. The conflict/control framework indicates that efforts to control urban disorder will vary positively with conflict itself; presumably, all three forms of conflict—class, ethnic, and cultural—rose through the nineteenth and twentieth centuries, down to World War II if not until the present. Thus, this framework predicts rising incidence of actual disorderly behavior and of control efforts—rising arrests for disorderly conduct—at least until about 1940. The framework that focuses on use of public space has somewhat less clear implications unless we can assume that the historical trend since 1850 in the use of public space had become progressively less heterogeneous as transport and housing alternatives had become more tailored to particular subgroups.[28] The spatial argument implies, then, a decline in control efforts, although, in contrast to the conflict/control framework, it implies nothing about the incidence or kind of actual public behavior. The third framework—including both the urbanization/alienation thesis and the urbanization/"urbanity" thesis—maintains that as urbanization continues, the incidence and control of disorder either increases with alienation or decreases with "urbanity." The fourth framework, the Victorian synthesis, implies a decline in incidence of and efforts to control public disorder until about 1920, with no clear implications for the subsequent era.

Of these various analytical frameworks, the conclusions suggested by this examination of arrest trends accord best with the framework that stresses the declining use of public space and with the one that claims that cities, as they age, become more orderly. Neither of these explanatory positions necessarily excludes the others. Nor do they exclude other explanations. Extending the Victorian synthesis down to the end of World War II would also neatly account for the data. This account finds support in recent studies of policing, which suggest that urban dwellers across class and ethnic boundaries wanted a modicum of urban order and seized on evolving urban police departments as one way of achieving this order.[29] This is not the place to resolve the explanatory problem but simply to point out that American historians have a new and interesting phenomenon to explain—the apparent rise of urban order.

APPENDIX: EFFECTS OF POLICE BEHAVIOR, LEGAL CHANGE, ALCOHOL CONSUMPTION, AND CITY DIFFERENCES

Four topics in this essay require more extended discussion. These include, first, the logical possibility that the decline in arrest rates paralleled the changing role of the police. Second, one must consider whether legal change created the visible shifts in arrests. Third, the relationship between levels of alcohol consumption and public drunkenness must be examined. And, fourth, because not all cities experienced simultaneous changes in public behavior and arrests, individual city differences must be contrasted.

1. One can argue that the decline in arrests in part reflected a rise in the informal police handling of public disorder to avoid the formality of arrest. According to Harold Pepinsky such a rise would parallel a shift in police role from proactive to reactive: from maintaining order to stopping crime.[30] This argument cannot be countered with empirical evidence, but an increase in informal behavior—beating, verbal humiliation, detainment without arrest—would certainly have been inconsistent with the trend in policing toward greater control of officers and more rule-bounded conduct. That the police simply ignored more disorderly behavior as their general focus shifted from class control to crime control is not consistent with one way in which police implemented crime-control strategies—that is, by arresting people who "looked like" criminals. Another argument to account for the decline in public-order arrests claims that the police themselves resisted making arrests, for the arrest and walk to the station house was an unpleasant business. This argument has more intuitive appeal for short-run changes or for the arrest practices in one city, but it could hardly account for a behavioral shift in policing over almost a century and in many cities. On the other hand, William A. Westley implies that police may not make order

arrests in those urban areas where they interpret disorderly behavior as a part of the culture.[31]

2. Did the decline in drunk and disorderly-conduct arrests come from legal change? As the overall downward trend in arrests is counterintuitive, the examination of the legal basis for arrest carries less explanatory burden than it otherwise might. For had arrests increased, we might expect that the number of arrestable offenses would have also increased, in part causing the arrest increase. To examine the question of legal change, I have examined all relevant state and federal court cases from 1800 to 1930 that were abstracted in the *American Digest*.[32] This analysis is therefore limited by the adequacy of the *American Digest* as a sampling tool. The procedure used was to analyze the mix of the content of the appellate cases by decade, asking, for instance, what proportion of all cases under drunkenness, disorderly conduct, and breach of peace came from the South or what proportion focused on language acts. Most of the results of this analysis were inconclusive, and those reported here include all of the conclusive results.

Two regions proved to be of interest. The Northeast's percentage of all disorder-related cases declined from 50 percent to 10 percent between 1860 and 1880, rose steadily back to the 50 percent mark by 1920, then fell to almost nothing in 1930. The South, whose percentage of cases has to be ignored for the 1860s, contributed a steady 50 percent of the cases from 1870 until 1910 when its contribution began to fall, dropping to about 10 percent by 1930. These regional differences suggest that public-order laws had different functions in these two regions. The South showed a consistent concern with definition of order until the onset of recession and depression drove the costs of disputing these definitions too high. The Northeast followed a more predictable curve, with urban growth and change in this section focusing more and more attention on the definition of public order.

Of more interest than regional location is the kind of behavior on which the judicial deliberations centered, especially over the question of physical action or verbal action. Consistent with the general conclusions of this article is the hypothesis that rising standards of public order and behavior would move the focus of order statutes from physical behavior in the early period to verbal behavior later on. To a very limited extent the data support this expectation: before 1870, at least 60 percent of the cases appealed concerned physical action; between 1870 and 1939, excepting the decade 1920–1929, 50 percent or fewer cases concerned physical action.

If part of the decline in order arrests came from increased access to private space for disorderly behavior, the location of the physical action should also have responded to this change, with an increased concern shown for behavior in private or semipublic places. The data on location are not consistent before 1850, but from 1850 to 1890 a steady 9 to 16 percent of the cases explicitly concern physical action in public places, while from 1891 to 1939 a steady 20 to 30 percent concern public places. Certainly these figures do not support the hypothesis that disorderly behavior slowly moved indoors, so to speak, but neither do they allow us to reject the thesis, for they may in fact reflect a generally low level of judicial concern with the location of behavior. One final approach to the question of physical action is to look at the mix of cases that did not concern language-based conduct. The distribution of these cases over time confirms the trends of cases that explicitly concered action–a high concern with action before 1850, lowered interest from 1850 to 1919, and more concern between 1919 and 1939. Finally, an impressionistic note: prior to 1920, the concept of reasonableness did not seem to enter the *American Digest*'s report of the appellate decisions, but during the 1920s this concept did crop up. This cannot stand as evidence of some new reasonableness test of public drunk and disorder offenses, but it does suggest the continuing concern with more precise standards for order offenses.

3. Did changes in alcohol consumption cause the decrease in arrests? If the per capita consumption of alcohol had also declined between 1860 and 1970 except for a surge between 1945 and 1946, then we would have no problem of explanation and a less interesting arrest series. Figure 17.2 presents three estimates of beverage alcohol consumed per capita in the United States from 1860 to 1975. The estimates suggest that from the mid-1870s, and possibly earlier, to 1910, alcohol consumption per capita rose steadily and gradually. Consumption then took a violent dip from 1915 until the mid-1930s, thereafter resuming its upward climb, though starting at a lower level than the prior high point of 1910. Because of the questionable accuracy of data measuring alcohol consumption per capita during Prohibition, one must doubt the precision of the measured dip between 1915 and 1935. The absolute amount of the decline is uncertain, and the drop in consumption may have been more gradual, perhaps continuing until 1940. A visual inspection of the alcohol data, however, shows two clear trends of increasing per capita consumption interrupted by war, Prohibition, and depression. The post–World War II increase in consumption reflects a resumption of the historical trend toward more per capita alcohol consumption, the data for 1970 finally assuming the level reached just before Prohibition. While an interesting phenomenon in itself, this trend probably comes from a combination of changing age structure, rising real wages, and changing styles of personal consumption. But, for the purposes of the analysis of public drunkenness and disorder, the level of alcohol consumption is irrelevant.

Note that if arrests for drunk and disorderly conduct were to be plotted against alcohol consumption, the result for each period of reliable and consistent measurement would be a negative curve. If one holds the view that arrests mirror precisely the amount of disorderly and drunken behavior and that alcohol consumption per capita drives this behavior, then the curve clearly rejects one of the two models—

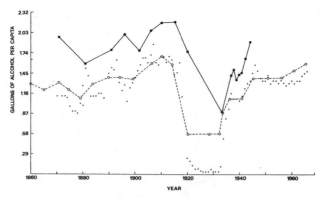

Figure 17.2 Estimates of United States Beverage Alcohol Consumption per Capita, 1860–1965*
*Large black dots and solid line estimate consumption per capita of the population fifteen years of age and older (see Jellinek); small circles and broken line represent five-year estimates of consumption per capita of the whole population (see Rorabaugh); small black dots present yearly estimates of alcohol produced, 1870–1910, and alcohol consumed, 1860, 1911–1965, per capita of the whole population.
Sources: U.S. Department of Commerce, Bureau of the Census, *Statistical Abstract of the United States: 1950* (Washington, 1950), 787; U.S. Department of Commerce, Bureau of the Census, *Statistical Abstract of the United States: 1964* (Washington, 1964), 793; U.S. Department of Commerce, Bureau of the Census, *Statistical Abstract of the United States: 1967* (Washington, 1967), 795; U.S. Department of Commerce, Bureau of the Census, *Historical Statistics of the United States: Colonial Times to 1970,* 2 vols. (Washington, 1975), 2: 690–91; E. M. Jellinek, "Recent Trends in Alcoholism and in Alcohol Consumption," *Quarterly Journal of Studies on Alcohol* 8 (June 1974): 8; W. J. Rorabaugh, "Estimated U.S. Alcoholic Beverage Consumption, 1790–1860," *Journal of Studies on Alcohol* 37 (March 1976): 357–64.

as alcohol consumption rises, arrests fall. On the other hand, should one hold the view that arrests do not so much measure drunk and disorderly behavior, but rather the deterrence efforts of the police, then the curve gives the coefficient of the relationship—and it is a highly successful one—an increase in arrests driving down the consumption of alcohol. Both arguments are wrong, however, for the models are inadequately specified and the data do not support the more elaborate techniques. In fact, both models provide classic examples of simultaneity.[33] The problem can be verbalized as follows. Let us assume that economic prosperity produces a higher alcohol consumption; let us also assume that arrests effectively deter alcohol consumption; finally, let us assume that increased public drunkenness produces greater pressures on police to make arrests, with additional operating expenses supplied during times of economic prosperity. As prosperity increases, it drives up the consumption of alcohol and therefore the incidence of public drunkenness; rising incidence of drunkenness produces greater demands for deterrence, which produce greater numbers of arrests, which in turn drive down the incidence of public drunkenness. Within this set of variables, it is impossible to analyze these compounding effects. To separate the two and allow the use of simultaneous equations, one needs a variable which operates on only one of the two causal systems—a "swing" variable—a variable very difficult to identify. In historical data the problem is in fact compounded, for we have no measure of the actual incidence of public drunkenness. But, in general, if deterrence is effective and if increased undesirable behavior provokes increased deterrence, then an analysis of the relationship is very difficult. This is why I do not begin to try to speculate on the deterrent effects of declined public order arrests, particularly since even a technically perfect untangling of the problem would be of less interest than a simple description of more directly observable rates.

4. The cities whose arrest trends do not conform to the national trend, 1860–1920, may be grouped by comparing simple Pearsonian correlations. While there are more than enough cases to pair cities and create a correlation matrix, there are enough randomly dispersed missing values to stop a more complex cluster analysis technique. This matrix indicates the existence of four main clusters—the first including Boston, Lowell, Buffalo, and Richmond; the second including St. Louis, Detroit, and Richmond; the third with Baltimore, Lowell, and New Haven; the fourth with San Francisco, Lowell, and New Haven. These clusters all show positive and statistically significant intercorrelations with one another, but in only two pairs are the R^2 values greater than .19. These two pairs, Baltimore with New Haven and Richmond with St. Louis, make more intuitive sense than the large clusters, for at least each pair is vaguely regional. None of the clusters point toward a substantively appealing interpretation, given the broad scope of this article. But the implication of these clusters of cities whose drunk and disorderly-conduct arrest trends differ from the national trends is that case studies of individual cities must pose questions which place the unit under intensive analysis in contrast to national trends. In significant ways public order in San Francisco differed from order in the bulk of large cities, and to understand this difference will illuminate both the individual city and the broad national trends.

Because of the postulated shift in the relationship of public-order arrests to depression and war, and also because more complete individual city data are available for the period before the 1910–1920 era, Table 17.1 has only given the slopes for the years prior to 1920. For fourteen of the original twenty-three cities in this study, reasonably complete data down to 1951 can be found. Of these fourteen, eleven have negative slopes, continuing the national decline on the level of the individual city, and three have positive slopes. (See Table 17.3.) Although these three nonconforming cities do not contradict the analysis in this article, they do suggest an interesting problem in need of further city-level research.

Table 17.2 Pearsonian Correlation of Drunk and Disorderly Conduct Arrest Rates for Cities Deviating from the National Trend, 1860–1920, Using First Differences

	St. Louis	Baltimore	San Francisco	Buffalo	Detroit	Richmond	New Haven	Lowell
Boston	.21***	.09 (ns)	−.11 (ns)	.26***	−.10***	.39*	0	.35*
St. Louis		−.03 (ns)	−.34*	.09 (ns)	.32*	.71*	−.01 (ns)	.06 (ns)
Baltimore			.13 (ns)	−.14 (ns)	.16 (ns)	−.13 (ns)	.60*	.28**
San Francisco				.08 (ns)	.06 (ns)	−.34**	.32**	.30**
Buffalo					.06 (ns)	.44*	.04 (ns)	.53*
Detroit						.34*	.42*	.02 (ns)
Richmond							−.01 (ns)	.28**
New Haven								.31**

* = statistically significant at .01
** = statistically significant at .05
*** = statistically significant at .10
(ns) = not statistically significant
Sources: see Table 17.1.

Table 17.3 Trends in Arrest Rates for Drunkenness and Disorderly Conduct for Individual Cities, 1920–1951: Slope and Significance

City	Slope	Significance
New York City	−.62	.00001
Philadelphia	−.16	.00002
Chicago	−.23	.00001
Boston	−.17	.07
St. Louis	−.11	.001
Baltimore	−.02	n.s.
Cincinnati	−.04	.0001
San Francisco	.06	.07
Buffalo	−.26	.00001
Newark	−.35	.00001
Detroit	−.12	.00001
Milwaukee	.10	.10
Rochester	−.11	.00001
Richmond	.43	.00001

Source: Annual reports of city police departments or annual mayor's reports. This list includes those cities from Table 17.1 for which data down to 1951 could be obtained. It excludes major cities, such as Los Angeles, which grew in rank and size in the twentieth century.

NOTES

1. Robert Brent Toplin, *Unchallenged Violence: An American Ordeal* (Westport, Conn., 1975), 265–69; Richard Maxwell Brown, *Strain of Violence: Historical Studies of American Violence and Vigilantism* (New York, 1975), 29–30; David Brion Davis, *Homicide in American Fiction, 1798–1860: A Study in Social Values* (Ithaca, N.Y., 1957), 257–65; Arthur Meier Schlesinger, *The Rise of the City,*

1878–1898 (New York, 1933), xv, 111-20. See also the fascinating popular works of Herbert Asbury such as *The Gangs of New York: An Informal History of the Underworld* (Garden City, N.Y., 1928). The portrayal of our past as uniquely violent has begun to be challenged. Rhodri Jeffreys-Jones analyzes the "myth" of industrial violence in the United States and flatly states that the argument "that the United States has had an exceptionally violent history is based on false or non-existent premises and is groundless." Rhodri Jeffreys-Jones, *Violence and Reform in American History* (New York, 1978), 28. For a useful literature survey of recent work on perceptions, see Steven Balkin, "Victimization Rates, Safety and Fear of Crime," *Social Problems* 26 (Feb. 1979): 343–58. For a sensitive analysis of American urban homicide, see Henry P. Lundsgaarde, *Murder in Space City: A Cultural Analysis of Houston Homicide Patterns* (New York, 1977).

2. Samuel L. Clemens (Mark Twain), *The Innocents Abroad, or the New Pilgrim's Progress* (Hartford, Conn., 1869), 112; Stephen Crane, *Maggie: A Girl of the Streets* (New York, 1896).

3. For an applied, if not explicit, historical/geographical notion of *at risk,* formulated in terms of action within the constraints of nineteenth-century urban space, see John C. Schneider, "Public Order and the Geography of the City: Crime, Violence, and the Police in Detroit, 1845–1875," *Journal of Urban History* 4 (Feb. 1978): 183–208; see also John C. Schneider, *Detroit and the Problem of Order, 1830–1880: A Geography of Crime, Riot, and Policing* (Lincoln, Nebr., 1980). The original insight into the different degrees to which social groups can be at risk for arrest came from Arthur L. Stinchcombe, "Institutions of Privacy in the Determination of Police Administrative Practice," *American Journal of Sociology* 69 (Sept. 1963): 150–60. Some of the methodological problems implicit in Arthur L. Stinchcombe's analysis are dealt with clearly in John I. Kitsuse and Aaron V. Cicourel, "A Note on the Uses of Official Statistics," *Social Problems* 11 (Fall 1963): 131–39.

4. This arrest categorization represents an aggregation of the major public-order arrest categories, which occasionally varied from city to city. These include drunkenness, disorderly conduct, drunk and disorderly, corner lounging, vagrancy, suspicion, and like categories. Of these, drunk and disorderly were by far the most numerous categories. For two very useful anthropological analyses of public drinking, see James P. Spradley, *You Owe Yourself a Drunk: An Ethnography of Urban Nomads* (Boston, 1970), and Robert B. Edgerton and Craig MacAndrew, *Drunken Comportment: A Social Explanation* (Chicago, 1969). For discussion of drinking patterns, see also Brian Harrison, *Drink and the Victorians: The Temperance Question in England, 1815–1872* (London, 1971), 37–63, 297–347, and Norman H. Clark, *Deliver Us from Evil: An Interpretation of American Prohibition* (New York, 1976).

5. Thorsten Sellin, "The Basis of a Crime Index," *Journal of the American Institute of Criminal Law and Criminology* 22 (Sept. 1931): 346. For a useful introduction to twentieth-century crime statistics, see Michael D. Maltz, "Crime Statistics: A Historical Perspective," *Crime and Delinquency* 23 (Jan. 1977): 32–40.

6. Because it is public, disorderly behavior is open to observation and interference strategies. Of course, the question of deterrence is much more complex than this observation might wrongly suggest. See Alfred Blumstein, Jacqueline Cohen, and Daniel Nagin, eds., *Deterrence and Incapacitation: Estimating the Effects of Criminal Sanctions on Crime Rates* (Washington, 1978), 5–6, 19–63.

7. Harold Garfinkel, "Conditions of Successful Degradation Ceremonies," *American Journal of Sociology* 61 (March 1956): 420–24.

8. The first radio car was introduced in Detroit in 1927. John L. Thompson, "Uniform Crime Reporting: Historical IACP Landmark," *Police Chief* 35 (Feb. 1968): 23.

9. Given the current trend toward decriminalization of alcohol-related arrests, one would like to believe this implication; however, a similar notion in the early twentieth century (the

so-called Golden Rule policy) failed. See Samuel Walker, *A Critical History of Police Reform: The Emergence of Professionalism* (Lexington, Mass., 1977), 94–98.

10. See, for instance, Paul Boyer, *Urban Masses and Moral Order in America, 1820–1920* (Cambridge, 1978), 67–84, 123–31. This book examines a century of middle-class battle with what appeared to be rising urban disorder. Another analysis asserts that police behavior ran counter to middle-class and elite wishes and perceptions. Especially when the police helped ensure the reelection of immigrant political machines, elite reformers attempted to reform the police who were indeed corrupt. For a lengthy discussion of various reform movements, see Robert M. Fogelson, *Big-City Police* (Cambridge, 1977), 67–92.

11. For the era he covers, John C. Schneider finds a perception of rising disorder. Schneider, *Detroit and the Problem of Order*, 64–77.

12. Eugene J. Watts, in a detailed study of St. Louis, has been able to adjust arrest data per officer's hours on patrol. Adjusting for the fewer hours on patrol still yielded declining order arrests per officer. Eugene J. Watts, "Police Priorities in Twentieth Century St. Louis," *Journal of Social History* 14 (Summer 1981): 649–74.

13. Compare, for instance, Schlesinger, *Rise of the City,* 360. Norman H. Clark implies a rise in drunkenness from 1810 to 1840 and a decline to 1850, followed by a rise to 1910, a decline to 1940, and a rise to 1970. Yet he asserts that Prohibition "became a social movement when public drunkenness became a social problem." See Clark, *Deliver Us from Evil,* 20, 146–47, 13. This implies a rise in public drunkenness, unless one reads the statement to indicate that drunken behavior simply became redefined as a problem.

14. For perceptions of tramps, see Paul T. Ringenbach, *Tramps and Reformers, 1873–1916: The Discovery of Unemployment in New York* (Westport, Conn., 1973), 5–12. In the second decade of the twentieth century, at least in New York, the disorderly person charge was expanded to include men who did not support their children, wives, or mothers, if in so doing they forced the abandoned ones to become charges. See the summaries of *City of New York ex rel. De Stefano* v. *De Stefano,* 196 N.Y.S. 482 (1921); *People on Complaint of Berman* v. *Berman,* 197 N.Y.S. 502 (1922); *City of New York* v. *Wasserman,* 196 N.Y.S. 325, 40 N.Y.Cr.R. 168 (1922); and *People* v. *Meyer,* 207 N.Y.S. 741, 124 Misc. Rep. 285 (1925); in *Third Decennial Edition of the American Digest: A Complete Digest of All Reported Cases from 1916 to 1926,* 29 vols. (St. Paul, 1928–1929), 10: 1140–41.

15. Kirk Jeffrey, "The Family as Utopian Retreat from the City: The Nineteenth-Century Contribution," in *The Family, Communes, and Utopian Societies,* ed. Sallie TeSelle (New York, 1972), 21–41.

16. J. C. Burnham, "New Perspectives on the Prohibition 'Experiment' of the 1920s," *Journal of Social History* 2 (Fall 1968): 51–68. For a useful, thorough survey of the measurable quantitative impact of Prohibition, see Clark Warburton, *The Economic Results of Prohibition* (New York, 1932), 101–2.

17. For an example of the impact of politics on reporting, see Mark H. Haller, "Historical Roots of Police Behavior: Chicago, 1890–1925," *Law and Society Review* 10 (Winter 1976): 303–23. This article shows how the Chicago police manipulated arrest data for short periods of time.

18. Arrests in Buffalo have been analyzed at least twice, each author finding support for his or her own particular theoretical perspective. See Sidney L. Harring and Lorraine M. McMullin, "The Buffalo Police, 1872–1900: Labor Unrest, Political Power, and the Creation of the Police Institution," *Crime and Social Justice* 4 (Fall–Winter 1975): 5–14; Elwin H. Powell, "Crime as a Function of Anomie," *Journal of Criminal Law, Criminology and Police Science* 57 (June 1966): 161–71.

19. Interestingly, two of these three atypical cities have been studied as cases. On Buffalo, see note 18. On San Francisco, see Eric Monkkonen, "Toward a Dynamic Theory of Crime and the Police: A Criminal Justice System Perspective," *Historical Methods Newsletter* 10 (Fall 1977): 157–65.

20. For a carefully reasoned argument for the greater reliability of criminal statistics that indicate a long downward trend, see Ted R. Gurr, "Historical Trends in Violent Crimes: A Critical Review of Evidence," *Crime and Justice: An Annual Review of Research* 3 (Sept. 1981): 295–353. Given the long rise in official attention to criminal offenses, an upward trend might only graph increased interest.

21. On the Progressives' fear of immigrants, see Richard Hofstadter, *The Age of Reform: From Bryan to F.D.R.* (New York, 1955), 176–83. Much of the Progressive anti-Catholicism came from a Protestant failure to deal with immigrants as well as did the Catholic Church. See Robert D. Cross, ed., *The Church and the City, 1865–1910* (Indianapolis, 1967), xxxiv–xxxv. For a discussion of Progressive reform and the working class that focuses on deviance and crime control, see Steven L. Schlossman, *Love and the American Delinquent: The Theory and Practice of "Progressive" Juvenile Justice, 1825–1920* (Chicago, 1977). On the male culture of pre-Prohibition saloons, see Jon M. Kingsdale, "The 'Poor Man's Club': Social Functions of the Urban Working-Class Saloon," *American Quarterly* 25 (Oct. 1973): 472–89.

22. Schneider, *Detroit and the Problem of Order,* 3–5, 40–52, 135–39.

23. For the classic exposition of the mechanism by which the city caused alienation, which in turn led to anomie and deviance, see Georg Simmel, "The Metropolis and Mental Life," in *The Sociology of Georg Simmel,* ed. and trans. Kurt H. Wolff (Glencoe, Ill., 1950), 409–24.

24. Eric H. Monkkonen, *The Dangerous Class: Crime and Poverty in Columbus, Ohio, 1860–1885* (Cambridge, 1975); Michael P. Smith, *The City and Social Theory* (New York, 1979).

25. Roger Lane, *Violent Death in the City: Suicide, Accident, and Murder in Nineteenth-Century Philadelphia* (Cambridge, 1979). For a related argument on drunkenness, see Harrison, *Drink and the Victorians,* 297–347.

26. For the clearest statement on Victorian America, see Daniel Walker Howe, "Victorian Culture in America," in *Victorian America,* ed. Daniel Walker Howe (Philadelphia, 1976), 3–28.

27. Thomas C. Cochran, "The 'Presidential Synthesis' in American History," *American Historical Review* 52 (July 1948): 748–59.

28. For one perspective on the suburbanization process, see Scott Donaldson, *The Suburban Myth* (New York, 1969). The phenomenon has recently been reconceptualized as the relationship of work to residence. Stephanie Wohl Greenberg, "Industrialization in Philadelphia: The Relationship between Industrial Location and Residential Patterns, 1880–1930" (Ph.D. diss., Temple University, 1977); Kenneth T. Jackson, "Urban Deconcentration in the Nineteenth Century: A Statistical Inquiry," in *The New Urban History: Quantitative Explorations by American Historians,* ed. Leo F. Schnore (Princeton, 1975), 110–42. How the decreased use of public space increased the proportion of homicide in the home from 30 percent to 50 percent is shown in Lane, *Violent Death,* 83.

29. I make this argument about the role of police in Eric H. Monkkonen, *Police in Urban America, 1860–1920* (Cambridge, Eng., 1981), 108–28. A growing body of research on working-class culture shows the cross-class basis of the temperance movement. See Ian R. Tyrrell, "Temperance and Economic Change in the Antebellum North," in *Alcohol, Reform, and Society: The Liquor Issue in Social Context,* ed. Jack S. Blocker (Westport, Conn., 1979), 45–67. Ian R. Tyrrell's view that temperance support came from workers and capitalists representing the emerging industrial order is supported by James R. Green, "The 'Salesmen-Soldiers' of the '*Appeal* Army': A Profile of Rank-and-File Socialist Agitators," in *Socialism and the Cities,* ed.

Bruce M. Stave (Port Washington, N.Y., 1975), 29. James R. Green further argues that the "working-class self-reform" of temperance "persisted into the twentieth century." This argument is congruent with John C. Burnham's analysis of the consequences of Prohibition; he claims that prior to Prohibition drinking and drunkenness centered on the saloon and on drinking as group behavior. During and after Prohibition drinking and drunkenness took on a new meaning of individualism, of social assertion of self, and sometimes of protest. Burnham, "New Perspectives on the Prohibition 'Experiment,'" 52–53, 63. The notion that in the late nineteenth century heavy drinking occurred mainly among men outside of the home is supported for all ethnic groups but the Irish by Robin Room, "Cultural Contingencies of Alcoholism: Variations between and within Nineteenth-Century Urban Ethnic Groups in Alcohol-Related Death Rates," *Journal of Health and Social Behavior* 9 (June 1968): 99–113.

30. Harold Pepinsky to Eric Monkkonen, Dec. 10, 1980.

31. William A. Westley, *Violence and the Police: A Sociological Study of Law, Custom, and Morality* (Cambridge, 1970), 10, 98–99.

32. *Century Edition of the American Digest: A Complete Digest of All Reported American Cases from the Earliest Times to 1896,* 50 vols. (St. Paul, 1897–1904); *Decennial Edition of the American Digest: A Complete Digest of All Reported Cases from 1897 to 1906,* 25 vols. (St. Paul, 1908–1912); *Second Decennial Edition of the American Digest: A Complete Digest of All Reported Cases from 1906 to 1916,* 24 vols. (St. Paul, 1917–1923); *Third Decennial Edition of the American Digest* (St. Paul, 1928–1929); *Fourth Decennial Digest, American Digest System: A Complete Digest of All Decisions of the State and Federal Courts as Reported in the National Reporter System and the State Reports, 1926 to 1936,* 34 vols. (St. Paul, 1937–1938).

33. For a clear explanation of the problem, see David F. Greenberg, *Mathematical Criminology* (New Brunswick, N.J., [1979]), 36–49.

18

American Cities and the Creation of Order

Do police bring order to cities? Are American cities disorderly because of their social composition? Are safe places dull places? And dangerous ones exciting? Does urban growth cause crime? And, given the decentralized federal American state, how do policing and city structure relate to the nation state? This essay deals with some of these huge issues. It is important for Americans to think about themselves from abroad, as I did when writing this. Our unique federal system looms larger as we struggle to explain how our system has evolved so differently. We think we have a national criminal justice framework, when we don't. The sworn police officers of New York City and Chicago, for example, outnumber the total number of federal officers involved in criminal investigation and enforcement (*Sourcebook of Criminal Justice Statistics,* 1995, Tables 1.51 and 1.6). Most criminal law enforcement is local, and local governments have enormous leeway in what they do and how they do it.

Hinted at in this essay are other issues about crime and creativity: why should the big cities have so much of the creative energy? Is it for the same reason that they have drawn in the disorderly? That is, urban economists talk about the economies of agglomeration; the biggest cities have economies that make possible the most exotic brain surgery, the elite jewelry markets, and high art. These same economies allow criminal subcultures to survive at the same time that they make bureaucracies like the police (or public schools) flounder. It is the urban economy that supports these very different activities

First published in Herbert Reinike, ed., *"Nur für die Sicherheit da?" Zur Geschichte der Polizei im 19. und 20. Jahrhundert* (Frankfurt: Campus Verlag, 1993).

and, blurring analysis, makes it seem as if the same impetus drives them all. It doesn't take crime to make art, just as it doesn't take a metropolis to make jewelry or support advanced surgery. But, the economic advantages of the metropolis do foster the consumption of special things.

Simultaneously, the same numerical imperative of the large city disadvantages virtually all social services: bigness hurts school systems, police departments, jails, social welfare systems, and public hospitals. So the places with the best of the times also overflow with the worst of the times.

Two contextual differences between European and U.S. cities must be considered when examining their histories of crime and policing. First, U.S. cities grew almost explosively in the second half of the nineteenth century, but neither law nor custom laid down models of modern municipal government. Most forms of government were simply copied from nearby cities or states, but few states stipulated what a city should do. As an example of this lack of control, when the small (population 8,000) city of Watertown, Wisconsin, decided not to pay its creditors in 1868, the voters elected to dissolve the city government (Monkkonen 1984: 140). The city corporation existed in law, but no actual people filled the governmental slots. The people were still there, the social entity we would call a small city still existed, but its formal governmental representatives did not exist. Second, these cities all had only those revenues they could raise through property tax, the rates of which were open to voter manipulation. Because of the white male franchise and relatively high proportions of working-class home ownership, voters constrained city spending.

The consequences for policing were that cities created their departments at different times, funded them at different strengths, and paid their officers differing wages. In addition, all police had local responsibilities, with little incentive or institutional mechanism for intercommunications or coordination. Police departments resembled one another very closely, though not because of law, but because of imitation: cities copied each other or turned to experts from other cities.

In spite of the historical variety across the landscape of U.S. cities and their individual police departments, recent research has produced some tentative generalizations about both policing and criminal behavior. When summarized, these present a series of contradictions. First, between 1850 and 1910, cities grew at dramatic rates; poor and immigrant populations doubled and tripled city sizes. Yet our collective research results now indicate that, as best we can measure, rates of criminal and public order offenses either remained stable or declined (Monkkonen 1981c: 73; Gurr 1989). Second, between 1890 and 1920, the police of major U.S. cities became rationalized, more explicitly oriented toward "scientific" crime control, and less concerned about disorder. Yet it appears that serious crime ceased its decline while the public order offenses of less concern to the police may have continued to drop—or, at least, their arrests did (Watts 1983; Monkkonen 1981a and 1981b; Bijleveld and Monkkonen 1991: 11; Wertsch 1987). And third, since the 1930s, the U.S. welfare state has expanded and made fairer its social provision, U.S. cities have attained relatively high standards of living, racial discrimination has moderated, and police practices have improved dramatically. Yet, by most measures, cities have seen soaring rates of violence and felony crime.[1]

Lane (1979) offers the most comprehensive explanation of these diverging events, arguing that urbanization and certain processes in nineteenth-century industrial cities, e.g., the orderly behavior required in factories, produced the increase in nineteenth-century urban order. Orderly behavior, he argues, was produced by social institutions enforcing rules that resulted in a new sense of order within individuals. Factory time, to paraphrase Gutman (1973) and Thompson (1967), became individual time, and crowded out the leisure and unpredictability which led to disorderly and criminal behavior.[2] In essence, Lane has reversed the classic model of Simmel, who conceptualized metropolitan life as leading to alienation, anomie, and individual deviance, if not disorder. For Simmel the psychopathic criminal symbolized the metropolitan personality; for Lane, it is the child/adult who shows up for work regularly, eats at a bell, and urinates only at set times of the day.

Lane's analysis conforms with known facts better than Simmel's because of our nearly century longer experience with the new urban world. The research conclusions of historians dealing with the criminal disorder of this world have sketched in the crude outlines of a now familiar picture: declining rates of criminal violence from the mid- or early nineteenth century to the mid-twentieth century, turning dramatically upward in the late 1950s. Except for the latest, none of the trends were in the direction Simmel's analysis would have predicted. But better fitting as it is, Lane's analysis, as a substitute for Simmel's, lacks precision and clarity in accounting for recent increases in crime as well as nineteenth-century declines. The vision of a transformed culture and personality of the new urban industrial workers simply argues too much, especially when one considers that not all workers experienced the factory regimen nor did all youth spend long periods in schools (Rodgers 1977).

The resolution of these three contradictions requires our serious attention. The first place to begin a consideration of these contradictions is with the base line on which the whole analysis rests: crime rates. Twenty-five years ago, historians considered the counting of crimes the most challenging part of understanding them. In fact, most who dealt with criminal justice history used various indicators of crime to reflect on the criminal justice system, not on crime itself. But more recently, when so many research results from across Western history converged, skeptical historians began to take more seriously the idea that the variety of ways of counting crime had a parallel if not exact relationship to the actual amount of crime (Gatrell and Hadden 1972, and Gatrell 1980).[3] Although still complex and subtle, there is now a general belief that some aspects of the criminal past are, in principle, recoverable.

The notion of measuring crime is complex. Elsewhere, I have argued that crime statistics tell us first about the criminal justice system (Monkkonen 1981c). By this I mean that our data about events come to us created by and filtered through various organizations created for purposes other than producing these measures. To begin to consider the measures as measures of anything other than the organizations that produced them we must first understand those organizations. To try to take the measures as direct assumes that the transmitting agencies are transparent and misses interesting information about the agencies themselves.

But this position does not imply that the data tell us *only* about the system that produced them. There are other reasons to think that we can know something systematic about crime. Homicide research, for instance, can come fairly close to finding out the actual number of homicides because of the consistent definitions of the crime and the regularity with which many societies have recorded it. In a data base built only on arrest data, new statistical techniques pull out variation which seems to be only explained as causes by variation in felony crimes (Bijleveld and Monkkonen 1990). But this is not an admonition to immediately interpret information generated by the criminal justice system as transparent; in particular, we should consider the process and purposes for which the data were created.

There are, after all, two distinctly different ways to view the subject of crime. The control system (and the social scientist) sees some sort of regularity—similar numbers, places, people, situations. This is because the conceptualization and state-created definition of crime as a category of events attends to the category first, the events second. But from the perspective of people in the social system, crime, when understood as actually experienced, is a sporadic and highly asymmetric event. Notable and traumatic crimes are rare and unusual. And all crimes are asymmetric in that a minor episode in the offender's life can take on deep significance in the victim's.

For the analyst, neither construction is correct or incorrect: each is appropriate to consider. But neither is appropriate for all analysis. This has immediate methodological consequences. To analyze organizations dealing with crime, regular variation is important. To analyze the social production of crime, its regularity must be open to question.

Attentive as we are to the organizations that produce the crime indicators, we would not make the claim that crime is only a construction of the organization. After all, in an empty place with no persons, even the most aggressive crime-control agency could produce no data. Similarly, a place with ten persons and a place with a million would have some differences, even if wildly different sources produced the information. This is why historians almost immediately turn to population as a denominator and produce rates. But for several reasons, this is a tricky move, first because it carries with it a parallel notion of the social production of crimes, and second, because we all too often use the wrong population figures. Both should be carefully examined.

The first, which I develop below, carries with it the heavy freight of our customary assumptions that criminal behavior is produced with regularity and that this regularity is indicative of the existence of social laws. Consequently, we are unwilling to accept irregularity, for it implies that no laws govern the production of criminal events. It would do us well to always hold in reserve the logical possibility that no overarching laws govern the production of criminal events.

But our genuine progress in understanding the criminal justice system and the statistics it produces has not seen similarly heightened informational sophistication and sensitivity to the denominator of crime rates—that is, the population figures by which the numbers of criminal occurrences are divided. This is the second problem we have to confront in our customary mode of presenting crime information.

Because the age and sex distribution of criminals and their victims is not the same as the whole population, one must be careful in percapitizing events. The total population as a denominator accurately tells about crime in the whole society, but it does not accurately tell about the reasons for its amount. A comparison of mid-nineteenth-century New York City murderers' and victims' ages with the age structure of the city's whole population shows, as one would expect, how age profile of the total population was not the same as the murderers and victims. The city's population shows the clear signs of immigration and high infant mortality with a bulge

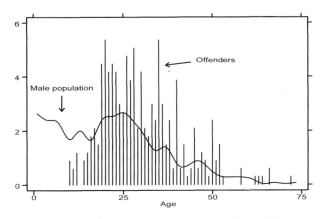

Figure 18.1 New York City murderer and total male population ages, mid-nineteenth century. Source: Monkkonen (2001).

in the population between fifteen and forty-five. The population of murderers and victims exaggerates this bulge, most falling between the ages of fifteen and forty-five.

A city with a large proportion of twenty- and thirty-year-old males will have a higher rate of crime per the total population. Relatively small shifts in the size of the crime-producing age group will provide larger per capita shifts in offenses, even if the rate of offending by age-specific groups stays the same. The more age-concentrated the subgroup which produces the crime, the greater the multiplier. For instance, a city in which the criminal offenses come from 15 percent of the population (adult males) and which experiences a modest 1 percent population growth all concentrated in this subgroup will experience nearly a 7 percent increase in total crime. For industrial cities with their typically high infant mortality rates and immigration-driven growth, the implications for order are enormous; short-term population swings driven by migration can be almost invisible to census enumerators but can cause larger variations in crime rates. The whole city's amount of crime and disorder may change dramatically, yet the change does not derive from any fundamental change in the nature of the society or in its crime-control apparatus.

A parallel circumstance can occur when the criminal behavior of a small crime-producing group changes its behavior slightly. The multiplier effect makes the small change seem very large indeed and can easily be misinterpreted by the analyst as indicative of some deep social change, so that when a relatively small group becomes more or less criminally active, its social impact seems quite large. This should make historians cautious in interpreting meaning. Consider a person who ordinarily gets drunk and starts a vicious fight three times a year but who now does so four times. This is a one-third increase in his personal crime rate (which criminologists customarily call lambda), but would we really want to interpret it as indicating a social-structural shift? In essence, from the point of view of the whole city, its social-control mechanism, and the additional victim perhaps yes, but as far as the historian's analysis of social change, probably not.

Figure 18.2 displays an estimate of the proportion of the total U.S. population composed of young adult males, rural and urban. The picture here is of a pre-1850 declining, then post-1850 rising proportion, until the beginning of the twentieth century. The long decline then lasts until the mid-twentieth century. Impressionistically, only the post-1960 increase in at-risk population corresponds with known trends in crime. No official separate age/gender compilation has been produced for nineteenth-century cities, so one must estimate the urban proportions of these young men. All evidence suggests that these estimates may undercount even though cities did have a larger number of women than men. Figure 18.3 focuses more on cities than does Figure 18.2, and the data it reports are also only estimates, for the same reasons. It pictures the proportion of the total population of U.S. cities which were males between fifteen and twenty-nine years old. The estimate seems right for the nineteenth century, climbing as cities grew throughout the century except for

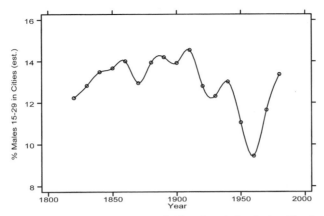

Figure 18.2 Estimated Proportion of Urban Population in Age/Gender Crime-Prone Group. Source: Monkkonen (2001).

the drop caused by Civil War mortality in 1870. They also suggest a decline roughly equivalent until World Wars I and II, then a rise, both for black males and whites. This latter conforms more with known crime trends of course.

In some contrast to these data distributions is my best estimate for New York City, which, one must caution, may not be representative of other cities as captured by Figure 18.4. The suggestion of the New York at-risk percent is that there was a steady rise in the crime-prone population for almost a century and a quarter until the 1930s, a decline throughout the 1950s, and another recent rise. Again, the latter is the one place where there is any clear agreement among all of these population plots, the sharp increase caused by the baby boom in the 1950s. This

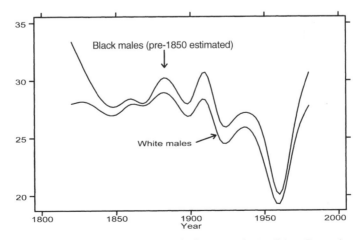

Figure 18.3 Estimated Proportion of All U.S. Males in Crime-Prone Age Group. Source: Monkkonen (2001).

269

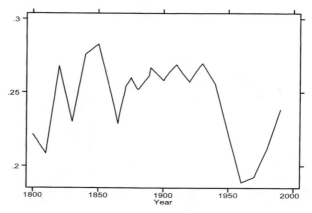

Figure 18.4 Estimated Percentage of Males 15–54 in New York City.
Source: Monkkonen (2001).

increase in the crime-prone population has been commented on extensively, and in some ways it may almost be classified as a lost generation which has not only caused an increase in crime, but which now has fathered the next generation of criminals.

Unless we are willing to concede that meaningless variations in individual lambdas are responsible for our crime measures, the overall effect of the pictures here is baffling: the at-risk population only matches the known offenses in the past few decades. The implication is that the nineteenth- and early-twentieth-century decrease in crime was even more dramatic than at first it appears, for the crime-prone population increased both absolutely and as a proportion of the larger population.

A final picture summarizes these puzzles. Figure 18.5 redisplays estimated crime-prone males in cities and the proportion in cities themselves, each decade

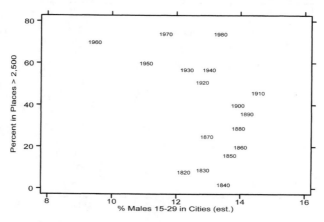

Figure 18.5 Percent of Urban Young Males, 1820–1980, United States.
Source: Monkkonen (2001).

indicated in the plot. The picture suggests that periods with known bursts in crime have virtually no clearly comparable characteristics, and we may ultimately have to turn to other explanations to unravel the problem of crime and urban growth.

Thus the demographic explanation of recent U.S. crime raises as many questions as it settles. Most importantly, prior to 1950, the demographic trends sketched in all three figures above contradict all that we know about rates of crime and disorder in U.S. cities, especially in the period from the 1850s to 1920, when all indicators point to either declining or stable offense rates per total population. These contradictions indicate that we need to work with extreme care and try for new levels of precision for both denominators and numerators. It is clear that the population estimates are inadequate and that more precision in identifying who was most likely to commit an offense and then discovering that population proportion will give us better understanding of and explanation for changing crime patterns. We can no longer accept as meaningful the total population as denominator. Until we know with some precision or reliability these basics, any broader explanatory efforts will be wasted.

Numerators have some special characteristics which we also need to rethink. Given the obvious potential for wild swings in the crime rates without any deep social/structural meaning (e.g., two fights a week to one, or changed lambdas), the wonder is that crime rates appear so very stable over long periods of time. Here I argue that the important word is *appear,* as it may turn out we have been more self-deceptive with the numerator or the crime counts in the crime rates than we admit. We are very careful and critical about legal definitions of crime, and we are equally careful about thinking about the possible biases in the sources of information. The customary way of dealing with disorder is to measure it in a way to smooth it and make it have the regularity we have taught ourselves to expect. So doing privileges a form of data manipulation, so that we do not discuss it.[4] Significantly, this issue is conceptual and methodological at once. Let me use the example of murder in New York in the nineteenth century as an example. Figure 18.6 shows the annual number of murders in New York City, unadjusted for population. The picture is a bit rough, and more sophisticated analysts would smooth using a three-, five-, or seven-year moving average as a customary practice; others might simply group into three- to seven-year clusters.

Smoothing Figure 18.6 with a three-year curvilinear line produces Figure 18.7. The philosophy behind making this image is that the scattering of detail in 18.7 has obscured a more "fundamental" trend. The missing information, the problem of 1834's lack of murders, and the various solitary peaks and valleys have disappeared in this plot, allowing us to concentrate on trends. But this step has thrown away information and masked the equally important observation that there are sporadic events in crimes.

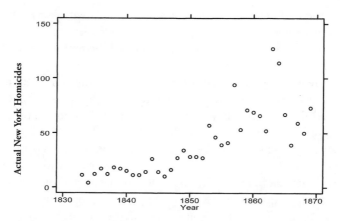

Figure 18.6 New York City Murders per Year. Source: Monkkonen (2001).

Yet is equally logical that the "fundamental" is not the trend but the unevenness and irregularity. Therefore, consider what we really mean by plotting the events over time and how we have played with that meaning. Counts per year (or 3 years) represent a way of averaging time intervals between events within the year. We choose wide time bands to create these averages. If we select a very small time band, then we would have plots with large gaps, days, say, when nothing happens. We often know within a day or two when an event occurred, but we arbitrarily choose to discard this information and look only at the year. Once we have accepted that this decision is arbitrary, then we have opened ourselves to rethinking crime "trends."

Only custom prevents us from examining this choice. Why do we not measure the precise time between events? Why should historians, who pride themselves on accuracy, ignore this dating? One reason, I think, is because such a measure demolishes our assumption of regularity, which we have pictured in the smoothed annual counts.

Figure 18.8 is the same set of New York City murders, only now pictured by time intervals between events, again unadjusted for population. One can see the intervals between events drawing briefer, the number per year increasing, but one can also see the sporadic and occasionally bunched quality of homicides. Throughout the thirty-six-year period analyzed, there were often long stretches of time between murders, followed by inexplicable clusters of unrelated events. And the more finely drawn the picture, the less even it would appear. Thus the regularity in Figures 18.6 and 18.7 is imposed initially by our determination to find it, not by any latent social/historical process.

The better denominators I have called for above may not resolve the three contradictions posed at the beginning of this essay, that is, first, city growth coupled

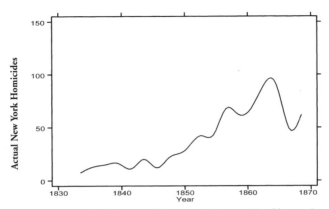

Figure 18.7 Smoothed Version of Figure 18.6. Source: Monkkonen (2001).

with per capita crime decline in the nineteenth century; second, police focus on crime control followed by rising crime in the twentieth century; and third, a simultaneous increase in social welfare provision and serious crime since the 1950s. Since we do not yet know the exact dimensions of the denominators, we can hardly analyze them. Moreover, we cannot assume that better measures will resolve contradictions, for the population estimates in all three figures tend to heighten the contradictions. For instance, the most precise population estimate, that for New York City, Figure 18.4, actually is negatively related to most of what we know about New York crime until the post–World War II era.

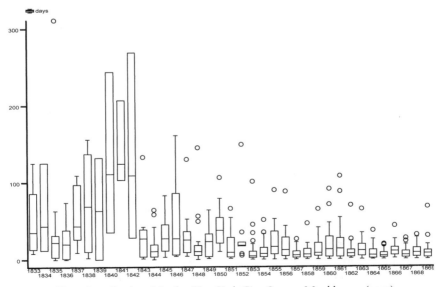

Figure 18.8 Days since Previous Murder, New York City. Source: Monkkonen (2001).

If our interpretive and empirical puzzles cry out for resolution, at least historians who work on crime and justice have become comfortable with a robust paradigm for understanding order. This paradigm derives in part from the influential work of Norbert Elias who has helped social historians of crime gain a modicum of understanding of the notion of order. In particular, we have become comfortable with the idea that modern social behavior exhibits control of impulse, consideration of others, and nonviolent and nonconfrontational social relations, with familiar people as well as strangers. Both Elias and Soman (1980: 21) have linked this aspect of private behavior to the growth of the state and the suppression of private vengeance. The order defined by Elias and Soman is communicated through various socialization and social-control processes, the logic of which requires successful communication, especially between strangers.

Industrializing cities of the nineteenth century often had large bodies of people from diverse cultures and language groups. By definition, these new cities contained the demographic ingredients for disorderly individual actions. And this, not class conflict, should contain the social logic for the formation of formal, local police with the emergence of the industrial city. Manifestations of class conflict, or more generally, violent political protest, were best suppressed by military action. On the other hand, the production of public order required attention to individual acts, the job for the police. Police acted, as Storch (1976) has put it, as "domestic missionaries," conveying the forms and norms of orderly behavior to individuals on the street. In the United States, such control focused on suppressing public drunkenness, behavior to which police officers were not in principle opposed. When in 1908 Cleveland Police Chief Fred Kohler ordered his officers to focus on felony crime and to help drunks home instead of arresting them, he called the new policy the "Golden Rule," the obvious implication being that public drunkenness was an acceptable off-duty behavior. The U.S. police were probably reluctant missionaries.

The concept of order and its relationship to the legal mechanism defining crime sketched above contrasts with the multiple definitions of order invoked in social history more broadly. These definitions range from societies without conflict or dissent to those in which individuals live without stress or in which social contradictions are absent. Still others emphasize more the power constellations forcing resolution or repression of contradictions. And others, stability.

The ambiguities of the concept can be expanded when the location of order is considered. Does the concept encompass the relationship of the various parts of society? Or is order merely a cognitive or perceptual state in an individual, group, or culture? That is, does it reside in the perceptions of an individual or is it present in the society? These are not necessarily mutually exclusive categories, and it may well be that one must consider both the society and its members separately. When order varies, does it vary in amount or in kind? Could its variation be the outward manifestation of a shift from public to individual? Is order simply social homogeneity, disorder social heterogeneity, as Richard Sennett argues? Is order consensus? Does the word "order" merely substitute for a moral judgment?

Let me diagram a two-dimensional social description of certain conditions on two lines of continua with attributes historians usually associate with order.[5] The vertical (Y) axis signifies the predictability of social relationships within the society. Note that this does not preclude change, but if there is change, it is predictable. By definition, a stable society on this continuum is one where relationships are predictable (upper portion), a chaotic society one where relationships are not predictable (lower portion).

The horizontal (X) axis refers to the cognitive processes of individuals and to the social aspect of these processes, intellectual life. A stagnant society on this continuum is one where thought does not develop, either in response to new conditions or to logical/creative processes (left side). A vibrant society is one where thinking adapts, creates, innovates, and where members may expect support and reinforcement of their new thought processes (right side). There are four quadrants, and a society can be located in any one of them, or it can be in more than one by overlapping on one scale or the other. The society's location can be plotted at the intercept of its location on the X and Y axes. Let me describe the ideal types, I, II, III, and IV.

I. While there is no intellectual growth, life is predictable and relationships of social forms are rational. No crime.

II. This society does not change or changes only predictably, but members can grow and create. It's *Gemeinschaft* with intellectual excitement.

III. An unpleasant place, where there is neither growth nor predictability; the structure of relationships and forms is relatively fixed in that consequences are neither predictable nor necessarily desired by members. High crime.

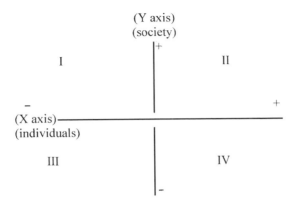

IV. While change and growth are not predictable or rational, they are not destructive, and members find intellectual growth.

An additional definitional problem comes from the likelihood that order is not constant through the society or its members. Class, neighborhood, ethnicity, occupation, family status, and gender no doubt have varying amounts or kinds of order, which will affect both the society and the individual members. Presumably individual differences, experiences, etc., also affect the subjective order for social members also. American reformers in the Progressive Era subjectively lived in a disorderly urban world, while at the same time corrupt urban political machines subjectively inhabited an orderly one. But the objective social world of the reformers was stable/orderly indeed; visions of Teddy Roosevelt, New York City police reformer before he was president, and other elite reformers moving through urbane social settings would certainly place them in quadrants II or IV.

On the other hand, the social world of actors in immigrant machines has posed an interesting historical problem. Oscar Handlin told us theirs was a disorderly world, where anomie, deviance, despair, and degeneration were the psychological consequences. More recently, historians have revised the Handlin description to find instead orderly worlds, where family, neighborhood, ethnicity, and work cultures all played a part in creating a social order quite invisible to urban elites.

To sort out these complications, it is first necessary to mention the object/subject problem. When discussing order, the problem is difficult, for the very congruence of the actor's subjective world and the objective world must also be a part of the order: lack of fit between the individual perceptions and the social situation certainly would be a kind of disorder. If all members subjectively operated in a world with a high degree of Type II order, but lived in a world with Type III order (or disorder), we would have to seriously consider whether it is possible to study such a society. Why bother to talk about objective social order if it is not the order perceived by the actor? We have to assume that correctly perceived or not, the objective social order made a difference in the lives of social members.

We cannot assume the obverse, for individual, subjective order would only affect objective order if there were widespread individual deviations from the objective order, which logically tells us that our description of the objective order is wrong. Individual deviations from objective social order of the kind or magnitude which would affect the objective order, would change the order so that the individual deviations would no longer be deviant.

This suggests that the place to study social order is in the larger, objective location. For the history of society, the individual perception of order is important only when it changes objective order, but objective order thus changed, one may only look at the objective order. On the other hand, one should not only look at an individual cognition of order alone, but must also examine objective social order. Obviously, should the change in order come from additive individual subjective change, then a proper account of the change in social order would examine individual order. Thus, my "resolution" of the object/subject problem is as follows. One may properly consider objective social order without considering subjective social order, narrow and limited as such an approach might be. On the other hand, one cannot examine subjective social order alone, but only in the context of objective social order. The best history would consider both, and examine their relationship, which would of course serve to validate and illuminate the two.

I have argued elsewhere (Monkkonen 1981c, 1983) that the role and practice of U.S. police changed from their first appearance in the 1850s. Until about 1890, the police focused on a broad range of public behavior, from felony crime and disorderly behavior to aiding the poor and controlling tramps. After 1893, they shed their broader social-control role and began to focus on crime control; for instance, they increased their felony arrests in response to variation in serious violent crimes like murder (Bijleveld and Monkkonen 1990). Recent work by Steinberg on Philadelphia and Rousey on New Orleans suggests an additional dimension. Prior to the creation of the uniformed police, citizens were able to privately prosecute minor offenses, personally bringing complaints to local magistrates who punished those found guilty. The volume of the activity, at least in Philadelphia, was higher than that the police produced. On the other hand, southern cities had police who functioned principally as a military slave-control organization, one that was abolished in the mid-nineteenth century in part because of the Civil War, and that was replaced after the war by a police organization modeled on the North.

These new findings help make a fuller picture of the role of U.S. police. First, they emphasize the great degree of local variation from city to city. Second, they suggest that the pre-uniformed police and criminal justice systems were even more focused on order maintenance than those that followed, those I have defined as order maintaining. If so, local criminal justice in U.S. cities has followed an even longer trajectory from order maintenance to crime prevention than I at first emphasized. This suggests that in the United States, prior to the industrial and urban expansion period of the second half of the nineteenth century, there was a development of policing which reinforces the concept of a long shift away from order control. This suggests two alternate interpretations. First, policing developments may have had little to do with the social changes associated with urban growth and more to do with the peculiar nature of the local American state. Or, second, a project by the state to create public order and crime control began before the industrial era, and having achieved order, turned toward the more intractable problem of crime.

NOTES

1. These contradictions can be resolved by arguing that various crime measures are *only* indicative of the activities of crime control institutions.

2. For an interesting and relevant critique of this notion, see Rodgers (1977), who says it has been accepted too uncritically as a part of modernization theory.

3. Here the role of the International Association for the History of Crime and Criminal Justice (IAHCCJ) in bringing together scholars in international context must be noted.

4. For a general discussion of the meaning of visual manipulation of data, see Tufte (1983).

5. G. N. Cantor helped me puzzle out this description.

REFERENCES

Adler, Jeffrey S. 1986. "Vagging the Demons and Scoundrels: Vagrancy and the Growth of St. Louis, 1830–1861." *Journal of Urban History* 13: 3–30.

Ayers, Edward L. 1984. *Vengeance & Justice: Crime and Punishment in the 19th-Century American South.* New York: Oxford Univ. Press.

Bijleveld, Catrien C. J. H. and Eric H. Monkkonen. 1991. "Cross-sectional and Dynamic Analyses of the Concomitants of Police Behavior." *Historical Methods* 24: 16–24.

Easterlin, Richard. 1980. *Birth and Fortune: The Impact of Numbers on Personal Welfare.* New York: Basic.

Gatrell, V. A. C. 1980. In Gatrell, Geoffrey Parker, and Bruce Lenman, eds., *Crime and the Law: The Social History of Crime in Western Europe since 1500.* London: Europa.

―――. and T. B. Hadden. 1972. "Criminal Statistics and Their Interpretation." In E. A. Wrigley, ed., *Nineteenth Century Society: Essays in the Use of Quantitative Methods for the Study of Social Data.* Cambridge: Cambridge Univ. Press, 336–96.

Gurr, Ted Robert. 1989. "Historical Trends in Violent Crime: Europe and the United States." In Gurr, ed., *Violence in America: Volume 1: The History of Crime,* 21–54. Beverly Hills: Sage.

Gutman, Herbert. 1973. "Work, Culture and Society in Industrializing America, 1815–1919." *American Historical Review* 77: 531–587.

Kyvig, David E. 1982. *Law, Alcohol and Order: Perspectives on National Prohibition.* Westport, CT: Greenwood.

Lane, Roger. 1979. *Violent Death in the City: Accident, Suicide and Homicide in Philadelphia, 1850–1900.* Cambridge: Harvard Univ. Press.

Monkkonen, Eric H. 1984. "The Politics of Municipal Indebtedness and Default, 1850–1936." In Terrence J. McDonald and Sally K. Ward, eds., *The Politics of Urban Fiscal Policy,* 125–161. Beverly Hills: Sage Press.

―――. 1983. "The Organized Response to Crime in the Nineteenth and Early Twentieth Centuries." *Journal of Interdisciplinary History* 14: 113–128.

―――. 1981a. "A Disorderly People? Urban Order in Nineteenth and Twentieth Century America." *Journal of American History* 68: 539–559.

―――. 1981b. "Toward an Understanding of Urbanisation: Drunk Arrests in Los Angeles." *Pacific Historical Review* 50: 234–244.

―――. 1981c. *Police in Urban America, 1860–1920.* New York: Cambridge Univ. Press.

Rodgers, Daniel T. 1977. "Tradition, Modernity, and the American Industrial Worker: Reflections and Critique." *Journal of Interdisciplinary History* 7: 655–682.

Rousey, Dennis C. 1983. "Hibernian Leatherheads: Irish Cops in New Orleans, 1830–1860." *Journal of Urban History* 10: 61–84.

Sennet, Richard. 1970. *The Uses of Disorder: Personal Identity and City Life*. New York: Vintage.

Simmel, Georg. 1964. "The Metropolitan Personality." In *The Sociology of Georg Simmel*. New York: Free Press.

Soman, Alfred. 1980. "Deviance and Criminal Justice in Western Europe, 1300–1800: An Essay in Structure." *Criminal Justice History* 1: 1–28.

Steinberg, Allen. 1989. *The Transformation of Criminal Justice: Philadelphia, 1800–1880*. Chapel Hill: Univ. of North Carolina Press.

Storch, Robert D. 1976. "The Policeman as Domestic Missionary: Urban Discipline and Popular Culture in Northern England, 1850–1880." *Journal of Social History* 9: 481–509.

Thompson, E. P. 1967. "Time, Work-Discipline, and Industrial Capitalism." *Past & Present* 38: 56–97.

Tufte, Edward R. 1983. *The Visual Display of Quantitative Information*. Cheshire, Conn.: Graphics Press.

Watts, Eugene J. 1983. "Police Response to Crime and Disorder in Twentieth Century St. Louis." *Journal of American History* 70: 340–358.

Weinberger, Barbara, and Herbert Reinke. 1989. "Law and Order in the Industrial City: An Anglo-German Comparison." Paper presented at the Social Science History Association Annual Meeting (Nov. 16–19); Washington, D.C.

Wertsch, Douglas. 1987. "The Evolution of the Des Moines Police Department." *Annals of Iowa* 48: 435–449.

References

Amenta, Edwin, Elisabeth S. Clemens, Jefren Olsen, Sunita Parika, and Theda Skocpol. (1987) "The political origins of unemployment insurance in five American states." In *Studies in American Political Development: An Annual* 2. New Haven: Yale University Press.

Ayers, Edward L. (1984). *Vengeance and Justice: Crime and Punishment in the Nineteenth-Century American South.* New York: Oxford University Press.

"Blighted Areas Are Revived as Crime Rate Falls in Cities." *New York Times,* May 29, 2000, pp. A1, A12.

Campbell, Ballard C. (1980). *Representative Democracy: Public Police and Midwestern Legislature in the Late Nineteenth Century.* Cambridge, Mass.: Northeastern University Press.

Claggett, William, ed. (Fall 1986). "Walter Dean Burnham and the dynamics of American politics." *Social Science History* 10 (Special Issue).

Courtwright, David T. *Violent Land: Single Men, and Social Disorder from the Frontier to the Inner City.* Cambridge, Mass.: Harvard University Press, 1996.

Daniels, Steve. (1986). "Explaining case load dynamics: the use of evolutionary models." Law & Society annual meeting.

Diamond, Stephen. (June 1983). "The death and transfiguration of benefit taxation: special assessments in nineteenth century America." *The Journal of Legal Studies* 12: 201–40.

Elazar, Daniel Judah. (1962). *The American Partnership: Intergovernmental Cooperation in the Nineteenth-Century United States.* Chicago: University of Chicago Press.

Elias, Norbert. (1978/1982). *The Civilizing Process,* tr. Edmund Jephcott. 1st American ed. New York: Urizen Books.

Emerson, Haven. (1941). *Population, Births, Notifiable Diseases, and Deaths, Assembled for New York City, New York: 1866–1938.* New York: DeLamar Institute of Public Health.

Friedman, Lawrence, and Robert Percival. (1981). *The Roots of Justice: Crime and Punishment in Alameda County, California, 1870–1910.* Chapel Hill: University of North Carolina Press.

Frug, Gerald E. (1980). "The city as legal concept." *Harvard Law Review* 93: 1059–1154.

Galambos, John. (1983). "Technology, Political Economy and Professionalization: Central Themes of the Organizational Synthesis." *Business History Review.* 57: 471–493.

Gere, Edwin A. (1982). "Dillon's Rule and the Cooley doctrine: reflections of the political culture. *Journal of Urban History* 8: 271–91.

Hindus, Michael S., Theodore M. Hammett, and Barbara M. Hobson. (1980). *The Files of the Massachusetts Superior Court, 1859–1959: An Analysis and a Plan for Action: A Report of the Massachusetts Judicial Records Committee of the Supreme Judicial Court, Boston, 1979.* Boston: G. K. Hall.

Jenkins, James Gilbert. (1864). *Life and Confessions of James Gilbert Jenkins: The Murderer of Eighteen Men.* Napa City, CA: Allen and Wood.

Kasserman, David Richard. (1986). *Fall River Outrage: Life, Murder, and Justice in Early Industrial New England.* Philadelphia: University of Pennsylvania Press.

Kelley, Robert. (June 1987). "The westward movement, reconceived within a transatlantic framework." *Reviews in American History* 15: 213–19.

Laurent, Francis W. (1959). *The Business of a Trial Court, 100 Years of Cases: A Census of the Actions and Special Proceedings in the Circuit Court for Chippewa County, Wisconsin, 1855–1954.* Madison: University of Wisconsin Press.

McDonald, Terrence J. (1987). "Building the impossible state: a polity centered approach to state building in America, 1820–1930." In John E. Jackson, ed., *Essays in American Institutions.* Ann Arbor.

———. (1987). *The Parameters of Urban Fiscal Policy: Socioeconomic Change, Political Culture and Fiscal Policy in San Francisco, 1860–1906.* Los Angeles: University of California Press.

——— and Sally Ward. (1984). *The Politics of Urban Fiscal Policy.* Beverly Hills, CA: Sage Press.

McGrath, Roger D. *Gunfighters, Highwaymen, and Vigilantes: Violence on the Frontier.* Berkeley: University of California Press, 1984.

Miller, Wilbur R. (Spring 1986). "Police and the state: a comparative perspective." *American Bar Foundation Research Journal,* 339–48.

Millspaugh, Arthur C. (1936). *Local Democracy and Crime Control.* Washington, DC: Brookings Inst.

Monkkonen, Eric H. (1984). "The politics of municipal indebtedness and default, 1850–1936." In McDonald and Ward, 125–60.

———. (1988). America Becomes Urban: *The Development of US Cities & Towns, 1780–1980.* Los Angeles: University of California Press.

———. (2001). *Murder in New York City.* Los Angeles: University of California Press.

———. (May, 1984). "Why is the history of crime in the United States different from the history of crime in Britain?" International Conference on Violence in History, Maastricht.

New York Secretary of State. (1857). *Report of the Secretary of State on the Criminal Statistics of the State of New York (March 13, 1857).* Senate Doc. No. 130.

New York Secretary of State. (1905). Annual Report on Statistics of Crime. Table D, pp. 99–159.

Palmer, Ian. (1985). "State theory and statutory authorities: points of convergence." *Sociology* 19: 523–40.

Pierson, Christopher. (1984). "Trend Report. New theories of state and civil society: recent developments in post-Marxist analysis of the state." *Sociology* 18: 563–71.

Scheiber, Harry. (1975). "Federalism and the American economic order, 1789–1910." *Law & Society Review* 10: 57–118.

Skocpol, Theda. (1987). "Social history and historical sociology: contrasts and complementarities." *Social Science History* 11: 17–30.

Skowronek, Stephen. (1982). *Building the New American State: The Expansion of National Administrative Capacities, 1877–1920.* New York: Cambridge University Press.

Steinberg, Allen. (1989). *The Transformation of Criminal Justice, Philadelphia, 1800–1880.* Chapel Hill: University of North Carolina Press.

Sylla, Richard. (1986). "The economics of state and local government sources and uses of funds in North Carolina, 1800–1977." *Research in Economic History.* JAI Press.

Taylor, W. B. (1985). "Between global process and local knowledge: an inquiry into early Latin American social history, 1500–1900." In Olivier Zunz, ed., *Reliving the Past: The Worlds of Social History.* Chapel Hill: University of North Carolina Press.

Teaford, Jon. (1979). *City and Suburb: The Political Fragmentation of Urban America, 1850–1970.* Baltimore: Johns Hopkins University Press.

———. (1984). *The Unheralded Triumph: City Government in America, 1867–1900.* Baltimore: Johns Hopkins University Press.

Teubner, Gunther. (1984). "Autopoesis in law and society: a rejoinder to Blankenburg." *Law & Society Review* 18: 291–301.

Valentine, David T. (1864). *Manual of the Corporation of the City of New York, 1864,* 104. New York.

Zimring, Franklin E., and Gordon Hawkins (1997). *Crime Is Not the Problem: Lethal Violence in America.* New York: Oxford University Press.

Index